Traumatic Imprints

The publisher and the University of California Press Foundation gratefully acknowledge the generous support of the Robert and Meryl Selig Endowment Fund in Film Studies, established in memory of Robert W. Selig.

Traumatic Imprints

Cinema, Military Psychiatry, and the
Aftermath of War

Noah Tsika

UNIVERSITY OF CALIFORNIA PRESS

University of California Press, one of the most
distinguished university presses in the United States,
enriches lives around the world by advancing
scholarship in the humanities, social sciences, and
natural sciences. Its activities are supported by the
UC Press Foundation and by philanthropic
contributions from individuals and institutions.
For more information, visit www.ucpress.edu.

University of California Press
Oakland, California

Library of Congress Cataloging-in-Publication Data

Names: Tsika, Noah, 1983– author.
Title: Traumatic imprints : cinema, military psychiatry,
    and the aftermath of war / Noah Tsika.
Description: Oakland, California : University of
    California Press, [2018] | Includes bibliographical
    references and index. |
Identifiers: LCCN 2018007649 (print) | LCCN 2018011047
    (ebook) | ISBN 9780520969926 (ebook) |
    ISBN 9780520297630 (cloth : alk. paper) |
    ISBN 9780520297647 (pbk. : alk. paper)
Subjects: LCSH: World War, 1939–1945—Motion
    pictures and the war. | World War, 1939–1945—
    Psychological aspects. | Nonfiction films—United
    States—History and criticism.
Classification: LCC D743.23 (ebook) | LCC D743.23..T79
    2018 (print) | DDC 616.85/212—dc23
LC record available at https://lccn.loc.gov/2018007649

Manufactured in the United States of America

27 26 25 24 23 22 21 20 19 18
10 9 8 7 6 5 4 3 2 1

Contents

Acknowledgments

Raina Polivka is an ideal editor—encouraging and enlightening—and I begin by thanking her. Raina saw and communicated the promise of this project at a particularly difficult time in my life, and her early support inspired me in more ways than I can possibly explain. It has been a pleasure and a privilege to work with her on this book. At the University of California Press, Zuha Kahn and Elena Bellaart were enormously helpful.

Material support for this project was provided by a PSC-CUNY Award, jointly funded by The Professional Staff Congress and The City University of New York. Additional support came from the Andrew W. Mellon Foundation, which generously provided back-to-back grants.

Clio Unger, my research assistant at the CUNY Graduate Center, helpfully tracked down and photocopied some key articles. I would also like to thank my students at the Graduate Center, especially Colleen O'Shea and Terrence Hunt, and my graduate students at Queens College, especially Juan Antonio Fernandez, Vanessa Dunstan, Michael Bass, and Keith Bevacqua.

Much of the research for this book was conducted at the National Archives and Records Administration's facility in College Park, Maryland; at the New York Public Library (especially the Manuscripts and Archives Division at the Stephen A. Schwarzman Building and the Schomburg Center for Research in Black Culture); at the Library of Congress; and at the National Library of Medicine, where Leonore

Burts, Miriam Meijer, Crystal Smith, and Linda Williams were ideal guides and generous interlocutors. I thank the intrepid archivists who remain committed to the careful preservation and classification of mid-twentieth-century military media, as well as the many staff members (especially Linda) who welcomed me day after day. At the New York University Archives, Danielle Nista was especially helpful.

I have been working on this project, off and on, for over ten years, and I have benefited from the input and expertise of a number of scholars, some of whom carefully read portions of the manuscript: Richard Allen, Michael Bronski, Amalia Córdova, Lee Grieveson, Martin Johnson, Jonathan Kahana, Moya Luckett, Rick Maxwell, Anna McCarthy, Dana Polan, Chris Straayer, Dan Streible, Haidee Wasson, Thomas Waugh, and Joe Wlodarz. True to form, Bronski never hesitated to alert me to any number of obscure films from Hollywood's classical period ("Quick—turn on TCM! Roz Russell is talking about combat fatigue!") The late Robert Sklar shaped this work in innumerable ways—including by showing me a 16mm print of John Huston's *Let There Be Light* when I was a particularly impressionable first-year graduate student. I hope that I have honored Bob's astonishing legacy, however modestly, with this book. Jonathan Kahana's influence is on every page: our conversations, email exchanges, and collaborative projects have been high points of my career. I am tempted to write that Jonathan taught me everything I know about documentary; he has certainly taught me how to be a better writer, a better thinker, and a more rigorous researcher.

Alice Lovejoy and Marlisa Santos, who read and commented on the manuscript multiple times for the press, were amazingly thorough and inspiring, including through the models of their own work. Alice, in particular, challenged me from the very beginning to rethink a series of assumptions, and I am immensely grateful for her meticulous criticism.

My remarkable parents, Mary Tsika and Ronald Tsika, let me stay with them for nearly three months in 2016, as I coped with my own post-traumatic condition, and it was while recovering in their house that I was able to return to this project. Their passion for film—especially documentary—has been a consistent source of inspiration, and their courage to grow is nothing short of awe-inspiring. My big brothers, Aaron Tsika and Adam Tsika, deserve special thanks, as well.

Adam Hobbins, thank you for everything.

This book is the product of two traumas—an attempted armed home invasion that occurred in the immediate wake of campus violence, and the sudden and quite unexpected end of my marriage—and it bears their imprints in ways that only I may be able to recognize. But it took a village to help me cope with the aftermath of a surprise divorce, and I would like to offer heartfelt thanks to the true friends who came to my aid as I was navigating the pain, confusion, and utter humiliation of that moment in my life, all while facing the residual effects of my late-night confrontation with a disturbed gunman: Phoenix Alexander, Max Andrucki, Brandon Arroyo, Lee Bailey, Beau Brinker, Jonathan Buchsbaum, Matthew Crain, Brooke Edge, Murtada Elfadl, Michael Fragoso, Dana Gravesen, Lindsey Green-Simms, David Greven, Kenneth Gyang, Amy Herzog, Sean Jacobs, Nikyatu Jusu, Amanda Ann Klein, Guy Lodge, Moya Luckett, Al Martin, Tara Mateik, Rick Maxwell, Kerry McBroom, Seán McGovern, Ryan McPhee, Michael Morgan, Tyler Morgenstern, 'Ṣẹgun Ọdẹjimi, Kimani Okearah, Nick Patton, Justine Peres Smith, Christopher Persaud, Nathaniel Rogers, Kieran Scarlett, and Joe Wlodarz. I risk "oversharing" here because I would like to impress upon the reader—as a sort of preview of one of the themes of this book—the possibility of recovery. The *possibility*.

It's possible.

Noah Tsika, New York City,
April 2018

Introduction

Documenting the "Residue of Battle"

"The aftermath of war is rubble—the rubble of cities and of
men—They are the casualties of a pitiless destruction. The
cities can be rebuilt, but the wounds of men, whether of the
mind or of the body, heal slowly."
—opening text of *Kiss the Blood Off My Hands*
(Norman Foster, 1948)

Tasked with explaining what war can "do to the mind," a Navy medical
officer stares into the camera and delivers a warning about cinema's
capacity to traumatize its spectators, especially those whose arena of
reception is the neuropsychiatric ward of a military hospital. Directly
addressing the vulnerable, "battle-fatigued" patients watching the film
from the relative safety of their hospital beds, this unnamed man offers a
gentle reminder about the diversity of formal devices that profitably constitute the category of documentary cinema. That these devices include
simulation in addition to the use of "authentic" footage means that a
traumatized war veteran will invariably fear more than just a "loud,"
star-studded, Hollywood-style recreation of the horrors of combat. He
may, in fact, fear the very film in which this medical officer appears—a
short, military-produced documentary designed, first and foremost, to
bolster the psychiatric treatment of those suffering from combat-related
"mental problems." After all, the officer's own segments—pedagogic
and therapeutic moments of direct address—are interspersed with dramatizations of various claims about war trauma, many of which recreate
ghastly battle conditions.

Introducing a series of staged sequences, the officer counsels the film's
hospitalized viewers to accept that, however vividly these sequences may

FIGURE 1. A Navy psychiatrist addresses the traumatized viewer in the service's
Introduction to Combat Fatigue (1944). Courtesy of the U.S. National Library of
Medicine.

evoke the very experiences that led to the viewers' psychological breakdowns, they are meant to indicate just how common—and, more to the
point, just how comprehensible—war trauma can be. As the officer puts
it, dramatic reenactments of combat are "painful" but "necessary"—
like the pulling of a bad tooth or the treatment of a broken leg. By
watching them, the battle-scarred soldier will learn how to recreate and
thereby exorcise his own traumatic past as a central part of the therapeutic process. Thus the film's own mimetic relationship to war is meant
to spur mimesis of a different order—the sort of "curative imitation"
that, performed in clinical settings under the close supervision of therapists, allows a soldier to "work through" war trauma.

This short Navy film, *Introduction to Combat Fatigue* (1944), demonstrates many of the principles that motivated the military's use of
documentary realism as a form of instruction and therapy during and
after World War II. Addressing hospitalized soldiers suffering from various symptoms of combat trauma, the officer-narrator also, at least
implicitly, addresses a number of other spectators for whom the film
was expressly produced: psychiatrists in "special Navy hospitals" where
film screenings were essential components of group psychotherapy;
nurses, hospital corpsmen, and medical officers not directly involved in

such psychotherapeutic sessions but nonetheless committed to the rehabilitation of the "war neurotic"; non-psychiatrists (both line and medical officers) likely to encounter cases of "battle fatigue"; and, finally, those charged with using trauma-themed documentary and realist films in order to "screen and diagnose" soldiers, "in a manner similar to Murray's thematic apperception and Rorschach's ink blot tests."[1] For the members of this latter category (committed, the Navy Medical Department maintained, to "a strictly limited experimental purpose"), cinema's diagnostic potential was tied to its capacity to "trigger" emotional responses, chief among these a fear of both the "real" (footage of combat) and the "faked" (dramatic reenactments and other staged performances).[2] The contradictory dimensions of this understanding of cinema—the sense that the medium was potentially traumatizing and, at the same time, potentially therapeutic—reflected broader contradictions in the military's frequently contentious engagements with the so-called "war neuroses" and their treatment.

If a Navy film like *Introduction to Combat Fatigue*, with its soft-spoken officer-narrator providing psychological counseling through direct address, was seen as a means of soothing the soldier-spectator, it was also, with its dramatic reenactments providing vivid reminders of the horrors of combat, viewed as a probable source of shock for men already primed to avoid all representations of war. Managing such a paradox was the job of the film itself, as the officer-narrator himself avers, pointing out the therapeutic value and documentary legitimacy of a skillful, "useful" combination of devices. But this obligation also extended to therapists responsible for leading pre- and post-screening discussions and, in the process, emphasizing that a documentary like *Introduction to Combat Fatigue* is, after all, "just a film," albeit one with the capacity to diagnose, treat, and even "cure" the titular condition.[3]

Introduction to Combat Fatigue may initially have been intended for hospital screenings, but, like a great many of its military-sponsored counterparts, it enjoyed remarkably expansive wartime and postwar itineraries—an indication not simply of the importance of war trauma as a cinematic subject but also of the proliferation of venues for nontheatrical nonfiction film. (As producer and critic John Grierson had observed in the interwar period, there is "more seating capacity outside the commercial cinemas than inside them.")[4] If the nontheatrical realm had previously been estranged from some of the military's cinematic efforts, the requirements of "total war" helped to change that. "War has broken these bottlenecks," wrote the editors of *Look* magazine in 1945, stressing that state-sponsored documentaries—including films about "the study and treatment of damaged minds"—would "be readily available for general use," especially in classrooms.[5] Faced with the "gigantic problem" of "mental disease" among members of the armed forces, military psychiatrists increasingly informed the public that they were "acutely aware of the psychic injury to an enormous number of servicemen, a far greater number than are diagnosed as psychiatric patients, or [than] ever get into the hospitals for that matter."[6]

Documentary film, in a variety of styles, was seen as a key means of alleviating concerns about the high incidence of psychoneurosis—a tool for treating soldiers, instructing medical officers, and assuring the general public that, paradoxically, the military was a place where mental health might be restored. "Joe Smith's mental health actually improved in the Army," claims the narrator of the service's *Shades of Gray* (1947), pointing to a pseudonymous enlistee who "could be any American," so effective and egalitarian is the military's alleged commitment to psychotherapy. Often coordinating its pursuit of the general public with the U.S. Office of Education (which had its own industrial training films to circulate), the military ensured that documentaries about trauma and psychotherapy would travel widely despite their exclusion from commercial exhibition. In the spring of 1945, the Office of Education prepared a "postwar proposal" that stressed the lasting value of military documentaries, noting that "the Army has stated that the use of training films speeds up training as much as forty percent," and that "the Navy reports that students learn thirty-five times faster and that facts are remembered up to fifty-five percent longer." Such claims, and their unqualified endorsement by the Office of Education, helped to normalize the use of military documentaries beyond the armed forces, including in businesses and schools.[7]

BATTLE SCARS

"Wars don't leave people as they were."
—Marina (Ann Baxter) in *The North Star*
  (Lewis Milestone, 1943)

This book considers the imprinting power of military psychiatry in its intersections with both theatrical and nontheatrical film. My title, *Traumatic Imprints*, is inspired, in part, by the 1945 Army Signal Corps short *The Atom Strikes!*, which insists that the trauma of the titular bomb has left traces—imprints—that only military expertise can identify, and that

only documentary film can adequately communicate.[8] These traces are both visible ("lines literally blasted into the stone" of a war memorial, the discoloration of a smokestack, flash burns on a lamppost) and invisible, both empirical and postempirical, explicitly recalling the lessons of wartime military psychiatry, which often insisted on trauma's dual character—its capacity to combine externalized symptoms (tremors, tics) with traits indiscernible on the surface.[9] The dead, charred trees of Hiroshima, like the razed buildings of that city, are thus juxtaposed with the imperceptible effects of radiation, which medical experts must explain in terms of an "inner development" akin to the progression of neurosis.[10]

If *The Atom Strikes!* tends to skirt the psychological traumas wrought by the bomb, focusing almost exclusively, in empiricist fashion, on its effects on buildings and bridges, other military documentaries of the period present the human mind as the principal bearer of war trauma. It was precisely the latter approach that rankled many military officials, including Army Chief of Staff General George C. Marshall, who, despite being a "zealous proponent of educational film," and despite his stated desire to "care for the minds of men as well as their bodies," balked at the prospect of producing documentaries about "invisible" ailments.[11] Hollywood films had addressed this dilemma throughout the interwar period. The traumatized protagonist of George Cukor's *A Bill of Divorcement* (1932), for instance, complains that his "invisible" condition generates "not honorable scars, not medals and glory," but merely "years in hell," remaining utterly imperceptible to others. In 1942, Marshall complained about such "invisibility" in a special report on war neuroses—an indictment of military psychiatry that was quickly leaked to a Washington newspaper. Rather than halting the development of documentaries about war trauma, the leaked report all but ensured their production, as curious Americans—including soldiers struck by the disconnect between official psychiatric policy and Marshall's own brand of empiricist bluster (which he shared with General George S. Patton)—were deemed in need of the interventions of educational films.[12]

War trauma had the force of a structure of feeling during and in the wake of World War II, informing a range of cultural productions, and its power was inextricable from the contradictions that it seemed at once to manage and exacerbate. Consider, for instance, a casual joke about war trauma in the film *A Letter to Three Wives* (Joseph L. Mankiewicz, 1949), which stands in stark contrast to the subject's sober discussion in the exactly contemporaneous *Home of the Brave* (Mark Robson,

1949).[13] Consider, as well, the era's tendency to depict the promiscuous character of war trauma—its capacity to bleed inexorably into civilian life. In Jean Renoir's *This Land Is Mine* (1943), the civilian protagonist suffers from a "nervous condition" that is worsened by thoughts of war. "I can't stand violence—it terrifies me," he confesses. "Noise and explosions—something happens to me." The severely traumatized daughter of a World War II veteran is compared to a combat soldier in MGM's *Shadow on the Wall* (Patrick Jackson, 1950), and she eventually develops "hysterical muteness," along with a range of other symptoms. "You're familiar with shellshock in adults?" asks a psychiatrist (played by Nancy Davis). "Well, children can be that badly upset, too."

Even Lassie, the canine character created by Eric Knight (who co-wrote scripts for the *Why We Fight* series and was instrumental in introducing the British documentary movement to Signal Corps filmmakers before his death in 1943), suffers from war trauma in *Courage of Lassie* (Fred M. Wilcox, 1946), surviving a horrific battle in the Aleutian Islands Campaign only to "crack up," initially lapsing into a catatonic state and later exhibiting violent behavior.[14] The dog's diverse symptoms inspire considerable terror, and it is up to a local rancher to explain war trauma as a common yet eminently treatable condition, one that extends not merely from soldier to civilian but also from soldier to dog.[15] That a rancher is capable of explicating the vagaries of war trauma suggests the sheer availability of psychotherapeutic discourses in the 1940s, and his eloquent disquisition provides *Courage of Lassie* with an instructive power, however partial and fleeting, that evokes documentary's translational character.[16] It is precisely because some of the traumas of World War II are "new"—as the rancher himself suggests—that they require creative interpretation, infiltrating even a children's film and forcing it to confront the challenges of rehabilitation and reintegration.

Defining a structure of feeling as "a social experience which is still *in process*," Raymond Williams offers a useful framework for thinking about the inchoate aspects of war trauma, as well as the capacity of new symptoms, diagnostic criteria, and treatment methods to spur public debate and encourage the hybridization of filmmaking strategies. The fluidity of war trauma was often sufficient to collapse previously sacrosanct distinctions in American public life, inspiring such catchphrases as "Are you fed up with the setup?" and "Are you nervous in the service?"[17] Thus while rhetorical convention clung to a binary opposition between soldier and civilian, the latter was, if employed in war production, considerably more likely to die or suffer serious injury, her traumas

encompassing the physical as well as the psychological.[18] Addressing these realities, military documentaries consistently couch war trauma as a universal phenomenon—a sweeping consequence of "total war" and, in particular, of shockingly destructive new technologies—while simultaneously striving to identify the peculiarities of combat-related neuroses.

Hollywood's wartime engagements with the subject of trauma occasionally emphasized its growing accessibility. Focusing on the dramatic experiences of the U.S. Merchant Marine, Victor Fleming's *Adventure* (1945), for instance, stresses the traumas to which civilian mariners are subjected, as well as the availability of information about the development and treatment of psychoneurosis. Visiting a public library, the traumatized Mudgin (Thomas Mitchell), who "lost [his] soul" after his ship was torpedoed, learns much about his condition from librarian Emily Sears (Greer Garson). Pointing to "some excellent studies"—including one by an American colonel, entitled *Facts on Combat Fatigue*—Emily explains that "the strain of war . . . sometimes causes psychoneurosis." She proceeds to confidently psychoanalyze Mudgin, doing her part to align him with combat soldiers—and to "prove," moreover, that "anyone" can comprehend the previously unknown etiologies of trauma.

Far from avoiding any resemblance to such star-driven, studio-bound representations, or denying that techniques of intervention and reconstruction constituted part of the terrain of documentary (in the manner of later objections issued, however disingenuously, by proponents of direct cinema), military filmmakers repeatedly linked trauma's diverse and sometimes contradictory symptomatology to a variety of documentary methods, arguing that the latter could ably serve the former, and vice versa. Describing documentary filmmaking as a realist enterprise whose restrictions all but disappear during times of institutional crisis and in the face of traumatic experience, Navy psychiatrist Howard P. Rome wrote in 1945 of a "realistic flexibility which has very few limitations." Because trauma's symptoms often included false memory and other fictive strategies of self-representation, and because its treatment entailed "creative reconstruction" (as in the psychodramatic interactions of patients and therapists, or the "memory work" of narcosynthesis), any attempt to document it had to embrace "drama and dynamics" that included "[scripted] words, music and sound, and even color."[19] Regarding the latter, Rome had in mind special effects that, however symbolic and anti-illusionist, would nevertheless "accurately illustrate" a patient's mental state. Thus if a traumatized combat veteran claimed that he could

see nothing but blood—both his own and that of his fallen comrades—
the filmic image of him could be given a red tint to reflect and perhaps
resolve this fixation, "desensitizing" him to his greatest fear.[20]

Traumatic Imprints considers some of the consequential intersections
among Freudian psychoanalysis, military psychiatry, and documentary
film in a period that long predated the codification of war trauma as
PTSD. At stake in my reevaluation of wartime and postwar military
media is a broader understanding of how war trauma and psychotherapy were articulated in and through documentary and realist film. Situated at the intersection of trauma studies and documentary studies, this
book considers some of the historically specific debates about, aspirations for, and uses of documentary as a vehicle for honoring, monitoring,
understanding, publicizing, and even "working through" war trauma,
while occasionally conceding trauma's contradictory and intractable
character. The diverse objectives toward which documentary was mobi-
lized are mirrored, in the films that I analyze here, by a diversity of formal strategies. Paying attention to trauma thus allows me to tell a more
nuanced story about films that are either tendentiously denied the label
of documentary or reduced to a limited, stable set of documentary techniques. It also demands that I address a number of films that, stored in
the National Archives and Records Administration and at the National
Library of Medicine, have not been cited in previous publications. As
pedagogic and therapeutic engagements with PTSD and the politics of
survival and recovery, these remarkable films merit close attention.

CHAPTER I

"Imaging the Mind"

Military Psychiatry Meets Documentary Film

"Wars today, accompanied by their terrific mechanical developments, create emotional stresses which are bound to hurt seriously large numbers of those engaged in them. It is the basic and major function of military psychiatrists to care for these people who have been made emotionally sick by the pressures of stresses of modern warfare."

—Dr. John Milne Murray, psychiatrist, Army Air Forces, 1947[1]

Between 1925 and 1940, the cost of caring for "psychologically disturbed" ex-servicemen, who occupied nearly half of all beds in Veterans Administration (VA) hospitals, approached one billion dollars.[2] By 1947, the situation had become graver still, with the VA forced to note that "the numbers of beds assigned to neurological and psychiatric patients exceed those of all other types put together," and that "there is nothing vague about these figures."[3] World War II had dramatically expanded the cultural visibility of post-traumatic conditions, compelling the military to directly address this pronounced "psychiatric problem" through documentary film. As early as 1942, medical officers were given crash courses in psychiatry at, among other establishments, the Army's School of Military Neuropsychiatry on Long Island, and psychiatrists were increasingly incorporated into the armed forces in an advisory capacity. World War II represented, as Rebecca Jo Plant puts it, "a major boon to American psychiatry"; it "spurred the ascendance of psychoanalytic and psychodynamic approaches and the destigmatization and normalization of mental disorders, setting the stage for the flourishing of postwar therapeutic culture."[4] Many at the VA nevertheless believed that more needed to be done to draw attention to the psychological problems that veterans continued to confront in the postwar period. As Dr. Daniel Blain, chief of the VA's Neuropsychiatry Division, put it in a 1947 report, "The size of the job to be done in this field has suffered from vagueness, exaggeration, misunderstanding, and sometimes a Pollyanna attitude of wishful thinking."[5] Such naïve optimism, Blain and others felt, could be countered through the ongoing distribution of "serious" films about trauma—works of nonfiction that, endorsed by the military, examined some of the practical difficulties of psychiatric treatment, particularly in understaffed or otherwise inadequate state facilities.[6]

Focusing on World War II and its immediate aftermath, this chapter offers a genealogy of a particular documentary tendency, one tied to the concurrent rise of military psychiatry and of the military-industrial state. As the psychiatric treatment of combat-traumatized soldiers gained greater institutional and cultural visibility, so did particular techniques associated with—but scarcely limited to—documentary film. In accounts of the period, American documentary is typically understood as having been stymied by the needs of a federal government that had previously (as with the formation of the United States Film Service in 1938) placed a premium on documentary's formal development as a tool for communicating government policy.[7] Some scholars go so far as to argue that the Second World War merely extended the constraints that the Great Depression had placed on documentary artistry, ensuring a "patriotic" homogeneity in the wake of congressional attacks on the arguably partisan work of Pare Lorentz and others. Michael Renov rehearses this claim when he writes, "The priorities enforced by the Depression and World War II reined in the experimentalism and unabashed subjectivity of expression that had so enlivened documentary practice in the 1920s."[8] This is, of course, hardly true if one considers the contributions to wartime documentary of such creative, often self-aggrandizing figures as Frank Capra, John Ford, and John Huston, who inscribed their "government work" with various authorial signatures. But it is perhaps even less true if one looks at the priorities of military psychiatrists and other psychological professionals, which reach expression in a number of films that have long been left out of accounts of documentary's development in the United States. Renov goes on to note that "[p]rivate visions and careerist goals have always commingled with the avowed social aims of collective documentary endeavors," demanding precisely the kind of reevaluation of wartime nonfiction that he does not undertake in his account of historically-specific conservatism—a reevaluation that would bring to light the vital impact of individuals who, while not nearly as famous as Ford and Capra, far outnumbered such uniformed auteurs.[9]

This book looks at some of the subjectivities—some of the "private visions" and "careerist goals"—of military psychiatrists and other psychological experts whose influence is abundantly evident in a range of "documentary endeavors," including those carried out both (and often simultaneously) by Hollywood studios and various military filmmaking outfits, from the Signal Corps Photographic Center to the Training Films and Motion Picture Branch of the Bureau of Aeronautics. Despite their substantial contributions to documentary praxis in the 1940s, these individuals have largely been ignored, including by the few scholars who have touched upon Huston's famous *Let There Be Light*, the production of which relied heavily upon the input and authority of four men: George S. Goldman, the psychiatrist who oversaw the military's multipronged development of "psychiatric documentaries"; M. Ralph Kaufman, a psychiatrist who had developed (and filmed) hypnosis techniques for the treatment of those traumatized in the Battle of Okinawa, and who was a member of the teaching staff at Mason General Hospital, where Huston's film was shot; John Spiegel, a psychiatrist who, with Roy Grinker, had advanced the use of sodium pentothal in a procedure known as "narcosynthesis"; and Benjamin Simon, a psychiatrist who served as a liaison between Huston and the others, and who supervised the scriptwriting efforts of the director and his co-author, Signal Corps Captain Charles Kaufman. However illustrious, Hollywood filmmakers were hardly essential to this diagnostic and psychotherapeutic institutional enterprise, and their ideas had to be vetted by psychiatrists and other psychological experts whose presence was rapidly expanding throughout the military. The number of physicians assigned to the neuropsychiatric corps increased from thirty-five in 1941 to twenty-four hundred in 1946, and it was in this context of psychiatric expansion and experimentation that documentary and realist films began to centralize war trauma as a common yet treatable condition.[10]

The experimental uses to which certain films were put, and their shifting meanings in the treatment of the combat-traumatized, recall Nathan Hale Jr.'s description of World War I as a "human laboratory" that "gave psychiatrists a new sense of mission and an expanded social role."[11] By World War II, this social role had come to encompass new duties associated with documentary film production, distribution, and exhibition. The military psychiatrist did not, however, enjoy anything like the privilege of final cut. In most cases, he was subordinate to the chief of the medical service, who, while not a psychiatrist, was often called upon to approve scripts about war trauma.[12] There is no evidence to suggest that any such chief actually rejected or even tweaked film scripts, but some were known to be "entirely uninformed or even antagonistic to psychiatry," and their mediating function was, at the very least, an odious source of delays for many psychiatrists eager to see their efforts translated from script to screen and disseminated to audiences.[13] Such efforts helped to ensure, as psychiatrist William C. Menninger suggested, "wider acceptance and better understanding of psychiatry," making war trauma and its treatment "evident to the layman."[14]

From the initial "narrow assumption that almost any type or degree of neurotic disturbance was a counter-indication for military service" to the later embrace of psychiatric treatment for active-duty soldiers, "psychiatrists' approach to military problems broadened during and, particularly, since the war," in the words of one former military psychiatrist who, looking back on his work, stressed how psychiatric concepts "were expanded in several major respects," including through the pedagogic and therapeutic use of documentary film.[15] "We psychiatrists are primarily doctors," said Air Forces psychiatrist John M. Murray in 1947, noting that, throughout World War II, "we were called upon to perform many auxiliary and secondary functions," not only supervising and participating in the production of documentaries but also contributing to debates about the potentially deleterious effects of Hollywood films that, through various fictive devices, "distorted" military psychiatry.[16] "World War II was a key point in the history of American psychoanalysis," argues Jonathan Michel Metzl; it "allowed for the first demonstrated 'success' in the treatment of neurotic symptoms in noninstitutional settings" such as the camps and convalescent centers near the North African front lines where Grinker and Spiegel administered "interactive" drug therapies, or the soundstages on which their psychiatric disciples made reenactment a central technique in military documentaries about war trauma—a way of "reviving" the recent past for therapeutic and filmic purposes.[17]

The rhetoric of visibility and invisibility would inform the work of psychological experts throughout the postwar period. The clinical psychologist John Watkins, for instance, would dedicate his 1949 casebook *Hypnotherapy of War Neuroses* "to the many veterans whose wounds, though real, are invisible," but his efforts were frequently coopted by filmmakers eager to visualize war trauma.[18] Watkins' wartime work at the Welch Convalescent Hospital in Daytona Beach, Florida, which involved exhorting hypnotized patients to imagine "a large movie screen" on which to unfold various fantasy scenarios, was occasionally filmed in order to be studied (and, of course, duplicated at other facilities), its commitment to "the inner unconscious content of the patient's emotional life" nevertheless constituting an object of visual documentation.[19] Set during World War II, the service comedy *Imitation General* (George Marshall, 1958) reflects this historical development, as a traumatized soldier (who's "really in terrible shape" and "ought to be in a hospital") confesses that "what's wrong" with him "is nothing you can see": "I think it must be what they call combat fatigue." Adding "You know what it is—you've seen it," the soldier points to a paradox that military documentaries were increasingly designed to manage—that of the sheer invisibility of a "mental disease" that cinema alone promised to make visible and knowable. "I can't find a scratch on him!" complains a hospital corpsman of one of his traumatized charges in the Navy's *The N.P. Patient* (1944); the film proceeds to "visualize" neuroses through the "psychodramatic," proto-Method acting of both experienced and nonprofessional performers. Using animation to indicate how the scars of tuberculosis may be seen via X-rays, the Army's *Shades of Gray* (1947) suggests that "psychiatric disturbances" are equally invisible to the naked eye, requiring the intervention of documentary film, which promises a "deeper understanding" of mental health, in order to achieve intelligibility.[20]

Shorts and features about unseen "matters of the mind" reliably contributed to the American documentary tradition that Jonathan Kahana has identified with the term "intelligence work," "making visible the invisible or 'phantom' realities that shape the experience of the ordinary Americans in whose name power is exercised and contested."[21] Following a period of medical uncertainty and official suppression, such films quickly became key mediators among multiple, at times competing systems of knowledge, lending trauma—especially war trauma—an audiovisual coherence made widely accessible via an abundance of state and private film distribution organs. That the identification and treatment of trauma continued to be characterized by professional disputes did not diminish but, rather, enhanced the documentary legitimacy of associated films. As Kahana argues, progressive documentary in the 1930s and 1940s tended to tackle that which was "not yet frozen in an established idea, position, or institution," even as it promised to concretize various complex political, medical, and sociological concepts.[22]

While it may seem paradoxical to align military-sponsored films with the progressive frameworks that Kahana explores, to polarize the two categories is to fail to recognize important formal as well as ideological continuities. As Alice Lovejoy argues, the state is necessarily multifaceted, the military often "at the vanguard not only of media technology but also of media aesthetics"—a "laboratory for film form and language," "a pioneer in cinema's applications and institutions."[23] By the 1940s, American military filmmakers were, to varying degrees, familiar with the writings of documentary critics John Grierson and Paul Rotha, and their ranks included (at least for a time) the Dutch socialist Joris Ivens, who worked for the Army Signal Corps.[24] State documentary remained, in this period, distinctly amenable to experimentation—at times rooted in actual clinical practice—while simultaneously offering, as Kahana puts it, "a means for grounding political abstractions like state, party, movement, and nation in the apparently natural formation of the American people."[25] Psychological traumas and their exploratory treatment constituted ripe terrain for documentary—a word that was widely used in this period, including to refer to "mere" military films made in a variety of styles. Take, for instance, a single 1944 issue of the trade paper *Motion Picture Herald*, which offered no fewer than ten uses of the term to describe military-sponsored films, at one point carefully explaining that William Wyler's *The Memphis Belle: A Story of a Flying Fortress* (1944)—a production of the Army Air Forces First Motion Picture Unit—is more than a simple "aviation report," and is in fact a "war documentary."[26] This liberal application of "documentary" extended even to military films that weren't made by Oscar-winning directors like Wyler—that, in fact, arrived as anonymous accounts of various mundane activities, or that, like many a dramatic treatment of trauma and psychotherapy, suggested the carefully staged action of a Hollywood studio production. Taking their cues from the military as well as from the widely circulated work of Grierson and Rotha, *Motion Picture Herald* and other publications regularly employed the term "dramatic documentary" throughout the war, echoing its use among psychiatrists and other psychological experts who believed that trauma could best be addressed via reenactment and other theatrical, even fantasmatic techniques.[27]

"The most misunderstood of all human ills are those due to problems of the mind," reads the opening crawl of the 1944 documentary *The Inside Story of Seaman Jones*. "It is, of course, impossible to fully cover this subject in any single book or picture, but this presentation, *made for you*, endeavors to clarify the most common, fundamental troubles that beset us as a result of emotional upset."[28] Produced by Paramount

Pictures as a Coast Guard training film, and based, in part, on psychiatrist Robert H. Felix's work at the Coast Guard Academy in New London, Connecticut, *The Inside Story of Seaman Jones* would soon become one of the most widely distributed of all military documentaries made during World War II, its depiction of "emotional disturbances" at once responsive to the unique realities of armed service and potentially relevant to individuals in all walks—and at virtually all stages—of life. As its official distributor, the Navy remained committed, for over two decades, to ensuring the film's broad circulation as both an instrument of instruction and a source of therapy. In short, *The Inside Story of Seaman Jones* was thought to be good publicity for the military, especially as the United States (like the film's young male subject) entered a new "life phase"—a postwar period of global leadership. By 1946, with the film reaching members of all branches of the armed forces as well as secondary schools, businesses, churches, and community centers nationwide, its opening address to the viewer could easily be recast as capacious in the extreme, the words "made for you" addressed as much to students in the classroom as to workers in the factory.[29]

One of many trauma-themed military films produced during and after the war, *The Inside Story of Seaman Jones* boasts sequences that purport to explain dissociation as well as a range of psychosomatic symptoms, crosscutting between cartoon characters (such as a censor whose job is to "police" the borders between the conscious and unconscious mind) and live-action subjects who simulate psychogenic illness and its careful treatment. The film focuses on the plight of Pat Jones, a former football hero—the star of his small-town high school—who begins to "crack up" upon entering the military, with its innumerable demands. "The change is a big one," explains the film's voice-over narrator, "and he's having a hard time adjusting himself to this new life. Seaman Jones is homesick, unhappy, and disturbed. Lots of things seem to be combining to worry him." He begins to struggle with his coursework, and, "panicked and lost," he develops acute anxiety, which leads to horrific nightmares. "Am I going nuts?" he asks himself. "Maybe I'm going nuts!"

Recognizing Pat's problem, the sympathetic narrator points out that, while anxiety can be crippling, "at least [Pat] can have [it] taken care of"—and by a "mighty good doctor," at that. Disturbingly, Pat starts to experience severe knee pain, but a non-psychiatric physician can find no organic cause. "What can be wrong?" asks the narrator. "[Pat] had better do something about it! He does—the most sensible thing he can

FIGURE 2. Pat Jones awakens from an "anxiety dream" in *The Inside Story of Seaman Jones* (1944). Courtesy of the U.S. National Library of Medicine.

possibly do: goes to the mental health department and sees the psychiatrist, for naturally an emotional upset must be treated differently from an organic illness." Close-ups of the books in the psychiatrist's library (with titles like *Mental Health, Diseases of the Mind,* and *Psychosomatic Medicine*) establish the seriousness of the man's endeavor, and the film proceeds to detail his credentials while presenting him as a "normal" and "natural" part of military life. The narrator praises this Navy psychiatrist for "not using a lot of strange, highfalutin terms," thus couching the film itself as a readily interpretable extension of his vernacular prowess—one whose messages are "easily understood."

The Inside Story of Seaman Jones suggests the expansive value of a docudramatic recounting of trauma and psychotherapy, and the film's influence can be felt in the Navy's *Combat Fatigue: Insomnia* (1945), whose narrator critiques "vague medical terms" and aspires to translate trauma into an intelligible vernacular—precisely, he says, the job of the "helpful," "patient" military psychiatrist. Various dramatizations reinforce this point: "You know, what you need is—" says one sailor to another, unable to finish the sentence with a reasonable prescription for the treatment of anxiety because he himself is not a psychiatrist. "Hell, I can't help him—that's the doc's job," he later admits. "Sure, see the doc!"

More than a "mere" training film intended to acquaint enlistees with the challenges and benefits of life in the armed services, *The Inside Story of Seaman Jones* is a similarly explicit advertisement for military psychiatry—part of an entire cycle of nontheatrical films designed to address the subject of war trauma, which, as Pat's case makes clear, is hardly limited to battlefield experiences. The demands of war are, the film suggests, so extreme—so psychologically disruptive—that they affect even those who, like Pat, have never seen combat. Luckily, however, the military is committed to "handling" as well as "preventing" mental illness. Anticipating America's postwar responsibilities, *The Inside Story of Seaman Jones* also stresses the military's capacity to "mold minds" both at home and abroad. "Today, we're making a scientific study of the mind," the psychiatrist tells Pat, "and we're finding some very encouraging things." Not only is military-psychiatric expertise responsible for effectively explaining to Pat that "emotions actually can cause real physical pain," but the psychiatrist himself is also available to "counsel" the young man, suggesting that "a lot of boys feel about the way you do"—including "a big, strapping lad" who won multiple Golden Gloves tournaments. Upon entering the wartime military, this "very pretty fighter" developed severe, psychogenic stomach pains. Like Pat, he was forced to see a military psychiatrist—an encounter that, the film suggests, changed his life for the better.

The universality of emotional disturbances—and of psychogenic illnesses in particular—is thus a central theme of *The Inside Story of Seaman Jones*, which endeavors to implicate all Americans as beneficiaries of military psychiatry. The eponymous enlistee, with his recognizable character flaws, is allegedly representative of his countrymen—"each one a Seaman Jones." Such rhetoric undoubtedly fueled the film's broad uptake in the postwar period. It proved so popular in secondary schools in part because it provided a clear object of identification in the Pat Jones who goes from high school football field to "new responsibilities," and it was perhaps equally welcome in factories because of its focus on Pat's prewar role as a junior foreman—a job that the film flatteringly (and strategically) links to military service.[30]

Fittingly, Pat is transformed into a source of useful information about mental health—a comprehensible conveyor of psychoanalytic wisdom, much like the film itself. Pat's psychiatrist hands him a pamphlet on "the mind"—a set of notes on his specific condition—that he studies before "advising" his fellow servicemen, who gather around him to discuss their troubles. If the film endorses the claims made in this

FIGURE 3. Expelled from the conscious mind, "self-pitying thoughts" attempt to arouse Unconscious Mind ("the dormant parent of all your emotions") in *The Inside Story of Seaman Jones* (1944). Courtesy of the U.S. National Library of Medicine.

FIGURE 4. After learning "the basics" from a plainspoken Navy psychiatrist, Pat Jones proceeds to teach his fellow enlistees about "matters of the mind" in *The Inside Story of Seaman Jones* (1944). Courtesy of the U.S. National Library of Medicine.

pamphlet—an actual "medical circular" seen in instructive close-up—it also supplants it, suggesting that documentary, with its capacity to assimilate everything from animation to staged reenactment, is a superior vehicle of psychiatric instruction. It is also, of course, an instrument of statecraft, as the narrator makes clear at the close of the film: "Sound mental health is our nation's greatest asset, and this we must maintain."

DOCUMENTING MENTAL HEALTH

"[W]hen the boys come home from the battlefields overseas, you will find they have changed. . . . The war has made Americans think, and they aren't going to be so interested in trivial, trashy movies anymore."

—Darryl F. Zanuck, 1945[31]

Responding to the deadliest conflict in human history, a series of American documentary and realist films—produced or commissioned by the United States military—developed an aesthetic of trauma in the 1940s and early 1950s. In their narrative emphasis on illness and recovery, rupture and rehabilitation, social isolation and gradual reintegration, these films sought to convert complex psychiatric concepts into vernacular terms and to disseminate those terms to as wide a public as could be gathered beneath the broadening umbrella of nontheatrical exhibition. New Deal documentary provided a template for much of this work, as the trauma of the Great Depression (and associated ecological catastrophes like dust storms and flooding) gave way to the work of rebuilding and re-enfranchisement encapsulated in such films as *The Plow That Broke the Plains* (Pare Lorentz, 1936) and *The River* (Pare Lorentz, 1937), with their optimistic emphasis on the state's reparative potential. Painfully aware of the political and psychiatric failures of an earlier era, when traumatized veterans of the First World War did not receive adequate attention for their conditions (particularly amid widespread debates about "malingering," pensions, and the stigma of asylums), military filmmakers fashioned a way of addressing war trauma as a national problem with emphatically national solutions. This figuration of trauma and rehabilitation was also a kind of visual and rhetorical shorthand for the military-industrial state.[32] For if that state was responsible for the treatment of war-traumatized Americans, including through the Veterans Administration (VA), it was also responsible for returning them to forms of employment that often explicitly involved contributions to military power.[33]

The remarkable survival of trauma-themed films through nontheatrical distribution helped promote the belief that psychic recovery could be attained through an individual's close, cooperative involvement with the military-industrial state. "The Second World War gave nontheatrical films their greatest chance for service and their greatest public recognition," wrote Gloria Waldron, a member of the educational staff of the Twentieth Century Fund, in 1949.[34] Seeking to account for the lasting popularity of military documentaries in particular, the educational researcher Charles F. Hoban observed that "their use involved little or no expense to the user"; production, distribution, and exhibition costs were typically "borne by [the Army, Navy, Air Forces, and U.S. Office of Education], *not by the user* of the films."[35] Corporations routinely acquired free prints for in-house use, including for explicitly "inspirational" and even "therapeutic" purposes. Businesses that had lost employees to combat were encouraged by the War Activities Committee to request filmed records of the deceased, such as John Huston's *San Pietro* (1945), which featured men of the 143rd Infantry Regiment of the Army's 36th Division, many of whom, after "playing themselves" for Huston, were killed in action in Monte Cassino.[36] Huston's earlier documentary *Report from the Aleutians* (1943) was even abridged as a special "home movie" to comfort the father of one of its "stars," a first lieutenant; with the blessing of the War Department's Bureau of Public Relations, the Signal Corps covered the cost of Kodachrome processing (of "corded off footages") by the Eastman Kodak Company.[37] Seven years later, the Army established a mere $30 licensing fee for each of a number of nonfiction films, which, sold to American television stations via a specialty distributor, were broadcast "over and over without further cost," filling federally mandated public service time.[38]

This transformation of wartime documentaries into postwar television programs was widespread, and it represented the logical evolution of films engineered to be vehicles of military public relations—to bridge gaps between a professional-intellectual class (whose membership increasingly included psychiatrists and psychologists) and the so-called "common man" whose very ordinariness could be telegraphed through his traumatic symptoms. These, the influential Army Air Forces psychiatrist John M. Murray maintained, "could affect anyone"—even, he added, "Everyman" (thus evoking historian Carl Becker's 1931 identification of "Mr. Everyman," who, despite or perhaps because of his very "normality," found himself "living history").[39] Paramount's glossy

Lady in the Dark (Mitchell Leisen, 1944), in which Ginger Rogers' high-powered magazine editor reluctantly undergoes psychoanalysis in order to resolve her romantic dilemmas, took a dramatically different approach to trauma, couching it as a distinctly bourgeois affliction—something reserved for an uppity "boss-lady"—and its box-office success seemed to portend a cycle of films predicated on the stylish trappings of the talking cure.[40] "Psychiatry in Technicolor," read a promotional headline in *Motion Picture Herald*, which later claimed that the success of *Lady in the Dark* was "tantamount to a starter's pistol signaling the opening of a new frontier for producers and writers to cross over and explore beyond"—a claim that David Bordwell endorses in *Reinventing Hollywood*, asserting that Leisen's film singlehandedly "launched the therapeutic cycle."[41] But *Lady in the Dark* hardly broke new narrative ground in 1944, and its depiction of psychoanalysis can be traced back at least to the interwar period—and even to another Ginger Rogers film, the RKO musical *Carefree* (Mark Sandrich, 1938), costarring Fred Astaire as a psychiatrist who experiments with sodium pentothal. If the deeply derivative, altogether misogynist *Lady in the Dark* symbolized anything for filmmakers and psychological professionals fundamentally concerned with war trauma, it was a misplaced approach to mental illness—an advertisement for psychiatry as a wealthy woman's pursuit, which films about "ordinary" yet "nervously wounded" men would have to counter, and quickly. The Austrian-American psychiatrist Jacob Moreno, whose work would influence that of Roy Grinker, John Spiegel, and many other doctors forced to confront war trauma, condemned *Lady in the Dark* as "abhorrent"—an albatross around psychiatry's increasingly public neck, its commercial success demanding corrective depictions of trauma as anything but rarefied.[42] Military documentaries about mental illness were, for Moreno and others, ideal ambassadors of psychiatric and psychological treatment. Their principal aim was to normalize trauma and psychotherapy as far removed from the sort of "feminine" exclusivity centered in a Technicolor extravaganza like *Lady in the Dark*, and their modest style was reinforced by their television appearances in the 1950s, which built upon earlier uses of the medium as an intimate therapeutic agent for "average Joes."[43] In 1944, for instance, the Radio Corporation of America (RCA) purchased a series of newspaper ads touting television as "a daily reality" for thousands of servicemen then being treated in Army and Navy hospitals, where its subsidiary NBC telecast allegedly salubrious images of "the outside world."[44]

While television stations were recycling them as nonprofit public service broadcasts in the postwar period, extending their strategic appeals to "everyday Americans," military films were also serving as key instruments of private enterprise, helping to fill corporate coffers by legitimizing continued production and, moreover, the sort of alliance identified—as early as 1947—with the term "the military-industrial complex."[45] Even the abovementioned "therapeutic telecasts" were intended to advertise NBC and RCA, which both insisted that the new medium was ready for massification despite concerns about broadcast standards. Such bold claims, which directly contradicted those of CBS and the FCC, depended upon the pronounced public relations value of media associated with veterans' education and rehabilitation, even as they were clearly part of the process by which, as Herbert Schiller put it, "television prematurely was hurried into the economy by impatient equipment manufacturers and broadcasting networks, eager to sell sets and screen time."[46] Anna McCarthy has documented the emergence of institutional advertising on American television, highlighting corporate sponsorship of public service programming, which was frequently designed to advance private interests via a liberal pluralist understanding of good governance.[47] Such interests were plainly compatible with those of the U.S. military during and after World War II, as "the future of advanced corporate capitalism" increasingly depended on "the efficient linkage of commercial objectives . . . and military conquest"—a "politico-economic structure" in a "powerful imperial system."[48]

From the perspective of the increasingly robust military-industrial state, cheaply produced military documentaries were, in promotional terms, scarcely different from the two-and-a-half-million-dollar *Lady in the Dark*. Like the latter, whose tie-ins included a special fragrance by Dorothy Gray and a high-end men's clothing line by The Kleinhans Company, military documentaries enjoyed numerous sponsors and generated at least as many commercial spin-offs. When the Allied co-production *Tunisian Victory* (Frank Capra et al., 1944)—which ads breathlessly described as "the real thing—filmed under fire!"—was exhibited at Loew's Columbia Theatre in Washington, it brought with it a "mammoth military display" that took up the entire block and included trucks and Jeeps, as well as a large 40mm anti-aircraft gun and range finder in a "complete action demonstration."[49] Reviewing *Lady in the Dark* alongside Wyler's *The Memphis Belle*, critic Manny Farber seemed to miss this capitalist connection, arguing that the two 1944 releases "resemble each other only in that they are both color films." In Farber's reading, the style of *Lady in the Dark* "makes each shot look like the domestic interiors in linoleum ads," relying as it does upon "the kind of costuming, interior decorating and makeup that occur most frequently in department stores' windows." He went on, "Scenes like the ones in the analyst's office amount to displays of what the well dressed analyst and analyzee [*sic*] should wear, what the one should write with and the other lie on: a special pencil gadget that unhooks from the belt, and a great green-leather monster that curves so you don't need pillows."[50] The "smart, effective," admirably "realistic" "opposite" of *Lady in the Dark*, Wyler's *The Memphis Belle* in fact shares—and arguably even exceeds—the other film's promotional imperatives, supplementing simple commodity fetishism with a more sophisticated form of institutional advertising designed, as Douglas Cunningham argues, to advance the political struggle for Air Force autonomy, precisely by presenting it in terms of anthropomorphic metaphors that made the titular "belle" seem in need of more appreciative (and more munificent) treatment.[51]

If *Lady in the Dark* functioned to enrich Paramount while selling perfume and other fast-moving consumer goods, *The Memphis Belle* and other military documentaries had even broader, more consequential capitalist goals. Wyler's film, in particular, was made not merely to support the continued manufacture of the Boeing B-17 Flying Fortress, but also to agitate for what would finally be achieved in 1947 with the signing of the National Security Act—namely, the establishment of the Air Force as a discrete service on a par with the Army and the Navy.[52] By the end of World War I, the American armed forces had become what Aeron Davis calls "promotional cultures," cannily borrowing strategies from advertising and public relations.[53] Writing in 1920, George Creel, former head of the Committee on Public Information, likened military-industrial activities to a vast "advertising campaign . . . shot through and through with an evangelical quality."[54] Numerous companies—including those devoted to arms manufacturing—remained committed to screening military documentaries like *The Memphis Belle* in order to encourage worker productivity, even long after the end of hostilities. Films about mental health were especially useful in such contexts because they insisted that psychological rehabilitation could enhance one's employability, and thus provided a model for companies interested in preparing individuals for the possibility of experiencing—and, eventually, recovering from—traumatic workplace accidents. Military documentaries joined a whole host of other films that purported to provide "industrial therapy" amid the postwar efflorescence of psychiatry and psychology.[55]

A major agent of cinematic exchange between the military and private industry was the U.S. Office of Education's Division of Visual Aids for War Training, which was established in 1941 in order to instruct millions of war industry workers. Producing "practical" as well as "inspirational" and even "therapeutic" films that often relied upon footage from the Army—and that just as frequently fed the Army's own compilation films—the Division of Visual Aids for War Training maintained strong yet complicated ties to the armed forces.[56] In some cases, the division considered its finished films sacrosanct, imposing numerous restrictions on military use. For instance, in 1946—its final year of production—the division complied with the Army's request for its "inspirational documentary" *Employing Disabled Workers in Industry* (1946), outlining its restrictions in a letter to the Signal Corps: "[The film] must be shown to audiences where no charge is made for the showing and it cannot be cut, changed, or altered in any manner whatsoever."[57] Those at the Signal Corps Photographic Center were apparently happy to comply, labeling *Employing Disabled Workers in Industry* a "War Department Official Film" and earmarking it "for distribution to film libraries of hospitals designated for amputee care," where it could better prepare veterans for postwar work than, say, a newsreel like *United News*, whose November 1945 edition featured a mere fifty seconds of footage of disabled veterans learning, as the voice-over narrator puts it, "the highly skilled trade of watchmaking."[58] By contrast, the twenty-minute running time of *Employing Disabled Workers in Industry* allowed the film to explore a range of employment options for injured veterans—including the "war work" (such as weapons testing and aircraft manufacturing) that so concerned both the Division of Visual Aids for War Training and the military itself.

When it was not working directly with the Signal Corps, the Office of Education was outsourcing film production to independent companies, whose work would reliably blur the line between documentary pedagogy and institutional advertising. The formal and ideological resemblance between military documentaries—including those about war trauma—and industrial and advertising films is at least partly attributable to such subcontractors, whose commercially opportunistic flexibility lent them a remarkably broad purview as early as the interwar period.[59] Consider, for instance, Castle Films: established in 1924, this relatively small producer-distributor made advertising films for major corporations; in the 1940s, the company began producing shorts and features for various branches of the armed forces, including the Navy, which commissioned Castle's *Film Tactics* (1945), a twenty-two-minute dramatization of how best to use actual military films in the classroom. In *Film Tactics*, which focuses on the "optimal utilization" of the Navy's 1945 instructional short *The Countermarch* (also produced by Castle), a voice-over narrator exhorts officers to "get [enlisted men] ready for the film"—to "prepare their minds" by saying more than that "regulations require that we watch it": "You've got to tell them what to look for in the film!" When a soldier becomes an inattentive film spectator, a hot, stuffy room may well be to blame, but "inner conflicts" are always worth considering, and they must be "overcome" not merely by the spectator himself but also by his superior officer, who must employ "psychological tactics" in order to "inspire" the serious viewing of a didactic short. *Film Tactics* takes us, as the narrator phrases it, "inside the mind," where distractions abound, and specific neuroses—anthropomorphized in a manner that recalls the style of *The Inside Story of Seaman Jones*, and that evokes the dream sequence designed by Salvador Dalí in the exactly contemporaneous *Spellbound* (Alfred Hitchcock, 1945)— conspire to prevent men from paying attention to potentially life-saving instructional films. Here, the arena of reception is at once a military classroom and a "cluttered mind" that must be cleared through the psychotherapeutic entreaties of a "film instructor."

This symbolic outsourcing of psychotherapy to non-medical officers, and the associated cultivation of techniques of self-management among all enlisted men, suggest the expanding influence of psychiatric and psychological discourses during World War II. Depicting the screening room as a workplace where "matters of the mind" must be "managed," *Film Tactics* reflects then-current beliefs—most famously voiced by John Grierson—that the social technology of documentary could effectively unite disparate classes, its translational character "responsible at once to the individual instance and the totality," as Jonathan Kahana puts it.[60] Grierson was a known quantity among the military's in-house filmmakers and subcontractors in the 1940s, his work providing some key templates for their efforts. It was Grierson who, upon becoming the inaugural commissioner of the National Film Board of Canada (NFB) in 1939, began subcontracting private companies (including Crawley Films and Associated Screen Studios) in order to meet the wartime demand for documentary, and his close personal ties to Hollywood producers— including Walter Wanger, president of the Academy of Motion Picture Arts and Sciences during World War II—did not go unnoticed in American military circles. Throughout the 1940s, numerous NFB filmmakers,

FIGURE 5. The "cluttered," neurotic spectatorial mind in *Film Tactics* (1945). Courtesy of the National Archives and Records Administration.

including George L. George, would go on to work for the U.S. Army Signal Corps on Grierson's recommendation—an informal exchange program that helped to situate Griersonian ideals at the center of American military filmmaking.[61] Establishing certain precedents for later military films, Wanger's *Private Worlds* (Gregory La Cava, 1935) features a psychiatrist (played by Claudette Colbert) who decides to work in a mental hospital in order to understand the "lost souls" of the "lost generation," including her lover, who, in a panic, fled the horrors of combat and was shot for cowardice. Both Grierson and Wanger were well acquainted with Walter Lippmann (Grierson had studied Lippmann during his tenure as a Rockefeller Foundation fellow at the University of Chicago, while Wanger had served alongside Lippmann as an officer in U.S. Army Intelligence and as a member of Woodrow Wilson's staff at the Paris Peace Conference), and Lippmann's famous insistence that a special cadre of experts was required for the management of American political and social life has its own analogues in military documentaries that tout psychiatrists and psychologists.[62] (Even *Private Worlds*, made over a dozen years after the publication of Lippmann's *Public Opinion*, features a Lippmannian collection of renowned psychiatrists who must learn to work together for the betterment of "all Americans.") "Although Grierson is usually associated with a specifically British framework of governmental and liberal-capitalist institutions," Kahana notes, "his programmatic statements from the 1920s through the 1940s presume a broadly Anglo-American philosophical and political field of discourse," and they certainly had a bearing on the production of military documentaries about war trauma and its psychiatric treatment.[63] Following the model of Grierson's National Film Board, the U.S. Office of Education commissioned Caravel Films, a New York-based producer of industrial, advertising, and training films, to turn out a series of shorts on war trauma as a "workplace problem," one tied to physical and emotional "handicaps." The resulting collection of films included the fourteen-minute *Establishing Working Relations for the Disabled Worker* (1946), which depicts the absorption of psychiatric and psychological expertise by a machine-shop supervisor forced to contend with a war veteran's "problems of readjustment." Subcontractors were not always required for the production of films about the therapeutic cooperation of the military and private industry. Produced and distributed by the U.S. Veterans Administration, the fifteen-minute *Day for Decision* (1953) addresses the VA's vocational counseling services, which, as depicted here, overwhelmingly emphasize the restorative potential of "work for the military."

Because such documentaries often addressed "the peculiar mental and emotional processes of the military mind," they remained relevant to the schools, churches, civic organizations, and community centers that increasingly accommodated military recruitment during the postwar period.[64] But they also, as the above examples indicate, spoke to the political-economic assemblage known as the military-industrial complex, often promoting "defense work" as a means of recovering and sustaining mental health—a source of therapy unto itself.[65] Building on the work of the military's "industrial incentive" programs, which entailed the production of films "'angled' to establish the relationship between production on the home front and success on the battle front," documentaries about trauma and rehabilitation tend to link "defense of the mind" to defense of the nation, defining therapeutic self-governance in terms of the dividends that it pays to the state.[66] Far from being a pathological and contradictory element of the military machine, the traumatized soldier, as a beneficiary of military-psychiatric treatment, became

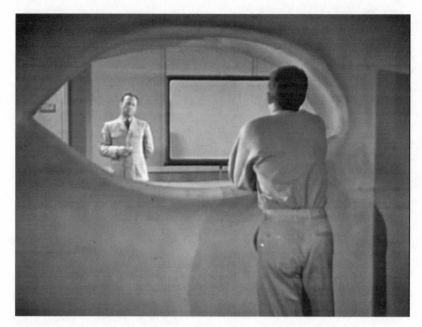

FIGURE 6. The "clean," focused spectatorial mind—free of any neuroses—in *Film Tactics* (1945). Courtesy of the National Archives and Records Administration.

the symbol of a new therapeutic order, one that was consistently limned through nontheatrical nonfiction film. As Michael Chanan argues, documentary "is one of the forms through which new attitudes enter wider circulation," and such was the function of military films committed to normalizing psychotherapy as an instrument of state power.[67]

Typically dismissed as "ephemeral films"—a designation that is often wrongly conflated with "nontheatrical films"—military documentaries were, in fact, designed to last.[68] This is particularly obvious when one examines the public relations directives of the Army, Navy, and Air Force, along with the related goals of the American Association for the Advancement of Psychology, the American Association for Adult Education, and the Carnegie Corporation, which often subsidized the production and distribution of military-approved films.[69] Numerous national organizations embraced these films long after the end of the war. For instance, the National Conference of Christians and Jews, which in the late 1940s had 325 local offices (each with its own film library), regularly acquired "old" military documentaries (particularly those about the Holocaust, atomic power, and psychotherapy), which it lent free of charge to community groups and other interested parties.[70]

Similarly, the League of Women Voters, various Junior Leagues, and the National Publicity Council for Health and Welfare Services all used military films to further their shared commitment to "mental hygiene," screening these documentaries alongside works produced by the National Film Board of Canada (such as *The Feeling of Rejection* [1947]) and the United Auto Workers (such as *Brotherhood of Man* [1946]).[71] At the same time, film societies—including Amos Vogel's legendary Cinema 16—were instrumental in cultivating appreciation for "films of fact and purpose," particularly those that featured psychological experiments (such as *Aggression and Destruction Games: Balloons* [1941], produced by a group of psychologists at Vassar College) and various other "psychological demonstration films" (such as works initially intended for military use).[72] Trauma-themed films produced by and for the armed forces remained very much at home in this environment—instruments and illustrations of a new therapeutic ethos.

So-called "mental health films" made their way to Cinema 16 thanks to the efforts of the New York University (NYU) Film Library, which, during the war, was made the exclusive distributor of these and other "psychological documentaries." That such films were valued for their pedagogic as well as therapeutic potential had much to do with precedents set by the military. "There is vast and effective use of films in the armed services, and the public is well aware of this," wrote the board of NYU's Educational Film Institute mere weeks after V-E Day.[73] Two years earlier, many at NYU were already envisioning ways of supplementing the work of the Office of War Information (OWI), the War Activities Committee, and other government agencies by ensuring the continued circulation of a variety of nonfiction films, including those produced by or for the military. "The war will revolutionize education," predicted Robert Gessner, chairman of NYU's Department of Motion Pictures, in 1943. "Over 3,500 Army and Navy training films are demonstrating that the human mind can be taught and trained in difficult subjects in a shorter time and in a more thorough manner than the old lecture-textbook method . . . Today an American soldier can say that one reel of training film is worth a thousand textbooks."[74]

With its reflexive emphasis on the effective translation of typed "psychiatric notes" into a dynamic documentary film, *The Inside Story of Seaman Jones* seemed to concur. When, in the early 1950s, the film was essentially "retranslated" into written form, the resulting mass-market paperback (entitled simply *The Inside Story* and written "under the direction" of Yale psychiatrist Fritz Redlich and VA psychologist Jacob

Levine) contained a "layman's preface" explaining that cartoons can be reliable conveyors of psychoanalytic insight. Much as the film features animated sequences that purport to visualize the "inner workings" of the human mind, the book boasts over one hundred cartoons portraying various "human predicaments"—all of them reminders of the film's mimetic flexibility, its insistence that psychoneuroses can be modeled in many ways.[75]

It is now widely accepted that, as Damion Searls puts it, "World War II was the turning point in the history of mental health in America."[76] Less understood is the role that cinema—and, in particular, nontheatrical nonfiction film—played in this process. If, in Ellen Dwyer's words, World War II "helped psychiatrists move out of the asylum and into the community at large," documentary films were among the most reliable vehicles for their transportation, not only translating medical knowledge into vernacular terms but also familiarizing audiences with the faces, voices, and clinical techniques of particular therapists.[77] The military had long since accepted the superiority of audiovisual media to more "static" pedagogic forms as a means of educating enlisted men and women about psychological matters. This institutional shift from written documents, such as the Selective Service's Medical Circular No. 1 (1940)—derided by psychiatrist Harry Stack Sullivan as "a child's guide to psychiatric diagnosis"—to more sophisticated audiovisual techniques laid much of the discursive and material groundwork for the later use of "therapeutic films" in a wide variety of civilian settings.[78]

Whether to communicate the military's "humanitarian" aims and its lasting commitment (ostensibly shared by the Veterans Administration) to rehabilitating its traumatized members, or simply to advertise the achievements of military psychiatrists increasingly responsible for treating civilian patients, these films were recycled via a range of nontheatrical distribution networks, surviving well past the cessation of hostilities and certainly irrespective of whatever labels ("classified," "restricted," "educational," "training," "orientation") were once nominally attached to them. John Huston's Army Signal Corps documentary *Let There Be Light* (1946) offers a key case in point. "Suppressed" by the military, which denied it a commercial theatrical release until 1980, the film was nevertheless given a very public "tour of the state" of Minnesota by governor Luther Youngdahl in the late 1940s—part of Youngdahl's campaign to improve conditions in state mental hospitals and promote a military-approved conception of psychiatric care. On a single day in January 1949, nearly three thousand Minnesotans saw *Let There Be*

Light in back-to-back screenings at the historic Lowry Hotel in Minneapolis, where Huston's "special attraction"—prints of which were
purchased from the VA by the State of Minnesota, their public use sponsored by such organizations as the Interclub Council and the Ramsey
County Citizens Committee on Mental Health—was upheld as a source
of inspiration and a catalyst for community action. The film remained a
magnet for Minnesotan audiences for years to come.[79] Scholarship on
the film has, however, routinely asserted that it went unseen until 1980.
Thomas Doherty claims that it was "withheld from public screening,"
while Mark Harris has more recently alleged that *"Let There Be Light*
would not be shown publicly for 35 years."[80] The film was, in fact, so
widely—and so publicly—circulated in the five months immediately following its completion that a Signal Corps memorandum from May
1946 bemoaned the condition of the much-used distribution print in
its possession. As one officer noted in a handwritten addendum, this
print was "mutilated beyond projection [or] duping," so frequently
had it been "borrowed" by medical educators within and beyond
the military.[81] Accepting one (erroneous) narrative—that *Let There Be
Light* was successfully "hidden" in response to Huston's "heroic" truth-
telling—has enabled widespread ignorance of the role that the film
played, along with a number of other documentaries, in publicizing certain practices of military psychiatry and their civilian applications. It
has also meant sustaining certain assumptions about the purposes of
state-sponsored documentary as well as a particular (and peculiarly
narrow) historiographic approach to the American armed forces and
their relationship to media.

A series of postwar articles in *Hollywood Quarterly* set certain myopic
precedents for scholarly accounts of military documentaries, bemoaning
the "little-seen" status of these films because their only metric was commercial theatrical exhibition, or focusing on Frank Capra and the *Why
We Fight* series (1942–1945) at the expense of the thousands of other
works produced.[82] What Michel Foucault calls "popular memory"—in
this case, memory of the many trauma-themed films screened in classrooms, churches, factories, offices, town squares, and elsewhere—appears
to have been blocked, or at least recast, by the apparatuses committed to
regulating historical knowledge. These include the "popular literature,"
schools, and academic studies implicated in Foucault's critique, but also
commercial media that, in the "heroic mode," invariably focus on the
exploits of Capra, Huston, John Ford, George Stevens, William Wyler,
and other directors-in-uniform.[83] The refusal to consider films made by

individuals other than these widely celebrated "great men" threatens the intelligibility not simply of a rich and revealing history of nontheatrical film production and distribution but also of the particular political and economic agendas that these "orphan films" directly and indirectly served. As Haidee Wasson points out, "there is another story to be told about cinema as a wartime apparatus, one not well addressed by focusing on the familiar." Wasson rightly recognizes "the wide range of film types made by and for the military in the 1940s," and it was within this wide range that documentaries about war trauma and psychotherapy functioned as instruments of education and vehicles of public relations—though they are all but forgotten today.[84]

In his account of the ideologically fraught struggles over the public memory of World War II, Foucault provides an important framework for understanding what is at stake in this neglect of films that exceed the familiar dimensions of "state propaganda." For Foucault, the regulation of memory and knowledge is more about meeting present ideological needs than about "accurately" rendering past events. An awareness of xenophobic, jingoistic propaganda on the order of Capra's *Prelude to War* (1942) is perhaps more palatable—more readily digestible—than knowledge of the subtler explorations of trauma and psychotherapy that helped through their therapeutic discourses to promote the solidification of certain aspects of the military-industrial state. Positing the ideological crudeness of the largely racist, warmongering *Why We Fight* films, and limiting one's analysis to them, means widening the gap between past and "enlightened" present—and thus, perhaps, absolving oneself of responsibility for investigating the links between trauma-themed films, with their broad uptake by the national mental health movement, and the consolidation of certain kinds of military-industrial power.

This carefully curated knowledge of the past—this production of "common sense" about what military documentaries were and what purposes they served—permits reformation, as Foucault puts it, only "along certain lines." "People are shown not what they have been but what they must remember they have been": not complicit in the normalization of the military-industrial complex, but regrettably tolerant of the historically-specific racism "required" to win the war, as well as of the embarrassing optimism allegedly characteristic of the period—ostensibly an easier problem to fix, because it is (allegedly) about the changing tides of taste and behavior, and not political-economic assemblages in a broader, less tractable sense.[85] Far from the simplistic "good war" of popular myth, World War II in fact "laid the structural foundations in politics for the modern American empire," as Michael Rogin points out. It effectively "established the military-industrial state as the basis for both domestic welfare and foreign policy," all while demanding the production of films that could reach recalcitrant Americans, conditioning them to accept the permanence and therapeutic utility of a large-scale military force.[86] That such coercion was deemed increasingly necessary is a testament to the confusions characteristic of the era. As a postwar psychiatric report pointed out, "there was little explicit agreement about goal norms among the American soldiers," who offered wildly divergent explanations for "why we fight."[87] Yet scholars of cinema and the Second World War have tended to rely on some rather narrow frameworks of interpretation. In his influential book *War and Cinema*, Paul Virilio goes so far as to allege that wartime military documentaries "were withdrawn from circulation"—rendered permanently irrelevant as "the convalescent joy of the immediate postwar period was gradually extinguished."[88] Virilio is wildly wrong on multiple counts, of course, for his assertion presupposes cheerful patriotism as a motif of all wartime military documentaries (a tired historiographic tactic even when *War and Cinema* was first published in 1989), while simultaneously ignoring the numerous nontheatrical distribution networks that, in reality, ensured that these films would *not* be "withdrawn from circulation"—and that, more to the point, they would persist in advertising the military establishment, whether as 8mm reduction prints for the private home, as audiovisual artifacts to be studied in school, or as television programs that aired in public service time.

Virilio's affection for florid overstatement—as in his equally misplaced assertion that cinema, after Abel Gance's day, "would be no more than a bastardized form, a poor relation of military-industrial society"—is all too easy to discredit by paying close attention to the nontheatrical sector, but it speaks volumes about the sort of scholarly myopia that maintains an investment in stale narratives of World War II.[89] Hence the widespread resistance to the study of "mere" training and orientation films—and the reluctance to bestow the lofty label of documentary upon them, which Alice Lovejoy rightly reads in terms of a "general mistrust of 'sponsored'" fare.[90] Frequently rejected out of hand, or consigned to the purgatory of YouTube, where they allegedly index the inanities of the mid-twentieth-century mindset, these were, in fact, remarkably durable works of "useful cinema" (to adopt Haidee Wasson and Charles R. Acland's indispensable term) that did more than just normalize war trauma and psychotherapy.[91]

Viewing these films today, one comes face to face with a particular public-relations strategy that hasn't gone away—that views diagnosis and therapy as the crux of institutional power and liberal individualism. David Serlin notes that, because of their noncommercial character, public health films are often wrongly assumed to "operate outside of the visual culture of modern consumerism and, in particular, genres of communication defined by advertising and marketing," when in fact they have long been central to such genres, linked as much to the pharmaceutical industry as to the aims of various political campaigns (like Governor Youngdahl's) and government agencies.[92] The films addressed in this book are key examples of works that proved instrumental first to the waging and winning of war; later to the emergence and popularization of the national mental health movement; and finally to the normalization of the military-industrial state, with its claims on defense of the national body as well as the individual psyche.

That we are still living with the consequences of these strategies—and still subjected to their coercive character, whether in the form of commercials for the armed forces (and such associated charitable organizations as Support Our Troops and The Wounded Warrior Project) or of docudramatic films like *American Sniper* (Clint Eastwood, 2014) and *12 Strong: The Declassified True Story of the Horse Soldiers* (Nicolai Fuglsig, 2018)—is all the more reason to scrutinize the period when they were relatively new. As Walter Benjamin warns, "every image of the past that is not recognized by the present as one of its concerns threatens to disappear irretrievably."[93] Losing sight of the formation and initial flourishing of a particular public relations tactic, we run the risk of misrecognizing that which remains very much an instrument of the military-industrial state.

TRAUMATIC TIMES

"We all have war jitters."

—Val Lewton, 1944[94]

Merely alluding to the high incidence of psychiatric disorders during World War II may seem controversial—even nonsensical. After all, as Penny Coleman points out, the war "is not associated with combat-related stress in the popular imagination." It is instead "remembered as the 'good war' whose soldiers defeated an unequivocal evil and returned with Gene Kelly optimism."[95] Yet even Gene Kelly, while serving in the

Navy, was called upon to portray a severely traumatized veteran in his directorial debut *Combat Fatigue: Irritability* (Gene Kelly, 1945), a work that was widely distributed as an entry in the Navy's five-part film series on war trauma. The persistent availability of such films—even outside of government archives—has seemingly done little to influence retrospective accounts. "Today, few Americans associate war trauma with the so-called good war and the greatest generation that fought it," writes Rebecca Jo Plant. "But the proportion of men discharged from the U.S. military on neuropsychiatric grounds was in fact significantly higher in World War II than in World War I, Korea, or Vietnam."[96] As the narrator of the Navy's *The N.P. Patient* (1944) puts it, "The size of the problem will startle you."

Discharge rates were so high, in fact, that films about psychoneurosis were developed, in part, to prepare inductees for the "exceedingly traumatic" experience of being "let go" because of a "mental problem."[97] World War II, which remains "the most destructive conflict humanity has yet seen," forced millions of Americans to confront the realities of war trauma.[98] The number of psychiatric patients in VA hospitals nearly doubled between 1940 and 1948; in 1946, roughly 60 percent of all VA patients were classified as "neuropsychiatric cases."[99] Such sobering figures demanded the fashioning of what Eva Moskowitz calls a "psychological front"—an unprecedented attempt to incorporate psychological expertise into the prosecution of war.[100]

Even before the United States entered World War II, the military was carefully cultivating the work of psychological experts, particularly through the Research Branch of the Army's Morale Division (later known as the Information and Education Division), which was established in October 1941.[101] By this time, the military's visual cultures reflected a deep investment in "matters of the mind." In 1942, the clinical psychologist Molly Harrower introduced the Group Rorschach Test, which involved projecting images of inkblots onto screens, walls, and curtains—a proto-cinematic experiment that, while never widely adopted by the military, still suggested a growing commitment to visualizing the psychological.[102] During the war, similar projections of diagnostic materials supplemented actual film screenings. The Army psychiatrist Daniel Jaffe, for instance, favored projecting the "cartoonish diagrams" originally published in the journal *War Medicine*, which purported to illustrate various emotional states, in order to educate officers about mental health.[103]

Contrary to conventional wisdom, military documentaries of the 1940s and 1950s insisted on the centrality of psychiatric and psychological treatment to the rehabilitation of veterans. Emphasizing the sheer diversity of "so much challenging clinical material," the institutional documentary *The Navy Nurse* (1952) notes that patients' "ills may be either of the body or the mind." Even films believed to have been beyond the ken of psychological experts in fact reflected their work. The psychiatrist and psychoanalyst John W. Appel, for instance, supervised the production of the *Why We Fight* films, which, as a result of his interventions, "exemplified a new kind of Signal Corps documentary," as Charles Wolfe argues, "one in which the historical and psychological conditions of combat took precedence over a narrow technical or tactical approach."[104]

Teaching filmmakers basic Freudian concepts, Appel was part of a movement within military psychiatry that embraced film for its pedagogic as well as therapeutic potential, and that sought to normalize psychoneurosis as a consequence of war.[105] "There is no getting used to combat," Appel wrote in December 1944. "Each moment of it imposes a strain so great men will break down in direct relation to the intensity and duration of their exposure. Thus, psychiatric casualties are just as inevitable as gunshot and shrapnel wounds in warfare."[106] As one character says to another in Sam Fuller's postwar drama *House of Bamboo* (1955), "You got battle fatigue. It happens to the best of us. It's nothing personal." For its part, the earlier *Sherlock Holmes Faces Death* (Roy William Neill, 1943) depicts "convalescent officers"—"all fine fellows, [with] wonderful war records and everything"—who are nevertheless "all victims of combat fatigue." It falls upon the titular detective to confidently proclaim that this is "not unnatural."[107]

For soldiers, military training increasingly entailed exposure to therapeutic rhetoric, with the average enlistee coming to learn that "nothing was wrong with seeking psychological help; in fact, to do so was a sign of unusual strength and maturity."[108] The first two years of American involvement in World War II were marked by a commitment to "screening out" anyone suspected of a "psychological deviation" (including "sluggishness," "overboisterousness," and homosexuality).[109] By 1945, after the establishment of the Army's Neuropsychiatry Consultants Division and the termination of the practice of automatically discharging psychologically "suspicious" inductees, the military had shifted toward an entirely different model, one premised on the efficacy of psychiatric treatment.[110] Medical centers (including Brooke General Hospital at

Fort Sam Houston, Lawson General in Atlanta, and Mason General on Long Island) acquired schools of military neuropsychiatry, all of which heartily embraced films as teaching tools, recognizing "the fact that tremendous educational value may accrue to the benefit of the Army, the public, and ultimately the individual psychiatric patient, through the utilization of carefully developed motion pictures and photographs of neuropsychiatric activities."[111] The film program at St. Albans, a hospital for war veterans located in Queens, New York, was especially advanced, screening a range of military-sponsored shorts and features.[112] Thanks in no small part to such visual aids—all of them premised on the treatability of various disorders—wartime military psychiatry achieved "a comprehensive 'normalization' that altered the subjects and purposes of clinical work by reorienting theory and practice away from mental illness and toward mental health."[113] This "normalization" was increasingly central to the military's public relations strategies: the armed forces were reconfigured as sites where mental health could be found, not permanently lost—places where the potentially disturbed could be treated, not peremptorily excluded.[114]

Drawing on the interpretive work of military psychiatrists, and presenting this work, in Fredric Jameson's terms, as "somehow complete and self-sufficient," trauma-themed films are fundamentally concerned with disabling a rather obvious question: if war trauma is as terrible as it is inevitable, why wage war at all—why continue to pursue military action around the globe?[115] In wartime and postwar military documentaries, then, trauma itself is not the "unthinkable" that needs to be repressed; rather, it is the questionability of military power that lies beyond the films' boundaries—that seems, in fact, to necessitate the presentation of trauma as a consequence of modernity that only the military, with its wide-ranging faculties, can adequately "handle."[116] Looking back on the consolidation of the military-industrial complex, Herbert Schiller and Joseph Phillips dismissed "simplistic notions of domestic conspiracy," positing instead a liberal-capitalist framework in which "open discussions" of military power are understood as "healthy": "Secrecy is not the essence of the relationship between the military and the large industrial corporations that are [its] principal contractors," they wrote in 1970.[117] Borrowing from Donna Haraway, Mimi White has suggested that therapeutic discourse "can be seen as organizing new forms of power"; in White's interpretation, it is a "discourse of transition," and that is precisely how I am using the concept here—as one of the pivots of the permanent war economy and of the military-industrial state more broadly.[118] In doing its part to normalize psychotherapy, the military was thus attempting to naturalize its own ascendance as an agent of massive transformations both at home and abroad.

By insisting on the ideological labor that nontheatrical nonfiction films were called upon to perform as pedagogic and therapeutic agents of the military-industrial state, I hope to move away from what Foucault called "this sacralising modesty that insists on denying that psychoanalysis has anything to do with normalization."[119] Psychotherapy is as much an instrument of state power as a mechanism of social control, and its initial appearance in military documentaries must be understood as such. This complex institutional role was neither inevitable nor easily won, however. It grew out of complex negotiations among government agencies, military psychiatrists, and civilian organizations concerned about how best to communicate to the general public the scale of the country's "psychological problem." In response to questions about the loss of military manpower through unprecedentedly high rates of "neuropsychiatric rejection," the War Department elected to impose a "publicity blackout" in 1943. Lasting until the spring of the following year, the blackout was intended to limit public knowledge of "mental illness among soldiers," but it was stymied by frequent leaks to the press—including to the *Washington Post*, which reported (accurately if with colloquial abandon) that the percentage of rejections due to "crackups" was significantly higher than in World War I.[120]

The blackout was therefore largely ineffective, failing to prevent, for instance, the radio program *The March of Time* from broadcasting, in the spring of 1944, a pair of special reports by the Surgeon General and the director of the Army's Neuropsychiatry Consultants Division.[121] It would, in any event, be naïve to assume the efficacy of any measure designed to limit trauma's intelligibility in the early 1940s. Exhibited in commercial theaters across the country, MGM's short film *The Woman in the House* (Sammy Lee, 1942), an entry in the series *John Nesbitt's Passing Parade* (1938–1949), opens with images of global war—from panicked populations besieged by bombs to traumatized Americans suffering from "night terrors"—and argues that, because of the war, "we have all come to know the meaning of fear as never before." Luckily, however, psychiatry provides a reason to hold out hope for humanity: "Because we are all afraid of something, a new science has sprung up which attempts to treat fear as a disease." This "new science of psychiatry" is, we are told, rooted in the horrors of war; "one of history's worst moments" is thus one of the best for psychiatry, which flourishes in such "troubled times." The film goes on to depict a "victim of fear" (played by Ann Richards) who is traumatized by news of her fiancé's death in combat, and it concludes with an awkward expression of gratitude to war trauma for "generating" so widely useful a profession as psychiatry. Similar arguments were offered in widely read publications of the period, including J.R. Rees' *The Shaping of Psychiatry by War* (1945).[122] Though marred by outmoded nomenclature and speculation regarding the role of carbon monoxide in the development of "shell shock," Norman C. Meier's 1943 book *Military Psychology* further introduced war trauma to a broad readership, arguing that it "may affect almost anyone."[123] Even Eleanor Roosevelt, writing in her newspaper column in the fall of 1942, emphasized the importance of giving each draftee "a sufficiently careful psychiatric examination."[124] At the time, notes Alison Winter, "there were fears that as many as *half* the troops might ultimately be lost to psychiatric problems," making the subject of war trauma difficult to avoid in American everyday life.[125]

Despite considerable pressure from the American Psychiatric Association to make pertinent information more widely available, the War Department remained committed, for a period of several months, to limiting public as well as institutional knowledge of psychoneurosis. This meant placing a moratorium on the Psychiatric Film Program recently established under the leadership of military psychiatrist George S. Goldman at the Office of the Surgeon General, which had yielded the Army documentary *Combat Exhaustion* in 1943.[126] Nevertheless, British documentary imports (particularly *Neuropsychiatry 1943* [Michael Hankinson, 1943], which insists that military psychiatry will "benefit not only the individual but also the society in which he lives") were widely screened in military settings prior to and during the blackout. In an indication of British influence on the development of the Psychiatric Film Program, the American military psychiatrists Lloyd J. Thompson, Ernest Parsons, and Jackson Thomas had made *Combat Exhaustion* at the 312th Station Psychiatric Hospital in England; when they returned to the United States, however, their film was virtually alone among American-made works that purported to teach psychiatric techniques, at least until the blackout was finally lifted in the spring of 1944.

Given the sheer impossibility of limiting public knowledge of the astonishingly high incidence of psychiatric cases in all branches of the armed forces, the War Department eventually pivoted toward an embrace of film's utility as a psychotherapeutic vehicle of public relations—a means not of denying the prevalence of trauma among American men but rather of convincing audiences of the military's capacity to treat and even prevent the condition. At least one of the military's own public relations specialists was discharged on the basis of a psychiatric disorder: Mike Gorman, who suffered from anxiety, anorexia, and insomnia, later became a renowned mental health lobbyist, pushing for the continued application of military-psychiatric lessons to all Americans, including through film.[127] Addressing the Army's belated production and distribution of "psychiatric documentaries," one psychiatric advisor noted that, in order to counteract any alarmism caused by the above-mentioned leaks (and by general press coverage of the military's "psychiatric problem"), "it was necessary that each film perform as many functions and reach as wide an audience as possible."[128] The publicity blackout did succeed in obscuring certain statistics and suppressing some carefully prepared documents—including a fact sheet entitled "The Mental Health of the U.S. Soldier," which was intended to assure "the woman in the home" that the men fighting for her protection were not, in fact, all "mental cases."[129] By 1945, however, the official message had changed. The War Department's goal was no longer to trumpet the mental health of all servicemen—that would have been impossible in light of revelations about discharge rates—but instead to normalize trauma, including and especially through film, adopting a confessional mode as the intimate scaffolding on which to build bold claims about military-psychiatric treatment and its implications for American power in the postwar world.

This new policy—one of "absolute frankness and honesty about the total situation"—required careful management.[130] In the fall of 1944, an investigation by the Army's Inspector General had led to the recommendation that the military's Bureau of Public Relations "assign a full-time public relations officer to handle the planning and execution of a program relative to publicity and public education of psychiatry in the Army."[131] That the recommendation was never followed speaks, in part, to the importance increasingly attached to film as a vehicle of public relations, for no one official could possibly be expected to oversee the promiscuous circulation of documentaries whose purpose was explicitly to "spread knowledge."[132] As Winter points out, military documentaries "were sometimes the primary form of enculturation that turned doctors from other specialties into rough-and-ready psychiatric practitioners," but they were also part of a "liberal policy of public education" that demanded their use in schools, factories, and a variety of other nontheatrical, nonmilitary locations.[133] Refining this policy in the early months of 1945, the Neuropsychiatry Consultants Division, rejecting the premise behind the earlier blackout, argued that "full publicity of the psychiatric problem should be given in a factual manner," with "factual" here signifying a certain documentary ideal.[134] Films about the military's "psychiatric problem" thus provided the occasion for debates about the nature and limits of documentary realism.

Discursively, psychiatric treatment, with its emphasis on individual minds, was often deployed as a useful rejoinder to the perceived regimentation and "mindlessness" of fascist fighting forces. The humanistic psychologist Carl Rogers, for instance, argued that American servicemen undergoing treatment stood in "contrast to marching troops who are 'men without faces,'" and military psychiatry, rather than concealed as a shameful index of weakness, was instead loudly touted in antifascist propaganda.[135] The tendentiousness of such propaganda is readily evident in its emphasis on Germans' allegedly congenital commitment to the community or *Volk* as opposed to the individual so identifiable— and so valued—by psychoanalysis.[136] In fact, numerous German and Austrian psychoanalysts (with the conspicuous exception of Sigmund Freud, who rejected the notion of film as a psychoanalytic instrument) had participated in the production of motion pictures in the interwar period, supervising, for instance, the making of G. W. Pabst's *Secrets of a Soul* (1926) in the very manner in which their American counterparts would later advise the shooting of such wartime Hollywood films as *Since You Went Away* (John Cromwell, 1944) and *Spellbound*.[137] The allegedly uniquely American dimensions of "therapeutic film" were nevertheless identified in and through wartime and postwar military documentaries, particularly as psychoanalysis was forbidden in communist countries where Freud himself was a banned author.[138]

The notion that documentaries could serve to fortify the minds of "fighting men" was widely embraced not only by the military but also by the American popular press. Even the editors of *Look* magazine insisted that "wounded soldiers derive unconscious therapeutic benefit" from film screenings.[139] In their 1945 volume *Movie Lot to Beach Head*, the editors argued that documentaries intended for the "treatment of psychoneurotics" represented the apotheosis of the military's "medical films"—works designed to "aid and protect our wounded."[140] Surveying how soldiers are "conditioned psychologically" by the use of nonfiction film, the *Look* editors emphasized the function of military documentaries as "therapeutic stimuli," particularly in such nontheatrical settings as field hospitals, rest camps, and troopships.[141] If such an investment in the "psychological dimensions" of cinema can be dated all the way back to the work of Hugo Münsterberg, whose *The Photoplay: A Psychological Study* was published in 1916, it was also influenced by new clinical developments. During World War II, military psychiatrists repeatedly identified "post-traumatic syndrome" as a principal "neuropsychiatric problem" plaguing current and former servicemen, and films reflected this discovery by insisting on the complexity of trauma's lasting effects.[142]

TRAUMATIC IMPRINTS

"To this day, that first face of death [in combat] is imprinted on my mind like a leaf in a fossil, never to fade away."
—Sam Fuller[143]

"Traumatic imprints" are both tangible—haptic in the sense epitomized by fallout from the explosion of the first atomic bomb, which contaminated faraway cornstalks used to package film for Eastman Kodak, whose shipments were irrevocably damaged as a result—and suggestive of the extent to which "war neuroses" function in tropological terms in American cinema.[144] Produced by Cascade Pictures of California for the Armed Forces Special Weapons Project (1947–1959), the short film *Self-Preservation in an Atomic Bomb Attack* (1950) vividly illustrates these two interpretations of traumatic imprints. The film opens with disturbing footage of the ruins of Hiroshima and Nagasaki, the sight of which, the voice-over narrator says, "sorta gave a guy the shakes."[145] Just as he is about to elaborate, the film strip breaks—and is thus revealed to have been constitutive of a film-within-a-film. At the outset, then, *Self-Preservation in an Atomic Bomb Attack* creatively suggests the traumatic impact of its own subject, literalized through the obliteration of the medium's very materiality. In this respect, the film recalls the Navy's 1945 short *This Could Be America*, which shows the death of the Army Air Forces cameraman responsible for much of its footage; his corpse carefully laid out for the camera, he is presented as a victim of the film's very subject. It also anticipates a remarkable moment in the anthology film *Far From Vietnam* (Joris Ivens, et al., 1967): while she was filming the activities of the Viet Cong, Michele Ray's camera "went berserk," as the narrator puts it. "She tore up the film, and perhaps the result"—which *Far From Vietnam* presents in all its Brakhage-esque abstractness—"resembled the cry she wanted to express."

Cutting from the film strip's spontaneous destruction (as though the celluloid itself were unable to sustain an investigation into the psychological effects of atomic warfare), *Self-Preservation* reveals a typical nontheatrical exhibition site—a military classroom, where four uniformed men (including a puzzled projectionist) have gathered to engage with images "imprinted" by nuclear weapons. Celebrating the tearing of the film strip, one soldier requests a replacement—"something easier to take," such as a "rootin'-tootin' western, with men fighting it out the old-fashioned way" (a request echoed by the narrator of *Let There Be Light*, who, ventriloquizing through patients forced to watch so many military-produced documentaries, asks, "How 'bout a good movie for a change?"). Another audience member echoes the soldier's resistance, denouncing upsetting representations of "that atom business." Both men must be schooled by an officer who somberly insists on the pedagogic value of "traumatic" documentaries—what *Self-Preservation in an Atomic Bomb Attack* itself represents.

The motif of imprinting is thus, in this book, a multidirectional one, as much responsive to a Bazinian conception of realism as to the efforts of military psychiatrists to use cinema as a means of training members of the armed forces (including fellow physicians). As Alison Winter argues, "it is likely that, in many cases, the on-screen instructor was the best that could be offered to [medical] trainees" amid the relative scarcity of military psychiatrists.[146] Documentaries about psychoneurosis and psychotherapy were thus intended, in part, to imprint medical staff members with an awareness of trauma's effects, cultivating certain psychotherapeutic patterns of clinical behavior. But they were also meant to reflect the dialectics of visibility and invisibility that could render intelligible various "unphotographable mental illnesses," as Brian Winston calls them.[147]

Numerous military psychiatrists insisted that, far from being impossibly elusive, trauma in fact imprinted the human mind, and that these imprints could be revealed through the diverse devices of documentary (from animation to reenactment to the on-camera, synch-sound interview). Roy Grinker and John Spiegel argued that combat trauma "is not like the writing on a slate that can be erased, leaving the slate as it was before. Combat leaves a lasting impression on men's minds."[148] By employing the motif of the imprint, I hope also to evoke Derrida's claim that psychoanalysis "does not, by accident, privilege the figures of the imprint and of imprinting"—that "its discourse concerns, first of all, the stock of 'impressions' and the deciphering of inscriptions, but also their censorship and repression."[149] For Derrida, such repression itself "leaves an imprint" whose traumatic character is rehearsed again and again—much as war, implicated as traumatic yet "vindicated" through the work of military psychiatry, has become a permanent condition of American power.[150]

PSYCHOLOGICALLY "USEFUL CINEMA"

"At present, I am working in Hollywood, as an advisor on
psychosocial pictures. That means I tell producers and directors
how different minds should react under different conditions in these
psychological pictures. It used to be you went to a theater, and you
sat down, you watched a picture, and you relaxed, and when you
walked out you said, 'Isn't that wonderful? The boy married the girl.'
You enjoyed yourself. *That's no good!* My job is to make you sit on
the edge of your chair and worry and suffer and figure out why this
should happen."

—Sid Caesar's parody of a Viennese psychiatrist in Columbia's
  The Guilt of Janet Ames (Henry Levin, 1947)

During and after the war, the military was able to aggressively pursue the broad and persistent publicizing and distribution of its own films as well as those that it had sponsored or otherwise "adopted." Contrary to conventional wisdom, these included numerous documentaries about war trauma and psychotherapy—subjects that, far from being anxiously denied, were in fact the fulcrum of postwar efforts to spread military influence through nontheatrical film. Such funders of the behavioral sciences as the Office of Naval Research (established in August 1946) and the Group for the Advancement of Psychiatry (established in May 1946) were committed to furthering the wartime cause of psychological rehabilitation through the sponsorship of nonfiction films, and their efforts dovetailed with the burgeoning mental health movement to ensure the survival of these films beyond limited institutional contexts.

Veterans and their families were among the most vocal proponents of the production and wide distribution of documentaries about trauma and psychotherapy, and their growing political influence, which helped lead to the passage of the National Mental Health Act in 1946, was a decisive factor in the military's continued commitment to "mental health films." Rebecca Jo Plant has written of "the curious development of American psychoanalysis in the immediate postwar years, a period of sustained professional growth and unprecedented popularization."[151] I argue that this development was made possible, in large part, by the film work of military psychiatrists, which circulated widely and for many years via an expanding nontheatrical distribution network. Nontheatrical nonfiction film thus played a crucial yet understudied role in the establishment and survival of a popular movement for mental health, and the roots of this movement in military psychiatry demand serious attention.

Military documentaries about trauma and psychotherapy were by no means uniform in their messages. In *The Inside Story of Seaman Jones*, the title character is told by his doctor that there is no such thing as a nervous breakdown—a claim that boldly contradicted those of many real-life military psychiatrists, who not only insisted on the legitimacy of the term "nervous breakdown" but also suggested that it was synonymous with "psychoneurosis."[152] Such contradictions inevitably spilled over into Hollywood fiction films, including Raoul Walsh's *The Man I Love* (1947), in which a sympathetic military psychiatrist explains, "Most people have the wrong idea about [psychoneurotic] soldiers. It's more like a nervous breakdown. They're not crazy—just overtired. They'll get well if you give them a chance." With these words, the doctor echoes the narrator of *Psychiatric Procedures in the Combat Area*, who refers to the victims of combat trauma by averring, "They're not quitters, but are truly ill." The basic psychological lexicon at the center of *The Inside Story of Seaman Jones*, with its principled eschewal of the term "nervous breakdown," is thus dramatically different from that employed not only in such fiction films as *The Man I Love* and Walsh's later *Glory Alley* (1952) but also in the Navy documentary *Combat Psychiatry: The Division Psychiatrist* (1954), which, in detailing "sudden, severe psychological trauma," characterizes it by "attacks of the nerves." Marlisa Santos has drawn attention to the similarly blatant contradiction between the "opening caution" of *Let There Be Light*, which warns against conflating war trauma and "peacetime neuroses," and the claims made in other psychiatric and cinematic discourses of the era—particularly those of film noir, which, according to Santos, emphasize the "scant difference" between soldiers and civilians in their shared vulnerability to various psychological disorders.[153] Such comparisons are taken to bizarre extremes in *Shades of Gray*, which likens lofty "military concerns" to worrying about a mortgage—or even "a letter two days overdue." The film, which purports to offer "a summary of experience gained in the prevention and treatment of neuropsychiatric cases in World War II," notes that "the stresses of military and civilian life" are "equally complex and important."

Because the condition seemed to demand a number of different, sometimes opposing modes of articulation and treatment, documentaries that tackled the contours of war trauma also adopted a wide range of approaches. Indeed, it is possible to perceive in certain trauma-themed military documentaries of the 1940s and early 1950s the seeds of direct cinema and *cinéma vérité*, as well as of the testimonial function of activist films like *Winter Soldier* (Winterfilm Collective, 1972) and *Interviews with My Lai Veterans* (Joseph Strick, 1971), among other styles informed by—even generative of—various configurations of trauma and psychotherapy. Just as the fantasy of a "pure" documentary, devoted entirely to "neutral" observation and predicated on the invisibility of filmmaker and filmmaking apparatus alike, is unsustainable in the face of innumerable challenges and thus no basis for documentary theory and criticism, the notion that trauma is limited to a familiar expressive repertoire and a stable generic context is insensitive to some of trauma's historical conditions and physical, psychological, and textual effects. Military documentaries about mental illness were designed to heal as well as to teach, and many a military psychiatrist proclaimed their success as therapeutic tools, echoing an institutional belief that these films "could accomplish literally anything"—including the psychic rehabilitation of the combat-traumatized soldier.[154] But they were also designed to recruit, as well as to perform a number of other institutional functions, serving as ideal instruments of public relations precisely because they *didn't* deny the traumatic effects of combat, or the incidence of soldiers needing extensive psychiatric treatment. In viewing some of these films today, it is tempting to regard them as the "truthful" alternatives to so many absurdly hyperbolic movies about the beauty and efficacy of American patriotism, and to praise their commitment to the psychic rehabilitation of their earliest audiences. However, as Anna McCarthy warns, "recounting governmental reason should not automatically affirm its efficacy, nor discount its close connections to private interest." [155] Wartime military documentaries may have enjoyed extensive afterlives in factories and secondary schools, their exhibition mandated by management as well as by various educational leaders, but that does not mean that their methods were automatically appreciated or their prescriptions unthinkingly followed. As Peter Miller and Nikolas Rose point out, "Things, persons, or events always appear to escape . . . the programmatic logic that seeks to govern them."[156] We should not assume that military documentaries did what many of them said they would do—"heal the mind" and "restore the spirit," to quote the Army's

Combat Exhaustion (1945)—and their identifiable ties to military and private interests suggest several reasons why we should not. As Haidee Wasson and Charles R. Acland argue, the paradoxical purpose of many examples of "useful" cinema is "to both promote change and to resist it"; films that reflect the ambitions of a particular institution inevitably "help to preserve and reproduce that institution," whatever their ostensible deviations from convention.[157]

In considering how military psychiatry shaped particular cinematic practices in the 1940s and early 1950s, I hope to avoid suggesting an uncritical appreciation of filmic innovation and institutional reform— hence my commitment to uncovering how even disturbing films about war trauma are implicated in the military-industrial complex and in political efforts to normalize the war-based economy. At the same time, I certainly do not want to underestimate the lasting pedagogic and therapeutic value of some of these films. Diagnosed with PTSD in the spring of 2016, I found myself turning, in addition to formal psychiatric treatment, to the Navy's *Introduction to Combat Fatigue* (1944), a film whose officer-narrator, in directly addressing the camera, seemed to speak sympathetically to my own condition. Communicating across the gulf of seventy-plus years and from within the functional dimensions of institutional documentary, *Introduction to Combat Fatigue* helpfully reinforced what I was learning about my own anxiety states, reminding me that I was neither dying nor "going crazy" (as I had long suspected) but instead suffering from a distinct and treatable disorder, one born (at least in part) of repeated exposure to the threat of gun violence.[158] ("Oh, no, you're not gonna die," says a soothing voice on the soundtrack of *Combat Fatigue: Insomnia*. "We know how you feel.") I do not doubt that a fair number of other viewers, forced to watch these films in classrooms and factories, have shared my sense of recognition across the longue durée of the American military documentary. Thus my own "transferential and affect-laden implication in the object of study," to quote Dominick LaCapra, is such that I cannot help but appreciate the reparative potential of so many wartime and postwar military documentaries, despite their obvious political shortcomings.[159] The usefulness of "useful cinema," then, may persist well past the point of contact between particular films and their initial audiences, animating instructive strategies and therapeutic regimens for years to come.

CHAPTER 2

Solemn Venues

War Trauma and the Expanding
Nontheatrical Realm

In 1943, the Army psychiatrist George S. Goldman was placed on full-time duty to develop a "general program" of "psychiatric films"—original documentaries that could "contribute to mental health" by "removing some of the mystery connected with psychiatry and by properly explaining many of the misconceptions commonly connected with this specialty."[1] The hope was that such films would not only help to rehabilitate "the great number of seriously sick returnees" but also to prevent future psychiatric casualties, in the process solidifying the military's reputation as a "healthful" set of institutions—or, at the very least, as eminently capable of providing effective psychiatric treatment for those in need.[2] Because the so-called "neuropsychiatric problem" had become "overwhelmingly large," threatening to "amount to the largest medical-social problem this country [had] ever faced," documentary film was deemed necessary as a flexible instrument of education, rehabilitation, and public relations. The genre was thus an ideal component of "a program of well directed, constructive publicity"—a means of "acquainting [Americans] factually with the problem involved."[3] Because all of the resulting films dealt, in some fashion, with "death and the fear of death," they were deemed widely—potentially "universally"—relevant, particularly during the nuclear age.[4] Their "focus is on the wartime patient," noted a 1953 manual, "but the psychodynamics portrayed are generally applicable," lending these films a "high instructional value and motivating power" for the population at large.[5] The postwar passage of the National Mental Health Act (1946) and the emergence of a bona fide mental health movement seemed to confirm this power, as government and civilian agencies continued to find new uses for "old" documentaries.

During and after the war, the military sought to formalize and expand the links between cinema and the social sciences, a process that required the close participation of psychological experts. Established in 1942, the Psychological Test Film Unit of the Army Air Forces Aviation Psychology Program, which studied cinema's effects on audiences, was maintained until well into the postwar period. Eventually, the Army Air Forces First Motion Picture Unit, based in Culver City, would coordinate its production activities with the Psychological Test Film Unit, based in Santa Ana. Under the direction of psychologist James J. Gibson, whose celebrated interest in visual perception hardly precluded considerations of war trauma and psychotherapy, the latter would help solidify connections between military filmmaking and psychological research, producing twenty-two "psychological test films" by 1946.[6]

While these "interactive" works—"tests on film," which included such titles as *Identification of Velocity Test* and *Aircraft Recognition Proficiency Exam*—were hardly the kinds of "therapeutic documentaries" that the Army and the Navy were producing at the time, they were used to identify "neurotic factors," and their verifiable pedagogic effects helped confirm cinema's value as a psychological and psychoanalytic tool in the military.[7] Furthermore, Gibson's films were commonly screened for newly admitted psychiatric patients, not only gauging the aptitude and intelligence of the recently traumatized but also serving as crucial diagnostic tools, "triggering" telling responses.[8] With Gibson getting such noteworthy results with his psychological test films, others—including psychiatrists—were encouraged to pursue their own cinematic experiments, becoming amateur filmmakers even while functioning as medical professionals. Adopting a Freudian metaphor, Charles Tepperman considers the extent to which amateur films "represent a *working through* of the relationship between creativity and technology, between individual and collective experience, and between local contingencies and the commercial aesthetics of mass media."[9] Such was the essence of psychiatry's embrace of filmmaking amid the seismic transformations of the 1940s, as "total war" raised new questions about the profession's obligation both to institutions like the Army and the Navy and to society as a whole.

TRAUMATIC ANTECEDENTS

"I know one guy from the last World War. He was shell-shocked—
people made fun of him. That made me mad. Nice guy, but he's down
in the dumps. He didn't care for nothing. Used to tell me about the
other war. Nice guy. I don't want to be that way myself. I want to go
home, but I don't want to be like that guy. He was dirty—nice guy,
though. No one could understand. They didn't know that the guy
was shell-shocked. They laughed at him and poked fun at him. And I
used to beat hell out of the kids—nice guy. I don't want to go home
like that, Captain. I want to be well and be able to have a family."

—Army corporal, 25, speaking under the influence of sodium
pentothal in a VA hospital at the end of World War II[10]

World War I and the interwar period witnessed numerous private and
state-sponsored efforts to render cinema useful to the treatment of war
trauma. Beginning in 1915, French and British physicians screened
Charlie Chaplin films in an attempt to restore speech in soldiers rendered mute by the horrors of combat, while Red Cross and, increasingly, YMCA centers at or near the front lines frequently served as
"therapeutic" exhibition sites.[11] Catalyzed by George Eastman in the
early 1920s, the "Hospital Happiness Movement" further touted film's
restorative potential, as the Eastman Kodak Company's Medical Division began advertising films, projectors, and screens to hospital administrators across the United States.[12] The company's careful cultivation of
the hospital as a source of revenue was coincident with its canny transformation of the classroom into an exhibition space of equal if not
greater profitability.[13]

That nontheatrical film was big business by the early 1920s, thanks
in large part to the introduction of nonflammable 16mm stock, helps
explain the zeal with which so many key players pursued the perpetual
circulation of military documentaries after World War II. Numerous
companies stood to profit from this pursuit, and not merely financially.
The inescapably high-minded dimensions of this activity—the moral
and quasi-medical cachet conferred upon those who ensured that
trauma-themed documentaries would be widely seen—represented their
own form of capital, one that could empower both civic participation
and the emergent practices of "corporate social responsibility" and
"cause-related marketing."

By the 1920s, profits may have motivated the uptake of "therapeutic
films" by various distributors and other nontheatrical interests (including Eastern Film and the Society for Visual Education), but the Red
Cross had already set several important precedents for the widespread

use of films to provide "medical education." As Jennifer Horne has shown, the Red Cross Motion Picture Bureau (1916–1922) used non-theatrical film to contribute to public health campaigns, even offering an entire film program on the physical and psychological rehabilitation of veterans.[14] Distributing its own original productions along with the Army's "hygiene films," the Red Cross reached Rotary halls, Kiwanis clubs, churches, bus stations, and gymnasiums with privately and federally funded films about war trauma, thus providing some of the discursive and infrastructural scaffolding on which later efforts would rest.

Commercial firms quickly adopted the Red Cross's approach, often collaborating with the government in order to make military films widely available to Americans. Between 1924 and 1939, Kodak's Kodascope Library, a rental and purchase system for 16mm films, had contracts with the U.S. War Department that allowed it to regularly distribute short, government-sponsored documentaries to nationwide audiences for home viewing. Advertisements for Kodascope Libraries frequently touted the availability of "official United States War Department movies of the World War, filmed in action by the Signal Corps." Additionally, so-called War Cinegraphs, two-hundred-foot one-reelers sold for $15 each, were available along with feature-length documentaries in the *America Goes Over* series, which consisted of "special authentic war pictures compiled and edited by military experts."[15]

Nonfiction films about the traumas of World War I were also sold by individual collectors who echoed Kodak's insistence that such films deserved to become "a permanent part of [one's] film library."[16] As Haidee Wasson has demonstrated in her work on 16mm, Kodak and other distributors were firmly committed to circulating "shocking," potentially traumatizing images of combat, with one advertisement going so far as to promise a "vast panorama of war," the "stark realism" of which could be "lived" and "relived" by audiences in the home.[17] Anticipating the overtly therapeutic use and reuse of films by military psychiatrists and others committed to rehabilitating battle-scarred veterans, Kodak's promotion of combat documentaries was, in Wasson's persuasive reading, part of a broader attempt to normalize war trauma—"a means by which the changes wrought by modern life would be made slower, safer and more easily contained."[18] Kodak, which began developing high-resolution aerial photography in 1919, thus positioned itself as more than just a facilitator of the military's image-making capabilities, circulating nonfiction films as a means of educating as well as "soothing" Americans made anxious by the traumas of modernity.[19]

In many instances, what was good business for Kodak and other companies was good public relations for the military, particularly in the wake of World War I. Kodak was hardly in the habit of embracing films of which the armed forces disapproved, and its military contracts often precluded precisely this gesture.[20] In the late teens, however, the nontheatrical circulation of Arthur Hurst's "imported" British documentary *War Neuroses* (1918), which recorded the treatment of severely "shell-shocked" patients at the Royal Victoria Hospital in Netley and the Seale Hayne Military Hospital in Devon, raised concerns among American military officials even as it inspired new therapeutic regimens.[21]

The use of film to directly address war trauma was plainly discouraged during the reign of such far-reaching regulatory organizations as the Community Motion Picture Bureau (headed by self-proclaimed "motion picture reformer" Warren Dunham Foster) as well as the far more familiar Committee on Public Information (CPI, also known as the Creel Committee), both of which were dedicated to censoring anything that smacked of an antiwar or anti-military stance. At the same time, however, cinema's realist potential—including its capacity to record traumatic combat experiences—was widely celebrated in accounts of "war pictures." Thus the difficulty of disentangling war trauma (potentially a source of negative publicity for the military) from discourses of realism (increasingly employed to tout the military's image-making capabilities) characterized the state-sponsored development of film production, distribution, and exhibition during and in the wake of World War I.[22]

These tensions between realism and public relations played out in a number of ways. With journalists routinely critiquing the capacity of visual media to "give rather too rose-colored an idea of the soldier's daily routine," the military was compelled to employ strategic doses of realism—often in the form of direct references to combat—in its recruitment efforts.[23] "It is a fact that the Government has nothing to conceal from any prospective applicant as to any feature of the different arms of the service," wrote Major R.C. Croxton in 1913.[24] And yet the War Department objected to Vitagraph's *Lifting the Ban of Coventry* (Wilfred North, 1915) on the grounds that the film, which is based on actual cases of social discrimination in the military, offered "a most unfavorable impression of the Army," forcing the National Board of Censorship to intervene with requested cuts.[25] American involvement in World War I would only intensify these censorial pressures, even as it offered new opportunities for a realist portrayal of combat.

For the military itself, producing realist motion pictures without so much as alluding to war trauma proved remarkably difficult. The Army Signal Corps began making films in late 1917, at which point it was tasked with producing a "Pictorial History of the War" that would serve as both proto-documentary "record" and reliable recruitment tool.[26] But the CPI, with its close ties to private industry as well as its narrow conception of "acceptable propaganda," became the sole distributing agency for Signal Corps films during World War I.[27] Committed to avoiding conflict with commercial film interests, the CPI's Division of Films often handed Signal Corps "actualities" to the American Red Cross and various state councils of defense, which tended to screen them free of charge to patriotic societies, schools, and churches.[28] Despite the CPI's injunctions against "demoralization," at least one Signal Corps film produced during World War I—1918's *His Best Gift*—dramatizes war trauma (in this case, combat-related blindness); its emphasis, however, is not on rehabilitation but, rather, on the need to purchase "war risk insurance."[29]

At the same time that the Signal Corps, in close collaboration with the CPI, was generally skirting the issue of war trauma, several commercial films were addressing it directly, if with disastrous consequences. In 1917, two pacifist films, *Civilization* (Thomas H. Ince, et al., 1916) and *War Brides* (Herbert Brenon, 1916), were banned by the Pennsylvania Board of Censors, who argued that the films "tended to discourage enlistment" by focusing on the traumatic consequences of combat.[30] After attending a screening of the latter film in Kansas City, Army and Navy recruiting officers asked the War Department to "suppress the picture," citing its "disturbing" dimensions.[31] In *Civilization*, all soldiers are, according to a title card, "grim specters of death"—individual agents of trauma in the age of mechanized war.

Remaining a key referent in interwar attempts to sketch the contours of trauma, World War I offered a sort of shorthand for films that sought to plumb psychological depths. Set in the war's immediate aftermath, the Howard Hughes production *The Mating Call* (James Cruze, 1928) features men who confidently diagnose shell shock in veterans exhibiting any hints of emotional distress. For its part, *In Paris, A.W.O.L.* (Roland Reed, 1936) uses footage of World War I in order to suggest a "traumatic flashback" experienced by a convalescing veteran—an approach shared by Ernst Lubitsch's 1932 melodrama *Broken Lullaby*, which additionally depicts the startle response of a traumatized man who mistakes the sounds of a celebratory parade for the sounds of battle.[32]

Unlike Lubitsch's film, the somewhat more disturbing *In Paris, A.W.O.L.* was not given a general commercial release in 1936 and was, instead, screened in special engagements organized by its sponsor, the American Legion, which hoped to raise awareness about war trauma and its lasting effects on veterans.

Hardly unique, *Broken Lullaby* and *In Paris, A.W.O.L.* were merely two among a number of trauma-themed films produced and distributed in the interwar period. These included George Cukor's *A Bill of Divorcement* (1932), which explores the relationship between war trauma and other forms of mental illness, as its suffering protagonist (played by John Barrymore) reveals that his "latent insanity"—a hereditary trait that threatens to strike his daughter (played by Katharine Hepburn)— was merely "brought on by shellshock." Stressing that war trauma, which is all too excruciating on its own, can also exacerbate preexisting conditions, *A Bill of Divorcement* looks forward to the military's postwar documentary *Shades of Gray* (1947), which insists that combat fatigue can "inflame" inborn neuroses, as well as to the Hollywood thriller *Niagara* (Henry Hathaway, 1953), which makes an identical claim in its depiction of a Korean War veteran. Consider, as well, Franchot Tone's performance of shell shock in John Ford's *The World Moves On* (1934), in which one man's callous comment—that "war is nature's way of eliminating surplus people"—inspires the female protagonist, Mary (Madeleine Carroll), to offer a powerful denunciation of the military-industrial complex, which functions, in her acidulous reading, "so that the guns shan't go hungry." Presciently denouncing what seem to her to be welfare programs for the military, Mary goes on to declare that "war is a disease—homicidal mania, on the grand scale, brought on by fear and jealousy." For its part, the contemporaneous mystery film *Charlie Chan in Paris* (Lewis Seiler, 1935) suggests the sheer intelligibility of war trauma—the production of common sense about the condition—in its depiction of criminals who disguise themselves as the same "unfortunate relic of the war," a pitiable figure suffering from "shellshock."

In the 1930s, the peace, isolationist, and anti-interventionist movements were united by a common commitment to raising awareness about war trauma, and individual antiwar organizations often produced their own films for distribution to schools, churches, amateur movie clubs, and fraternal organizations. These included *Must War Be?* (Walter Niebuhr, 1932), a production of the Peace Films Foundation that enjoyed a broad nontheatrical circulation (and was directed by the former coordinator of motion picture photography for the Signal Corps); *Dealers in Death: The Story of the War Racket* (Burnet Hershey, 1934), which implicates the military-industrial complex in the production of war trauma (as the narrator puts it, "Profits increased in direct proportion to the ever-growing lists of dead and wounded—stock prices and casualty lists skyrocketed together," creating "a pagan holiday for the dealers in death"); *Lives Wasted* (1936), a widely screened anti-war drama produced by the New Film Group, focusing on the plight of a "crippled" and otherwise traumatized veteran living in abject poverty; and a variety of shorts and features screened through the Peace Films Caravan, whose portable 16mm projectors enabled screenings in an array of public locations, from town squares to fairgrounds.[33]

Some films produced in the interwar period focus directly on war trauma and its psychological symptoms. Set during and in the immediate aftermath of the First World War, the aptly titled *Shock* (Roy J. Pomeroy, 1934), for instance, explicitly depicts the traumatic effects of combat. The film's opening credit sequence features several explosions, the sound of which is practically deafening and the smoke of which obscures the titles—a shock for the spectator, a sort of violation of convention that, in its own way, seeks to reproduce the intolerable experience of technological war. *Shock* emphasizes the sheer inevitability of war trauma, as the "tough" officer Derek Marbury (Ralph Forbes) succumbs to shell shock, which leads to amnesia. The remainder of the film is devoted to psychiatric and lay efforts to restore Marbury's memory—efforts that eventually hinge on a therapeutic reenactment of combat.[34] *Shock* ends with Marbury, his memory restored, finally aware of the epidemic proportions of war trauma—and of the federal government's responsibility to care for veterans. Should the government fail in this regard, Marbury and others will simply have to "march on Washington."[35]

When, in the 1940s, the U.S. military began producing and commissioning films about war trauma, it was partly as a form of social and political management—a means of reclaiming war trauma from anti-war filmmakers and of preventing the sort of protest movement promised in *Shock* and other films. With the military itself acknowledging the extent of the problem, there would perhaps be no need to march on Washington—and certainly no need to suggest that the state cruelly ignores the struggles of so many men. First, however, the matter of distribution would need to be addressed, and with it the potential scope of nontheatrical nonfiction film.

DISTRIBUTING TRAUMA

To claim that any film was "produced by the United States military," as I do throughout this book, requires some qualification. The military was, in the 1940s, hardly a monolithic entity, and my attention to its multivalent character is in keeping with the work of scholars who insist that it was, and remains, not one institution but, rather, a network of institutions with variant relationships to—and aspirations for—cinema as a source of instruction, instrument of public relations, and agent of psychological rehabilitation.[36] I use the term "military documentary" to describe films produced by actual military studios (the Signal Corps Photographic Center, the Training Films and Motion Picture Branch of the Bureau of Aeronautics, the Army Air Forces First Motion Picture Unit) as well as by nonmilitary organizations that collaborated with the armed forces, including Hollywood studios, the U.S. Office of Education's Division of Visual Aids for War Training, and an array of small production companies devoted to nontheatrical nonfiction film. I thus consider a film a military documentary, and refer to it as such, even if it was produced by the Jam Handy Organization or Chicago Film Studios, since the production orders frequently came directly from the armed forces, which, in many cases, oversaw production and enjoyed something like final cut. My intention is not to deny the specificity of a nonmilitary organization, subsuming it under the totalizing banner of the armed forces, but rather to foreground the diverse utility of films for a military that has long been in complex dialogue with a diversity of producers, distributors, and audiences. Contesting the naïve "paradigm of military versus society"—the familiar binaries separating martial and civil spheres—Alice Lovejoy writes of "military cinema's close intertwining with 'civilian' cinema," and her scare quotes are instructive: they point not only to the close cooperation between the state and profit-seeking producers—the public-private partnerships that make commercial filmmaking possible, particularly in the United States (albeit in ways that differ from the Czechoslovak contexts that centrally concern Lovejoy)—but also to the understudied influence of "nonfiction, short, and 'useful' film" on more "mainstream" fare. Lovejoy's ironizing of "civilian" speaks to the need to revise received wisdom regarding what qualifies as state-sponsored cinema—a task taken up by political economists like Richard Maxwell and Toby Miller, who have long insisted on the centrality of government support to the ever-broadening Hollywood machine.[37]

By 1945, the armed forces were heavily involved in efforts to influence—even dictate—the dimensions of Hollywood's fictional engagements with war trauma, often demanding a certain instructional flair and singling out erroneous and otherwise offensive representations. For example, the military's Bureau of Public Relations cited RKO's romantic fantasy *The Enchanted Cottage* (John Cromwell, 1945) as a pernicious source of misinformation—a fiction film that "presents a completely false impression of Army rehabilitation policy."[38] Premised, the bureau argued, on the paranoid notion that "war-crazed" veterans were being denied the benefits of military psychiatry, the film features a battle-scarred protagonist whose recovery requires nothing short of the sheer magic of the eponymous cottage, which effects the "extraordinary transformation" of this "broken, bitter shell of a man"—a sort of psychological conversion without psychotherapy. This odious exception seemed to prove a new rule, one that would extend well into the postwar period: when it came to depicting war trauma, Hollywood's realist techniques—the industry's systematized production of verisimilitude—increasingly depended upon close collaboration with the military, a set of institutions that often enjoyed script approval (vetoing misleading or otherwise objectionable representations of war trauma, as in the original draft of Raymond Chandler's screenplay for *The Blue Dahlia* [George Marshall, 1946]) and even dispatched officers and enlisted personnel to "play themselves" in projects deemed in need of a patina of documentary legitimacy.[39]

Military filmmaking, whether at the Signal Corps or the Bureau of Aeronautics, was no less artisanal than the work of the Hollywood studios, which David Bordwell has described as a mode of production "in which each worker adds something distinctive to the result, and the 'product' is a complex blend of overlapping and crisscrossing contributions."[40] Military documentaries rarely bear the names of directors, owing to an institutional tradition of attributing authorship to the sponsoring service branch. Many such films were made in a truly collaborative fashion, and one of my goals is to emphasize the function of military psychiatrists who participated in the filmmaking process, often directing actors and storyboarding scenes according to certain therapeutic and pedagogic objectives, their contributions scarcely recognizable to auteurist discourse. The "domain of the anonymous, the uncelebrated, and the amateur," the nontheatrical sector was also informed by the efforts of psychiatric professionals who attempted not merely to make names for themselves but also to take their work out of the asylum (long a site of exhibition for "therapeutic film") and place it in classrooms, churches, civic organizations, and museums.[41] Military-sponsored nontheatrical film was thus a key vehicle of psychiatry's movement "from asylum to community"—a means of transporting it from the stigmatized margins to the teeming center of everyday life in the United States.[42]

The military, through its various branches, had multiple ways of pursuing film distribution in wartime America. The Army's Industrial Services Division, linked as it was to the War Department's Bureau of Public Relations, maintained a commitment to the free distribution of documentaries to a vast nontheatrical audience of "managers and war workers engaged in the production of war materials." Dubbed "incentive films," these documentaries were hardly limited to cheerful records of industrial productivity. They included films designed to "show the realities of war"—to "bring home to American war workers and to industrial management . . . a full sense of the immediacy" of combat-related traumas. The point, as articulated by the likes of Undersecretary of War Robert Patterson and Lieutenant General Brehon Somervell, was to inspire a serious-minded dedication to one's job (and, perhaps, to obfuscate the connections between that job and the traumas depicted in various documentaries). Incentive films, which ran the gamut from the shrill *Why We Fight* series to more reflective works about war trauma and psychotherapy (such as *The Inside Story of Seaman Jones* and *Introduction to Combat Fatigue*), reached an estimated six million spectators per month by the summer of 1944. Millions more were added with the increased cooperation of industrial managers, such as those in Mobile, Alabama, who screened incentive films on a nightly basis in a public park. Others, like the managers of the Glenn Martin Company, an aircraft manufacturer in Baltimore, elected to rent commercial theaters for twice-weekly screenings of Army documentaries for employees and their families.[43]

Despite the period's reputation for monotonous propaganda and top-down instruction in patriotic citizenship, the war years witnessed the largely nontheatrical distribution of a wide variety of military films for an equally wide variety of purposes—including, eventually, the purpose of normalizing war trauma and its state-sponsored treatment. Some of the military's more reflexive films confirm this expansiveness: the Coast Guard's *Sunset in the Pacific* (1945), for instance, proudly suggests that the institution's documentaries "get around," while the Army's *The Role of the Combat Cameraman* (1952) similarly insists that such films "serve many important purposes," from "visual documentation" to "intelligence work" to "emotional" rehabilitation.

Military documentaries about trauma and psychotherapy were especially welcome in American universities during and after the war. As Dana Polan has demonstrated, the study of film was a prominent, if occasionally awkward and contentious, part of university psychology departments as early as the 1920s, and this history of film's "psychological" use in higher education would exert an appreciable influence on the wartime embrace of cinema as a therapeutic as well as pedagogic instrument. Consider, for instance, Boris Morkovin's Auditory Visual Kinesthetic Clinic at the University of Southern California, which the comparative literature professor established in 1938, and which, during World War II, "took as one of its charges the rehabilitation of wounded soldiers," building on pedagogic precedents long since set in the classroom.[44] If interwar advances in the study of film reliably informed the convalescent experiences of veterans and influenced as well the military's wartime uptake of "therapeutic film," the military, along with such agencies as the Office of War Information (OWI) and the New York State War Council, would forcefully return the favor as early as 1944, ensuring that the latest war-themed documentaries would be screened in university classrooms—including, on numerous occasions, Morkovin's own.[45]

In many instances, military spectatorship was upheld as a model for future forms of "film education." "Nine million young men and women have seen over 3,500 training films," wrote NYU's Robert Gessner in December 1943. "Those returning to college or entering anew will be visual-minded."[46] Catalyzed by wartime needs, close collaborations between the armed forces and various institutions of higher education frequently involved the donation of military documentaries to university film libraries and the subsequent screening of these documentaries as key components of curricula. By 1944, the School of Military Neuropsychiatry at New York University was regularly offering screenings of military documentaries (including the Army's *Psychiatric Procedures in the Combat Area* and the Navy's *Introduction to Combat Fatigue*), prints of which were provided by the NYU Film Library.[47] NYU was, in many ways, well positioned to employ such documentaries as teaching tools: in the 1930s, Frederic Thrasher's for-credit course on film appreciation had included special lectures from representatives of the American Social Hygiene Association and the American Psychiatric Association; the psychiatrist A. A. Brill, whose guest lecture for Thrasher was entitled "Psychiatric Aspects of Motion Pictures," argued for film's capacity to both reflect complex psychological states and to convey such complexity to spectators, including psychiatrists-in-training.[48]

State and federal agencies may have facilitated the distribution of military documentaries to colleges and universities, but they had divergent views regarding other sites of exhibition. Much as the Creel Committee had placed certain constraints on the production and circulation of films during World War I, new organizations attempted to regulate cinema during American involvement in World War II. Established by President Roosevelt in June 1942, the OWI, headed by Elmer Davis, faced considerable Republican opposition and, beginning in 1943, major budget cuts. But it managed to play an important part in the wartime cultivation of nontheatrical nonfiction film, as Charles R. Acland has shown. The agency's objectives were, in Acland's words, "to capitalize upon and expand existing school and community media facilities, thereby helping to orchestrate channels through which government information could reach local audiences." The OWI's National 16mm Advisory Committee, which helped to coordinate nationwide screenings of nonfiction films, paid particular attention to nontheatrical venues, from labor unions to women's clubs, and it succeeded in reaching an estimated three hundred million viewers by the end of the war. In 1946, the Advisory Committee was transformed into a civilian operation known as the Film Council of America. Run by volunteers with funding from the Carnegie Corporation and other donors, it continued to promote nontheatrical nonfiction film—often in explicitly Griersonian terms—as a vehicle of "good citizenship."[49]

The OWI distributed 16mm prints of such "exceptional," broadly educative military documentaries as *The Negro Soldier* (Stuart Heisler, 1944) to unions (including the United Auto Workers), PTAs, prisons, museums (including MoMA), and the American Council on Race Relations.[50] Though it rarely received the cooperation of the armed forces, and occasionally ignored the demands of other government agencies (as when it elected to release the notorious *Japanese Relocation* [Milton S. Eisenhower, 1942] despite sound warnings from the War Relocation Authority), the OWI remained at least nominally committed to identifying nontheatrical distribution streams for military films, as Acland's research reveals. By 1944, the OWI had deposited seventy films (including many produced by the Army Signal Corps) at the NYU Film Library, which regularly distributed them to war plants, secondary schools, and various "adult organizations."[51]

Even before its budget was cut, however, the OWI was arguably far less powerful than the War Department's Bureau of Public Relations, which "helped regulate the flow of information to the American people," and which often clashed with the other agency.[52] (Such clashes are parodied in the wartime comedy *The Doughgirls* [James V. Kern, 1944], which features the apocryphal "Administration of Inter-Bureau Coordination," and a character who complains "the OEW telephoned the DMA that they can't act on that WMP matter until they get an OK from AIBC.") The OWI, which was "keenly aware" of the military's "psychiatric problem," was caught between the impulse to follow the urgent recommendations of military psychiatrists (who wanted their work publicized) and the need to comply with the War Department's initial injunctions against informing Americans of the "epidemic" of war trauma. Confronted with these conflicting demands, the OWI hastily prepared "psychiatric" press releases without conferring with either the Surgeon General's Office or the Army's Neuropsychiatry Consultants Division, leading to the dissemination of "many erroneous facts," in the words of psychiatrist William C. Menninger. As Menninger recognized as early as 1942, military psychiatrists would need to prevail upon the Signal Corps and other military filmmaking outfits to begin production on documentaries that could counteract the misinformation for which the OWI was partly responsible.[53]

By 1942, the military had access to a growing number of facilities for the production of its own films. Certain establishments predated the war, among them the Army's Training Film Production Laboratory at Fort Monmouth, New Jersey, and the Army War College photographic libraries in Carlisle, Pennsylvania. Recognizing the need for a centralized film unit that would save the Army money, the Signal Corps purchased the former Paramount studios in Astoria, New York, establishing the Signal Corps Photographic Center (later the Army Pictorial Center) in 1942.[54] Several other facilities were sold to or temporarily occupied by the military. The Office of Strategic Services, for instance, took over the Department of Agriculture's Motion Picture Division for the duration of World War II, while the Navy requisitioned a vast movie studio in Glenview, Illinois, the property of David A. Smart, a co-founder of Coronet Films.[55] As Anthony Slide points out, "America's entry into the Second World War provided a major boost for nontheatrical film production and underlined the prominence that the U.S. government could command in the field through its various production activities."[56]

The fruits of this production were distributed in several ways. First and foremost, military documentaries—including those about war trauma and psychotherapy—circulated among all branches of the armed forces. As early as the summer of 1941, the Bureau of Aeronautics began providing films for use throughout the Navy, Marines, and Coast Guard. Later, the Navy would produce films in its own facilities, including the Photographic Science Laboratory at Anacostia, DC ("built to Hollywood standards," as Peter Maslowski points out), and the Navy Photographic Services Depot in Hollywood, California, and then distribute these to other branches.[57] While the Navy could, by way of the Bureau of Aeronautics, claim authorship of the 1944 documentary *Introduction to Combat Fatigue*, the film was quickly adopted by the Army for use in Army hospitals and other convalescent centers.[58]

Throughout the 1940s, the military was constantly discovering "new film uses," "more effective utilization methods," and, perhaps most importantly, new sites of exhibition.[59] "Therapeutic films" became staples on hospital ships carrying psychiatric patients, and, by 1944, all Army and Navy transport vessels were equipped for 16mm film screenings. *Medicine in Action*, a series of short documentaries produced by the Navy between 1944 and 1946, often identified the institution's "auxiliary hospital ships" as spaces of film exhibition, insisting on cinema's therapeutic function for men recovering from "the wounds of war." While the military's use of cinema was often understood—and often publicized by the armed forces themselves—in terms of a pronounced commitment to instructing the greatest number of people in the shortest amount of time, it was never intended to replace flesh-and-blood teachers—or, for that matter, flesh-and-blood therapists. In the words of an official statement from the Army, films "supplement but do not supplant the work of instructors."[60]

In the armed forces, film was part of a multimedia economy that also embraced radio broadcasts and transcriptions, phonograph records, pamphlets, and symposia. Produced in collaboration with the Army, the CBS radio series *Assignment Home* was devoted to "veteran readjustment," its scripts tending to detail trauma and psychotherapy in accordance with official military films. In fact, at least two episodes of the series were explicit "tie-ins" to the Navy's 1945 documentary *Combat Fatigue: Assignment Home*, which the Army had adopted for its own use.[61] Radio and, increasingly, television broadcasts were intended to supplement film instruction in ways that were difficult to achieve with such traditional conveyors of institutional information as recruitment officers. Indeed, *Assignment Home* was designed to duplicate "live instruction" and disseminate it to a broad swath of radio listeners, much as the Defense Department's public-service television program *The Big Picture* (1950 – 1975) would later seek to spread information—including information about trauma and psychotherapy—via syndication.[62]

These new protocols were necessitated by the military's broadening commitment to providing information about war trauma and psychotherapy. With the help of Chicago Film Studios, an independent company specializing in nontheatrical nonfiction film, the Navy's Bureau of Medicine and Surgery made a series of "essential films" for hospital corpsmen, many of them addressing the subject of psychoneurosis.[63] At around the same time, the Signal Corps was adapting psychologist John Dollard's 1943 study *Fear in Battle* into its *Fighting Men* series of training films.[64] Dollard, a psychologist at Yale University's Institute of Human Relations, had studied three hundred veterans of the Abraham Lincoln Brigade of the Spanish Civil War, his work helping to familiarize the Army with an array of psychosomatic symptoms ("feeling faint or weak," "roaring or ringing sensation in ears," "dryness of mouth and throat").[65] Dollard, and the Signal Corps films based on his study, thus helped normalize trauma as a diversely symptomatic experience. *Time* magazine covered this confluence of academic inquiry and military training in November 1943, and Dollard, whose work emphasized the vast differences between the technologies of the two world wars, told Americans to expect more and greater cases of distress and anxiety.[66] But if film could reflect the results of Dollard's study, so could it assure spectators of the reliability of military-psychiatric treatment. As an Army technical manual put it, filmmaking and filmgoing were among the "mental hygiene activities" intended to cultivate "a deeper appreciation on the part of military personnel of the wide range of individual personal and social needs and desires"—and of the accessibility and effectiveness of treatment.[67]

A number of military documentaries reflexively address this "therapeutic" use of film, directly depicting screenings designed to teach as well as to "heal." The Air Force's short *Wings Up* (1943), for instance, emphasizes the pedagogic as well as rehabilitative function of nontheatrical films, while the Army's *Follow Me Again* (1945) presents motion pictures as key elements of the Army Education Program, assisting veterans in their transition back to civilian life. Similarly, the Army documentaries *Diary of a Sergeant* (1945) and *Half a Chance* (1946) both feature nurses who screen nonfiction films meant to "aid rehabilitation,"

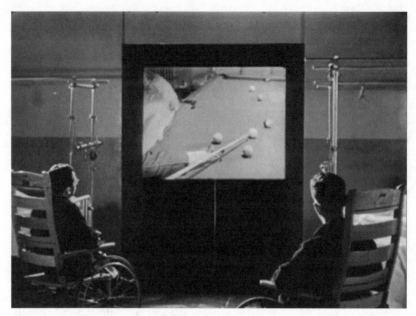

FIGURE 7. A therapeutic film screening for hospitalized servicemen in the Army's *Diary of a Sergeant* (1945). Courtesy of the National Archives and Records Administration.

but they also, in showing their traumatized protagonists' return to civilian life, suggest new uses for these institutional works.

To be sure, some films were hardly "timeless"—hardly ceaselessly relevant amid seismic changes in military routines, objectives, and treatment protocols—but what was no longer needed in the armed forces could easily be made to matter to civilians. Often, a "declaration of obsolescence," conveyed through a classified publication like the monthly *Catalog of Training Films*, came with recommendations for a film's eventual use "beyond the armed services."[68] This repurposing of "expired" documentaries was a major way in which the military, in David Culbert's words, "contributed to what could be termed an audiovisual revolution in American higher education."[69] The promiscuous spread of military documentaries via ever-expanding networks of nontheatrical distribution was difficult if not impossible to stop, as the Army itself discovered through its unsuccessful attempts to destroy all extant prints of the problematic *Why We Fight* entry *The Battle of China*, which continued to circulate, often in "minor," sometimes literally underground locations (such as church basements) far beyond the surveillance capabilities of the armed forces.[70]

More frequently, however, the military actively encouraged this pro-
miscuity even in the handling of films long believed to have been "banned"
or otherwise "suppressed," such as *Let There Be Light*. "At no time in
our history has it been so important that the layman have some grasp of
[psychiatry's] principles," wrote William C. Menninger in 1946.[71] The
military that had made Menninger a brigadier general seemed to agree.
When Menninger's words appeared in print, the disturbing realities that
had precipitated the War Department's temporary "publicity blackout"
were no less conspicuous, and they required constant intervention in the
convenient form of films (many of them limited to just two reels) that
could be screened in a variety of nontheatrical locations. As Martin Halliwell writes, "despite the supreme confidence that many had in science
and medicine, the number of cases of combat fatigue during World War
II indicated that the nation, which seemed purposeful and prosperous on
the surface, underneath suffered from uncertainty and anxiety."[72] It was
documentary, with its lofty, Griersonian associations, that offered a way
of exposing and, ultimately, managing this traumatic underside of institutional and everyday life—promising to reveal, as Paul Rotha had written in 1935, the "meaning *behind* the thing and the significance *underlying* the person."[73]

TRAUMATIZING DOCUMENTARY

The trauma-themed films that the military produced—or that it merely
adopted, inspired, or critiqued—should be understood as documentary
and realist works by dint of their direct, evidential engagement with
trauma as a verifiable yet elusive consequence of World War II, one
whose comprehension and eventual treatment was seen as requiring
a number of creative strategies typically taken to be beyond the ken
of such categories as "instructional film," "industrial film," and "training film." While such overlapping categories arguably "belong," in
some fundamental sense, to documentary as a capacious parent genre,
and while they were certainly used throughout the 1940s to describe
military-produced works about war trauma, they tend to signify a rote
functionality far removed from the actual patterns and purposes of
trauma-themed films, which sought not merely to teach, and not merely
to promote (in the sense intended by institutional advertising), but
also to inspire and even rehabilitate.[74] Inspiration and rehabilitation
were hardly incompatible with the aims of instruction and public relations, but they demanded a formal and discursive flexibility capable of

accommodating everything from therapeutic role play to diagnostic encounters between troubled servicemen and the sights and sounds of combat (particularly as captured on film). Military psychiatrists played a key role in shifting the military's nonfiction films away from the terrain of the strictly functional and toward the more imaginative, experimental territory claimed for documentary at the time, particularly by John Grierson (whose films and film writings were hardly unknown in military circles), Joris Ivens (whose unfinished film *Know Your Enemy: Japan* was intended for the Army Signal Corps, from which Ivens was summarily dismissed in 1944), and Paul Rotha.[75]

There was considerable governmental precedent for the military's official position on documentary as an instructive, creative, and potentially therapeutic genre. During the 1930s, for instance, the U.S. Department of Agriculture had worked to situate its "uninspiring but necessary films" as "true documentary pictures," laying some of the discursive groundwork for the military, which throughout World War II insisted that it was producing "motion pictures of documentary importance," whatever their subjects and formal features.[76] Grierson, in his "First Principles of Documentary," may have denigrated educational, scientific, industrial, and training films as "lower categories" of filmmaking far removed from the lofty echelons of documentary proper, but many producers of such films—including Raymond Evans, chief of the Division of Motion Pictures at the Department of Agriculture—firmly disagreed with him.[77] "That the straight 'nuts and bolts' training film, like the juvenile classroom film, exists outside rather than strictly within the documentary film area proper is a common opinion," wrote Richard Griffith in the aftermath of World War II, as he looked back on what he called "the use of films by the U.S. armed services."[78] "Common opinion" was hardly sacrosanct, however—something that Griffith appeared to misunderstand as he insisted that the "productions of the U.S. Army and Navy, remarkable and important though they were, do not really fall into the historic reading of documentary."[79] That may be true of certain examples, but "psychiatric motion pictures" (as George S. Goldman and others called them) force us to contest Griffith's claim that the military's documentary enterprise failed to "further or even notably continue documentary's main function of shaping or spreading constructive opinions and ideas for the good of mankind."[80] More recently, Charles Musser has stressed the importance of developing "less prescriptive ideas in regard to the representational methods appropriate for documentary," which would permit the reincorporation of long-marginalized films into the documentary tradition.[81]

It may be tempting to dismiss all military-produced films as mere "propaganda" artlessly designed to advance particular institutional objectives, but war trauma—a widely and often hotly debated topic in the 1940s—required nothing less than the "creative treatment of actuality," to quote Grierson's famous description of documentary, embellishing the blunt fact of trauma with strategies intended to teach as much as to treat and contain. As Cathy Caruth has written, trauma is characterized by "its refusal to be simply located," whether spatially or temporally, as well as by "its insistent appearance outside the boundaries" believed to effectively separate fantasy from reality, fiction from nonfiction.[82] In the influential terms of trauma studies, the seemingly fictive—a fantastical vision of danger, say—may well be factual as a specific experience of trauma, and admissible as one of its all-too-real symptoms. "Some types of sensory disturbances are accurate hallucinatory reproductions of sensations originally experienced in the traumatic event," observed the American psychiatrist Abram Kardiner in 1941.[83] The field of trauma studies, with its respect for the psychoanalytic category of "subjective truth," thus presents unique challenges to typical understandings of documentary evidence, as Janet Walker has argued.[84] Long before the appearance of Caruth and Walker's groundbreaking work, however, the United States military was engaged in efforts to reimagine documentary according to the soldierly experience, psychiatric treatment, and public perception of war trauma, raising key questions about trauma's historical relationship to representation.

The debates about documentary that had flourished in various North Atlantic countries in the 1930s were made intelligible to America's wartime military in multiple ways. The writer Eric Knight, who studied British documentaries under the guidance of his friends Paul Rotha and John Grierson, took this knowledge to the Signal Corps in the early 1940s. Knight was merely one among many ambassadors of the British documentary movement and of Griersonian principles in particular, reliably influencing the development of the military's "therapeutic films" by helping to circulate their British forbears.[85] With Knight (co-author of scripts for the *Why We Fight* series) came a number of influential British documentaries, including *Neuropsychiatry 1943*, a largely observational record of real patients, and *Field Psychiatry for the Medical Officer* (1944), which relied entirely on professional actors. Memorably, the latter film ends with its protagonist, an ambitious medical officer, being diagnosed with combat fatigue—a not-so-subtle suggestion that the condition may affect anyone, regardless of rank or experience. ("I would never have figured it could happen to him!" exclaims a character in Fox's *Twelve O'Clock High* [Henry King, 1949], referring to the impact of combat fatigue on Gregory Peck's brigadier general, who goes into a "state of shock—complete collapse.") Whatever its melodramatic qualities and dependence on polished performers (including a young Trevor Howard, who plays a colonel who, despite his smugness, becomes a reasonably reliable source of "psychiatric knowledge"), *Field Psychiatry*'s relationship to documentary lies in its careful reconstruction of various clinical practices, from drug treatment to physical therapy to "diagnostic interviews."

Like other "imported" films, *Field Psychiatry for the Medical Officer* was widely distributed within and beyond the American military during World War II, and it helped normalize the extension of familiar techniques of documentary reconstruction to the challenging subjects of trauma and psychotherapy. In the well-known Griersonian view, documentary differed from mere "films of fact," which were exclusively reliant upon the camera's "reproductive capacities"; the latter, then, offered "a method which describes only the surface values of a subject," while documentary "more explosively reveals the reality of it."[86] Military films about trauma and psychotherapy, which are very much devoted to "uncovering" and comprehending the "hidden" realities of the human mind, seemed thus to exemplify the distinctiveness of documentary, at least as Grierson had outlined it. Numerous military documentaries literalize this mode of inquiry through animation, figuring the "inner workings" of the mind as so many unruly cartoon characters (as in *The Inside Story of Seaman Jones*), or simply suggesting an "X-ray effect" that permits the viewer to see the deceptively "normal" brain inside the psychologically disturbed man.

Take, for instance, the Army film *Our Job in Japan* (1945), which insists that "problems of the mind" are the chief challenges to postwar reconstruction. Since these problems are invisible—even when "Japanese brains," which are "physically no different from any other brains in the world," are brought into view—Americans must simply assume that they are present among the masses of conquered Japanese citizens, who proved themselves susceptible to imperial propaganda and are now, in their defeated state, just as susceptible to "reeducation" in the form of American psychological intervention. Analogous claims are made in the harrowing *Here Is Germany*, produced by the Signal Corps in 1945, which insists on the psychoanalytic dimensions of postwar work, as the voice-over narrator exhorts the soldier-spectator to "look deeper," treating "the German mind" as a "puzzle that we've got to solve." Documentary is explicitly positioned as a useful tool in this regard, as gruesome images of corpses and of starved concentration camp survivors are employed as indications of what underlies seemingly comforting images of individuals who, with their whiteness of skin, "look like us."

The similarly themed *Your Job in Germany*, produced by the Signal Corps in 1945, sought to condition the members of the U.S. Army of Occupation to look *beneath* surfaces, *behind* objects, and *within* the ruins of cities, arguing that, as the voice-over narrator puts it, "The problem now is future peace." "Don't relax," he commands, "be suspicious"—especially since "every German is a potential source of trouble," all too willing to present a patina of "phony peace" beneath which simmers the true intentions of a "disturbed" national psyche. In order to illustrate this point, the film incorporates footage of dead American soldiers being placed in body bags—footage also included in Huston's *San Pietro*, and that, as Peter Maslowski's research reveals, consisted at least in part of living GIs merely simulating postmortem conditions.[87] The Signal Corps was certainly aware of these simulations when it repurposed the footage for *Your Job in Germany*, whose point— that the human imagination must be sufficiently active to "see inside" the minds of Germans—hardly depended on the strictest standards of observational realism. What mattered was less the indexical dimensions of this footage than its capacity to promote recognition of a particularly disturbing reality.

The military-psychiatric approach to documentary was essentially— and often by design—Griersonian, and thus also evocative of the work of Walter Lippmann: it posited a class of professionals (military psychiatrists and other psychological experts) capable of "mending minds" and cultivating self-knowledge among "ordinary" soldiers. More than just theoretically useful, however, the documentary label was also a strategic mechanism through which to guarantee a film's longevity through nontheatrical distribution. By the end of the war, the NYU Film Library was classifying several military films as "documentary classics," a label under which they continued to be distributed well into the 1960s.[88] This favorable label was hardly limited to conventional combat films and other nakedly patriotic works. The NYU Film Library distributed the British feature *Psychiatry in Action* (1943), which its catalogues classified as "a scientific documentary film," beginning in 1944, shortly after it had been "adopted" for use by the U.S. Army.[89]

A documentary-style emphasis on the availability of psychiatric treatment in the American armed forces was, in many ways, an extension of earlier efforts to tout the military's commitment to physical rehabilitation. As Maslowski points out, "realistic," even "grisly" images of combat victims—commissioned by President Roosevelt as a means of "correcting" complacency on the home front—"invariably showed them getting help—being assisted or carried to the rear by fellow soldiers, tended by battlefield medics, or surrounded by white-garbed doctors and nurses." If, as Maslowski suggests, the "implication was that prompt medical attention was always available for wounded Americans," this attention was increasingly expanded to include psychiatric treatment in films made after 1943.[90]

Military films about war trauma and psychotherapy occupy various positions on the continuum of documentary reconstruction that runs, in Brian Winston's productive formulation, "from complete non-interventionist surveillance through to totally fictional set-ups."[91] All of them emphasize the importance of prior witness—in this case, that of psychiatrists and other psychological experts who had come into sustained professional contact with those suffering from various forms and degrees of war trauma. Describing the act of witnessing—and the testimonial function that it may serve—as part of documentary's "essential foundation," Winston argues that the "crucial element is always witness"—that "there can be no claim on the real, no 'documentary value,' no documentary" in its absence. If rooted in verifiable experience—and, in particular, in clinical practice—reconstruction is thus, in Winston's terms, "no straightforward threat to documentary value."[92] Nor, of course, is extensive narrativization. Winston writes, "The presence of narrative in documentary, being inevitable, means that it is no marker of fictionality: documentaries cannot be held to be identical to fiction because they are narratives."[93] But narrative enjoyed an additional legitimacy in wartime and postwar documentaries about war trauma. Narrative—the telling of a story—was, after all, deemed necessary as a therapeutic measure, making its ultimate function in trauma-themed documentaries all the more defensible, especially by psychiatrists focused on the clinical construction of chronology and causality. Psychoanalytic inquiry is thus inherently a form of "creative treatment," whether embodied in the heuristic strategies of actors tasked with reenacting traumatic battle experiences or evident in the tentative pedagogy of an officer directly addressing the camera with a series of claims about the human mind.

If, as Stuart Legg argues, "documentary has always flourished in times of trouble," the epidemic experience of war trauma gave the genre a new remit in the 1940s, pushing it beyond the realm of instruction and into that of clinical therapy.[94] Education and recovery were among the official goals of the military documentary—"purposes" in the Griersonian sense—intended not merely to enrich and "mend" minds, but also to rehabilitate the public image of the military itself, particularly in preparation for its unprecedented postwar permanence as a large-scale enterprise. "A decisive change in motion pictures dealing with the human mind was brought about by the psychiatric realities of World War II," argued a team of physicians and medical educators in 1953. Singling out the Navy's *Combat Fatigue* series, they called its constituent films "outstanding examples of the fusion of imaginative psychiatric thinking and artistically splendid visualization in presenting such difficult concepts as unconscious guilt [and] the fear mechanism."[95] They concluded, as I do here, that military films about trauma and psychotherapy deserve recognition as crucial components of documentary history.

WHITEWASHING WAR TRAUMA

Realism was hardly the exclusive provenance of state-sponsored documentary during the 1940s, but its role in classical Hollywood cinema has often been understood strictly in terms of an Althusserian critique of its reputedly bourgeois pretensions. It was at the height of the Vietnam War, in fact, that Jean-Louis Comolli and Jean Narboni first offered their influential argument that, insofar as cinema can be said to "reproduce reality," the reality that it reproduces is merely that of bourgeois ideology—an argument echoed by, among others, Colin MacCabe (who later recanted, citing the prevailing pressure to create an "Althusserian straw man" out of theories—such as those of André Bazin—that seemed, in retrospect, far less reducible to such dimensions).[96] In the emerging field of film studies, then, the Althusserian critique of realism gained force precisely as Vietnam veterans' advocacy groups were beginning to confront and contest the military-industrial construction of the "realities" of soldiering, a process recorded in such trauma-themed documentaries as *Winter Soldier* (Winterfilm Collective, 1972) and *Interviews with My Lai Veterans* (Joseph Strick, 1971), which helped turn traumatized ex-combatants into a political collective with strong moral claims on the nation's attention.[97] Remarking on the need to reject a monolithic realism understood as inevitably bourgeois, Robert Stam helpfully insists on "a proliferation of 'realisms.'"[98] War trauma demanded such proliferation, its sheer complexity challenging certain mimetic traditions in both documentary and fiction film.

The term "war trauma" best accommodates the diversity of war-related symptoms that affected soldiers as well as civilians. At once specific and inclusive, the term "trauma" was widely used in the 1940s, despite presentist assumptions about its current popularity and diagnostic use-value. Zadie Smith, for instance, writes, "Trauma itself—now such a familiar tool in the writers' arsenal—was, in the forties, still something to be wrangled with, fresh theory rather than (generally) accepted fact."[99] But "trauma"—first theorized in organized psychological medicine in the 1870s—held sway as more than just a popular rhetorical tool during and after the Second World War, and I am by no means applying the term retroactively.[100] "It means shock," explains the psychiatrist in Universal's *Harvey* (Henry Koster, 1950), who proceeds to spell the word: "T-R-A-U-M-A. . . . There's nothing unusual about it!"

"War trauma," as it appears in these pages, is hardly anachronistic. In 1942, the Office of the Surgeon General, in a report on the condition, issued detailed descriptions of "post-traumatic states," "post-traumatic personality disorders," and "post-traumatic mental deterioration," while the first edition of Abram Kardiner's *War Stress and Neurotic Illness*, published in 1941, was titled *The Traumatic Neuroses of War*.[101] Six years later, Kardiner and John Spiegel would go so far as to suggest that "the stresses of war create only one syndrome which, though not unique to war conditions, is extremely frequent," and best characterized as "trauma."[102] The word was hardly uncontroversial, however, and the military's own public relations apparatus was often resistant to its potentially stigmatizing use. As Kardiner and Spiegel pointed out in 1947, "public responsibility and public prejudice have made their own contribution to [official] classification," leading to the occasional replacement of "disturbing" and "offensive" terms like "trauma" and "neurosis" with "misleading euphemisms like 'combat fatigue.'"[103]

Throughout World War II, "trauma" continued to be used in military-psychiatric documents as well as in documentary and realist films, even as euphemistic characterizations of mental illness became central to the military's public relations strategies. In the late 1940s, William C. Menninger noted that a "lack of agreement as to causes [of psychic distress] has resulted in a confusion in diagnostic terms," and argued for the utility of "trauma" as a convenient catchall.[104] During the war, Army psychiatrists had officially "differentiated between combat-incurred and noncombat-incurred neuroses," reserving the term "war trauma" for a broad set of war-related symptoms, from battle-induced nausea to the psychological distress that beset Harold Russell, the subject of the Army documentary *Diary of a Sergeant*, who lost both of his hands in an accident during the production of a training film at Camp Mackall in North Carolina.[105] In popular media especially, however, the term "psychoneurosis" was often confused with "psychosis," even when it was meant to designate "simple adult maladjustment."[106] As Menninger wryly noted, "psychoneurosis" was routinely "attached to anything from a transient emotional upset to a severe hysterical paralysis," and it often competed with colloquial labels like "gangplank fever," "old sergeant's syndrome," "shipboard jitters," "flak happy," "reple-deple exhaustion," and "war weary"—not to mention any number of terms carried over, however misleadingly, from the First World War.[107]

Compounding the problem, individual branches of the armed forces often diverged in their efforts to name psychic distress, despite the War Department's 1943 injunction against the use of certain "stigmatizing" psychiatric terms. For the Navy and the Air Force, the terms "combat fatigue" and "operational fatigue" were, during World War II, "mandatory for neurotic illness which developed on duty overseas," and they served the laudatory purpose of ensuring that the victim of war trauma would receive pay while hospitalized.[108] The Army, by contrast, continued to prefer the far less euphemistic "psychoneurosis" in its filmmaking activities, content with having jettisoned the antiquated and altogether misleading "shellshock" (traces of which nevertheless remain in more than a few Signal Corps documentaries, although the Hollywood film *Tonight and Every Night* [Victor Saville, 1945] critiques it as "quaint"). First used medically in 1915, "shellshock" was termed a "grievous misnomer" as early as 1922, its suggestion of explosive harm to the soma at odds with strictly psychogenic conceptions of war trauma.[109] By the 1940s, the term had largely been superseded by "combat exhaustion" and "combat fatigue," which posed their own, intractable challenges, including, as Menninger put it, "the disadvantage of implying that physical exhaustion or fatigue played a more major role than it did."[110] Nevertheless, such "replacement" terms for war trauma entered cinema almost immediately. For instance, "combat fatigue" is central to *Sherlock Holmes Faces Death* (Roy William Neill, 1943), whose plot pivots around the psychiatric treatment of war-traumatized British and American veterans in a remote estate. The even earlier *The Gay Sisters* (Irving Rapper, 1942), which is set mostly in the months immediately preceding the attack on Pearl Harbor, acknowledges the term in its efforts to connect the shell shock of 1918 to the "nervous strain" of 1941.

Wartime films show a growing sensitivity to terminology. The narrator of Jacques Tourneur's *Experiment Perilous* (1944), for instance, makes a point of using "mentally ill" in place of less charitable designations (a somewhat anachronistic move, given that the film is set in 1903, but one that clearly reflects wartime lessons).[111] In contemporaneous military documentaries, "combat fatigue" informs institutional efforts to promote the notion that, in the words of Abram Kardiner and Herbert Spiegel, the "normal state for the soldier in battle is fatigue and fear."[112] This is not to suggest, however, that military psychiatrists were somehow unaware of contradictions between their own, empathic approaches to certain "disorders" and those of a discriminatory military establishment. So-called "homosexual panic," while considered a "nontraumatic condition" by sympathetic and reform-minded psychiatrists, was nonetheless grounds for a psychiatric discharge, as the "exposed" homosexual was "no longer fit for duty" according to military protocol.[113] Some liberal psychiatrists working for the military, such as Harry Stack Sullivan (himself a gay man), believed that homosexuals were "particularly vulnerable to psychological strain in military life."[114] In colluding with homophobic institutions like the Army and the Navy, such professionals came to believe that they were in fact protecting the mental health of gay men by barring them from service, particularly after 1944, when the influential military psychiatrist John W. Appel, who had spent six weeks studying war trauma in the Italian theater, proclaimed the inevitability of "neuropsychiatric casualties" among combatants.[115] Naoko Wake argues that the pursuit of a non-homophobic military policy was deprioritized as psychiatrists gained national recognition through their work with the armed forces, settling for the professional opportunities that military service afforded them, and failing to question various racist and anti-queer measures.[116]

As a result of this strategic suppression of anti-homophobic and anti-racist inquiries, military documentaries about psychiatry and psychology tend to exclude considerations of the social ecologies of war trauma. As Yoosun Park and Joshua Miller suggest, experiences of inequality are central to social ecologies, as the "most disadvantaged members of the most disadvantaged communities suffer the greatest losses when disaster strikes"—a point that Sullivan and other psychiatrists anticipated in their emphasis on the disproportionate vulnerability of gay men in the wartime military.[117] While well aware of "the great variations of stress within the military environment," psychiatrists hardly adopted what, in today's parlance, would be termed an intersectional approach to trauma.[118] In military documentaries, women are only rarely mentioned as actual and potential victims of war trauma, their status as noncombatants seemingly sufficient to shield them from specifically "soldierly" neuroses. In reality, however, nurses and other female enlistees were victims of combat—just as likely to die or suffer grievous wounds in the line of duty as their male counterparts, a point that Yvonne Tasker has emphasized.[119] In cinema, the traumatic potential of "women's work" is evident as early as 1930, with the release of MGM's *War Nurse* (Edgar Selwyn, 1930), which insists that nurses are, in the words of one character, "soldiers, just as the men are." The film proceeds to illustrate how they, too, can be traumatized by war—and even by such patients as a shell shock victim who turns violent and must be "strapped down."[120]

Other films reflect a certain resistance to this militarization of women, even as they feature female characters suffering from psychoneurosis. The narrator of the thriller *Bewitched* (Arch Oboler, 1945), for instance, describes the "war-torn world"—"a world filled with sudden death," in which trauma is all but inescapable—and the film's focus is firmly on a woman who, though an American civilian, manages to succumb to what one character calls the "dark corners of the human mind that we know little about—very little about." For its part, the thriller *Shock* (Alfred Werker, 1946) allegorizes war trauma through its depiction of a woman who suffers a "nervous collapse" after witnessing a murder, her condition precipitated, in part, by the "built-up" stress of worrying about her soldier husband, who spent two years as a prisoner of war, but who is improbably untouched by trauma when he finally returns to the United States. "The mind is a delicate, fragile thing," says a psychiatrist, but such fragility seems only to apply to the film's female characters. Ayn Rand's script for the melodrama *Love Letters* (William Dieterle, 1945) similarly displaces war trauma onto the figure of a woman driven mad—and amnesiac—by the murder of her husband. She spends one year in a prison psychiatric ward, whereas the film's male protagonist, a soldier in the Italian campaign, spends time in a "regular" military hospital, his wounds strictly physical.[121]

Rand's reactionary script was written at a time when questions of gender integration were hotly debated. The Women's Army Auxiliary

Corps, created as a civilian organization in July 1942, became a military unit (the Women's Army Corps) in July 1943. Approximately 150,000 women served in both organizations between 1942 and 1945, and psychiatric discharges were 10 percent higher in this group than they were among servicemen.[122] Smaller women's branches, such as the Navy WAVES (which accepted approximately 100,000 women), the Women Marines (which accepted about 23,000), and the Coast Guard SPARS (which saw roughly 13,000 serve), were equally subject to psychiatric and, increasingly, homophobic surveillance, as the so-called "lesbian problem" became a matter of national concern.[123]

Like black and Native American enlistees, women were officially psychologized according to longstanding social prejudice, and disproportionately discharged as "psychoneurotic." Indeed, "neurotic potential" was generally believed to be highest among women of color, forced to contend with, at once, racism, misogyny, and the horrors and hardships of modern technological war. In 1946, the Chicago Institute for Psychoanalysis produced a study of the psychological effects of war, insisting that gender-segregated military service was traumatic in itself, constituting as it did "a threat to the not yet well-entrenched heterosexuality of the late-adolescent"; the inevitable "stimulation of homosexual tendencies" was thus both symptom and cause of "anxiety and trauma."[124] The study went on to report that, once in the Army, "women were faced with the problems of emotional adjustment which were in some respects more difficult than those of the men." Many were "willing 'to pay the price,' willing to share the dangers and hardships of life close to combat zones," but they were denied diagnoses of "operational fatigue" and "traumatic neurosis," despite the obviousness of their posttraumatic conditions.[125]

Rather than focusing on the treatment of these conditions, the "WAC Program" at Drew Field, an Army Air Forces base in Florida, was entirely devoted to the prevention of "actual breakdown," citing "the social disadvantages of formal referral to the Mental Hygiene Unit." While men who broke down were routinely referred to this unit, women who broke down were simply discharged so as to spare them the "stigma" of being treated for "neurotic illness."[126] Reflecting on this shameful history, William C. Menninger would later stress the dangers of integration, writing, "[T]here is no question whatever that the Women's Army Corps was an extremely valuable and effective segment of the Army. It must be recognized that it was, however, a pioneering effort somewhat contrary to the concept of femininity in American culture. . . .

We must accept the many psychological hazards that are connected with a Women's Corps in the Army."[127] Despite (or perhaps because of) such alarmist pronouncements, women were largely excluded from military documentaries about war trauma—except, of course, as concerned daughters, wives, and mothers. *Shades of Gray*, for instance, focuses in reactionary fashion on the culpability of neurotic mothers—including one "over-anxious" woman—in the cultivation of "psychiatric disturbances" in their sons.

If military psychiatrists failed to effectively address the structuring of homophobia and misogyny within the armed forces, they also tended to divert attention from the traumatic dimensions of institutionalized racism, despite recognizing that "the Negro experience" represented "a special problem" of immense "psychiatric importance."[128] Rejected by the Selective Service far more often than their white counterparts, black men were victims of the biological racism that underwrote an array of military policies.[129] Largely confined to service units, they often broke down from the stresses of life in the Jim Crow military, in which simply complaining about segregation was grounds for psychiatric rejection.[130] Oscar Micheaux's *Birthright* (1938) features a remarkable representation of racism's exacerbating effects on war trauma: a recipient of the Medal of Honor, the black war hero Tump Pack (Alec Lovejoy) develops a debilitating stutter only when in the presence of white people, the traumas of racism sufficient to awaken and inflame the latent traumas of combat. Eventually, these combined traumas prove too much for Tump Pack, who pulls a gun on the film's protagonist and is last seen obsessively reenacting military drills, weeping and shouting "Attention! About-face!" His symptoms include auditory hallucinations—whizzing bullets and explosive blasts—that Micheaux, in an empathic gesture, incorporates into the film's soundtrack, forcing the audience to share some of Tump's distress. *Birthright* thus offers an exceptional account of racial trauma, presciently detailing symptoms that would become all too obvious just a few years later. During World War II, "rare conversion hysterias"—psychosomatic or somatization reactions to trauma—were abundantly evident among segregated dockworkers, along with a range of other "unique" conditions.[131] The military establishment's discrimination against "Negro cases" meant that the lion's share of psychiatric treatment for black servicemen had to be provided by the Tuskegee Veterans Administration Hospital in Alabama, although integrated hospital units (such as the facility depicted in John Huston's *Let There Be Light*) operated during and after the war.[132]

Of the ten American "case studies" examined—and filmed—by an American military psychiatrist stationed in Trier, Germany, the lone black man was the only patient whose condition showed no signs of improvement after therapy. This patient ("Case I") and the lone gender-nonconforming patient ("Case J") were the only men who received a diagnosis of "dementia praecox" (in contrast to such "lesser" diagnoses as "psychoneurosis" and "anxiety").[133] "Case J," who was white and spoke in a soft, "feminine" voice, was often mistaken for a cross-dressing girl; his treatment involved a form of "psychodrama theater" in which he was forced to act out scenes from Thorne Smith's comic novel *Turnabout* (1931), "in which a man turns into a woman and has a baby"—a scenario whose "absurdity" was presented as akin to the patient's own "deviant" performance of gender. His therapy culminated in a "program of training" in which he was "assured" of his masculinity, taught to speak "with a deep masculine voice and to walk with a vigorous, manly gait"—a process dramatized in the Hollywood film *There's Something About a Soldier* (Alfred E. Green, 1943), as well as in the Army documentary *Combat Fatigue* (1943), in which the focus is on "walking like a soldier."[134] ("The Army psychiatrist straightened me out," says a character on a 1955 episode of *The Phil Silvers Show* [CBS, 1955–1959]; similarly, in *The Strip* [László Kardos, 1951], Mickey Rooney's traumatized Korean War veteran thanks the psychiatrists at a VA hospital in Kansas for "helping to straighten [him] out.") Throughout the war, experiences of racism and homophobia were recognized as "neurotic determinants" even as they were compounded by various treatment regimens. When, in 1980, post-traumatic stress disorder was finally recognized by the American Psychological Association in the third edition of the Diagnostic and Statistical Manual of Mental Disorders (DSM-III), it helped to displace the pathologization of homosexuality that had persisted for decades—although homosexuality would not disappear from the DSM until 1987.[135]

Of the extant, trauma-themed military documentaries produced during and in the wake of World War II, only Huston's *Let There Be Light* comes closest to suggesting how war trauma is compounded by social and economic experiences of racism—a subject that even later films, such as the Navy's *Preventative Psychiatry: In or Out* (1961), studiously avoid, but that Wendell Willkie directly addressed in a 1942 article on "war psychology," drawing attention to the "threat to individual and minority rights inherent in every war and its aftermath."[136] Even as they emphasize the racial diversity of the integrated armed forces,

FIGURE 8. A traumatized veteran weeps before a military psychiatrist at Mason General Hospital in John Huston's Army documentary *Let There Be Light* (1946). Courtesy of the National Archives and Records Administration.

incorporating numerous close-ups of black recruits, these later films firmly deny that the military has a responsibility to address the psychological effects of racism. As the voice-over narrator of *Preventative Psychiatry* puts it, the 1961 Navy offers "a true cross-section of the nation," one in which everyone—black as well as white—is equally vulnerable to "neuropsychiatric problems." The film's ultimate message is much like that of *Let There Be Light*: the military offers expert psychiatric treatment, regardless of race. This simple claim extends even to the otherwise outré territory of *The Manchurian Candidate* (John Frankenheimer, 1962), which not only addresses the complicated post-traumatic condition of a black man (played by James Edwards, a frequent avatar of racial trauma in postwar American cinema), but also depicts the efforts of a black psychiatrist (played by Joe Adams) to treat him and others like him, including the film's white protagonist (played by Frank Sinatra). Similarly set in the wake of the Korean War, Toni Morrison's novel *Home* (2012) contests—or at least complicates—this optimistic approach, focusing on a severely traumatized black veteran who, despite having been in "a desegregated army," comes to understand that, as another character puts it, "custom is just as real as law, and can be just as dangerous."[137]

Whatever its merits, Huston's *Let There Be Light* is structured by many of the strategic exclusions cited above, leading a group of physicians and medical educators to proclaim in 1953 that its effectiveness as a teaching tool derives from its careful, allegedly audience-friendly omission of queer men: "There is no suggestion of femininity or homosexuality," they approvingly wrote, despite recognizing the presence of queer patients in places like Mason General Hospital, where Huston's film was shot.[138] Their point is that, like so many other trauma-themed military documentaries, *Let There Be Light* is best approached not as a comprehensive record of military-psychiatric treatment but as a generalized, even sanitized advertisement for psychiatry itself, one that was particularly useful amid what Hans Pols has termed the "postwar political project of American psychiatry." Committed to promoting psychiatry's capacity to "contribute to the social and cultural transformation of society as a whole," such a project required the production and nontheatrical distribution of documentary films that could telegraph the successes of military psychiatrists without raising "uncomfortable" questions about their patients.[139] "It is almost impossible for any psychiatrist to describe all the phenomena seen in psychiatric combat casualties," wrote Abram Kardiner in 1947.[140] This does not, however, excuse the strategic omissions that characterize military documentaries about war trauma, which suggest a form of "restricted realism" rooted in efforts to normalize psychotherapy.

These films belong, in a certain sense, to the tradition of the Griersonian "victim documentary," which, Brian Winston suggests, "substitutes empathy for analysis" and "privileges effect over cause," carefully avoiding, in this case, the question of the state's own role in the spread of mental illness.[141] Such is how one character uncharitably understands military films in RKO's postwar thriller *Split Second* (Dick Powell, 1953): newly escaped from prison, the disturbed Army veteran Sam Hurley (Stephen McNally) explains, "I was a 'hero' for three years— watching all my pals get their heads blown off." Self-identifying as "another one of the vast army of young men who were ruined by the war," Sam in his post-traumatic state cynically suggests that he is now an ideal subject of documentary reporting, if only because "the people want to feel sorry for me." *The Hoodlum Saint* (Norman Taurog, 1946) offers a similarly cynical take on "human interest stuff," as the editor of a Baltimore newspaper asks a destitute veteran to do an exploitative

"Sunday series on the returning soldier—real names, hospitals, handi-capped guys!"

To be sure, many of the films analyzed in this book offer naked appeals to public sympathy for such traumatized figures. But they also suggest what Bhaskar Sarkar and Janet Walker have identified, in a far different sociopolitical context, as a "critical shift from a politics of 'victims' and victimhood to one of 'survivors' and agency," showing how the state, in collaboration with the psychiatric profession, offers opportunities for psychic recovery and promotes social and economic reintegration, albeit in the form, most frequently, of a return to "war work" (whether in the military or private industry).[142] Admittedly, there is something formulaic—and certainly nationalist and masculinist—about this emphasis on the agency of survivors, who, as straight, white American men, are upheld as uniquely capable of completing the hard work of psychic recovery. But a key component of the films' collective project is to suggest that war trauma is surmountable—that those affected by it are no less soldiers, and certainly no less Americans, for experiencing a disturbing array of symptoms and having to submit to the ministrations of psychiatrists, psychologists, and other professionals tasked with their rehabilitation. These films configured war trauma as a modern problem with institutional solutions. Therein lies their signal contribution not merely to documentary history but also to the field of trauma studies. Yet if they give us pause, that is at least partly due to their implication in an emergent military-industrial complex, which I explore in greater detail in the next chapter.

CHAPTER 3

Selling "Psycho Films"

Trauma Cinema and the Military-Industrial
Complex

"We do not simply name war trauma because it is there; we
make choices about how to view the suffering which can
result from combat experience and the history of this
suffering."

—Tracey Loughran[1]

Trauma-themed military documentaries served a variety of promotional
purposes—many of them strictly corporate—during and after World
War II. John Huston's *Let There Be Light* (1946), which features shots
of hospital patients making long-distance telephone calls "without
cost," was particularly attractive to the New York Telephone Company,
which maintained a Telephone Center at the Edgewood Annex of
Mason General Hospital, where the film was shot. Writing to the Signal
Corps Photographic Center while *Let There Be Light* was still in production, a representative of the telephone company announced his
intention to eventually acquire a print of the film from which the relevant scene could be excerpted for promotional use. With its attention to
the therapeutic value of long-distance telephone calls ("After months
and years of silence, familiar voices are heard once again"), *Let There
Be Light* depicts the wide and benevolent reach of the New York Telephone Company, helping to fashion its corporate image as a socially
responsible one.[2]

The company was hardly alone in seeking to circulate those portions
of state-sponsored "medical films" that revealed aspects of the "constructive," even "therapeutic" relationship between the military and private industry.[3] In fact, its uses of *Let There Be Light* were characteristic

of corporate efforts to co-opt wartime and postwar military documentaries to serve their own ends. In his 1952 article "Buy Them and Edit Them," the physician and medical educator David S. Ruhe advocated just that, calling on corporations to make the most of their cameo appearances in military films.[4] These fleeting appearances were hardly accidental, however. In many cases, they were a direct and strategic reflection of the military's commitment to situating trauma and psychotherapy in a recognizable context, one whose "curative" dimensions pivoted around the presence of large corporations and the availability of industrial employment.

REFINING "THERAPEUTIC FILM"

"A schizophrenic national condition has been created which finds mounting material well-being for large numbers of the population alongside of and largely dependent on omnipresent and numbing terror."

—Herbert Schiller[5]

While empathic depictions of trauma and psychotherapy are seemingly at odds with the bellicose approach of, say, Frank Capra's stridently racist *Prelude to War* (1942), and while they certainly contradict received knowledge about wartime documentaries, they were increasingly compatible with the aims of an emergent military-industrial state whose armed forces were repeatedly envisioned as global "watchdogs"— proponents of peace and agents of humanitarianism, as opposed to mere "war machines." (Besides, as Michel Foucault would put it in 1976, "One has to recognize the war underneath the peace."[6]) MGM's postwar documentary *The Secret Land* (1948) is a military-sponsored advertisement for precisely this "humanitarian" expansion, featuring footage of the Navy's "Operation Highjump" (an effort to explore and map the "hitherto unknown" Antarctic region) and exhorting the viewer to appreciate the military's commitment to science and industry "for all mankind."[7]

Trauma has a part to play in *The Secret Land*: it encapsulates the effects of the Antarctic on the brave men who travel there, and whose recovery is contingent upon new military technologies (a state-of-the-art icebreaker to rescue them, a naval vessel capable of accommodating a vast sick bay where therapeutic films may be screened, and so on). Thus even when military documentaries shift their focus from combat to a concern with cartography and "scientific discovery," they tend to retain a relatively stable sense of trauma and psychotherapy. In both cases, the military's responsibility for trauma—its institutional role in sending men to the battlefield as well as to the perhaps equally dangerous "nether region" of Antarctica—is mitigated (if not entirely displaced) by its commitment to providing immediate and effective psychiatric treatment. A key component of this tendency, in *The Secret Land* as in other such documentaries, is reenactment—particularly the process of "playing oneself": Secretary of the Navy James V. Forrestal, Chief of Naval Operations Chester W. Nimitz, Rear Admiral Richard E. Byrd, and Rear Admiral Richard H. Cruzen all "play themselves" in an opening sequence that permits them not simply to (woodenly) reenact official meetings but also, the film suggests, "work through" their emotions regarding "Operation Highjump" as a perilous, historic endeavor.

Something similar is at work in films about civil defense in the Atomic Age. After 1945, the act of "playing oneself" acquired a new purpose in public exercises designed to prepare civilian populations for atomic attack. As Tracy C. Davis points out in her history of civil defense as an inherently theatrical enterprise, Western governments "conceded that the public had to be a vigilant part of Cold War readiness, not to prevent conflict but to mitigate its consequences."[8] Several films illustrate Davis' claims in their attention to the act of rehearsing nuclear war. Produced by RKO for the Air Force, the short documentary *Sentinels in the Air* (Howard Winner, 1956) promises that all American cities and towns will one day boast centers for air reserve training, helping to make "the general militarization of American society"—or, as Hanson Baldwin put it in 1947, "the militarization . . . of the American state of mind"—complete.[9] The film was shot in and around one such center in Marietta, Georgia, and local residents—including reservists—"play themselves," in the process "proving" their capacity to assume "military responsibilities." As the voice-over narrator (actor and Air Force veteran Robert Preston) puts it,

> In every emergency since 1776, our country has ultimately come to depend on civilians to man its armed forces. But today, with weapons of instantaneous and total destruction at the disposal of unfriendly powers, there's not likely to be much time for a long buildup following an enemy attack. That's one big reason why reservists stay active—to be ready to defend their families and homes and communities in time of need.

Non-reservists are seen participating in "practice air raids" in the town square. Playing themselves playing "victims of enemy attack," they remain on the ground while their counterparts take to the newly militarized skies. "Today," Preston's narration continues, "no one challenges the Air Force's claim to be our country's first line of defense. And no one questions the need for this great sky barrier to be strong. For today, everyone knows what could happen if an invader were to push his way through this vast protective screen."

The film next cuts to stock footage of an atomic bomb being detonated in the Nevada desert—an American weapons test carried out on American soil in November 1951. (The footage is also included in RKO's 1953 thriller *Split Second*, which takes place at the Nevada Proving Grounds.) If such imagery undermines the film's main argument—that the militarization of America is therapeutic ("soothing and strengthening") rather than traumatizing, and that all threats come from "external foes" rather than, say, domestic weapons testing—its very existence seems to substantiate the narrator's insistence on a kind of statistical sublime ("no one challenges," "no one questions," "everyone knows"). How else to explain the permissibility of nuclear weapons testing—and in Nevada, no less? The mass consent that it requires is mirrored in the dutiful playacting of the Marietta residents, all of them scrambling to defend their town while the narrator claims that such mimetic actions are cathartic—and proof positive of the military's fortifying influence on everyday life.[10]

These experiments in institutional advertising, with their emphasis on the therapeutic dimensions of extensive militarization, were hardly limited to the postwar period. In a fundamental sense, they originated with the military's wartime efforts to contain widespread concerns regarding war trauma—efforts that met the militant tone of certain orientation films with a more measured, even somber reflection on the psychic costs of combat. As Dana Polan has suggested, "the war period is potentially a quite contradictory moment," one that forces us to question conventional wisdom.[11] Considering some of the circuits for nontheatrical nonfiction film in this period, it requires that we take seriously the contributions to institutional debates of those who, like military psychiatrists and their patients, are rarely cited in accounts of 1940s cinema, but who were instrumental to the development of films that, whatever their relationship to government policy, were widely distributed for decades. "The question of the forties, then, is also immediately a *theoretical* question," argues Polan, pointing to the importance of reevaluating received knowledge about the wartime and postwar aims of a military heavily if contentiously involved in the production of documentary film.[12]

Produced by the Army Signal Corps toward the end of the war, the documentary *G-5 in Action* (1945) is exemplary of the military's understudied efforts to use nontheatrical nonfiction in order to confirm its "humanitarian" mission while simultaneously advertising the equipment—including the Fairchild C-119 Flying Boxcar and other military transport aircraft, "delivery tanks," and various naval vessels—instrumental in carrying out that mission. For its part, the War Department's *Seeds of Destiny* (1946), which won an Oscar for Best Documentary (Short Subject), touts the capacity of the U.S. military, along with international agencies like the United Nations Relief and Rehabilitation Administration (UNRRA), to cope with the "lingering marks" of war trauma among the world's children. Describing psychological rehabilitation as "the last battle" of world war—and lingering on footage of a ten-year-old girl who "lost her senses when shells swept her Dutch village"—the voice-over narrator does not mention the military's complicity in the spread of mental illness, emphasizing instead its responsibility for treating such illness, even when it affects a Dutch civilian.

Like so many postwar military documentaries, the later *This Is Korea!* (John Ford, 1951) similarly emphasizes the disproportionate vulnerability of children to the traumas of war, as well as the military's largely "humanitarian" mission.[13] According to the film's voice-over narrator, the children of Korea were "homeless [and] hungry until *we* fed them," and altogether traumatized until "*we* stepped in." The containment of communism is thus presented as coextensive with "welcome" interventions of aid in the form of food and psychotherapeutic rhetoric. But it is also equally dependent upon industrial prowess, as the Korean War drama *One Minute to Zero* (Tay Garnett, 1952) attests, its narrator (Ann Blyth) stressing the "global need" for American military technologies: "The South Koreans started preparing to defend themselves against invasion. Their methods were primitive—their equipment, pitifully crude." It is only by "generously" bestowing better equipment upon them—and with it plenty of psychological insights—that the American armed forces manage to help South Koreans "fight for freedom." Advertising new equipment is thus coextensive with advertising psychotherapy, as the South Koreans are taught to "trust themselves" as well as to "trust their machines"—the individuated, techno-optimist essence of the film's anticommunism.[14]

This intricate approach to the material aspects of the military-industrial state was honed before the U.S. entered World War II. Produced by Castle Films, *Salute to the Navy!* (1941), which focuses on "the armaments of war," shows not merely how "mechanical genius joins with the muscle of millions of men," but also how workers are psychologically conditioned to "suit" their ships—to "serve" a ten-billion-dollar fleet. MGM's short film *Aeronautics* (Francis Corby and S. B. Harrison, 1941) reflects a similar argument, its voice-over narrator offering paeans not merely to the "sleek sky monster, ready to roar off into the blue," and to "Uncle Sam's mighty ships of the sky, the last word in flying perfection," but also to the therapeutic dimensions of this "fascination with machines," which promises to fortify "the average American youth of today." Later films go even further in fusing familiar techniques of institutional advertising with new shorthand references to psychotherapy. The widely seen OWI film *The Autobiography of a "Jeep"* (Joseph Krumgold and Irving Lerner, 1943) suggests how psychological expertise can assist the titular motor vehicle, famously anthropomorphized and granted a first-person voice-over narration, through which "he" expresses considerable anxiety and self-doubt. As an advertisement for the Jeep, the film is fundamentally about the ego building of this general-purpose vehicle and its close, almost symbiotic relationship with the American soldier.[15] Carrying this approach to its logical conclusion, Basil Dearden's *The Ship That Died of Shame* (1955) poetically suggests how war trauma ultimately sinks the titular vessel. "I know about ships," says the film's protagonist, a World War II veteran, in voice-over. "They're wood and metal and nothing else—they don't have souls, they don't have wills of their own . . . or so I told myself a thousand times." After "witnessing" the struggles of the postwar years, however, the film's central ship simply "gives up"—"in anger, and in shame."

If, by the 1940s, "total war" had traumatized the world and, in particular, the combat soldier, the American military-industrial state was increasingly deemed the only apparatus capable of ensuring that so extensive a conflict would "not happen again" (to quote the 1944 Army film *He Has Seen War*). This particular claim is central to a number of wartime military documentaries; like most of them, *He Has Seen War* was intended as an illustration of the veteran's "readiness to work," despite—or perhaps because of—the "profound changes" he has undergone. ("Work's the best thing for you fellas coming back," says a character in the Navy's *Combat Fatigue: Assignment Home* [1945].) For its part, the Army documentary *Combat Exhaustion* (1945), which focuses on the psychiatric treatment of war trauma, emphasizes the effectiveness of "sensible occupational therapy projects," which not only assist in the immediate mental recovery of the "psychoneurotic" soldier, but also promise "constructive ends" beyond the context of rehabilitation—including in "postwar work." Far from denying the realities of combat trauma, the military was committed to presenting, through documentary film, the treatment of this condition as well as the industrial dividends that such treatment would ultimately pay. As the War Department put it in May 1945, "returnees will be the greatest single potential pool of high-grade employees for years to come."[16]

Positioning veterans as "the hope of every American community and business of the future," the War Department distilled the arguments of numerous military documentaries that insisted that trauma could be overcome—"faced, and understood, and worked out," to quote the Navy film *Combat Fatigue: Irritability* (1945)—for the sake of postwar productivity. "He has seen and experienced things which should not happen under God, which should not happen under the sun," proclaims the narrator of *He Has Seen War*, referring to the traumatized war veteran. "He is no longer illusioned, he is no longer a boy." But precisely because he has "fought for a future," the veteran is the ideal agent of replenishment for American industry, a figure eminently capable of using his hard-won strength, knowledge, and maturity to "fuel" postwar production: "Here is your man."

Psychological rehabilitation was only one of the purposes to which "therapeutic motion pictures" were put during and after World War II, and a number of key players worked to delineate the adaptability of these works. "Training films will repeat their wartime accomplishment," promised a 1944 advertisement in *Business Screen*.[17] A year later, Ray-Bell Films, a company that produced numerous documentaries for the Navy's Bureau of Aeronautics, directly addressed American businesses, declaring that their "motion picture problem" could be solved by adopting military films for instructional and therapeutic purposes.[18] By 1948, a professor at Harvard Business School could confidently write, "The extensive and successful use of films and other audiovisual training aids by the Armed Services stimulated the imaginations of educators and industrial training directors alike." Calling for the continued uptake of military documentaries by private industry, he suggested that such films were as "instructive" as they were "therapeutic," their potential to improve workers' lives "proven" by their use in the armed forces.[19]

For their part, military psychiatrists repeatedly identified their work in relation to economic considerations, touting occupational therapy as a means of ensuring the postwar productivity of traumatized servicemen.

"Opportunities for education and training for lifetime careers are regarded as part of our job as we prepare these men to go back to a varied group of duties," proclaimed Army Air Forces psychiatrist John M. Murray in 1944.[20] However varied the duties of which Murray and other psychiatrists spoke, they were united by a single factor: they were all "military-friendly" occupations whose relevance to the armed forces was seen as part and parcel of their therapeutic utility.[21] According to this logic, removing a recovering soldier from "the military scene"—carefully extricating him from anything that smacked of militarization—was tantamount to enabling his anxieties and even cultivating new phobias.[22] "The psychiatrist with the combat organization is in the same position as the mechanic who maintains the airplane or the mechanical equipment," argued one military psychiatrist in 1949. "[H]e is there to keep the humans in fighting condition."[23]

Such analogies between man and machine are unmistakable in *Shades of Gray*, which repeatedly describes psychiatric patients as having been "salvaged for duty" and "salvaged for service" to the military-industrial state: "Until proven otherwise," the narrator claims, "even the most serious cases are regarded as salvageable."[24] John Frankenheimer's *The Manchurian Candidate* (1962) astutely shows a Chinese agent, Dr. Yen Lo (Khigh Dhiegh), working to expose such analogies as morally bankrupt, critiquing American psychotherapy by appropriating its "distracting" rhetoric, and ultimately referring to the brainwashed Sergeant Raymond Shaw (Laurence Harvey) as a mere tool—something to be "handled" by "operators." This dehumanizing language has deep roots in military psychiatry, which often strained to align itself with other military duties through various semantic acrobatics. Writing of the "aggressive rehabilitation" of soldiers during World War II, Alison Winter notes that military psychiatrists "sometimes affected to treat a buried memory as a military surgeon might a buried bullet."[25] According to the narrator of the Navy's *Combat Fatigue: Insomnia* (1945), soothing oneself is as difficult as sharpshooting: "Relaxing's a skill, like hitting a target. It takes practice, concentration, and more practice."

Addressing the high incidence of "psychiatric discharges" in 1943, the War Department noted that, in some cases, "men who have been returned to the community were told that they were 'crazy' or were given some other equally tactless reason," when they should have been encouraged to pursue "war work"—to accept that they "could serve [their] country better in a defense industry" than on the battlefield.[26] If documentary could help de-stigmatize mental illness, it could also be used as a tool for returning the discharged "psychiatric casualty" to some form of military service as a civilian, counseling him to assume a "useful" position in a permanent war-based economy. Restoring the veteran's capacity for industriousness was a central objective of President Roosevelt's rehabilitation plan, which expressed faith even in traumatized ex-combatants, carefully explaining how, through various treatment methods (including occupational therapy), such men could eventually "become a national asset."[27] Similarly, the sociologist and World War I veteran Willard Waller, in his 1944 book *The Veteran Comes Back*, outlined strategies for "pushing" the veteran toward a "competitive position" in the postwar workforce, stressing an "art of rehabilitation" tied to the synergy of the military and private industry.[28]

Directed by George L. George, formerly of the National Film Board of Canada, the Army's Oscar-winning documentary *Toward Independence* (1947) is a thirty-minute advertisement for precisely this synergy. Outlining what the narrator refers to as "recent developments in medical management," the film reflects the era's insistence on the therapeutic dimensions of "mechanical work." It focuses on the plight of disabled hospital patients, all of whom "play themselves," reenacting the processes by which they came to accept and "manage" their post-traumatic conditions. These reenactments are performed with a painstaking attention to detail designed, the film suggests, to instruct and even "inspire" others. Here, rehabilitation—both physical and psychological—is repeatedly defined as a job, one that often involves new equipment (prosthetic limbs, crutches, wheelchairs) in need of "mastering." One patient, who was wounded when his Jeep overturned during maneuvers in Kansas, describes his gradual psychological recovery in terms of a growing orientation toward "defense work." Suddenly, he says, "I dreamed about being back at my old job at the plant"—a "nautical instruments laboratory" that supplies the Navy. The film ends with his triumphant return to this facility—the place toward which the military's employment counselors confidently "steered" him after their psychiatric counterparts had helped to "free [his] personality" from post-traumatic depression.

"Licking" war trauma was thus, in many instances, presented as akin to overcoming impediments to employability in the postwar period, precisely because the regimentation of so many industrial jobs evoked the conditions of military service; to succeed in one arena, including by "rising above" its endemic traumas, was to succeed in the other—provided, of course, employers could be "cured" of their irrational aversion to battle-scarred veterans. Numerous mass-market books offered this equation

FIGURE 9. The process of physical and psychological rehabilitation involves "defense work" in the Army's Oscar-winning documentary *Toward Independence* (1947). Courtesy of the National Archives and Records Administration.

between military service and civilian employment, consistently positing a close resemblance between technological war and industrial production. From 1945's *Psychology for the Returning Serviceman*, a mass-market paperback whose chapters were written by Army and Navy personnel, to Charles Bolté's *The New Veteran*, published in the same year, such books suggested that the best way to conquer the traumas of war was to engage in some form of "useful" work that, in most cases, sounded a lot like war production—a lot like the "naval support" that the disabled protagonist of *Toward Independence*, though a victim "only" of Cold War preparedness, comes to provide.[29]

Bolté, himself a veteran of World War II and the founding chairman of the American Veterans Committee (whose motto was "Citizens First, Veterans Second"), insisted that, "in a modern technological society," veterans would need to surmount their neuroses—and "correct" considerable public prejudice—in order to find work in the "new material world" that the war itself had created, and that was likely to reproduce the traumas of combat even in the ostensible service of peace (in "atomic energy, in air transport, in rocket and jet propulsion, in the techniques of mass production").[30] The psychoanalyst Abram Kardiner was considerably less hopeful, however, suggesting that the veteran's psychic rehabilitation simply could not survive his employment in sectors that, with their close ties to the military, invariably "complicate and aggravate the already existing medical problem."[31] But Kardiner's proved to be a rare, almost radical voice among American psychological experts during and in the immediate aftermath of the war, when confronting trauma so often involved acceding to its sources—industrial and otherwise.

Indicating their recognition and acceptance of the emergent military-industrial state, several psychiatrists began in the immediate postwar period to press for the "exportation" of military psychiatry to private industry. Efforts to find a home for psychotherapy in industry date back at least to the teens, with the publication of Hugo Münsterberg's *Psychology and Industrial Efficiency* (1913) and other tomes devoted to the shaping of labor through therapeutic techniques. World War I had a major part to play in the emergence of this "psychology of industry," its obvious and increasingly controversial ties to private enterprise inspiring considerable interest in "transferring" military psychiatry, with its focus on the traumatic effects of technological war, directly to the factories in which war technologies were produced. In 1920, the American psychiatrist Elmer Ernest Southard published an article entitled "The Movement for a Mental Hygiene of Industry," in which he argued that the study of "war neuroses" had provided the justifications for psychiatry's entrée into big business.[32] "Had it not been for the war, this fusion of physical-health ideas and mental-health ideas for the betterment of industry might have been postponed a decade or a quarter of a century," he wrote, stressing how the growth of "war work" had made military psychiatry uniquely suited to civilian labor.[33] In Southard's view, it "takes but half an eye to see" that military psychiatry is not only "relevant" but also "essential" to industrial operations, so closely entwined had the military and private industry become by 1920. Even if industrial risks are "perhaps not so acute as the war risks," they still bear a startling resemblance to the latter, if only because of the common role of "technologies of war"—what the soldier uses and the worker produces.[34] For Southard, then, industries "partaking largely of the nature" of technological war—what he classified in terms of "the business of war"—could only benefit from the psychiatric study of war neuroses.[35]

Southard was hardly alone in touting the benefits of military psychiatry for private industry, offering a sophisticated understanding of the military-industrial complex over a decade before the so-called "munitions inquiry" led by Senator Gerald P. Nye of North Dakota and the publication of H. C. Engelbrecht and F. C. Hanighen's bestselling *Merchants of Death* in 1934 would spotlight the sheer profitability of military contracts.[36] The psychiatric social worker Mary J. Jarrett, in a 1918 study subsidized by the Engineering Foundation, concluded that "analogues of shell shock in civilian life" were most abundant in industry, while the psychiatrist Thomas Salmon, medical director of the National Committee for Mental Hygiene, argued in 1919 that the "extraordinary effects of modern war upon the human nervous system" derived from such "eminently practical work as gassing, bombing, shelling, and bayoneting our enemies"—work that, Salmon pointed out, was made possible by "vulnerable" war workers in private manufacturing plants.[37] Each such plant represented an arm of what the activist documentary *Dealers in Death* (Burnet Hershey, 1934) calls "the armaments octopus." Depicted through an animated sequence in which the creature's tentacles spread menacingly throughout Europe, the armaments octopus is transformed—one might say contained—in the later *Why We Fight* films, whose strikingly similar animated maps reconfigure it as "the fascist menace."

The advent of "total war" in the 1940s, coupled with fading memories of earlier proprieties, helped to reduce the likelihood that films—both theatrical and nontheatrical—would avoid carrying military-industrial messages. Indeed, the sudden frequency with which such messages were relayed cinematically marked something of departure for the medium as it was regulated in the United States. During World War I, the Committee on Public Information was particularly wary of "commercial propaganda taking advantage of the wartime screens," and it promptly banned Universal's *The Yanks Are Coming* (1918), a film produced in close collaboration with the Dayton-Wright Company, an airplane manufacturer, for which it served an obviously promotional purpose.[38] By 1918, the Creel Committee had good reason to be wary. Three years earlier, the Edison Company had worked with the War Department on *The Manufacture of Big Guns for the Nation's Defense*, which was shot in (and invariably became an advertisement for) an actual armaments factory. At around the same time, the Vitagraph Company was collaborating with the Maxim Munitions Corporation in order to produce a series of interventionist films, including *The Battle Cry of Peace* (J. Stuart Blackton and Wilfrid North, 1915), while Universal was busy shooting *The Eagle's Wings* (Robert Z. Leonard and Rufus Steele, 1916) in, and partly for, a rival munitions plant.[39]

The Creel Committee's clampdown on "commercial propaganda" was short-lived, however—not to mention mired in suspicions regarding its true origins and purpose. After World War II, the promotional forms epitomized by the abovementioned films would become par for the course—so pervasive as to go unnoticed by many critics and commentators, with the conspicuous exception of Pare Lorentz, who asked, "Who puts the Navy in every newsreel?" and answered, "The Bethlehem Steel Company."[40] In the postwar period, institutional advertising increasingly embraced psychotherapeutic rhetoric, with many films going so far as to depict military-industrial expansion as essential to an individual's psychological recovery. Produced with the assistance of the Air Force, *Toward the Unknown* (Mervyn LeRoy, 1956) is the story of Major Lincoln Bond (William Holden), a pilot who "cracked under stress" in a "Red prison camp," but who hopes to "prove his stability" by testing the Bell X-2 rocket at Edwards Air Force Base in California. The film explicitly links the military to private industry, and psychotherapy to technological "progress," in a scene in which Brigadier General Bill Banner (Lloyd Nolan) tells a visiting senator about the Air Force's "mission," which is not only tied to an American entrepreneurial spirit but also deemed capable of "curing" the traumatized Bond. Confessing his persistent war trauma—"a mental thing," he calls it—Bond discovers that the key to its cure is simple submission to the military-industrial state, which, for the sake of his recovery, enlists him in the testing of the X-2. One officer even goes so far as to invoke William Faulkner's Nobel Prize acceptance speech, couching Faulkner's famous words ("I believe that man will not merely endure: he will prevail") as descriptive of the military-industrial capacity to "manage" war trauma.

The cruel irony of the films examined in this book is that, for all their compassion for the combat-traumatized soldier, and for all their psychiatric and pseudo-psychiatric savvy, they point to an unacknowledged repetition-compulsion in the new national character. For in depicting the relationship between psychotherapy and industrial production, these films speak to the durability of a military-industrial state that will only produce new "neurotic cases." In the Hollywood drama *Till the End of Time* (Edward Dmytryk, 1946), for instance, the battle-scarred protagonist learns to cope with his anxieties primarily in order to succeed in his job as a repairman of radios and other communication devices that, the film makes clear, are crucial to the winning of wars—and that will thus play their own parts in the production of future forms of psychoneurosis. In the later *Battle Hymn* (Douglas Sirk, 1957), a traumatized veteran of the Second World War reenlists at the outset of the Korean War, upsetting his wife, who protests, "It doesn't make sense, it doesn't—going back to war! That's where your problem began!" "Don't look for any sense in this," he calmly replies. "You won't find it." In congressional hearings on the proposed National Neuropsychiatric Institute in 1945 and 1946, some went so far as to favorably align efforts to federalize mental health services—a major and unprecedented undertaking—with the Manhattan Project. The formation of the National Institute of Mental Health was thus equated with the creation of the atomic bomb—a point that, intended to trumpet the power of scientific research, merely pointed to the disturbingly paradoxical underpinnings of a mental health program in an advanced national security state.[41]

This awkward, even contradictory reliance on World War II as a reference point can be found in any number of films that assert the healthful effects of combat. The Warner Bros. musical *Starlift* (1951)—a weak retread of such patriotic fare as *Thank Your Lucky Stars* (David Butler, 1943) and *Hollywood Canteen* (Delmer Daves, 1944)—signals its own reiterative status through a studio executive who says, "We supplied shows for the armed forces all through the last war. All they have to do is call on us and we're ready again!" But the film also depicts a young Air Force flyer who wants desperately to be transferred to a combat unit. Being kept from the front lines of the Korean War proves traumatizing to him—it "makes [him] crazy," much as being restricted to messenger duty is a cause for alarm among the men of John Ford's *We Were Expendable* (1945). "All I do is fly back and forth, back and forth, between here and Honolulu," he complains, stressing his fear of "going out of [his] mind." As another flyer observes, "That kid's getting ready for a psycho ward!" Thus as *Starlift* suggests the continued capacity of Hollywood studios to furnish patriotic spectacles amid a new conflict in Korea, it also revives an earlier representational approach to the "common soldier," who here, as in the similarly structured musicals *Private Buckaroo* (Edward F. Cline, 1942) and *Thousands Cheer* (George Sidney, 1943), is unaccountably eager to see combat, which he couches in therapeutic terms—as a "cure" for boredom, feminization, and more. Combat's capacity to negatively affect its participants remains unstated, but it is nonetheless discernable in this film—evident, at the very least, in its not-infrequent references to "going crazy," "psycho wards," and "mind problems." Addressing Freud's "Remembering, Repeating, and Working-Through," M. Guy Thompson acknowledges Freud's insistence that the "solution" to a psychic problem may, in

Thompson's words, "harbor acts of sabotage that help preserve the symptom," and it is in this sense that military cinema, understood as a state project whose influence extends to the terrain of commercial films, undermines the psychiatric "cure" both practically and symbolically.[42]

NONTHEATRICAL NONFICTION AND
THE MILITARY-INDUSTRIAL COMPLEX

"Out of the American experience of global war during the
years 1941–1945 came habits, ambitions, and expectations
that left a large and lasting imprint on virtually all subsequent
matters related to national security."
—Andrew J. Bacevich[43]

"Our problem is how to live with our machines."
—Robert Flaherty[44]

Trauma-themed documentaries had a part to play in efforts to forge a permanent relationship between the military and private industry, laying some of the discursive and even practical groundwork for what would later be known (and denounced) as the military-industrial complex. Widely distributed to American manufacturing plants (particularly those with military contracts), such documentaries as the Navy's *Combat Fatigue: Insomnia* (1945), which explores ways of overcoming the potentially negative psychological consequences of "repetitive work," and the Air Forces' *Recognition of the Japanese Zero Fighter* (Bernard Vorhaus, 1943), which reenacts the experiences of a "typical" pilot who learns how to emotionally recover from a near-fatal mistake, were touted as useful lessons for employees in various industries, testifying to the adaptability not just of documentary film but of the very concept of trauma itself. These equations between military and industry were so frequently and so nakedly proffered that servicemen began to scoff at the now-sacrosanct assertion that they were fighting a "good war" for freedom at home and abroad. Asked for their "*own personal* opinion[s] about what the United States is fighting for," 5 percent of soldiers in the Army responded with "cynical attitudes" about "capitalists."[45]

The notion that wartime military documentaries could "boost" industry persisted well past V-J Day. As late as 1961, the U.S. Office of Education was promoting such wartime documentaries as *Introduction to Combat Fatigue* and *Combat Fatigue: Assignment Home* as "widely beneficial" films with the potential to "improve morale" among students

FIGURE 10. An enlisted man confronts his "inner voices"—his "other selves"—in the Navy's *Combat Fatigue: Insomnia* (1945). Courtesy of the U.S. National Library of Medicine.

and all manner of industrial workers.[46] Distributed for public use by the U.S. Department of Health, Education, and Welfare, they were advertised alongside industrial documentaries designed to enhance worker efficiency and boost business enterprise. In order to lend the film a broader relevance, the Navy cut those sections of *Introduction to Combat Fatigue* in which a medical officer stares at the camera and addresses the hospitalized spectator, preparing a version that would speak not to a psychiatric patient but to the "average working man." If the so-called "patient's version" of *Introduction to Combat Fatigue* reflected the Navy's belief in documentary's capacity to rehabilitate victims of war trauma, the so-called "working man's version" signaled the institution's growing commitment to addressing the needs of private industry.[47]

Highlighting what it saw as the "problem" of anxious and handicapped employees, the Navy authorized the *New York Times* to include its films *Voyage to Recovery* (1945) and *Combat Fatigue: Assignment Home* in a 1947 directory of agencies and organizations "concerned with rehabilitation and services to the handicapped." Presented as a public service—an extension of the newspaper's avowed commitment to

"the cause of the millions of Americans who are physically and emotionally handicapped"—the directory credits the rehabilitation programs of the armed services and the Veterans Administration for increasing the visibility of trauma and its treatment in social and national life,
listing the two Navy films as instrumental agents in this process. Cited
alongside the films is information about their availability: at the time,
the American Medical Association provided both documentaries "on a
temporary loan basis," while the home-movie distributor Castle Films
(which had just been purchased by the nontheatrical division of Universal Pictures, a studio that had lent considerable production support to
the Navy during World War II) was selling 16mm as well as 8mm reduction prints "for home use."[48]

The increasing availability of military documentaries about war
trauma and psychotherapy is thus partly explicable in terms of the postwar growth of film societies and small-gauge film libraries, with distributors like United World Films and the Visual Training Corporation
among the "growing body of commercial firms seeking to service the
growing market for nontheatrical audiences."[49] Even before the war,
such firms had worked to cultivate appreciation for the sort of "bal-
anced" film program that brought together institutional documentary
and Hollywood entertainment. As Eric Hoyt has pointed out, Eastman
Kodak's 16mm Kodascope Library (1924 – 1939) conditioned consum-
ers to curate their own film festivals, offering a monthly newsletter that
stressed the importance of "a thoughtfully selected program" of films
that prominently included nonfiction.[50] Thus when the U.S. Office of
Education began distributing *Introduction to Combat Fatigue* in 1952,
it relied on Kodak's rhetoric of balance and completion, presenting the
film as a means of rounding out "public educational fare."[51]

Caravel Films, an independent production company based in New
York, praised the Navy's wartime use of documentaries as a model for
"the Sales Managers of American Businesses." Arguing that these managers must adopt military documentaries "if they are to do their part
in providing worthwhile opportunities for returning veterans," Caravel
repeatedly advertised "war-time training films for peace-time use,"
pushing "for [their] general release." The company, which had produced a number of films for the Navy and other branches of the military, had a vested interest in seeing these films survive as teaching tools
and "sources of inspiration." Even when the Navy handled distribution
on a nonprofit basis, Caravel stood to benefit from the enhanced visibility of its work, particularly in the postwar circulation of such titles as

Dealing with the Dissatisfied Employee (1944) and *Creating Job Interest* (1945).[52] The military's commitment to nontheatrical film thus paid dividends for independent production companies as well as for manufacturers of screens and projectors, some of which sought to fashion an image of corporate social responsibility out of their association with military documentaries about trauma and psychotherapy. Billing itself as "the most progressive force in 16mm," the International Theatrical & Television Corp. (ITT) cited its acquisition of thousands of films produced by the Walter O. Gutlohn Corporation, including those about war trauma—films that ITT distributed "for ALL USES" ("Instruction for the home . . . the factory . . . the school"). Promising that "vision and progress shall ever be the watch-word" for the corporation, ITT demonstrated that the sheer public relations value of trauma-themed films extended to civilian businesses as early as 1945.[53]

The longstanding involvement of the American Medical Association and the U.S. Department of Health, Education, and Welfare in the nontheatrical distribution of military documentaries suggests an abiding medical and governmental belief in the films' instructive and perhaps even curative potential. Such lofty aspirations, articulated in terms of the public good, coexisted with—and in some cases motivated—the military's ambition to use its wartime documentaries (especially "therapeutic films") to manage aspects of its own, growing relationship with private industry. The trade journal *Industrial Relations*, which began publication in 1942 and targeted "war work" (a category encompassing a range of manufacturing activities), routinely ran advertisements for military documentaries that were readily available for use in factories and plants, further establishing a rhetorical equivalence between soldiers and civilian workers. Since the concept's introduction in public discourse, the military-industrial complex has been critiqued for its perceived effects on the psychology of working Americans, whom military psychiatrists had repeatedly aligned with "warriors" in efforts to spread their therapeutic gospel and secure a prominent place for themselves in the postwar United States.[54] As one military psychiatrist put it in 1945, "the employee in a large factory and the man in military life have to live pretty close to the line."[55] Eight years later, another military psychiatrist confessed, "The more I see of military life the closer I see it allied to big business operations."[56] Echoing the OWI's familiar reminder that "men and women on the production line . . . are as much a part of the battle front as the soldier in the battle zone," military psychiatrists helped to popularize the notion of the industrialized self—an ideal of institutional conduct toward which American workers were exhorted to strive.[57]

Transforming workers into unwitting (or, more disturbing still, conscious) assistants to various "merchants of death," the military establishment was held increasingly responsible for dramatically reducing labor's usefulness to American social and cultural life, particularly at a time when the labor movement was hardly antiwar—when, for instance, AFL and CIO policies were strongly pro-military, opposed to anything that smacked of resistance to the Cold War consensus. As Sidney Lens put it in 1970, "The American labor hierarchy became a segment of the military-industrial complex partly to protect millions of jobs dependent on armaments, partly because of its conservative philosophy."[58] In the postwar period, labor unions increasingly embraced military documentaries as durable therapeutic instruments, ensuring that they wouldn't "just stand in the library to gather dust." Unions like the UAW-CIO (which "makes the Army roll and go," as Pete Seeger sang during the war) regularly screened these films at chapter meetings and made them available for use by such community groups as the Detroit Fire Department, the Jewish Community Center, the Office of Civilian Defense, the Police Safety Department, the House of Correction, "and all sorts of church, women's and youth groups." The UAW-CIO prided itself on owning prints of over two hundred military documentaries, which the union claimed to have screened for "a total of five and a half million persons" in 1944 alone. Well into the postwar period, the UAW-CIO continued to circulate these films—including the Army's *The Negro Soldier*, which it used as a tool for "raising the morale of the Negro people" and as a therapeutic bulwark against racism in the workplace.[59]

Long before Eisenhower's 1961 warning against the "unwarranted influence" of the military-industrial complex, the military establishment was devising ways of using its documentaries to suggest that the traumatic or merely mundane aspects of "war work" could be alleviated through exposure to "therapeutic film," thereby fortifying—and, in a sense, "psychologizing"—the relationship between the armed forces and private industry. Deemed successful as a tool for treating combat-traumatized soldiers, this type of film had also, one Army Air Forces officer maintained, effectively "returned them to work," both within and beyond the military. Documentary's pedagogic and psychiatric efficacy was thus understood to be coextensive with its capacity to promote industriousness; remedying mental illness meant instilling a "healthy" work ethic.[60] In the Army's *Psychiatric Procedures in the Combat Area*

(1944), for instance, some "seriously shaken men"—those who, suffering from "chronic anxiety," have "reached the limit of their endurance" on the front lines—are prescribed work in a quartermaster unit, and told that continued service "behind the lines," more than just a duty, is in fact a therapeutic blessing.

In the Army, victims of war trauma were increasingly told that their conditions "could best be overcome by continuing at [war] work."[61] At the same time, civilian workers were told that they, too, were vulnerable to the sort of psychological "breakdown" that bore a close family resemblance to combat fatigue. In his 1943 book *Military Psychology*, Norman C. Meier insisted on this homology between war trauma and "other forms of psychoneurotic or psychasthenic trauma (shock) that are not uncommon in industrial mishaps."[62] Depicting the early stages of the Cold War, numerous films dramatized threats to American factory workers, promoting a further blurring of the lines between soldier and civilian. For instance, in the Warner Bros. docudrama *I Was a Communist for the F.B.I.* (Gordon Douglas, 1951), horrific industrial accidents are perpetrated by communist foremen against those workers who do not carry party cards, creating considerable confusion as to the boundaries between enemy and ally, battlefront and home front. If trauma could not be avoided in war, then neither could it be avoided in peace. There was thus little reason for the combat-traumatized veteran to avoid returning to "war work," at least according to psychologists like Meier, who maintained that continued support for the military establishment could only be therapeutic—and clear evidence of one's rehabilitation—even if the workplace remained a potential threat to one's safety.[63]

A number of military documentaries reflect this logic, presenting "re-militarization"—understood as coextensive with therapeutic self-confidence and self-discipline—as essential to a traumatized soldier's psychological recovery, whether or not the soldier is returned to actual combat. The labors of psychological rehabilitation map easily onto those of industry in these films. As the narrator of the Navy's *The N.P. Patient* (1944) puts it, referring to the titular figure, "Now, [after psychotherapy], all his extra horsepower can be used on something constructive and helpful." The film proceeds to show him performing a series of militarized tasks that help him to get "back into an organized routine, where he feels himself the member of a group." Interviewing a young man suffering from "a mild anxiety state," a psychiatrist outlines the therapeutic dimensions of "work with guns" in *Psychiatric Procedures in the*

Combat Area: "You'll get a chance to have your confidence back," he promises the patient. "When was the last time you shot your rifle? We'll give you a chance to shoot it." After all, the psychiatrist suggests, panic is "just a safety valve"—one that may be "controlled" through a therapeutic devotion to "the mechanics" of war. The film shows how, in order to test whether their patients are truly "on the road to recovery," psychiatrists give them rifles and field equipment, "which must be cared for properly." In the Army's *Shades of Gray* (1947), hospital patients (played by actors) throw live grenades as part of their therapy, and the film insists that serving as weapons instructors can "cure" patients of depression—that "confidence in weapons" can restore (and is itself a sign of) mental health. In learning to "be well again," these victims of war trauma also learn how to be "good workers" and "good gunners." If one soldier can regain his psychological fitness by eventually returning to combat, another can regain his by assembling and maintaining "war machines." Numerous Hollywood films share this insistence on the therapeutic value of munitions work.[64] The biopic *Carbine Williams* (Richard Thorpe, 1952), for instance, opens with a depiction of the Winchester Repeating Arms Company in New Haven, Connecticut, which routinely receives orders from the Army ("Good news from Washington!"), profiting from the accomplishments of the titular figure, who "perfected" the M1 carbine ("The first carbine adopted by the United States Army in 40 years") while in prison for his involvement in the death of a deputy sheriff. Tellingly, the film presents "work with guns" as therapeutic; it restores Williams to his own "best self" as well as to the good graces of society, earning him an official pardon. Released from prison so that he may make a "greater contribution" to the military-industrial state, Williams proudly sees eight million of his carbines "go to war," thus filling Winchester's coffers—and then some.

Psychoanalytic equations between battlefield and factory were pervasive during and after the war.[65] In 1947, psychologist Thomas Arthur Ryan published *Work and Effort: The Psychology of Production*, which explicitly linked the treatment of "war neuroses" to the psychological "development" of civilian employees, arguing that the lessons learned during the war could enhance the productivity of industrial workers.[66] As mental illness was increasingly configured as something one could live with, it was also touted as something one could work with.[67] "Much of the work of the world, and much of the very best work, is done by persons not in the best of mental health," wrote the sociologist Willard Waller in his widely read 1944 book *The Veteran Comes Back*.[68] Such is the argument of the Navy's *Combat Fatigue: Assignment Home*, the Army's *Let There Be Light*, and a number of other films that insist on the essential employability of those who have undergone psychiatric treatment. (These include several industrial films, such as U.S. Steel's *Unfinished Business* [1948], which emphasizes the importance of "re-employing veterans.") It is no surprise that *Let There Be Light* focuses so pointedly on occupational therapy: as in other military documentaries about war trauma, this style of treatment is not only therapeutic in itself; it is also a form of job (re)training—evidence that the patient is ready to "return to work."

Hollywood fiction films reliably reproduced these claims during and after the war. Set in the neuropsychiatric ward of a military hospital, the opening sequence of the romantic comedy *She Wouldn't Say Yes* (Alexander Hall, 1945) reflects this military-approved connection between psychotherapy and "getting back to work." Visiting the hospital as an ambassador of civilian psychiatry, Dr. Susan Lane (Rosalind Russell) meets with each patient, learning that many are worried about the discrimination they may face from potential employers. One veteran, a young man named Johnny, tells Dr. Lane that he fears "being out of a job": "See, my father was shell-shocked in the last war, and he never was able to get a job." Dr. Lane takes the opportunity to tell him, "We don't have shell shock anymore—it's old-fashioned." Johnny nods, assenting to the new terminology and even repeating, in his own vernacular terms, Dr. Lane's professional opinion: "War neurosis—or whatever you call it—you can get well from!" Dr. Lane then moves to a section of the ward in which patients are "proving" their aptitude for hard work by engaging in occupational and recreational therapy, some of them producing elaborate sculptures.

If this sequence anticipates the spirit of *Let There Be Light*, with its focus on recovery from war trauma, it also suggests the extent to which Hollywood fiction films shared the initial purpose of Huston's institutional documentary—namely, to cultivate appreciation for the curative function of psychotherapy and its compatibility with the quintessential American work ethic. For if hospitalized "mental patients," far from malingerers or maladapted outcasts incapable of contributing to the military, were to be seen as "working through" their war trauma (as in both *She Wouldn't Say Yes* and *Let There Be Light*), they were also to be appreciated for their potential contributions to the postwar economy. After outlining some of the harsh realities of war (and especially of combat), the Army documentary *Welcome Home* (1945) similarly strives to debunk the notion that veterans are, to varying degrees, "maladjusted"—that they have been "brutalized by war" and subsequently neglected by the military. "Do not think the average serviceman comes out of the army able only to fire a rifle or crawl on his belly," warns the voice-over narrator. "He returns armed for a civilian future with training and skills adapted to an amazing variety of civilian jobs." Even the postwar melodrama *Pete Kelly's Blues* (Jack Webb, 1955), though set in the 1920s, reflects this conviction: while one character—a civilian played by Peggy Lee—ends up confined to a "state hospital for the insane," another character—a veteran of the First World War, explicitly identified as a victim of shell shock—remains reasonably functional, able to perform a variety of duties in and around a Kansas City speakeasy.

While *Let There Be Light* can scarcely be said to show patients becoming reacquainted with combat (except, of course, through narcosynthesis, which "activates" memory), it nevertheless echoes the rhetoric of the military establishment in insisting on the militarized labor so widely required in the postwar period. As the narrator says of the patients undergoing occupational therapy, "Now, in an environment of peace and safety, all the violence behind them, they are building rather than destroying." But building what, exactly, and for whom? The film is perhaps deliberately vague on this point, noting only that "some find relaxation in mechanical jobs"—and that "peace and safety" require constant vigilance and an ever-increasing military strength. *Let There Be Light* may, as its reputation suggests, be antiwar. But it is certainly not anti-military. The film's acknowledgment of the debilitating effects of war trauma merely sets the stage for a particular form of institutional advertising characteristic of the era, and its investment in the armed forces extends from an essential (and resounding) endorsement of military psychiatry into territory best understood in terms of emergent Cold War politics.

Symbolized by Boeing's decision to rename its B-29 Superfortress "The Peacemaker" in 1945, the military's postwar commitment to "peace and stability operations" signaled a humanitarian turn that films like *Let There Be Light* were intended to anticipate.[69] According to this logic, psychiatry was merely one component of a broader humanitarianism that ably extended to foreign countries as well as to refugees from those countries, as in *The Cummington Story* (Helen Grayson and Larry Madison, 1945), an OWI production that insists on the power of occupational therapy to "bring people together." If the profit-driven dimensions of this matrix are sublimated in *Let There Be Light*, they are nonetheless perceptible in its textual and institutional commitment to "getting back to work." The political activist Sidney Lens would later condemn this strategic use of therapeutic discourse to advance corporate and political objectives, writing in 1970, "We are expected to believe that a society based on private profit sternly subordinates this motive in dealing with foreign countries, and that for the first time in history military bases abroad are no longer an instrument of empire-building but of helping harassed peoples achieve 'self-determination.'"[70]

The film critic James Agee may have celebrated Huston's "intelligent, noble, fiercely moving" efforts with *Let There Be Light*, but his colleagues were less generous, some of them going so far as to attack all films that purported to address war trauma, drawing attention to their disingenuousness in language that often anticipated that of Lens.[71] In his 1947 book *Magic and Myth of the Movies*, Parker Tyler identified the decade's "strategic" representations of war trauma as "hobbling" true political critique, noting that, in a number of documentary and fiction films, "a man must be mentally or physically maimed to simplify his moral problems in our time."[72] Offering as a case in point the 1944 film *I'll Be Seeing You*, a melodrama about a serviceman suffering from psychoneurosis, Tyler stressed the deflective potential of seemingly progressive films about war trauma, which, far from conveying antiwar sentiments, in fact insidiously served the interests of the military-industrial state. Tyler's compelling argument is perhaps most applicable to films that he does not address—that are plainly beyond the scope of his Hollywood-centric analysis. They include military-sponsored nontheatrical films that, in prescribing psychotherapy for the treatment of war trauma, also prescribe a return to work, citing the needs of such manufacturers as the Lockheed Corporation and Raytheon and thus serving as audiovisual instruments of an emergent, Cold War military-industrial complex.

At work in such prescriptions was, of course, a desire to prevent the formation of antiwar, even anti-state sentiment—to stave off the temptation to oppose war and the state's prosecution of it. Thus a film like *Psychiatric Procedures in the Combat Area* insists that "war work" represents not a "frightening" and "demoralizing" pursuit but rather "a situation in which [traumatized veterans] can prove to themselves how well and able they have again become." In this manner "they can go on fighting the war," albeit far from the front lines. "They can do a useful job once again" while simultaneously "regain[ing] their sense of personal value," these "men who will be the healthy citizens of tomorrow." Depicted as a site of rehabilitation, the munitions factory is a place where men can "handle guns" and other weapons of war—and thus discover the therapeutic dimensions of such repetitive "mechanical work." That these labors may be carried out in peacetime—that they will, in fact, be *required* in peacetime, as *Let There Be Light* suggests—further blurs distinctions between war and peace, much as military psychiatrists had insisted on effacing divisions between combatant and noncombatant.

In many instances, normalizing war trauma meant normalizing its causes, if only because military psychiatrists remained publicly committed to the aims of the institutions (the Army, the Navy, the Air Forces) that had sponsored their career-defining work, providing them with a major platform from which to launch postwar mental health initiatives. As Ellen Herman points out, millions of Americans were "brought into the orbit" of military psychiatry during and after the war, and individual psychiatrists, in transitioning from the armed forces into civilian practice, effectively "translated" military ideology into terms intelligible to their new patients.[73] This process is vividly depicted in the reform-school melodrama *So Young, So Bad*, directed by former Army Air Forces filmmaker Bernard Vorhaus and released in 1950. In the film, a psychiatrist played by Paul Henreid goes from working in an Army rehabilitation center to a job as head of the Elmview Corrective School for Girls, and he carefully describes, in voiceover, this shift from "combat casualties" to "social casualties," and the translational flair that it requires of him.

In their book *Men Under Stress*, Roy Grinker and John Spiegel had written extensively of this need to "retain" the lessons of war, devoting an entire chapter to "applications from military to civilian psychiatry." The authors, like many of their counterparts, called for the survival and dispersion of "military goals" in the postwar period, thus further contributing to what Catherine Lutz calls "the militarization of the psychological."[74] Far from shedding their wartime association with the armed forces, psychiatrists and other psychological professionals tended to trumpet it. Just as they were complicit in the institutional racism, misogyny, homophobia, and classism that characterized the war years (and that, to varying degrees, persisted after 1945), they remained complicit in the military's ambitions as an agent of postwar imperialism—at least until some of them began to critique the war in Vietnam and call attention to traumatized veterans as unwitting victims of a mendacious, expansionist state.[75] As Lutz puts it, "the political economy and culture of permanent war used and shaped psychological science"; "professional and popular psychological discourses . . . bloomed with the emergence of the national security state."[76] This was a notably reciprocal process, as Melvin Sabshin pointed out in the early 1970s, looking back on the legacies of *Men Under Stress*: "Indeed, the history of military psychiatry since World War II . . . indicates that psychiatric leaders in the Department of Defense have taken full advantage of the concepts introduced by Grinker and Spiegel."[77]

This is not to say that individual psychiatrists and other psychological professionals failed to speak out against the political economy of war. In an address before the Columbus Academy of Medicine in June 1942, William C. Menninger drew attention to the flourishing military-industrial complex when he said, "We [have] developed a schism between our democratic ideals and our economic greed. It is a sad commentary that one of our symptoms of weakness is now manifesting itself as Japanese bullets made from American scrap iron."[78] At the time, Menninger still believed that, as he put it, "America is capable of surviving the disease *War*"—what he elsewhere described as a form of psychosis, a "pathological outpouring of aggression and destructiveness."[79]

The prolific Menninger may have been paying mere lip service to antiwar sentiment, however, for he would later stress the importance of national defense in ways that resonated with the military establishment's strategic equation between the national body and the individual mind, both of them deemed in need of "protection" during the Cold War. Despite the occasional antiwar statement, such as the 1945 "Psychologists' Peace Manifesto," psychological experts remained remarkably responsive to military needs throughout the postwar period—and distinctly, even disturbingly willing to recognize the professional benefits of aggressive militarism, much like the corporations that saw further profits in American foreign policy. As Herman so pungently puts it, paraphrasing the sentiments shared by such complicit figures, "Where will future data for behavioral experts come from if not from future wars?"[80] Herman is here using "wars" in the broadest sense, encompassing both "hot" and "cold"—and everything in between. Global conflict on the order of World War II was, of course, hardly required for the military-industrial complex to function; as William D. Hartung notes, Lockheed Martin and other major corporations have long been "profiting rather nicely from the [American] projection of soft power—diplomacy, humanitarian relief, peacekeeping, reconstruction, and development activities aimed at curbing or preventing conflict."[81] The psychiatric establishment was another beneficiary of this system, however, and the institutional function refined by military psychiatrists during the Second World War would survive across future conflagrations (despite setbacks at the start of the Korean War) and into new areas of American life, as *So Young, So Bad* attests.

"TRAINING FOR CITIZENSHIP"

Psychiatrists and other psychological professionals certainly had no desire to relinquish the gains that wartime military service had supplied, and their continued association with military strategy meant that it was increasingly difficult to distinguish between foreign policy (particularly at the time of the Truman Doctrine) and official psychiatric aims for average Americans: both promoted individual liberty and self-government, and both informed the landscape of American cinema in the postwar period, when the forbidding of psychoanalysis in communist countries became a popular target of opprobrium. "We don't go in for brainwashing," claims an Air Force colonel in the film *The Iron Petticoat* (Ralph Thomas, 1956). "That's communist procedure—not ours." He goes on to discuss "the subconscious" of a Russian pilot (played by Katharine Hepburn) who defects after she is passed over for a promotion, and he concludes, in reference to the communists, that their estrangement from psychoanalysis "may very well be what's the matter with them." Ironically, psychiatry was also aligned with communism in some political circles; the John Birch Society and the Daughters of the American Revolution considered it a "communist plot" akin to fluoridation.[82] But in the immediate postwar period—and later during the presidencies of John F. Kennedy, who signed federal mental health legislation just weeks before his assassination in 1963, and Lyndon Johnson, whose Great Society initiatives extended his predecessor's commitment to federal funding for mental health services—psychiatry was frequently presented as a bulwark against communism, a tool of containment in its own right.

It is no surprise, then, that the communist Yen Lo, who refers at one point to Andrew Salter's famous postwar critiques of psychoanalysis, denounces psychological professionals in *The Manchurian Candidate*, acidulously referring to "those uniquely American symptoms—guilt and fear." Set in a prisoner-of-war camp run by the Chinese, Columbia's *The Bamboo Prison* (Lewis Seiler, 1954) features a telling exchange between representatives of East and West: a communist captor attempts to goad a black American prisoner into "becoming a collaborator," saying,

"They call you a 'nigger' there, don't they? They lynch you there!"
In response, the prisoner (played by Earle Hyman) declares that, despite
the racial traumas to which he is routinely subjected "back home,"
he would "much rather be black than Red!" Sam Fuller's *The Steel Helmet* (1951) similarly depicts black resistance to communist entreaties:
a Manchurian captive (known simply as "The Red" and played by
Harold Fong) recites a litany of Jim Crow laws, but a black medic
(played by James Edwards) simply says, in mitigation of his country's
racial sins, "There's some things you just can't rush, buster." Later, in
response to additional reminders of inequality in America, another character of color—Sergeant Tanaka (Richard Loo)—offers a similar, proto-
neoliberal defense of incremental change and personal responsibility,
painting a contradictory portrait of a post-racial America and proudly
declaring, "In our country, we have rules—even about war."

Produced by the Disabled American Veterans in collaboration with
the Department of Defense and the Association of Motion Picture Producers, the 1951 film *One Who Came Back* ("a true document, photo-
graphed as it happened," according to an opening title) offers a familiar
anticommunist argument in its focus on a man whose leg is severely
injured in Korea, but who immediately receives expert physical and psychological treatment, both at a mobile Army surgical hospital and later
at Letterman General Hospital in San Francisco (a key site of "neuropsychiatric rehabilitation," as depicted in the roughly contemporaneous
film *The Crooked Way* [Robert Florey, 1949], as well as in the later
Niagara, in which it is casually described as "an Army hospital—mostly
psycho," and *The Rack* [Arnold Laven, 1956], in which it serves as a
clearing station for former prisoners of war). Benefitting from "military
medicine," the subject of *One Who Came Back* testifies that it "makes
you realize that this is some country, where any guy that's wounded—
white, brown or black, plain GI or general—receives the same treatment. That's democracy! It's different in some of the other countries
that yell the loudest, but where life is cheap and where the lives of one
or even millions of human beings are expendable."

To the extent that such representations of military hospitals served the
purpose of public relations, their success can perhaps best be seen in a
number of Hollywood's fictional representations of war trauma. Consider, for instance, *The Chase* (Arthur Ripley, 1946), in which severely
traumatized veteran Chuck Scott (Robert Cummings), destitute and suffering from a range of symptoms (including amnesia and unaccountable
flashbacks), finds himself caught up in the criminal underworld. His

anxiety mounting, Chuck finally flees not to the police but to the U.S. Naval Hospital in Miami (whose façade, complete with bronze plaque, is shown in reverential close-up). There, Chuck is reunited with the Navy psychiatrist who treated him during the final phases of the war, and who now helps him further understand his "anxiety neurosis." The thriller *Shock* (Alfred Werker, 1946) offers a strikingly similar depiction of an Army hospital to which a veteran returns whenever he needs "someone to talk to." Its psychiatrists providing lasting friendship, the facility serves as a dependable reminder of "democratic values"—precisely what the veteran missed during his two years as a prisoner of war.

For its part, *The Rack* suggests—accurately enough—that Letterman General, which made viewings of such military documentaries as *Psychiatric Procedures in the Combat Area* and *Let There Be Light* mandatory for all doctors, nurses, corpsmen, and social workers starting in 1946, is at the forefront of psychotherapy.[83] Army officers readily distinguish "the talking cure" from what one of them calls "the new duress"—a communist "program of confession and mental agony." Further describing "this new moral perversion where the mind can be placed upon the rack and made to suffer agony for which there is no measure," the officer in question recalls a military-psychiatric truism familiar from the previous war—that "every man has his breaking point, his horizon of endurable anguish, and that this point can be come upon without bodily pain." While communist captors allegedly attempt to "turn the Army into a nightmare school" that erases the hard-won lessons of military psychiatry, Letterman General and other stateside facilities seek to "reeducate" veterans—particularly those who have spent time in prisoner-of-war camps—renewing their "democratic" commitment to "therapeutic basics."

Other films insist—in keeping with the objectives of Truman's national security state—that "mental hygiene activities" are necessary in order to preempt communist influence. In so doing, they suggest a darker dimension to therapeutic discourse in the postwar period, one rooted in a renewal of certain forms of psychological warfare as well as in an obsessive scrutiny of self and other. "Having become a permanent front, the mind was now a dangerous thing," writes Catherine Lutz. "Unearthing psychological problems became a matter of national security" after 1945, providing new and enhanced justifications for circulating "old" films about war trauma and psychotherapy.[84] "War continues everlastingly in this world," wrote Arthur Edwin Krows, a historian of nontheatrical film, in 1939. Stressing the "salvage value" of military

FIGURE 11. An instructor promotes proper mental hygiene before screening a documentary in the Army's *Film Tactics*. Courtesy of the National Archives and Records Administration.

documentaries produced during the First World War, Krows anticipated the recycling of later entries in the genre after 1945. A military film, Krows understood, could easily be repurposed as an industrial film, evolving from a "war document" into "a potent instrument for the expansion of markets."[85] Krows was especially prescient in recognizing the psychological and public relations role that nontheatrical film could play in the military-industrial complex, helping to connect a variety of interests through its promiscuous reach. "To keep America strong, we must strive to improve the physical and mental health of the whole nation," announces the narrator of *Shades of Gray*, which reflexively suggests that military documentaries, if widely circulated, can promote a "deeper understanding" of important matters, "supplying basic information on psychiatric questions."

Evidence that these films functioned more to sell a certain notion of the military establishment and its relationship to the public interest than to secure psychiatry's place on the front lines can be seen in the Army's disastrous decision to do without psychiatrists at the outset of the Korean War—a decision that was swiftly and mercifully reversed.

("They sent me home with battle fatigue!" complains a Korean War veteran in *Niagara*, shortly before denouncing "occupational therapy" as a source of further distress—something designed to make him a mere cog in the military-industrial machine, instead of a strong and self-sufficient individual.) It would therefore be naïve to assume that the military was solely invested in improving the lives of its enlistees and working to prevent combat-related neuroses. Clearly, it sought to benefit from psychiatry as an instrument of public relations, one that could—through the wide reach of nontheatrical film in particular—achieve a number of related aims, from increasing defense spending to establishing a public consensus about the importance of "national security." By the late 1960s, Ellen Herman convincingly argues, various "movements for community mental health had effectively undermined the legitimacy of distinctions between private emotions and public policy, between clinical work and the business of politics and government."[86] The psychiatrist Robert H. Felix had helped promote this blurring of distinctions as early as 1945, when he formally proposed a federal mental health program, and nontheatrical films were uniquely effective in serving his agenda of "carry[ing] the concepts of mental health to every corner of American society."[87]

The "psychologization" of American life, and with it the normalization of the military-industrial state, had the occasional fierce opponent, such as Senator J. William Fulbright, who in the late 1960s contested the politically expedient notion that conscious support for foreign policy was at the heart of workers' commitment to a permanent war economy:

> It is not an enthusiasm for war but simple economic self-interest that has drawn millions of workers, their labor unions and their elected representatives into the military-industrial complex. For all of them the antiballistic missile means prosperity, not war. For the industrialist it means higher profits, not war; for the worker, new jobs and the prospect of higher wages; for the politician, a new installation or defense order with which to ingratiate himself with his constituents. These benefits, once obtained, are not easily parted with.[88]

A number of nontheatrical films of the 1940s sought to cultivate the very conditions of which Fulbright spoke, focusing on the figure of the unemployed veteran and prescribing a return to "war work" as an individually therapeutic contribution to national defense. "There ain't gonna be any jobs for guys like me!" exclaims a disgruntled (and evidently psychologically disturbed) platoon sergeant in the Army's *Follow Me Again*

(1945)—to which the film responds with an upbeat dramatization of the Army's commitment to returning all veterans to "useful" work, including in defense industries.

Exhibited in classrooms and factories well into the 1950s, such films served to contest, among other critical accounts, Eisenhower's 1953 "Chance for Peace" speech, in which the newly inaugurated president characterized military-industrial expansion as a form of "theft" that ignored the needs of the most vulnerable Americans. Like *Combat Fatigue: Assignment Home*, *Follow Me Again* suggests that the downtrodden— including victims of war trauma—would "rise again" through their support for the military-industrial state. As the film's voice-over narrator puts it, being a "good citizen" in the postwar period would mean contributing to national defense. Explicitly rejecting this approach, the fiction film *Confidential Agent* (Herman Shumlin, 1945), which is set in 1937, offers a trenchant critique of the exploitation of labor by military forces. "I know this means a year's work to you, but it means death to my people!" shouts the film's Spanish protagonist (played by Charles Boyer) to a group of chronically unemployed men and women assembled to celebrate a sudden, seemingly inexplicable military-industrial expansion. But the film's principal referent is the Spanish Civil War, its impassioned critique of the military-industrial complex not only cleanly separated from the American context but also safely restricted to the historical past.

Numerous state-sponsored documentaries of the 1940s reflexively emphasize the military's capacity to promote liberal citizenship through the medium of film. *Follow Me Again*, for instance, cites cinema as a key source of "general education and training for citizenship," insisting that documentaries can "teach war" as well and as profitably as they can "teach peace." Produced by the Division of Motion Pictures at the Department of the Interior, the Veterans Administration film *Service to Those Who Served* (1945) reflexively configures its own, extensive non-theatrical reach as a measure of the massive federal expenditures associated with the VA. As the voice-over narrator puts it, echoing Robert H. Felix, "The helping hand of the United States government, extended through the Veterans Administration, reaches into every corner of the United States and its possessions—into practically every crossroads town and hamlet in America, as well as into foreign countries where American citizens may be temporarily domiciled." Such films provided the democratic (re)education that, Herman argues, was a key component of military psychiatry and psychology during and after the war, as clinicians strived to "recapture any democratic impulses that had been lost in the crush of wartime regimentation, and perhaps even generate attractive new styles of democratic conduct and decision making."[89]

These new styles inevitably involved accession to and active preparation for nuclear war. Retooling "democratic cooperation" as submission to a military-industrial state committed to nuclear armaments, a number of military-sponsored films suggest the economically as well as psychologically beneficial dimensions of such submission. Serving as a 1955 episode of the Defense Department's public service television program *The Big Picture*, the Army documentary *The Atom Soldier* focuses on a particular anxiety produced by the Atomic Age: the ground soldier's fear of his own obsolescence in the face of nuclear weapons. Introducing the film in his capacity as the episode's host, Sergeant Stuart Queen explains that its purpose is to "allay any unreasonable fears of the A-bomb" by revealing how the development and use of nuclear weapons will not only create jobs but cultivate therapeutic confidence in the well-equipped and globally dominant United States. Recycling footage from the Army's own *The Atom Strikes!* (1945), *The Atom Soldier* displaces anxieties about the bomb's destructive power with strictly economic anxieties regarding potential job loss. "We can live through an atomic attack," says one officer in the film, "and live to fight another day!" Fighting is thus aligned with employment—a source of economic and psychological stability for "all Americans."

The film carefully reveals how, far from rendering human labor obsolete, nuclear weapons in fact demand it: weapons testing, for instance, requires considerable manpower, and the transportation and storage of nuclear armaments involve the contributions of innumerable individuals. "Find out what there is to be afraid of and what we don't have to fear," advises one officer, who calls the mushroom cloud "one of the most beautiful sights ever seen by man"—a sublime, "soothing," downright therapeutic image whose sublimity is such that one needn't consider the destruction that it indexes. The film ends with an on-camera, synch-sound interview with a participant in a nuclear weapons test, thus underscoring "the human element" and emphasizing that even radiation is "nothing to worry about." As the narrator puts it, "The atom has revolutionized the mechanics of warfare, but the basic element—the fighting man—remains unchanged. No one is more aware of this than the men of the United States Army." Taking over on behalf of *The Big Picture*, Sergeant Queen explains that the preceding documentary has demonstrated the importance of contributing to nuclear defense—both for the sake of one's wallet and of one's sanity. "It is historical fact that military weakness is an invitation to aggression," he says, arguing that mental preparation will allow Americans to win the next war "in advance."

Such films were hardly exaggerating when they insisted on the economic significance of the postwar military establishment. By the 1950s, the Department of Defense was well on its way to becoming the country's largest employer, and the entrenchment of the national security state was coextensive with that of psychiatry and psychology, which were normalized alongside the concept of a large peacetime standing army. Rapid demobilization in the wake of World War II was soon reversed by the growing demands of the Cold War. As the conservative political scientist Samuel P. Huntington put it in 1957, "the complex technological requirements of the modern armed forces brought a significant permanent defense industry into existence for the first time in the United States."[90] The harnessing of psychological research to this swelling defense industry is attributable to any number of state agencies, private firms, and think tanks: the Human Factors Division of the Naval Electronics Laboratory; the Missile Systems Division at the Lockheed Aircraft Corporation; Princeton's Institute for International Social Research; the RAND Corporation; the Institute for Defense Analysis; the Human Resources Research Office; Hudson Institute; the Group Psychology Branch of the Office of Naval Research; Harvard University, where napalm was invented amid investigations into the psychological dimensions of chemical warfare; and many other research sites that boasted the daily presence of former military psychiatrists.[91] "Already suffused with power as the war ended," wrote Sidney Lens, "the military had no intention of relinquishing it," and psychological expertise helped to ensure its ascension in American life.[92] But this ascension was also guided by the continued production and nontheatrical circulation of military-sponsored nonfiction films. Insisting on the wide relevance of psychological insights associated with the armed forces, many such films were provided free of charge to American schools by the Department of Defense, which also "donated" psychological and vocational tests designed to aid recruitment.[93] Published in 1946, the Bureau of the Budget's *The United States at War* cited the costs associated with such gestures—after all, film prints had to be processed and shipped—as it indexed the Army's efforts to gain "total control of the nation."[94] Distributing films to factories and especially classrooms was a key if hardly inexpensive strategy in the military's efforts to become a "respected, even revered senior partner in running American society."[95]

MILITARY INTERESTS

Nontheatrical films helped to fashion the military as an interest group—a precondition, Samuel P. Huntington argued, for the establishment of a permanent defense sector in American society. It is no accident that the military became an established interest, in Huntington's terms, at the very moment that psychiatry and psychology expanded their reach amid the national mental health movement. Documentaries about war trauma and psychotherapy, which often strategically suggest more expansive narratives of emotional rehabilitation applicable to all Americans, played their own part in permitting the military to "rapidly acquire new salience to the broader society." The promiscuous circulation of films like *Introduction to Combat Fatigue* and *The Inside Story of Seaman Jones* (1944) helped to establish a high degree of correspondence between the military as an interest group and "dominant public interests."[96] This alignment of the armed forces with "public needs" took place even as defense spending dropped significantly in 1946 and 1947, setting the ideological stage for the dramatic and ongoing expansion of the defense sector initiated by the outbreak of the Korean War and justified by the aims of containment.

By the 1950s, military documentaries about war trauma and psychotherapy were being recycled on American television, as *The Big Picture* attests. *On Guard* (1955–1957), a thirteen-episode syndicated series produced by Aerojet-General, purported to cover "all aspects of defense," serving as both a recruitment vehicle for the armed forces and a form of institutional advertising, often depicting how employment by the sponsoring corporation has fulfilled a restorative function for veterans.[97] The syndicated anthology series *The Silent Service*, seventy-eight episodes of which were broadcast between 1957 and 1958, was sponsored by the Department of Defense and the Navy, and it similarly considered the curative dimensions of Cold War "military readiness," occasionally recycling Navy films (such as *Introduction to Combat Fatigue* and *The Inside Story of Seaman Jones*) in order to celebrate the continued availability and wider societal relevance of military-psychiatric treatment.

If military psychiatry helped establish a private market for psychoanalysis in the postwar period, it also helped constitute a specialized government market for missiles, aircraft carriers, and other weapon systems, precisely by insisting on the importance of returning the traumatized veteran to some form of "soothing," war-related work. At the same time, efforts to convince the civilian worker of her warrior-like usefulness to the military establishment were well underway. Configuring psychiatry as immensely relevant to all Americans, the military also presented the arms economy as a reliable source of employment and thus emotional stability for the service veteran, as in the aptly titled *Follow Me Again*. ("Veterans make good in all professions," reads a newspaper headline in RKO's *The Tattooed Stranger* [Edward Montagne, 1947].) Clear precedents for this emphasis on supplying the military with "weapons of war" can be found not only in the War Production Board's "industrial incentive" series of short documentaries but also in OWI films produced for overseas audiences, such as Willard Van Dyke's *Oswego* (1943), *Steeltown* (1944), and *Northwest U.S.A.* (1945), which insist on the economically as well as psychologically rehabilitative potential of "war work."

Building upon this earlier approach, films about war trauma and psychotherapy tend to focus on how the military serves the interests not merely of active-duty soldiers but also, through its sponsorship of psychological research, of all Americans—the "millions of Seaman Joneses" invoked in *The Inside Story of Seaman Jones*, or the "you" so inclusively addressed by the narrator of *Introduction to Combat Fatigue*. As a means of psychological manipulation, the military documentary thus represented one facet of a multipronged effort to turn the military into "an interest group unto itself rather than a mere instrument of public policy."[98] Joel Pfister has written of the nineteenth- and twentieth-century production of "'psychological' individuals, 'psychological' families, and 'psychological' bodies"—to which can be added the production, during and after World War II, of "psychological" institutions like the Army and the Navy.[99] While this production arguably predated the war in the elaboration of industrial and organizational psychology in the 1920s, it acquired a new force in the context of World War II and its aftermath. If, in Pfister's terms, "the psychological" is a historically specific cultural category, it is arguably constituted as much by public institutions as by private firms—and, of course, as much by nontheatrical as by theatrical film.

Numerous military documentaries reflect a desire to turn traumatized veterans into "useful citizens" whose usefulness might directly serve the armed forces for years to come. *Combat Fatigue: Assignment Home*, for example, which begins with the release of veterans from a psychiatric hospital, proceeds to show how their "full recovery" involves reintegration into systems of production (agricultural, industrial, intellectual) that "helped win the war"—and that, the film implies, will help win future ones. "The civilian is taught how to become a soldier, but the soldier is not taught how to become a civilian again," complained the Chicago Institute for Psychoanalysis toward the end of the war.[100] In addressing this complaint, *Assignment Home* deliberately blurred the boundaries between soldier and civilian, showing how the emergent military-industrial state came to depend upon "the militarization of everything"—and how the veteran could, in fact, avoid having to "become a civilian again" simply by getting a certain kind of job.

The much-debated "notion of a revolving door between the military and its contractors," which James Ledbetter traces to the 1930s, was given full expression in wartime and postwar documentaries that themselves forged various institutional connections, their spheres of influence shifting from the military to the industrial and back again.[101] As early as 1944, *Billboard* noted that the military's own "16mm films are being released in ever-greater quantities . . . to show the public that the armed forces continue to need war material ranging from bombs to insect repellant," and to "help" those civilians identified as "war workers."[102] This pseudophilanthropic gesture was, however, not so much about assisting individual workers as it was about strengthening the relationship between industry and the military, using nontheatrical film to convey subtle (and sometimes not-so-subtle) reminders about military needs and military successes, particularly psychiatric ones. As Walter J. Klein would write in 1976, "After religion the largest single source of sponsored films is—surprise—the United States Army," which "make[s] almost every other sponsor look like novices."[103] After all, if military psychiatry could, as numerous documentaries claimed, effectively restore the combat-traumatized soldier to mental health as well as to productive civilian work, corporations could return the favor by counseling their workers to take pride in manufacturing goods for the armed services. Increasingly after 1945, to be a recipient of a military contract was also to receive military films, many of which sought to demonstrate that strategies of "mental upbuilding" were as effective for the combat-traumatized as for the laborer on the assembly line.[104]

Such close connections between military and industrial uses of cinema were hardly new. Exhorting civilian workers to meet the diverse material needs of the armed forces, the War Production Board's "industrial incentive" series had proposed reciprocity—an exchange of techniques between the military and private industry—as a condition of "worker education." Defining soldiers as workers, the Signal Corps and other military organizations requested training films from various industrial corporations, which they subsequently screened for enlisted personnel deemed in need of education and inspiration. This two-way process was motivated, in part, by the claims of military psychiatrists and industrial psychologists, who maintained that the language of psychotherapy, communicated through film, could help individuals overcome the traumas of the industrialized workplace. In 1945, the Signal Corps acquired the industrial documentary *Combat Team* (1944) from the Chance Vought Aircraft Corporation (a major recipient of military contracts during and after the war), ensuring that it would be widely screened within the Army.[105] Two years earlier, an executive at the Empire Plow Company, which manufactured aircraft landing mats for the military, acquired John Huston's Signal Corps documentary *Report from the Aleutians* (1943) for mandatory screenings in its plants, on the assumption that the film would not only "inspire" but also teach workers how to cope with the tedium of labor.[106]

If such gestures would seem to trivialize trauma, reducing it to the dimensions of an everyday annoyance, other strategies emphasized the gravity of the situations explored in certain military documentaries, even as they promoted the use of these films in schools and factories. In 1950, the United Nations Department of Public Information (DPI), promoting the nontheatrical distribution of nonfiction films, placed *Combat Fatigue: Insomnia, Combat Fatigue: Assignment Home*, and several other related military documentaries in a global context, situating them on a continuum of films that included a Turkish short on institutions for mentally ill youth and a Czechoslovak account of the "long shadow" of war trauma. If such films could be grouped together, it was because of the seriousness of their subjects, which, the DPI maintained, rendered them deserving of the widest possible distribution, including to "major manufacturing industries."[107]

FROM EXPERIMENTAL THERAPY TO CLASSROOM INSTRUCTION

Private industry may have been a major beneficiary of the military's wartime experiments in "therapeutic film," but it also helped to catalyze them. Throughout the 1940s, trade journals identified the military's commitment to new cinematic technologies as evidence of its orientation toward American production. According to this logic, the military's interest in acquiring "even color films" reflected a broader hunger for materials that various industries might produce—"enough of every kind of apparatus and supply and shipping," in the words of the Navy documentary *Return to Guam* (1944). A number of different color technologies proved immensely popular among military psychiatrists who used films to help treat their combat-traumatized patients. In 1944, psychiatrists at Crile General, a military hospital in Cleveland, Ohio, began using Auroratone films, which featured abstract color patterns produced using crystallizing chemicals and polarized light, to treat psychotic combat veterans.[108] *Motion Picture* magazine immediately began advertising Auroratone as "a new kind of sound film which is being shown to patients in military hospitals everywhere."[109] At around the same time, Captain William Eddy, chief of the Navy's radar training center in Chicago, patented a device called the Kaleidoscope, which used records to produce color accompaniment to music. Eddy insisted that his Kaleidoscope films, like Auroratone films, were capable of "benefiting veterans." As *Billboard* magazine put it, "The effect of the color combined with the music is supposed to 'induce a natural state of relaxation and inspiration,' and doctors have found it effective in that respect."[110] A third technology, known as Musicolor, similarly sought to "visualize music" through the use of "soothing," "sedative" color patterns, comprising "a therapeutic aid to relax wounded vets."[111]

Developed by English psychologist Cecil Stokes (founder of the Hollywood-based Auroratone Foundation of America Inc., which regularly shipped prints to military hospitals free of charge), Auroratone films were said to "have real therapeutic value" in their capacity to both visualize mental states (including dream states) and soothe those suffering from war trauma.[112] "Into the constricted limits of human suffering comes the Auroratone!" reads an advertisement from 1947, which touts the technology's "documentary value"—its capacity to supersede the limitations of language and reproduce what the psychotic patient sees "in deep dreams forgotten in the waking consciousness."[113] According to a 1946 article in *Psychiatric Quarterly*, the primary function of Auroratone films was to "make military patients with psychotic depressions more accessible to individual and group psychotherapy"—to, in other words, "open their minds" to psychiatric treatment.[114]

Evangelizing on behalf of his invention, Stokes found homes for his Auroratone films in military hospitals throughout the country, as psychiatrists endeavored to use a diversity of moving-image styles in the treatment of combat-traumatized soldiers.[115] American hospitals forced to expand or convert their operations to handle the specificities of "war neuroses" tended to adopt all manner of aids, including audiovisual ones. At a time when the military's documentary enterprise embraced hybrid forms and considerable taxonomic flexibility, such experimental contributions as the Auroratone films were welcomed not merely as imaginative sources of a "soothing" spectatorial experience but also, in their own ways, as "documents of reality."[116] Such "rhythmic-art films," as Stokes called them, were thought to approximate actual mental processes, particularly "disordered" ones characteristic of a traumatic psychic landscape.[117]

Sharing an investment in documentary as a uniquely adaptable genre, but also recognizing its capacity to "shock or offend," military psychiatrists like Howard P. Rome, Herbert E. Rubin, and Elias Katz carefully scrutinized films before screening them for hospitalized soldiers. As Katz put it, all documentaries "should be carefully selected and evaluated by psychiatric and psychological criteria before exposing mental patients to them."[118] Considerably less care appears to have been taken with the distribution of these documentaries to private industries, community groups, labor organizations, scientific societies, and secondary-school classrooms, where "captive audiences and compulsory spectatorship" allowed the military to continue to advance certain claims about trauma and psychotherapy.[119] If the vulnerable, hospitalized victim of combat trauma could not be shown "just any movie," the average autoworker or high school senior could allegedly "handle"—and, more importantly, benefit from—any number of military documentaries, including those about psychosis.[120]

Initially reserved for Coast Guard use, *The Inside Story of Seaman Jones*, which dramatizes a young man's psychosomatic symptoms and their psychiatric treatment, was acquired in 1948 by the Nassau County School District for mandatory use in health education classes throughout the county. In addition, the Nassau County Tuberculosis and Public Health Association made arrangements for all adult groups and secondary schools in the vicinity to obtain prints of the film free of charge, while the Freeport *Leader* informed readers that they could obtain these prints from health education consultant Grace Bryant, whose mailing address the newspaper published. Sending copies of *The Inside Story of Seaman Jones* and other "mental health films" to DeLuxe Laboratories for extensive duplication, the Navy had in mind their wide circulation beyond the military's borders, and it began furnishing prints to Bryant and other public educators as early as 1944.[121]

The growing postwar emphasis on distribution to secondary schools was rooted in wartime activities. In 1942, as part of its "commitment to winning the war," the NYU Film Library had begun to distribute documentaries (including Army, Navy, and OWI shorts) to schools in the Mid-Atlantic states, thus equipping them "with vital aids to curricula geared to wartime needs."[122] Much as industrial workers were aligned with soldiers in various therapeutic discourses, students were increasingly understood to resemble enlistees in their "openness" to visual education. Writing in 1946, the educational researcher Charles F. Hoban noted that "the broad objectives for which war-training films were used are the same *in kind* as those of civilian education."[123] Many wartime military documentaries were simply shortened and retitled for ongoing distribution to schools and civic organizations. In the summer of 1947, for instance, the *Why We Fight* entry *War Comes to America* (Frank Capra and Anatole Litvak, 1945) was rechristened *War Came to America*, and, framed as a retrospective account of a particular historical moment, "secured a place in Cold War American culture as a publically circulated civics text."[124]

If education was one objective of this postwar distribution pattern, recruitment was another. By the early 1950s, the military had commissioned small production companies to make a series of films that could be adopted by secondary schools in order to prepare students for service. This opportunistic targeting of public educational institutions did not go unnoticed by those willing to speak out against the military-industrial complex. Sidney Lens, for instance, argued that it represented a significant component of the military's postwar attempts to "assert sovereignty over the nation's youth."[125] Frederick Wiseman's *High School* (1968), which so famously suggests that the titular institution is little more than a factory committed to churning out a homogenous product, also emphasizes the school's key function within the military-industrial state. War trauma is calmly and unquestioningly accepted by teachers and administrators eager to send male graduates to Vietnam. One educator cheerfully describes, in almost fetishistic detail, the physical injuries sustained by a former student in the line of duty, while another, having read aloud a letter from a young man who admits that the war has made him "jumpy," happily concludes that the school was "very successful" in setting him up for military service. The trauma to which the letter alludes is thus normalized in the context of what might reasonably be termed a military-industrial-educational complex—one that, of course, so often centralized the nontheatrical exhibition of military documentaries about war trauma (as in Wiseman's later documentary *Basic Training* [1971], which the filmmaker has repeatedly compared to *High School*).[126] While the postwar campaign for universal military training ultimately failed, the military nevertheless managed to mount, as Lens put it, "a propaganda drive on its behalf such as the nation had never seen before."[127]

The fourteen military-sponsored shorts produced by Coronet Films in 1951 vividly illustrate Lens' claims. Dubbed *Are You Ready for Service?*, the series was, its producer maintained, "designed solely to help high-school students plan for military service *well in advance of induction or enlistment.*"[128] The second, untitled entry in the series suggests that, in the military, "you learn how to learn": "War has become a highly technical proposition. A lot of men receive vocational training and experience that they can carry right on into civilian life." The sixth entry, entitled *Getting Ready Emotionally*, adopts a more psychotherapeutic approach, exhorting the viewer to "take stock of yourself—*think.*" Recognizing a widespread awareness of war trauma, the film's voice-over narrator provides reassurance: relatively few enlisted men see combat, even during wartime, and those who are actually wounded—whether physically or psychologically—receive effective treatment from the military, and thus "make out alright." Arguing that "it takes all sorts of people to make up a world," the narrator does his part to normalize psychoneurosis, in keeping with the military's own longstanding strategy, and promises a life of profound self-reflection for the young man bound for the armed forces: "When you leave home and go into the service, you're going to come face to face with yourself." Returning to the subject of war trauma, the narrator offers a qualification: "Now, I don't want to scare you by suggesting that every guy in service cracks up—of course they don't." But service brings "new challenges"—and only service can teach a man how to surmount them.

While the widely distributed series proved intensely controversial (the National Council Against Conscription denounced its capacity "to make training for war sound like training for peace"), films more explicitly concerned with trauma and psychotherapy were less likely to be met with opprobrium.[129] After all, such films were often adopted—by businesses and secondary schools alike—as "a motivational device for enlightening the public and altering its opinion of the nature of psychoneuroses."[130] The military's efforts to enlarge the influence of its wartime documentaries were thus abetted by a range of organizations, all of them committed to the belief that such films "should not be confined to teaching skills and building information and facts" for the enlisted man, but should "travel widely," displaying their "demonstrated value in creating attitudes, motivating behavior and in developing morale."[131] In

1947, the U.S. National Commission for UNESCO published a booklet entitled "UNESCO and You," in which it exhorted readers to "give [their] aid and support to the public, nonprofit showing of educational and documentary films." Singling out military documentaries "made during the war years," the booklet stressed that these were "still very useful" in the postwar period: "Your local and regional 16mm. film distributors have many of them. Check their lists."[132]

Lest the military seem wholly and admirably committed to public health education, however, it is necessary to reiterate the internal benefits that it expected to gain through the wide and ongoing distribution of its influential documentaries. Military films about psychiatry were part of the system of soft power in which "public service" was increasingly indistinguishable from institutional recruitment. "Soft power," in Joseph Nye's influential definition, refers to the assertion of political and corporate interests through means other than military force.[133] While the term is not typically associated with activities aimed at Americans, it is an apt description of the joint efforts of the military and private industry to, as Lens put it, "assert sovereignty" over the population. Screened for presumably impressionable high school students, a film like *The Inside Story of Seaman Jones* was meant to combine "useful" instruction on trauma and psychotherapy with subtle yet unmistakable invitations to the viewer to see the Navy—and the military more generally— as an ultimately hospitable, even curative place where treatment for mental illness may readily be found.[134] As a team of physicians pointed out in 1953, the common theme of wartime and postwar military documentaries about "psychiatric disturbances" is simple: "sick soldiers are healed" by the military itself.[135]

The legacies of this particular approach span the diverse landscapes of American film. In the Hollywood melodrama *Autumn Leaves* (Robert Aldrich, 1956), for instance, a young man is severely traumatized not by combat but by the sight of his wife sleeping with his father, and he finds respite in a military whose influential contributions to psychiatry enable his eventual recovery in a civilian hospital. Released in 1964, the war film *36 Hours*, directed by George Seaton, features an even more explicit endorsement of military psychiatry, as a character confidently proclaims that "[soldiers] with battle fatigue and nervous breakdowns were cured" in a matter of months—even if they'd suffered "complete mental breakdowns" and become "catatonics." By 1962, a character in *The Manchurian Candidate* could convincingly say, "The Army's got a lot of things wrong with it, but it does take care of its own people." In the 1973 Marine Corps film . . .*And a Few Good Men*, the institution is presented as a thoroughly reliable source of treatment not merely for psychological traumas but for all manner of ills: "Those that need glasses will get them," announces the voice-over narrator. "If any bad teeth are found, they'll be taken care of."

Historically, such examples of soft-sell recruitment tactics have also been used, in a familiar strategy of public relations, to divert attention from explosive revelations about the inadequate and sometimes nonexistent treatment of war veterans—especially mentally ill ones—in military hospitals and other federally (under)funded sites of rehabilitation. More recently, the Veterans Health Administration (VHA) scandal of 2014, which involved numerous reports of negligence in the treatment of military veterans, unfolded as the VHA was completing a series of documentaries about PTSD.[136] Paying close attention to the range of nontheatrical venues for military-produced nonfiction film is thus necessary for a better understanding of how the armed services have historically used war trauma in attempts to defuse potentially explosive controversies, manage public expectations, and honor private interests.

CHAPTER 4

Psychodocudramatics

*Role-Playing War Trauma from the
Hospital to Hollywood*

Toward the end of the war, in response to high turnover and absentee rates in aircraft manufacturing plants, and in a desperate effort to boost production and morale, the Navy placed "war-battered bomber planes" on display in various facilities, along with "crew that had flown the bombers on dozens of occasions over Germany." These veterans—some of them as "war-battered" as the planes—were asked to "play themselves" in efforts to alter "performance norms" among war workers, their mere presence in plants deemed capable of "correcting" a propensity for cynicism and lethargy.[1] By "playing themselves," the veterans were reportedly able to convince their civilian counterparts to better perform the roles assigned to them by the wartime economy, "inspiring" them to relinquish their laziness and cynicism, as well as to "act like soldiers [of production]." At the same time, their performances "as themselves" were thought to serve a therapeutic function for these veterans, helping them to take pride in their accomplishments—to transform what had made them "war-battered" into a source not of ongoing traumatization but of emotional strength.[2] As Joris Ivens had suggested, "acting to play oneself" was hardly easy, and veterans who visited war plants had to be given considerable direction, often by foremen in collaboration with the military's public relations officials, all of them endeavoring to stage-manage these "inspirational" stunts.[3]

Such challenges were well known to military psychiatrists, who consistently confronted the "bad" or otherwise inadequate acting techniques of traumatized patients asked to recreate battle conditions. "Many patients have a tendency to be narrators rather than actors," complained the Army psychiatrist Ernest Fantel, reporting from the 138th Evacuation Hospital, a four-hundred-bed installation in Trier, Germany. "We induced them to act as much as possible. No script was used and all acting was impromptu."[4] A number of wartime military documentaries address the importance of this sort of improvisatory, largely physical or gesticulatory acting, highlighting the therapeutic superiority of "doing" over merely "reciting." From this perspective, the Freudian "talking cure" was hardly sufficiently curative on its own; it had to be supplemented with "action"— the physical performance of emotion and identity. "If you don't feel like yawning, fake one," instructs the narrator of the Navy's *Combat Fatigue: Insomnia* (1945), drawing attention to what would later be termed neuroplasticity—the brain's basic changeability, including in response to consciously performed actions. Exhorting the insomniac to recreate synaptic connections associating the act of yawning with the onset of "sleepiness," the narrator of *Combat Fatigue: Irritability* speaks to the rehabilitative value of "acting rather than narrating."[5]

Prominent military psychiatrists consistently touted the value of performance—even of an explicitly Hollywood-style simulation—in the treatment of combat trauma, with Roy Grinker and John Spiegel, in their widely read book *War Neuroses in North Africa* (1943), going so far as to promote the direct participation of the therapist in the studiously stage-managed reenactment of battlefield terror. The two psychiatrists would inject their patients with a barbiturate (usually sodium pentothal), which was thought to "loosen their tongues," turning them into loquacious performers of their own pasts. But such patients needed even more prodding if they were to become actors; they needed scene partners. "The therapist plays the role of a fellow soldier," suggested Grinker and Spiegel, "calling out to the patient in an alarmed voice, to duck as the shells come over, or asking him to help with a wounded comrade."[6] Grinker and Spiegel's "dramatic scenes," as routinely enacted in a military hospital near the front lines, were thus equal parts "real" and "simulated," combining the "truth" of personal recollection (a narcotized patient's recovery of traumatic memories) with the "play-acting" of a therapist assuming a relevant role. Both performances, Grinker and Spiegel maintained, were examples of reenactment: the patient, undergoing what Grinker labeled "narcosynthesis" (and what detractors dubbed a "crude mental enema"), was in fact "re-enacting" his own trauma with the aid of barbiturates, while his therapist ably followed

suit, carefully taking his histrionic cues from the patient's pained narration and using these as the basis for plausible reconstructions of front-
line military service.[7]

This chapter examines the rise of "psychodrama," with its insistence
on the importance of performing one's own traumatic past, in the growing field of military psychiatry.[8] Developed by the Austrian-American
psychiatrist Jacob Moreno, psychodrama was a technique that required
both acting and reenacting, both imagination and memory. Moreno not
only anticipated the therapeutic performances of Grinker and Spiegel,
introducing his influential theories of "role play" as early as the 1920s;
he also called for their incorporation into the filmmaking process, both
in hospitals and in Hollywood, so that the therapeutic collision of "reality" (a patient's traumatic memory) and "simulation" (the psychiatrist's
imitation of trauma) could become, through cinema's mechanical repro-
ducibility, a "repeatable event of cathartic benefit" to "innumerable
audiences."[9] Moreno even co-produced what he called a "psychodramatic film"—a blend of observational footage of therapeutic treatments
and a nearly shot-by-shot simulation thereof—screening it at a meeting
of the American Psychiatric Association in 1935. By the end of World
War II, he had widely promoted the combination of what he called the
"patient-actor method," in which "playing oneself" contributed to the
emotional recovery of a trauma victim, and the "ego-actor method," in
which an "auxiliary" figure—a therapist or trained performer untouched
by trauma but willing to learn from, imitate, and "participate with" its
victim—completed the psychodramatic process, enabling its commitment to film.[10]

However eccentric Moreno's premise may seem, it reflected the growing popularity of a technique that the National Committee for Mental
Hygiene called "dramatization therapy."[11] Also known as "psychodramatic acting," it combined a Freudian conception of "working through"
trauma with a type of performance that was soon to be codified, in a
particular theatrical milieu, as "the Method."[12] The point, as one military psychiatrist put it, was for a person to "bring to the surface" a
tendency that may have been suppressed—a personality trait hidden
behind a façade of propriety, and reachable only through committed
psychoanalytic methods.[13] So widely intelligible was this notion that
even newsreel filmmakers, in their commitment to reenactment and
other methods of reconstruction, were beginning to embrace it in the
early 1940s. *The March of Time*, a documentary film series that bore a
family resemblance to the newsreel even if it "was not a newsreel in any

accepted sense," helped to popularize a conception of "fakery in allegiance to the truth" (in the words of *Time* cofounder Henry Luce) that the military would extend into explicitly therapeutic territory with its wartime and postwar battle reenactments and dramatizations of trauma and rehabilitation.[14] "Are newsreels news?" asked the documentary filmmakers Robert Stebbins and Irving Lerner in 1937, to which Louis de Rochemont, who oversaw *The March of Time*, offered a tacit answer, striving to expand the newsreel format to encompass the "working through" of problems whose solutions could be communicated by the end of two film reels.[15]

Shortly before the United States entered the Second World War, de Rochemont established himself as a key mediator of filmmaking activities at the Bureau of Aeronautics, which oversaw the production of Navy documentaries. A veteran of World War I, de Rochemont maintained close ties to the Navy throughout his career, and he was called in to assist the Bureau of Aeronautics in 1941, bringing a *March of Time* associate, Thomas Orchard, with him. Orchard, who would go on to organize a training film unit under the auspices of the Navy's Flight Division, helped de Rochemont expand the influence of the *March of Time*, sharing prints of various shorts with the intention of establishing certain stylistic guidelines for Navy filmmakers.[16] Orchard's unit, which would become the Training Film and Motion Picture Branch of the Navy, produced over a thousand films by 1945. Among these were a series of docudramas about combat fatigue, many of them premised on the notion that a serviceman might be able to manage his own dark impulses by "acting them out."

Military psychiatrist George S. Goldman would have a chance to test this theory while overseeing the Navy's production of *The N.P. Patient* in 1944. Initially intended for the training of hospital corpsmen confronted with a growing number of neuropsychiatric (or "N.P.") cases, the film was eventually screened for servicemen throughout the military, showing them not only what to expect should they find themselves hospitalized for "mental problems," but also how they might act in order to preempt such problems. As a group of physicians and medical educators pointed out in the early 1950s, drawing attention to the film's wide and continued circulation, "the objective was to acquaint hospital corpsmen without medical background with the principal psychoses and neuroses. Actors were chosen for this job because they could bring out the general features more schematically than would have been possible with real patients."[17]

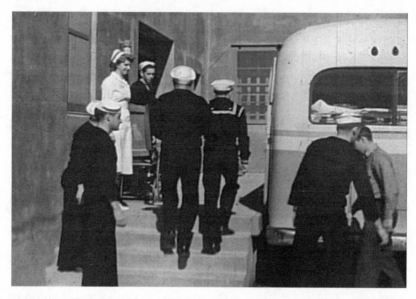

FIGURE 12. Observational footage of the arrivals at a psychiatric facility in the Navy's
The N.P. Patient (1944). Courtesy of the U.S. National Library of Medicine.

The N.P. Patient opens with an establishing shot of an unnamed
facility for the treatment of "battle-scarred" sailors. Following the credits, the film transitions to remarkable observational footage of severely
traumatized men being placed on stretchers and loaded onto ships and,
later, buses for transportation to a Navy hospital. This reliance on
sobering actuality footage soon gives way to staged sequences in which
various men must accept that they are, in fact, "N.P. patients"—and
that, moreover, war trauma may produce diverse and even contradictory symptoms. One man, a brash sailor named Bennett, who has no
conscious awareness of his own condition, enters the hospital prepared
to fight, snapping at anyone who gets in his way, while another lapses
into a catatonic state, staring blankly at the floor. To the former, whose
extreme combativeness is plainly symptomatic of the trauma that he has
endured, the latter seems unaccountably quiet—readily identifiable as
"crazy." Part of the point of the film is thus to emphasize the importance of acceding to a formal diagnosis of a neuropsychiatric condition,
whether combat fatigue or something more insidious—something cruelly rooted in one's own psychic makeup and recently "awakened" by
the stresses of war.

Under the watchful eye of de Rochemont, the makers of *The N.P. Patient* tasked Navy personnel with "impersonating" a series of "recorded cases" of men who had recently been hospitalized for psychiatric treatment. One Navy psychiatrist, Howard P. Rome, invoked Freud's theories of reenactment as an ambiguous activity—strongly suggestive of a "compulsion to repeat," but also a potential means of mastering an "unpleasurable" event. Paying particular attention to the mechanics of reenactment, Rome, who participated in all phases of the production of *The N.P Patient*, asked that Navy actors portray "sufficiently typical" neuropsychiatric "cases," so that each could "with little difficulty substitute himself and his reactions."[18] In Rome's view, an actor's recreation of the documented past needed to double as a strategy of self-analysis and, ultimately, self-discipline. As the occasion for blurring some of the boundaries between a "healthy" Navy actor and the "sick" patient he portrayed, reenactment was a tool not merely for de-stigmatizing mental illness but also for desensitizing soldiers to some of the effects of war trauma—a process that Rome saw as extending from actors to audiences.

Under the direction of Rome and other psychiatrists, the Navy's mostly nonprofessional actors exhibited a wooden performance style whose very artificiality was viewed as a therapeutic tool unto itself—a way of "shielding" both actor and audience against "a too great emotional release which is likely to produce additional psychological symptoms in self-defense."[19] Awkwardly performing a range of traumatic symptoms—and watching the filmed record of such a performance—was thought to be a way of familiarizing servicemen with some of the most common behavioral and psychosomatic responses to trauma, so that these responses might seem less daunting, and more "manageable." Thus the performance of reenactment was open to those who, in a sense, "played themselves"—including patients at St. Elizabeths Hospital (formerly the Government Hospital for the Insane) in Washington, DC, who appeared in *The N.P. Patient* in order to recreate and thus "work through" their own symptoms.

The notion that reenactment often entailed a "trance state" was not new, nor was it confined to psychiatric discourses. For Freud, reenactment—the assiduous repetition of past actions—threatens to "give the appearance of some 'daemonic' force at work" (hence, perhaps, the fashionable, quasi-Freudian notion that the Method actor may be "possessed" by a role performed on the basis of painful introspection). Freud's famous account of his eighteen-month-old grandson playing the "*fort/da*" game provided the basic framework for his theories of reenactment: a traumatic event (for Freud's grandson, the sudden and unaccountable departure of his mother) can be "tamed" by turning it into a game to be played over and over again—a simulation to be repetitively, perhaps even obsessively performed. In Kaja Silverman's gloss on the "*fort/da*" game, the child "reenacts his mother's departures in order to tame the unpleasure they evoke through symbolic and linguistic repetition"; he thus "renegotiates his relation to an event by shifting from a passive to an active position."[20]

It was precisely this shift that many military psychiatrists hoped to facilitate when they asked enlisted men—some of whom were actual psychiatric patients—to simulate many of the more disturbing responses to war trauma. *The N.P. Patient* reflects Goldman's commitment to turning the filmmaking process itself into an occasion for therapeutic repetition. Working with filmmakers from the Bureau of Aeronautics, including de Rochemont, Goldman helped to ensure that those servicemen cast in *The N.P. Patient*, whether actual "neuropsychiatric casualties" or those relatively untouched by trauma, would understand their contributions in Freudian terms. Performing the same actions in take after take, they were counseled by on-set psychiatrists and psychiatric social workers to accept that they were working toward the mastery not merely of history (in the form of the heavily documented psychiatric conditions they were simulating) but also of their own impulses. The military psychiatrist Z. M. Lebensohn, who served as a technical advisor to the producers of *The N.P Patient*, was particularly concerned about the high incidence of psychotic conditions among naval officers, and he insisted that psychosis—the simulation of which, he maintained, could prove both instructive and therapeutic—remain a key theme of the film.[21]

Part of the Navy's *Care of the Sick and Injured* series of short documentaries, and eventually adopted by the Army, *The N.P. Patient* was produced in order to supplement ("but in no way duplicate") the earlier *Ward Care of Psychotic Patients* (1944), an animated film made by Disney under the supervision of military psychiatrists. *The N.P. Patient* was meant to approach the topic of war trauma "from a different angle," replacing one form of simulation (cartoons) with another (live-action "impersonations" of actual cases).[22] Since Lebensohn had recorded numerous instances of window-smashing and other acts of destruction committed by psychotic servicemen, *The N.P. Patient* depicts Bennett's growing aggressiveness as he breaks window after window with the heel of his shoe—a striking scene intended to suggest "possession by psychosis," both for Bennett the historical character and the actor playing the role, who performs these acts of vandalism with believable abandon, perhaps signaling the sort of latent impulse that the film's production, as an exercise in therapeutic role play, was designed to keep in check.

However "typical," Bennett is only one among a whole host of patients suffering from various "disorders of the mind." According to the film's narrator, an unnamed medical officer (played by an actor) who occasionally appears onscreen, directly addressing the viewer after each reenactment, Navy hospitals provide "the best possible medical care" for an array of patients whose diverse conditions demand different treatments. Staring at the camera, the officer-narrator carefully elucidates the distinctions between, say, psychosis and catatonia, explicitly speaking to the educational needs of hospital-corpsmen-in-training. Constituting the film's first audiences, these corpsmen were learning how to assist psychiatrists in the treatment of war-traumatized servicemen—a process that *The N.P. Patient* was designed to outline and facilitate. "These men are suffering from everything," says the narrator, referring to all of the patients admitted to a "typical" military hospital like St. Elizabeths. "Some are sick from physical causes . . . others are just as sick from mental causes." Declaring that "all sick people require treatment," he reinforces the common goal of military psychiatrists, who often struggled to legitimize their own position among medical officers, repeatedly proffering analogies between physical and mental illness.

Reminding the hypothetical student-spectator that he is "chiefly interested in the mentally ill," the narrator proceeds to emphasize the importance of accepting the severity even of "invisible" conditions, counseling trainees to scrutinize all patients for evidence of psychoneurosis: "For the most part, they appear more or less normal, but if you look carefully, you will notice that some of them show definite signs of their illness. These patients are really sick—otherwise the doctors would never have sent them to the hospital. As hospital corpsmen, you will help in the treatment of many types of mental illness—and each requires a different approach." Strictly in terms of its direct address to corpsmen-in-training, the primary function of *The N.P. Patient* was to advocate professionalism and empathy in the treatment of those traumatized by war—an approach that mirrors that of the actors in the film, who were instructed to take seriously the plight of those they portrayed, viewing it as a condition to which they too were vulnerable. The film's reliance on equations between physical and mental illness, coupled with

FIGURE 13. A medical officer explains the use of dramatic reenactments in the Navy's *The N.P. Patient* (1944). Courtesy of the U.S. National Library of Medicine.

its insistence that the latter is "deeply serious" despite its occasional "invisibility," and that it takes a truly observant, admirably committed professional to recognize the signs and symptoms of psychoneurosis, suggests that *The N.P. Patient* was produced not simply for the instruction of hospital corpsmen but also for the satisfaction of a distinct public relations goal, cultivating acceptance of psychiatry as an indispensable, even admirable institutional pursuit.[23]

Reflecting this goal, the U.S. Office of Education released the film for public educational use in 1952, following an eight-year period in which it was reserved mainly for use in military and civilian hospitals throughout the country.[24] That the makers of *The N.P. Patient*, including the Bureau of Aeronautics, had this adaptability very much in mind, projecting future educational uses of the film beyond the basic training of hospital corpsmen, is evident from the way in which the film repeatedly couches empathy as a "universal" virtue in the "handling" of the mentally ill—a strategy for de-stigmatizing psychoneurosis as a means of assisting in its psychiatric treatment. For if psychiatrists were clearly in the minority among medical officers, as well as in the American medical

FIGURE 14. Patients arrive in the admitting room in the Navy's *The N.P. Patient* (1944). Courtesy of the U.S. National Library of Medicine.

community at large, the task of rehabilitating the mentally ill would have to be shared not merely by hospital corpsmen (the film's initial address-ees) but also by anyone with a stake in "the health of the nation"— including those who, like the film's performers, may one day fall victim to psychoneurosis, war having made trauma "quite common."[25]

Recognizing the "basic human" ties that tethered them to their patients, hospital corpsmen could model a form of compassionate treat-ment for the civilians who would one day be forced to contend with war-traumatized returnees, and who viewed *The N.P. Patient* in a wide range of schools, churches, and community groups beginning in 1952.[26] "Treat-ment of an N.P. patient begins from the moment he arrives in the admit-ting room," says the film's narrator, but it does not, he later makes clear, end with the activities of psychiatrists and their assistants. It extends to all who encounter the mentally ill, marking the narrator's use of the word "you," which initially refers to corpsmen-in-training, as an ultimately expansive gesture. Noting that "your manner, approach, and the way you handle the patient makes a difference," the narrator cautions, "Remember, they are more sensitive than those who are physically ill."

One man, Miller, complains of insomnia, saying that he feels "terrible"—a condition that the narrator describes as "dazed and slowed down." Outlining Miller's depression, he carefully explains its chronic nature and close connection to war trauma. "You've been in the dumps too," he says to the hypothetical spectator, "but you've always been able to snap out of it. That's normal." Miller, by contrast, is so depressed that he cannot eat. Reenactments show him lethargically refusing food, until a dedicated and competent corpsman comes along, his gentle entreaties prompting Miller to finally accept a few bites of breakfast. The next shot is of the officer-narrator seated behind his desk, looking directly at the camera and describing the preceding reenactment as having outlined the "proper" approach to a patient's depression—an approach that, praised in hospital records and "accurately" reconstructed for the film, was meant to be repeated by all corpsmen encountering depressed patients.[27]

Perhaps the most challenging aspect of the corpsman's job, at least according to the narrator, is the sheer inconsistency of mental illness, which militates against the adoption of a singular approach to treatment. Generative of a range of symptoms (some of them strikingly contradictory), psychoneurosis demands adaptability on the part of the corpsman, who must become a performer in his own right—an actor able and willing to "modulate," moving from the almost maternal warmth of a spoon-feeding session (as depicted in the film's reenactment of depression and its "gentle," "soothing" treatment) to the pokerfaced strength required of an encounter with a manipulative, unrepentantly mendacious patient. "There are many different types of mental illness," the narrator intones. "Some [patients] will be slowed down, others will be tense and on edge." This range of war-traumatized "types"—from "the unreliable psychopath" to the "very depressed, suicidal patient" and the catatonic—requires the corpsman to "adapt" to any number of scenarios. Once again, the acting analogy serves to discipline a dauntingly dynamic context, as corpsmen are counseled to see themselves as capable of "improvisation"—as "acting to meet the demands" of diverse patients ("Some may be mixed up . . . others with more energy than they can use . . . [and] all require different treatment"). Since "it is the corpsman, not the doctor, who will be with the patient most of the time," he must master the many techniques of a truly versatile performer while also serving as a conduit of vital medical information, becoming, in effect, "the eyes and ears of the doctor."

Despite his insistence on the value of spontaneity and improvisation in the handing of neuropsychiatric patients, the narrator furnishes a series of lines for the corpsman—scripted statements that suggest the dangers of

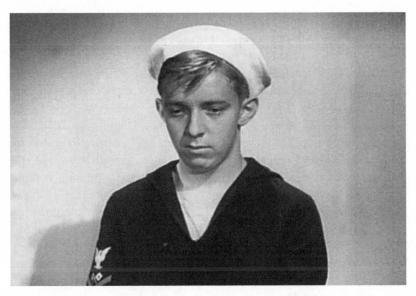

FIGURE 15. A severely depressed man awaits treatment in the Navy's *The N.P. Patient* (1944). Courtesy of the U.S. National Library of Medicine.

misleading the victims of war trauma, who, in their daily suffering, are desperate for credible signs of hope. Cautioning the corpsman against being "too optimistic in [his] answer" to any given question from a patient, the narrator advises that the "safest thing to say" is "I don't know, but I'll try to find out." This contradiction at the heart of the film reflects broader tensions between acting (especially improvisation) as a therapeutic tool and more structured instruments of rehabilitation, such as drug treatments and individual sessions with a doctor. If some military psychiatrists, influenced by Jacob Moreno and other proponents of "psychodrama," felt that acting—especially in the service of a documentary film—could serve a uniquely salutary purpose, others feared that the freedom to perform, with or without a pedagogic objective, could only lead to more suffering, the role-playing pleasures of the stage quickly giving way to confusion regarding the boundaries between fantasy and reality.

DRAMA TEAMS

While it is relatively well known that Hollywood actors like Ronald Reagan (whose character is "too anxious" in the Army Air Forces' *Recognition of the Japanese Zero Fighter*), Dick York (whose character is "wound up like a top" in the Navy's *Combat Fatigue: Insomnia*), and Arthur Kennedy (whose character learns how to "open up" in the Army's *It's Your America* [1945]) portrayed troubled servicemen in wartime military documentaries, less recognized are the contributions to such films of nonprofessional performers tasked with recreating and thus "working through" their own traumatic experiences. A major example of the military's work in nontheatrical nonfiction is the so-called "drama film" produced with hospitalized patients required to undergo a four-part process of "catharsis and desensitization": in the first stage, the patient was asked to ad lib after encountering various "emotional triggers"; in the second, he was made to reenact his traumatic combat experiences; in the third, he had to "act out" a number of scripted scenarios; and in the fourth, he was told to portray his "behavioral opposite"—someone whose demeanor seemed far removed from his own. Throughout World War II, military psychiatrist Lewis Barbato oversaw the use of such "drama therapy" in the neuropsychiatric ward of Fitzsimons Army Hospital in Aurora, Colorado. Having studied with Jacob Moreno, who taught numerous military psychiatrists and "psychiatric assistants" in his famous courses on psychodrama at the University of Denver, Barbato assembled a "drama team" consisting of "a dramatic director who is an enlisted man having an M.A. degree in dramatics from Kansas State College and Washington University, an assistant who is a civilian nurse with considerable experience on a military psychiatric ward and as an amateur actress, and a stenographer." At Fitzsimons, drama therapy was limited to "closed ward patients having both psychotic and psychoneurotic diagnoses," and its purpose was to demonstrate that such patients "learn best by doing."[28]

Barbato's "drama teams" epitomized a strategy of military psychiatry that would become a hallmark of Hollywood combat films produced toward the end of the war and well into the postwar period. Bringing professional, amateur, and entirely inexperienced performers together for the same cause, this strategy suggested the lasting popularity of Moreno's methods of psychodramatic role play. The reputedly therapeutic dimensions of this process appear to have survived its transformation into Hollywood convention, as in films whose voice-over narrators, title cards, and credit sequences tout the memorializing and even cathartic function of "playing oneself" for soldiers asked to reenact their combat experiences alongside civilian movie stars. But it also became a marketable sign of authenticity for filmmakers pursuing a documentary aesthetic (as well as implicitly competing with the excitement and evidentiary power of combat footage captured by military cameramen). In any case, the importance of reconstructing one's own past, using one's own mind and body, was scarcely in dispute, evoking Vanessa Agnew's definition of reenactment as "a body-based discourse in which the past is reanimated through physical and psychological experience," or Jane Marie Todd's notion of "autobiographics as cure."[29]

Echoing Joris Ivens' earlier emphasis on the pedagogic and therapeutic value of "playing oneself," this particular performance strategy also resonated with contemporaneous techniques of Hollywood docudrama, in which historical reconstruction was presented as tantamount to psychological rehabilitation. MGM's *Battleground*, as the opening credits tell us, features "the original 'Screaming Eagles' of the 101st Airborne Division, who play themselves," reenacting the traumatic experience of the Siege of Bastogne alongside professional actors like Van Johnson and Ricardo Montalbán, in the process—presumably—exorcising combat-related demons. Wellman's earlier *The Story of G. I. Joe* (1945) reflects a similar psychodramatic approach, and the film's opening credits list "as themselves, combat veterans of the campaigns in Africa, Sicily, and Italy," who interact with the likes of Burgess Meredith and star-in-the-making Robert Mitchum. On leave when the film was shot, these real-life soldiers—many of them doomed to die in the Pacific, along with the film's subject, Ernie Pyle—lend the film a haunting quality that transforms it from active psychodrama into somber memorial. At Fitzsimons and other military hospitals, drama therapy may not have brought psychiatric patients into close contact with Hollywood stars, as in the model of *Battleground* and *The Story of G. I. Joe*, but it did require them to see themselves as part of a semi-professional "drama team" legitimated by the extensive experience and educational credentials of that team's director.

Moving beyond the hospital, drama teams increasingly embraced activities performed in specific sites of trauma—a psychotherapeutic turn that anticipated major developments in documentary film. In Jean Rouch and Edgar Morin's *Chronicle of a Summer* (1961), for instance, a woman's traumatic memories of the Gare de l'est in Paris are "activated" as she is forced to walk through that very site—a tacit endorsement of location shooting as a potential "trigger," a means of awakening historical trauma, as in earlier docudramatic films like *The Big Lift* (George Seaton, 1950) and *Decision Before Dawn* (Anatole Litvak, 1951), which place "actual soldiers" (who, the credits say, "play themselves") among the European ruins that they themselves helped to produce.[30] Werner

Herzog's *Little Dieter Needs to Fly* (1997) similarly suggests the re-traumatizing potential of the original sites and characteristic gestures of trauma, as the film's titular subject returns to Laos in order to reenact his experiences as a prisoner of war there. Despite the motor-mouthed awkwardness of Dieter Dengler's performance of the traumatic past, and despite the lethargy of some of the Laotian villagers enlisted to participate in this historiographic and pseudotherapeutic process, the film occasionally indicates that re-traumatization is a constant threat for those who, like Dengler, are bravely willing to "go back" (both temporally and spatially). "Uh-oh, this feels a little bit too close to home," Dengler says at one point, as his hands are being tied behind his back. "Of course," Herzog interrupts in voice-over, "Dieter knew it was only a film, but all the old terror returned as if it were real." Believing that he can "chase the demons away," Dengler persists in spite of his terror. Later, he seems to recognize reenactment's potentially traumatizing effects on performers other than himself. Turning to a stoic, speechless participant in this strange psychodramatic process, he puts his arms around the other man and says gently, "It's just a movie—don't worry about it."

For Lewis Barbato, whose work was necessarily confined to a military hospital, trauma was *supposed* to be triggered by acting exercises—ways of performing the past in the absence of its material traces (save bodily wounds and other tactile reminders of combat trauma). Whatever their shortcomings, Barbato viewed his methods as akin to those of a Hollywood filmmaker forced to toil within the boundaries of a studio, striving to activate and cauterize trauma in both filmed participant and future spectator.[31] The truth claims of his dramatizations were thus rooted in precisely those autobiographical strategies that lent a series of contemporaneous documentary and realist films—from the military's *Combat Exhaustion* to Hollywood's *The Story of G. I. Joe*—a testimonial authority tied to the art of "playing oneself."

FEAR OF REALISM

Writing in 1945, Navy psychiatrist Howard P. Rome claimed that a fear of documentary realism was "almost universal" among hospitalized spectators suffering from various forms of war trauma.[32] Alleviating this fear could be accomplished, Rome suggested, through regular screenings of realist documentaries. While his colleague Elias Katz believed that "traumatizing" films should never be screened for hospitalized soldiers undergoing treatment for combat fatigue, Rome maintained a commitment to what he called "aversion therapy," screening "shocking" documentaries in an effort to "de-sensitize the psychoneurotic." According to Rome, "in new patients unprepared for the realistic portrayal of a commonly traumatic experience, there is an almost critical exacerbation of symptomatology; however, in sharp differentiation those patients who have been in therapy for even a brief period"—and who have been exposed to "more than one" realist documentary—"are better able to integrate their experiences and therefore profit by an opportunity to abreact and analyze their induced reactions, either in personal terms or vicariously in terms of the film characters."[33] The Navy documentary *Introduction to Combat Fatigue* (1944), which Rome took to be exemplary of "therapeutic film," provided opportunities for two forms of identification: the self-identification encouraged by the officer-narrator, who directly addresses the camera, invoking a vulnerable "you"; and identification with the traumatized characters created through dramatic reenactments, whose symptoms are said to be "typical"—characteristic of the conditions from which the film's addressees (its hospitalized, psychoneurotic spectators) were suffering.[34]

If these reenactments succeeded in reproducing some of the traumatic realities of combat, they could also, Rome believed, succeed in setting the stage for rehabilitation, precisely by desensitizing the spectator to her own traumas. The film's visible narrator seems to endorse Rome's approach even while echoing Katz's concern regarding "troubling images" and filmic "triggers." Staring into the camera, he offers what is today popularly known as a "trigger warning": "To explain the causes of your symptoms to you, we're going to show you, among other things, some combat scenes—scenes just like those some of you have been in. Now, they may upset you, but just remember that no one ever had an operation, or an illness, or had a broken leg fixed, without experiencing a little pain." *Introduction to Combat Fatigue* thus positions its own reception—and film spectatorship more generally—as painful but necessary. "Expect it to hurt a little," says the narrator, "and, strangely enough, you'll find it doesn't hurt half as much as you anticipate." Later, introducing another battle reenactment, he provides a final trigger warning: "Oh, and, by the way, this is the last of our really noisy scenes, so please bear with us."

Addressing cinema's capacity to traumatize its spectators, *Introduction to Combat Fatigue* reflexively apologizes for its own psychological impact. The film's unnamed officer-narrator thus functions as the calm, almost folksy ambassador of Rome's belief in docudramatic aversion

therapy, couching "upsetting" images as curative, provided the spectator "powers through" their initially distressing effects, eventually realizing that they—and, by extension, his own symptoms—are "not so bad
after all." Responding to *Introduction to Combat Fatigue* and other
military films that insist on the benefits of exposure to their intense battle reenactments, Katz (perhaps grudgingly) acknowledged their therapeutic efficacy, writing, "Films of graded intensity of sensory stimulation have been used to 'desensitize' 'combat-fatigue' casualties." Katz's
intervention was to demand that such "therapeutic motion pictures" do
more than just "shock" the spectator into overcoming trauma; he
insisted that they also conform to "psychodramatic principles" in their
very production. Citing "the selection of conflicts, the construction of
plots, the choice and training of cast," Katz argued that all production
decisions "must be made in accord with" theories of psychodramatic
psychotherapy.[35] A filmed battle reenactment needed to be "simple" and
thus further reproducible, its intensity deriving from acting rather than
elaborate special effects. If the hospitalized spectator was going to be
"shocked" by a film screening, he would need to be able to put his emotions to immediate use, joining others, in classic psychodramatic fashion, in the "live recreation" of a traumatic reality.[36]

If Katz, long cautious about the potentially scarring effects of documentary spectatorship, eventually acceded (with caveats) to Rome's
form of filmic aversion therapy, other military psychiatrists insisted that
certain cinematic examples simply should not, under any circumstances,
be shared with combat-traumatized veterans. Chief among these, perhaps unsurprisingly, was the combat film, which proved particularly
distressing to patients at Don Ce-Sar, an Army Air Forces facility in
Florida that William C. Menninger called "an excellent specialized psychiatric hospital for the treatment of neuroses."[37] It was at Don Ce-Sar
that Grinker and Spiegel were forced to consider some of the traumatizing effects of film spectatorship. While watching a combat film, one
pilot developed "coarse tremors which embarrassed him"; another had
to flee the screening room. For Grinker and Spiegel, such excruciating
spectatorial experiences seemed to prove cinema's utility as a barometer
of anxiety disorders. If such disorders could be diagnosed, in part,
through the observation of "pained" spectatorship, recovery from them
could be confirmed by a patient's capacity to sit through an entire
screening without becoming anxious.[38]

The Navy's *Combat Fatigue: Insomnia* (1945) illustrates these lessons, opening with a group of sailors entering a recreation hall for a

FIGURE 16. "Triggered" by the Donald Duck short *Early to Bed* (Jack King, 1941), a young man looks away from the screen in the Navy's *Combat Fatigue: Insomnia* (1945). Courtesy of the U.S. National Library of Medicine.

screening of a Donald Duck short entitled *Early to Bed* (Jack King, 1941), in which sleep cruelly eludes the cartoon character. Though an animated comedy, *Early to Bed* hits "too close to home" for one spectator, an anxious young man who himself suffers from insomnia, and who reacts to the screening with considerable discomfort.[39] Compounding matters, the sailor soon realizes that he alone is upset by the film—that his fellow spectators are all laughing uproariously, seemingly oblivious to the real problem of insomnia. Thus even as it purports to offer comic relief in the form of an anthropomorphized duck, *Early to Bed* manages to accurately index some of the causes and symptoms of insomnia—an implicit defense of animation's documentary potential, which here proves tremendously upsetting to an anxious serviceman.

Numerous Hollywood fiction films take up this spectatorial dilemma, representing the psychoneurotic soldier as fearful of documentary realism. In the Dore Schary production *I'll Be Seeing You* (William Dieterle, 1944), severely traumatized veteran Zachary Morgan (Joseph Cotton), on a ten-day leave from a military hospital, reluctantly purchases a ticket to a Hollywood combat film. Entitled *Make Way for Glory*, this apocryphal film (whose poster features the tagline "Thrill to the fighting Yanks!") so upsets Zachary that he can scarcely look at the screen.[40] For its part, the Army's 1947 documentary *Shades of Gray* indicates the traumatizing potential of combat footage, incorporating images of corpses that, the narrator suggests, are nearly as disturbing to see on the screen as they are to encounter on the battlefield: "The set-up is ideal for psychiatric breakdown," he says. Toni Morrison's 2012 novel *Home* addresses these themes through the experiences of a severely traumatized Korean War veteran who, unable to cope with a screening of the John Garfield thriller *He Ran All the Way* (John Berry, 1951), afterward resorts to "clenching his fist in silence"—precisely the coping tactic of the sailor unable to "handle" a Donald Duck film in *Combat Fatigue: Insomnia*.[41] For their part, films that model a kind of moral spectatorship through the diegetic incorporation of documentaries about the Nazi death camps also suggest the traumatizing potential of images of atrocity. In Orson Welles's *The Stranger* (1946), and to a still greater degree in Basil Dearden's *Frieda* (1947), such images risk "damaging" the very viewers they are meant to educate; in the latter film, a sequence set in a movie palace features a jarring, altogether unexpected transition from a light romantic feature to a newsreel entitled *Horror in Our Time* (the actual, April 1945 issue of *Gaumont British News*), which, with its footage of corpses being bulldozed into mass graves, proves deeply distressing to a German refugee played by Mai Zetterling, who is rendered temporarily mute—and nearly catatonic—by what she sees.

In its own, ultimately sentimental way, *I'll Be Seeing You* reflects some of the military's revelations regarding the spectatorial experiences of its psychoneurotic soldiers. Beginning in 1942, the Army Air Forces Aviation Psychology Program, overseen by James J. Gibson, maintained a Psychological Test Film Unit that sought, in part, to engage with the subject of spectatorial trauma. Building on Gibson's findings, a 1949 report by the Army Medical Department found that many traumatized veterans continued to avoid Hollywood combat films, which they tended to view as "too upsetting." The report describes a "typical" case—an anxious ex-soldier who "had to be persuaded to go to the movies and walked out if the film dealt with war." "It was unavailing," the report continued, "to assure him that he would not be returned to combat." For him, combat films seemed to confirm trauma as a "living reality"—"alive" on the screen in front of him, maintaining, however temporarily and artificially, a present tense for the very experiences that had made him ill in the first place.[42]

THE SHOCK OF THE "REAL"

As Jacob Moreno put it in 1946, "a good film producer, with a brilliant script on hand and an excellent cast, is not able, by himself, to know how to produce a truly therapeutic motion picture," just as "a competent psychiatrist or psychoanalyst is not, by himself, able to know how to produce one which has value." The former requires the additional "shock" of reality, while the latter needs to embrace artifice, yielding to the participatory benefits and sheer productivity of "role play."[43] Interspersed throughout a number of documentary and realist films of the 1940s, graphic footage, so illustrative of historical traumas, evokes the interruptions of the "expressionless" that, for Walter Benjamin, shatter any pretenses to wholeness or mastery.[44] Numerous films situate these interruptions—"caesurae" in Benjamin's terms—as the means by which to traumatize spectators, particularly civilians, in order to bring about not comprehensive historical knowledge but, rather, a kind of catharsis occasioned by exposure to the historical "real."[45]

Famously enamored of "wooden acting" as a guarantor of "honesty" and "authenticity," Moreno provided several justifications for the use of nonprofessional performers in films about global traumas, anticipating Italian neorealism and its theorization by such figures as Cesare Zavattini, André Bazin, and Gilles Deleuze. Moreno reserved special praise for what he called the "undramatic and unesthetic" qualities of therapeutic motion pictures—films whose production required "parting from the many subtleties and niceties of regular picture-making." The results were far from "picture-perfect and smooth"; they were instead—and precisely by virtue of this deliberate departure from "studio-bound" filmmaking—"authentic." The non-actor ensconced in the stark (and hardly Hollywoodian) setting of an actual psychiatric hospital, like the non-actor tasked with walking through the disturbing ruins of postwar European cities, was participating in a realist filmmaking practice of enormous importance for audiences while also engaged in his own, complex psychological rehabilitation. Not only would the nonprofessional performer avoid "over-acting" and other "melodramatic effects" (thus pleasing audiences eager for something "real"), but the unfamiliar demands of film performance would also allow him to "find himself and get relief": "[He] is not an actor, he is just tormented by a certain experience and in living through this experience, he is serving himself and as a by-product, producing the film which may help many of his fellow-sufferers."[46]

The nonprofessional, whose performance style inevitably seemed "false" and even "awkward" when viewed in terms of the standards associated with "conventional motion pictures," in fact demonstrated through his very awkwardness the authenticity of his "painful experiences."[47] He was, as Moreno pointed out, demonstrably "fake" in his "acting"—but therein lay his pedagogic as well as therapeutic significance. Moreno's theories of "therapeutic motion pictures" thus resonate with Bazin's remark that "realism can be achieved in one way: through artifice."[48] As Justin Horton argues, Bazin's theories of realism were hardly monolithic, despite longstanding complaints about his "ignorance" of their ideological implications. Far from being a "naïve literalist," Bazin in fact offered "a remarkably nuanced and flexible theorization of realism," one whose genealogy must be seen as including the work of Moreno and other psychological experts attuned to the therapeutic as well as pedagogic potential of motion pictures.[49] Like Moreno, Bazin would demand "a more active mental attitude on the part of the spectator"—a determination to read artifice in relation not merely to historical trauma but also to collective rehabilitation. Bazin's conception of realism as an "attitude of mind" thus has important precedents in Moreno's writings, which insist on the sort of psychodramatic clashes between fact and fantasy that numerous American films would take up as a therapeutic project of national importance in the immediate postwar period.[50]

PERFORMING PSYCHONEUROSIS

As military psychiatrists continued to promote their certainty that all combatants would eventually "wear out" and exhibit traumatic symptoms—"developing," in the words of psychiatrist John Appel, "an acute incapacitating neurosis or else becoming hypersensitive to shell fire, so overly cautious and jittery"—film productions that brought the "healthy" together with the "sick" served the interests of institutional surveillance, as documentary became not just a diagnostic but also a regulatory apparatus.[51] Resonating with Michel Foucault's notion that cinema and psychoanalysis are among the major technologies of supervision that developed in the late nineteenth century, the military's documentary enterprise, in increasingly inviting psychiatric oversight, allowed the institution to collect data on performers who, through the helpful reenactment of traumatic symptoms, invariably became barometers of psychoneurosis unto themselves.[52] If a "healthy" actor was, in a sense, both playing himself and reenacting the experiences of a "sick" serviceman, the film in which he appeared could be embraced both as a form of historical documentation and a source of insight into the "mechanisms of response" of performers whose every move could seem suspect—a possible indication of a propensity for psychic breakdown.[53] Performers in military documentaries were objects of analysis, their nuanced responses to direction becoming units of data—along with their every improvisatory gesture—in institutional efforts to determine the extent of the "spread of psychoneurotics" in the armed forces.[54]

Even famous performers were subjected to this treatment, as the experiences of Gene Kelly, who appeared in the Navy's *Combat Fatigue: Irritability* (1945), powerfully attest. Tasked with reenacting a particular "case study"—that of "a combat-fatigued sailor from Pacific action" —Kelly, in his directorial debut, was expected to help the Navy's psychiatric patients understand "just what their own problem is and how they must help themselves toward recovery."[55] But he was also, for the Navy, an object of study unto himself, his particular approach to the project of "cinematic rehabilitation" potentially revelatory. Responsible for marshaling his acting expertise in order to help "explain the problem of 'battle nerves'" and to "show psychiatric patients the road to recovery," Kelly was also an enlisted man, and thus subject to institutional scrutiny.[56] Portraying a well-documented historical "case," and reenacting "the various hospital steps in his recovery," Kelly was asked to bridge some of the gaps between his own experiences and those of the combat-traumatized, and his approach to this task would provide useful fodder for military psychiatrists committed to the pedagogic and therapeutic use of documentary film. If, according to the Navy, Kelly "proved" his mental health by calmly accepting the high incidence of psychoneurosis among his fellow enlistees, he also managed to substantiate emergent institutional efforts to treat film acting as a multidirectional form of therapy whose documentary legitimacy could not be denied.[57]

In order to reenact the experiences of a far less fortunate man, from initial traumatization to later breakdown and ultimate recovery in a Navy hospital, Kelly had to encounter "actual cases"—hospitalized men whose visible symptoms Kelly could imitate, though only after checking them against those described in the archival documents pertaining to his

FIGURE 17. Gene Kelly's severely disturbed sailor breaks down in the Navy's *Combat Fatigue: Irritability* (1945). Courtesy of the National Archives and Records Administration.

particular role in *Combat Fatigue: Irritability*. Kelly, who directed the film under the supervision of military psychiatrists (including George S. Goldman and Howard P. Rome), checked himself into St. Elizabeths Hospital, where he effectively impersonated a patient, "absorbed the routine," and gathered evidence that would provide the basis for cinematic reconstruction.[58] This painstaking process of observation, impersonation, and verification was widely promoted as "proof" not only of Kelly's commitment but also of documentary's capacity to accommodate acting and of acting's capacity to "teach" as well as to "heal."[59] It was also far from unique, as a number of individuals, both famous and unknown, impersonated doctors and patients in an effort to achieve cinematic realism. Parts of Billy Wilder's *The Lost Weekend* (1945), for example, were shot on location at Bellevue, where star Ray Milland had himself "committed" in order to prepare for his role in the film, much as Kelly had voluntarily "checked into" St. Elizabeths.[60]

In 1946, the mass-circulation magazine *Popular Photography* covered Kelly's "process"—with prose that paraphrased Navy psychiatrists—in an issue that repeatedly touted the military's documentary enterprise, including advertisements placed by commercial production outfits under military contract (like the Jam Handy Organization and Caravel Films).[61] Presenting the actor as an agent of rehabilitation (both his own and that of his institutional counterparts), *Popular Photography* persistently blurred distinctions between Kelly and the role that he played, pointing to "Kelly beginning to understand his problems and making a constructive effort to work [them] out." This slippage between Kelly and a historical "case study" was hardly accidental, however. It was part of a developing psychiatric doctrine that placed a premium on acting as a therapeutic exercise, and it was almost certainly prescribed as such by the public affairs strategists who, representing the interests of the Navy, shared with *Popular Photography* and other mass-circulation magazines information about the making of *Combat Fatigue: Irritability*, a docudrama whose famous lead actor provided an appealing point of entry for readers unaccustomed to coverage of "therapeutic film."[62]

As depicted in *Combat Fatigue: Irritability*, the function of a Navy rehabilitation center is to restore "happy equilibrium" to traumatized men, but the function of film acting was far less stable, if only because of the risks (Freudian and otherwise) attached to the reenactment of trauma. *Popular Photography* goes so far as to suggest that acting, as observed by military psychiatrists, offers a way of figuring out if a performer is "ill and needs treatment."[63] Rooted in a sociological respect for the pervasiveness of role playing in everyday life, this investment in acting as a barometer of mental illness is central to the representational strategies of *Combat Fatigue: Irritability*, in which Kelly's character, forced to assume the role of a war hero when visiting his demanding friends and family members, fails miserably (by, in fact, "performing inappropriately"), thus "proving" his need for immediate psychiatric treatment.

If Kelly passed his own performance test, simulating psychoneurosis with professional aplomb and an empathic doggedness that signaled a certain inner strength, other performers (particularly inexperienced ones) were thought to require opportunities to act precisely because they were "psychically scarred"—unable to behave "normally" without guidance.[64] Such men may have been monitored by those institutional agents eager to stamp out psychoneurosis, but a more generous understanding of their participation in documentary production often pivoted around an appreciation for acting not merely as a pedagogic vehicle but also as a form of occupational and recreational therapy. For professional performers like Gene Kelly, the opportunity to perform psychoneurosis in a documentary film offered challenges that were beyond the scope of commercial cinema—and, in particular, of a Hollywood governed by the restrictions of the Production Code, which plainly forbade the sort of expletive-laden outbursts so central to Kelly's simulation of psychosis. Kelly's pedagogic and therapeutic turn in *Combat Fatigue: Irritability*, then, was understood as benefitting both the hypothetical spectator and Kelly himself. A form of occupational therapy for a man who had already appeared in a number of Hollywood fiction films (including the war-themed *Pilot #5* [George Sidney, 1943] and *The Cross of Lorraine* [Tay Garnett, 1943], both of which touch upon the topic of war trauma), the performance of psychoneurosis was thought to acquaint Kelly with the condition in the idiom of his own profession.[65]

Honing their vocational skills, Kelly and other professional actors not only served the military's documentary enterprise but also, in pedagogic and psychotherapeutic terms, aided their own minds (however "strong" they seemed). By contrast, the performance of psychoneurosis by nonprofessional actors (including hospital patients) was promoted as a distinct yet related treatment method—a form of recreational therapy designed to "aid in the maintenance of one's good adjustment."[66] The commingling of professional and nonprofessional performers· brought occupational and recreational therapy together in a way that, for William C. Menninger, assured the military's place among "progressive psychiatric institutions."[67] Situating film acting on a continuum of "hobbies or recreation interests," Menninger and others upheld it as likely to yield "therapeutic benefits," aligning it with psychodramatic "role play" as a treatment method that "can be learned."[68] Thus the use of professional performers served the immediate purpose of training their nonprofessional counterparts in some basic techniques of acting for the camera, but it also functioned to offset the suspicion that film acting, like other forms of recreational therapy, was mere "child's play." Noting that this suspicion "may be a hangover from our early American heritage when play was frowned upon," Menninger explained that, for many servicemen (including traumatized patients desperate to recover their erstwhile "balance"), "play is still a child's game." Conceivably, then, professional performers like Kelly could embody and promote the concept of film acting as a respectable adult pursuit but also "an important factor in maintaining . . . good adjustment to life," and, moreover, one of military psychiatry's "most effective therapeutic measures."[69]

However successful in helping to legitimate film acting as pedagogically and therapeutically effective, professional performers inevitably muddied the waters of reenactment, introducing emotive techniques that, in some cases, contradicted or at least obscured the documented symptoms of war trauma that they were asked to simulate. As enlisted men (and thus, according to an emergent psychiatric logic, at risk of experiencing war trauma firsthand, even if their service was strictly stateside), these performers were expected to draw upon their own authenticity as servicemen (thus helpfully "playing themselves" while reenacting "case studies"), but their familiarity to spectators was such that their "auras" often eclipsed whatever symptomatologies they were expected to express, impeding some of the aims of historical reconstruction. This was especially true of Gene Kelly (repeatedly and misleadingly billed as a "former cinema actor" in military memoranda), whose attempts to satisfy the demands of therapeutic reenactment ran to promotable extremes. Kelly "spent three weeks in a rehabilitation hospital taking treatments himself and working with psychiatric patients"—an "extreme strategy" that the Navy immediately relayed to the popular press in an attempt to further advertise documentary reenactment as a pedagogic and therapeutic component of institutional rehabilitation policy, a means of "encouraging . . . patients' cooperation in helping Navy doctors facilitate their cure."[70]

In *Combat Fatigue: Irritability*, Kelly's character is "surly and quick-tempered," but Kelly's own exuberant athleticism—already familiar from a number of Hollywood films—threatened to confuse spectators, even as military psychiatrists repeatedly cautioned against taking too narrow a view of the titular condition. Literal physical exhaustion was far from inevitable as a consequence of war trauma, but Kelly's limber movements and generally energetic demeanor often seem ill suited to the representation of combat fatigue, suggesting that irritability is a consequence of excessive stamina rather than emergent psychosis. The Navy thus struggled to couch Kelly's performance, however reflective of a developing star persona, as a form of reenactment rooted in an actual case of combat fatigue and its "crippling effects," frequently relying on associations between military filmmaking and historical documentation. Drawing attention to "actual Navy hospitals" as shooting locations for *Combat Fatigue: Irritability*, public relations officials consistently emphasized the needs of military psychiatrists and their patients, which prominently included the "recording of history" as an educative and therapeutic strategy. Even scenes in which Kelly's character visits his family, which were not shot in Navy hospitals and thus, with their customary *mise-en-scène*, threatened to resemble "typical" Hollywood fare, were in fact "filmed by Navy camera crew," marking them as reenactments simply by virtue of their adherence to institutional records.[71]

Military filmmakers, like the psychiatrists with whom they collaborated, did not always couch repetition as therapeutic, however. Occasionally, they identified it in Freudian terms, as a symptom of mental illness—a compulsion in need of treatment. In many cases, carefully avoiding any semblance of this repetition compulsion meant focusing on "simple observation"—a style of documentary filmmaking that some psychiatrists identified as least likely to "damage" war-traumatized participants, some of them believed to be so "far gone" as to be completely unaware of the presence of the cameras that recorded their actions. In January 1944, Captain Lewis L. Robbins, director of the Mental Hygiene Unit of the Drew Army Airfield near Tampa, Florida, prepared a series of guidelines for the treatment of the "maladjusted." In a section entitled "Recording," Robbins described the importance of documenting—of committing to print as well as to various audio and audiovisual formats—a patient's symptoms in addition to their treatment. Here, Robbins distinguished between two competing vehicles of documentary evidence: the strictly observational, with its capacity to "quote the patient directly" rather than "reconstruct" his remarks and "interpret his feelings"; and the speculative or "imaginative," which allowed for the presentation of "non-factual data" as it emerged from a "history-taking interview" with the patient—data that included "associative patterns" and "emotional processes" that could be performed according to a carefully prepared script.[72]

Addressing these two categories of documentary, Robbins suggested that the former—the strictly observational—was of most use to the patient himself, who could benefit tremendously from the opportunity to hear his own words, in his own voice. Indeed, in the Mental Hygiene Unit at the Drew Army Airfield, patients were given the option of watching "filmed records" of their responses to a series of questions posed in intake interviews.[73] If these "history-taking" interviews had provided the foundations for various institutional biographies, helping psychiatric social workers to construct a number of "life stories" (such as those that would serve as the basis for Gene Kelly's reconstruction of a specific instance of combat fatigue), their "replay" for interviewees was thought to serve a potentially curative function, forcing patients to confront their own conditions.[74]

For Robbins, techniques of reconstruction were more useful as attempts to teach not patients but, rather, current and future social workers—to show them, through a range of didactic methods, how to do their jobs. A number of short films were produced for precisely this purpose at the Drew Army Airfield, with local actors and enlisted men simulating war trauma and its treatment, often on the basis of strictly observational shorts.[75] Produced for the psychiatrists' less qualified assistants (and withheld from their patients), Drew Army Airfield films that "dramatized" the identification and careful handling of war-traumatized patients do not appear to have survived, but archival evidence indicates that they often took liberties in depicting psychiatric treatment as a smooth process with universally beneficial, even downright curative effects.[76] It is likely that, given the style of related films archived at the National Library of Medicine (such as *Combat Fatigue: Psychosomatic Disorders* [1946] and especially *The N.P. Patient*), these non-extant works exhibited a cheerful faith in the psychotherapeutic process, inviting spectators to see battle-scarred soldiers as scarcely different from men with minor (and even major) bodily injuries.[77] Adapting particular (and evidently "encouraging") case histories, as well as inventing scenarios designed for educative purposes, these "imaginative documentaries"— entirely scripted and performed—were pedagogic instruments to which patients in the Mental Hygiene Unit at the Drew Army Airfield Hospital simply did not have access, owing to a site-specific emphasis on the therapeutic value of "straight records."[78]

"ARRESTED REMNANTS"

Military psychiatrists had good reason to be wary of reenactment as a tool for treating the combat-traumatized. Doctors at Don Ce-Sar Place, an Army Air Forces convalescent center in St. Pete Beach, Florida ("the only AAF convalescent hospital receiving cases of war neuroses," according to Roy Grinker and John Spiegel), noticed that war films (or "movies of combat," as Grinker and Spiegel called them) were extremely unpopular among recovering servicemen, many of whom expressed enthusiasm for the center's prominent inclusion of film spectatorship as a form of recreation and therapy but balked at the prospect of reencountering the sights and sounds of battle.[79] True convalescence would have to entail the serviceman's separation from war even in cinematic form, a conclusion that some military psychiatrists reached after observing the "triggering" effects of various audiovisual reminders of combat, which seemed to demand a series of soothing (if somewhat infantilizing) correctives.

Produced in 1944, a non-extant short film welcoming new patients to Don Ce-Sar was designed to suggest a cheerful sort of "letter home," carefully describing conditions at the convalescent center and the serviceman's (sanitized) reasons for being there. The basis for this untitled film, which was most likely screened for all new arrivals in the facility's vast recreation hall, was an illustrated postcard, its epistolary prose celebrating Don Ce-Sar in the occasionally irreverent words of a hypothetical patient addressing a civilian friend or family member. "At last I have found a home in the Army where I could be happy," it read. "I am at the A.A.F. Convalescent Hospital, formerly the Don Ce-Sar Hotel, which was a haven for tax dodging millionaires. I have been sent here by the A.A.F. to recuperate from the fatigue of my work overseas, and the doctors are helping me a lot."[80]

The inclusion of flippant asides (such as the reference to "tax dodging millionaires") was apparently meant to establish an impudent contract between this document and its seasoned addressees (a not-uncommon strategy of wartime military media, as the *Private Snafu* series [1942–1945] of bawdy animated films attests) and to inspire trust in more earnest claims about the convalescent center itself. However appealingly cheeky, such a cartoonish mode of address belied the strictness of the ward rules, which included injunctions against "boisterous actions, loud noises, profane language, loafing and loitering, interchange of towels, toilet articles or articles of clothing"; telephone, typewriter, and elevator use; and which required servicemen to temporary relinquish all their possessions (including "soothing" talismans and other good-luck charms). Patients were not allowed to leave the hospital for the first forty-eight hours, and their actions were closely monitored thereafter, with harsh punishments (including restrictions on mobility) meted out to those who missed or were late to appointments with psychiatrists and other medical officers, including dentists. Drafted by Captain J. E. Maynard in the fall of 1944, the ward rules of the Don Ce-Sar convalescent center were designed, in part, to regulate psychiatric treatment according to the strictest of military regimens.[81]

Where other hospitals and convalescent centers took a far more liberal approach to treatment, incorporating improvisatory role play and even documentary filmmaking as essential forms of recreational and occupational therapy, Don Ce-Sar was structured by the assumption that its patients would eventually return to service. More flexible treatment regimens, such as those at St. Elizabeths Hospital (where Gene Kelly could impersonate a psychiatric patient and documentary production could serve as a multidimensional source of pedagogy and therapy), were typically reserved for those who would be returning not to the rigid discipline of the armed forces but to the shifting—yet still, in many cases, militarized—demands of civilian life. Patients at Don Ce-Sar, unlike those at St. Elizabeths, were expected to be "back in the air" immediately following their stay at the hospital, and they were repeatedly reminded not only of this institutional expectation but also of the harsh regulation of psychotherapy as a newly "militarized" pursuit, one that, contrary to popular stereotypes of undisciplined chatter, could be reined in by the very institutional protocols governing other aspects of service.

Requiring all patients to sign his ward rules upon their arrival at Don Ce-Sar, Maynard reminded them that the facility, whatever its past uses, was now "a military post" and that "each officer and enlisted man ordered here for observation and treatment is still a member of the United States Army and as such is subject to all military rules and regulations." Recognizing the Army's interest in each patient receiving "all consideration possible for his health and welfare," Maynard's contract nevertheless promised that "any flagrant violations of existing rules and regulations will be dealt with in a strictly military manner."[82] Such strictness proved controversial among military psychiatrists, however, with many of them advocating a less punitive, more "open" approach. Arguing that rigidly "militarizing" psychotherapy could backfire by forcing patients to inhabit the very pressurized psychic spaces that led to their breakdowns, some psychiatrists at Don Ce-Sar suggested that, just as war films were having a negative effect on recovering servicemen desperate for a temporary reprieve from all echoes of combat, the continued emphasis on regulation and punishment could only sustain and possibly even exacerbate trauma.[83]

Looking back on the wartime treatment of battle-scarred soldiers at stateside hospitals and convalescent centers, the Army psychiatrist A. J. Glass noted in 1952 that "the demoralizing effect of combat stress [was] strongly heightened" in heavily regulated and often punitive conditions like those at Don Ce-Sar.[84] An Army training manual from 1950 similarly cited Don Ce-Sar in its critique of "authoritative or persuasive efforts to get . . . patients to use their 'will' to overcome the symptoms of their illness which are interfering with their daily lives."[85] Beyond the unwelcome reminders of institutional traumas encoded in the hospital's

draconian ward rules, patients at Don Ce-Sar and elsewhere had opportunities to encounter "grim evidence" of the horrors of war and even of
their own mental conditions through the viewing of both documentary
and fiction films, leading one military psychiatrist, Elias Katz, to caution
against the indiscriminate inclusion of films in hospitals and convalescent centers. For Katz, films needed to be "carefully selected"—curated
according to concerns about their possible psychic effects—with combat
films being all but inadmissible, given their capacity to "reawaken"
trauma.[86] Echoing Katz nearly a decade later, Glass described the condition of patients diagnosed as "severely combat-traumatized," pointing
out that this condition was "subject to exacerbation by battle noises
that produce violent efforts to run or frantically dig in the ground with
their bare hands." That these noises included those in motion-picture
soundtracks meant that, as Katz had so passionately argued, "film therapy" needed to be approached with an understanding of what sounds
and images might "trigger" a negative response.[87]

Partly set at Letterman General Hospital, an Army facility in San Francisco, MGM's *The Rack* (Arnold Laven, 1956) depicts Katz's ideal scenario: in the hospital's recreation room, former prisoners of war gather
to watch not a disturbing documentary but, rather, a frothy comedy—
the Debbie Reynolds vehicle *The Affairs of Dobie Gillis* (Don Weis,
1953), which brings them great pleasure. By contrast, the Hollywood
docudrama *Task Force* (Delmer Daves, 1949) suggests the traumatizing
dimensions of film spectatorship for Navy pilots made anxious by the
demands of their job. Focusing on one pilot (played by Gary Cooper)
who "proves the value" of a series of aircraft carriers (starting with the
Langley in 1922), the film suggests that the emotional bonds forged
between men and their machines are so strong as to generate anxieties
regarding the latter's possible destruction. On the day the *Langley* first
docks, a group of pilots board the carrier, immediately repairing to its
wardroom for a mandated film screening. There, they watch a didactic
short about airplanes "making mistakes"—to which they initially respond
with condescending laughter. Later, however, as the film begins to feature
footage of planes actually crashing, the men grow agitated, leaning forward in their seats, recoiling, and generally demonstrating the traumatizing potential even of "boring" institutional films. (Werner Herzog's *Rescue Dawn* [2006], a star-driven "remake" of his 1997 documentary *Little
Dieter Needs to Fly*, features a similar depiction of the "redemption" of
a military training film that is first a source of laughter and finally of useful, even life-saving lessons, which the film's protagonist implicitly puts

into practice during his escape from a prisoner-of-war camp.) Following his exposure to traumatizing images of "aircraft disasters," the protagonist of *Task Force* develops "operational fatigue"—a condition that derives, the film makes clear, "merely" from the paranoid expectation of such disasters.

Precisely because Don Ce-Sar was reserved for "mild cases of emotional illness," its rules and regulations had to be strict in the extreme, befitting the expectation that its patients would soon return to service. As a place where "the process of unwinding from the tension of battle experiences takes place," it was uniquely positioned to test the boundaries of cinema as a therapeutic enterprise.[88] By the spring of 1944, military psychiatrists installed at Don Ce-Sar had so wearied of the traumatic effects of war films on their patients that they began advocating the sort of "active approach" to trauma being undertaken at the time in places like St. Elizabeths Hospital, where psychodrama theater provided opportunities for the cathartic simulation of combat. It is an indication of the rapidly increasing popularity of dramatic acting as a therapeutic as well as documentative practice that, eventually, even the heavily rule-bound Don Ce-Sar became a site of "traumatic reenactment," as patients were encouraged to overcome their resistance to combat films by "reliving" (and thus "exorcising") their own combat experiences.[89]

With psychodrama theater among its major points of reference, the Army Air Forces attempted to retrofit Don Ce-Sar, installing "an adequate staff of leading men in the psychiatric field to pioneer the development of new techniques for the definitive care and rehabilitation" of patients.[90] Don Ce-Sar was thus a significant testing ground for efforts to demonstrate the potential of "therapeutic reenactment" as a tool for returning the "mildly emotionally ill" soldier to service: "The aim in the treatment is to uncover and relive painful, repressed residuals of war experiences and then, by ego supporting and development, to re-build the flyer for useful service in the Army Air Forces."[91] Promoted in frequent dispatches to the public, psychodrama theater, documentary reenactment, and other "fresh techniques" were said to create a new category of trauma victim, one far removed from the abject experiences of the inadequately treated (and otherwise neglected) veterans of World War I. Indeed, the Army Air Forces was convinced of the unprecedented efficacy of these newly refined therapeutic methods: "We feel that many cases which in the last war developed into chronic so-called war neuroses or 'shell shock' will be returned and sent on their way with a reasonable expectation of a normal and healthy life."[92]

As usual, however, reenactment seemed a double-edged sword, at once traumatizing and therapeutic—both Freudian symptom and new-fangled cure. Like many of his fellow military psychiatrists, A.J. Glass was particularly concerned about the dangers of reenactment, given the neurotic tendency of his war-traumatized patients to recreate combat conditions in a desperate effort to master them in the Freudian sense. As Glass pointed out, "A fragment of previous activity may remain in the form of an arrested remnant of the traumatic battle experience, such as the clutching of the captured enemy bugle, or the wearing of a steel helmet under all circumstances." Worse off was "the delusional patient, who talks and acts as if still in battle, mistakes friendly personnel for enemy troops, hears voices of his dead buddies and reacts with marked startle reaction to battle noise."[93] In assessing the value of reenactment as an organized form of therapy, including in the production of documentary film, Glass echoed Freud's insistence on reenactment's paradoxical character. For Freud, reenactment—understood as a compulsion to repeat or "relieve" the traumatic experience of combat—was the principal symptom of war trauma, its therapeutic potential tied to innumerable psychic risks.[94] Calling attention to the "defensive tics and ceremonials" characteristic of the post-traumatic condition, Abram Kardiner noted that reenactment can "represent . . . the most highly organized form of response to the unconscious activity of the traumatic event," threatening to re-traumatize through its neurotic character, as Freud had warned.[95] Psychodrama theater, with its emphasis on improvisation and the free play of identity, was not nearly so rigidly organized, however, and it was increasingly embraced as a bulwark against the potentially negative psychic consequences of reenactment.

Looking back on the wartime uses of psychodrama at St. Elizabeths, a 1959 publication claims that the hospital "helped carry the idea [of psychodrama theater] to international recognition," "proving" its pedagogic and therapeutic utility and inspiring its adoption in other psychiatric hospitals as well as in a vast array of universities and "educational institutions."[96] Indeed, the influence of psychodrama theater—particularly as practiced at St. Elizabeths and other facilities requisitioned by the wartime military—can be seen in MGM's postwar film *Shadow on the Wall* (Patrick Jackson, 1950), which dramatizes the use of the procedure (renamed "play therapy") on a traumatized child. First involved in what a psychiatrist calls a "play interview"—a role-playing question-and-answer session designed to "awaken" memory and inspire speech—the child is later subjected to an intense reenactment of the murder that she has witnessed, and that has driven her into a severely traumatized state. "This is play therapy with a vengeance!" observes the psychiatrist, who proceeds to carefully explain the "curative" purpose of this procedure, whose lineage can be traced back to wartime experiments at St. Elizabeths.

After consulting with Jacob Moreno, a social worker named Margaret Hagan, who also served as Field Director of the American Red Cross, began assembling a psychodrama theater at St. Elizabeths in 1939. By 1942, when victims of combat trauma started pouring into the facility, Hagan had managed to partition a portion of St. Elizabeths to include "a low, three-tiered circular stage with a table, a settee, and several chairs" ("the only props used").[97] The "psychodramatic sessions" that took place there were often guided and monitored not by psychiatrists but by social workers like Hagan, the assumption being that patients would feel freer to perform around the latter. Reflecting the strategic translation of psychiatry from specialist discourse into lingua franca, Hagan's mission was a key component of the military's efforts to ensure that psychiatry would be "disseminated and utilized at all levels," even in the absence of actual psychiatrists. The social worker was thus expected to contribute to "the broad application of sound psychiatric principles," often guiding the kinds of "creative tasks" that psychiatrists were not always on hand to oversee—and that they may have deemed "beneath" their expertise, in any case.[98]

Documentary filmmaking was, Hagan and others maintained, among the "modern methods" that could "indoctrinate personnel in the basic concepts of modern psychiatry," and it was frequently used to instruct psychiatric social workers, who, like clinical psychologists and hospital corpsmen, were required to watch such films as *Introduction to Combat Fatigue* and *The Inside Story of Seaman Jones* as part of their training.[99] The "didactic teaching" that documentary film could provide—the genre's capacity "to indoctrinate the principles of modern psychiatry in all personnel who are in immediate contact" with psychiatric patients— was part of a broader purpose that included "inspiration" and "therapeutic treatment," as indicated in the distribution of films like *The N.P. Patient* and *Combat Fatigue: Psychosomatic Disorders* to chaplains.[100] Unlike corpsmen and social workers, chaplains were hardly required to study basic psychiatric principles, but they were expected to benefit from exposure to documentaries that, in addition to providing specialist instruction, also offered advice on how to comfort the traumatized. If, in order to meet the demands of a growing number of battle-scarred soldiers, psychiatric expertise had to be distributed among "flexible specialized medical teams" that consisted of more than just physicians, documentary as a tool for disseminating useful information had to be equally pliant—"flexible and readily adaptable to any local situation."[101]

It was not by accident that documentary filmmaking became a factor in Hagan's experiments at St. Elizabeths, nor was this process merely a reflexive concession to the ideals of documentation that the military was broadly cultivating at the time. Documentary's malleability made it an apt means of contributing to—and not simply recording—the strategies of psychodrama theater, which could be tested and refined through the filmmaking process itself. When portions of *Combat Fatigue: Irritability* were shot at St. Elizabeths, psychodrama theater provided a model for all of the film's performers—both experienced actors like Gene Kelly and some of the nonprofessionals who were, at the time of shooting, actual psychiatric patients. Appearing in a documentary film, whether as oneself or in the guise of somebody else, was not, therefore, an entirely unfamiliar experience for men who had already staged various scenarios of breakdown and recovery in Hagan's psychodrama theater. Documentary filmmaking was, in other words, far from an interruption or a travestying of treatment in places like St. Elizabeths. It was, rather, continuous with therapeutic methods that placed a premium on acting as a way of "reviving" the frightening past and modeling "healthy" future actions.[102] Hagan's efforts were, in fact, strikingly compatible with the claims of various documentary producers and critics, including Paul Rotha, who wrote in 1936, "What we mean by 'acting' is, in fact, closely bound up with the whole principles of the documentary method."[103] Psychodrama theater helped to further justify and solidify this linkage in its wartime encounters with documentary film.

In helping to oversee the transition of psychodrama theater from military hospitals like St. Elizabeths to medical schools and other "educational institutions," Hagan was adamant that "no teaching staff [be] present" at performances, so that students could "make a lot of noise" and—like patients at military hospitals who had felt freer to perform beyond the scrutiny of their psychiatrists—improvise with impunity. Recognizing the potential of acting to "dredge up" uncomfortable experiences, Hagan recommended that clinical psychologists and psychiatric social workers—none of them actual university instructors—be present at all times in the psychodrama theater, providing counseling after each performance.[104] When, in 1945, the United States Public

Health Service began loaning both *Combat Fatigue: Irritability* and *The Inside Story of Seaman Jones* to various state and territorial health boards (such as the Hawaii Board of Health), it promoted the very procedures that Hagan had helped to codify, including "post-screening question-and-answer sessions" led by "licensed therapists or social workers."[105]

These paeans to the therapeutic power of reenactment reached their apex, at least in terms of critical acclaim, with the production of *We, the Mentally Ill . . .* in 1955, the year Congress passed the National Mental Health Study Act. Sponsored by the pharmaceutical company Smith, Kline, & French, with additional support from the American Medical Association, *We, the Mentally Ill . . .* aired as part of NBC's series *The March of Medicine*, fulfilling Margaret Hagan's goal of publicizing psychodrama theater to a nationwide audience. Recorded on 16mm via the kinescope process, the program was also widely distributed as a nontheatrical film. (As Anna McCarthy observes, "When we talk about educational television in this pre-PBS era we are often, necessarily, talking about nontheatrical film at the same time."[106]) The twenty-nine-minute *We, the Mentally Ill . . .* is set largely at St. Elizabeths Hospital, where patients reenact key events in the history of psychiatry, including the founding of the hospital itself by Dorothea Lynde Dix (described here as a "mental health crusader" with a particular interest in the treatment of the "indigent insane"). The film begins with the silhouette of a man seated in front of the camera, his voice resonating through the darkness as he tells his own story: "I am a mental patient at St. Elizabeths Hospital in Washington, DC," he says. "For ages people like us have been hidden in darkness. Families don't like to talk about their members in mental hospitals. People seem to think that there's something worse about being mentally ill than being ill with pneumonia. But it isn't true, and because it isn't true, tonight, mental patients all over the country are gathering together to strip away that darkness." At this point, the man's face is suddenly illuminated by an overhead light, which serves the additional purpose of revealing that he is seated in the middle of a simple stage—the very same stage that Hagan had constructed some sixteen years earlier, and on which many a hospitalized soldier reenacted his traumas during World War II.

"Now you can see me," the unnamed narrator continues, "and in a moment you will see others like me. You will learn from us how mental patients used to be treated, the conditions of our hospitals today, and the new hope we have now that we will get better again." Rising to his feet,

FIGURE 18. A hospital patient portrays Dorothea Lynde Dix in a "therapeutic reenactment" of Dix's life and legacy in *We, the Mentally Ill . . .* (1955). Courtesy of the U.S. National Library of Medicine.

he guides the camera toward a portion of the stage on which a group of female patients, clad in the elaborate costumes of an earlier era, are already engaged in the performance of a play—one that, the narrator points out, "we wrote," and that (like the film itself) is to serve as a means of celebrating the hospital's centennial. Reenacting the life of Dorothea Lynde Dix ("our founder"), the patients of St. Elizabeths pay tribute to a figure whose courage and compassion, as described in fulsome terms by the narrator, opened the doors to the sort of "performance therapy" that we see. Telling the camera that "each person in the play is a mental patient," the narrator carefully notes that "each one and his doctor and his guardian gave his permission that you might see us do it, that you can better understand the present by understanding the past." Further praising Dix's foresight in pushing for flexible treatment regimens for the mentally ill, the narrator addresses the seemingly incongruous, almost Sadean performance on display for the cameras at St. Elizabeths: "Mental patients like us doing a play for the public—a thing like that is astonishing enough today, but it could not have happened a hundred years ago."

With this invocation of the past, *We, the Mentally Ill* . . . signals the historicizing function of the unnamed play being performed by patients at St. Elizabeths—a function that, we are repeatedly reminded, doubles as a form of therapy. The documentary value of reenactment is thus explicitly tied to its therapeutic potential, as patients, in recreating the past for a national television audience, not only satisfy their own creative urges but also remind themselves of the enviable position that they occupy vis-à-vis the mental patients of yesteryear. Playing abject, neglected "crazies" of the past, these patients give voice to the sufferings that led Dorothea Lynde Dix to advocate on behalf of the mentally ill. In the role of Dix, one patient, encountering a group of women deemed criminally insane, screams, "Oh, what a horrible sight! Why, these people are half-naked! They look starved, and so utterly helpless!" Tracking down their jailer, she cries, "Why, you don't even treat them like human beings!" Dismissing the prisoners as "practically corpses," the callous jailer prompts Dix to devote her life to improving conditions for the mentally ill. Such cruelties as she has seen are, she says, "inhuman"— "And I think something should be done about it!"

Following a few contextualizing words from the narrator, who recapitulates his earlier points about the pedagogic and therapeutic value of acting, the film offers an elaborate reenactment of Dix's impassioned testimony before the Massachusetts state legislature. "I have seen these patients beaten, stripped of their clothing, and chained—put in living quarters not fit for swine!" she cries. "I come as the advocate for the helpless, forgotten, insane and idiotic men and women." Subsequent reenactments depict the founding of St. Elizabeths, with black patients portraying construction workers engaged in the creation of a "new sort of facility," one where all manner of creative endeavors—including documentary film production—may be pursued by the mentally ill. Underscoring this institutional potential, several patients gather to perform an interpretive dance for Dix, the driving force behind a true therapeutic revolution.

Stepping onto the stage where the dance is being performed, the narrator interrupts to remind us that acting is far from the only option available to amateur filmmakers committed to instruction and therapy. Besides, he says, there are time constraints to consider, and they preclude our exposure to the panoply of performance styles open to patients at St. Elizabeths. "Our play takes two hours to tell the full story of what Dorothea Lynde Dix did for us," the narrator informs the camera, somewhat apologetically. "But now that you have seen conditions

FIGURE 19. A hospital patient participates in psychodrama theater in *We, the Mentally Ill . . .* (1955). Courtesy of the U.S. National Library of Medicine.

as they were in her day, let's go to another mental hospital and hear from patients themselves about the conditions common today even at such a progressive place as the New Jersey State Hospital in Trenton." The next segment of *We, the Mentally Ill . . .*, shot on location at the Trenton hospital, features the unscripted testimony of several patients who tell the camera of their troubles. One elderly woman, sitting on her hospital bed, invites us to "come inside and see what I see every day."

What follows is observational footage of the overcrowding that plagues this particular hospital, where staff shortages prevent the adequate treatment of patients, much less the development of the kind of creative pursuits for which St. Elizabeths is known. More than just a legitimate documentary method, "mere" observation reflects the very conditions that characterize the New Jersey State Hospital, where anything more creative than direct testimony is simply impossible. The power of this observational style is evident to the elderly patient, who proclaims, "Now you see what I mean!" Shortly thereafter, however, she qualifies her praise for this form of documentation, claiming that its limitations are largely acoustical—that synch-sound cinematography is not yet sufficiently developed to capture more than just her own testimonial speech. "You don't hear the noises that we hear all day—it rings in your ear all day!" she cries.

Other patients assemble in front of the camera in order to describe their experiences, broadening the scope of this sequence, which seems at once proto-*vérité* and a reminder of such uses of the on-camera, synch-sound interview as Arthur Elton and Edgar Anstey's *Housing Problems*, made for the British Commercial Gas Association in 1935. One patient, an elderly man, describes conditions among the men—some psychotic and destructive, others quietly suicidal, and all of them underfed and underserved. One middle-aged woman evokes the legacy of military psychiatry by describing her own "branch" of the hospital—a run-down "colony" on the outskirts of the facility that was once "temporary housing for the Navy," and that still shows numerous signs of Navy occupancy (including conspicuous insignia from the Second World War). "They moved us out here because it was too crowded in the hospital," she explains, directing the camera to take in just how small this satellite facility is, its main room now a site of the very overcrowding that it was designed to alleviate. Lest we question the accuracy of statements made by "mental patients," a psychiatrist named Bennett appears in order to corroborate such claims, looking into the camera and saying, "I'm one psychiatrist for over six hundred patients. What can you expect?" The wry Dr. Bennett suggests that the problems that dogged military psychiatry throughout the Second World War—especially those related to staff shortages and fundamental disagreements regarding treatment methods—have persisted well into the postwar period, marking the New Jersey State Hospital as a tragically inadequate facility for the treatment of the mentally ill.

Despite these sobering realities, hope marks the horizon of psychiatry in the mid-1950s, as new psychotropic drugs promise relief from innumerable symptoms. Following the film's excursion to New Jersey, the narrator returns to address "positive developments," including those that stand to make up for the continued dearth of psychiatrists in public facilities. "For you, the public, who pay the bills, and for us, the mentally sick," these advances in research offer a reason to resist purely pessimistic narratives about the pervasive "problem" of psychoneurosis. A subsequent observational sequence, filmed at the Manhattan State Hospital, shows the treatment of psychotic patients with new drugs (particularly the antipsychotic Promazine), which restore speech to the mute and make others more "sociable"—and far less agitated. Dr. Herman Denber, a psychiatrist at the hospital, talks to the camera about the significance of new psychotropic drugs: "These new medicines have effected a tremendous change," he says. "As a result of their use, patients who were hitherto unmanageable or untreatable or have resisted all other forms of treatment" can finally be exposed to psychotherapy. "These drugs have given American medicine . . . the greatest opportunity of this age—to reduce the huge burden of mental illness which falls on us all." Back at St. Elizabeths, Dr. Wilfred Overholser, the hospital's superintendent (who headed the national neuropsychiatry committee that advised the military during World War II), testifies to the usefulness of these "new tranquilizing drugs," telling the camera, "We're on the verge of an entirely new era in the treatment of mental illness." At St. Elizabeths, electroshock therapy—a treatment option that, given its gruesome nature, was intentionally left out of the wartime military documentaries made at the hospital—has been "virtually discontinued," as new psychotropic drugs take the place of some of the "harsh" methods of yesteryear. As Dr. Overholser puts it, "the problem of mental disorder, vast as it is, is not an insurmountable one."

As a form of institutional advertising, *We, the Mentally Ill* . . . sought to cultivate faith in psychiatry and appreciation for the progress that Smith, Kline, & French had purportedly brought to the field in the form of drugs like Promazine. But it also forged a powerful link between the pharmaceutical advances of the postwar period and the psychodramatic experiments of the early 1940s, suggesting that the fears of reenactment that often qualified the method's wartime employment in places like St. Elizabeths—the specifically Freudian concern regarding its family resemblance to the repetition compulsion—can be assuaged by the softening influence of new psychotropic drugs. But publicizing Promazine wasn't the only goal of Smith, Kline, & French when it elected to sponsor *We, the Mentally Ill.* . . . By the mid-1950s, the company was widely associated with the epidemic of amphetamine abuse affecting veterans of World War II, who had been prescribed the drug in an effort to boost their "morale" and help them overcome mild "neurotic" depressions. Amphetamine had a disturbingly iatrogenic effect, however: not only did it lead to dependence, it also made anxiety disorders worse. It was partly to escape the taint of amphetamine, the synthetic adrenaline derivative that it had marketed rather aggressively before and during the war, that Smith, Kline, & French sponsored *We, the Mentally Ill* . . ., a mode of corporate social responsibility meant to install a far different image of the Philadelphia-based firm in the public's mind.[107]

In situating the reenactment of Dix's life and career on a continuum that implicitly includes *Combat Fatigue: Irritability* and *The N.P. Patient*, the narrator of *We, the Mentally Ill* . . . makes his case for medication, asking, "What better evidence of [its effectiveness] than mental patients joining tonight with our hospital staff to tell you the history of our past and the hope for our present?" At St. Elizabeths, drama therapy was never entirely dependent upon the use of psychotropic drugs, but Promazine and other medications have, the narrator suggests, enabled greater freedom in the realm of performance, providing the safety net of sedation that military psychiatrists had long sought in the form of group therapy and other methods that, far from disappearing with the rise of Promazine, were simply no longer required as "cushions" for reenactment. If, in the words of one administrator at St. Elizabeths, the hospital is waging "a war against mental disease," drama therapy, when combined with drug treatment, can permit a patient to "work through" this particular war—and on the very stage that Margaret Hagan had helped to construct in 1939. Billed as "the first public program ever enacted and narrated by mental patients," *We, the Mentally Ill* . . . built upon precedents set during the Second World War, and in particular upon the representational styles and mode of address of *The N.P. Patient*, in which a narrator periodically appears onscreen in order to interrupt reenactments designed to instruct as well as to heal.

Such appeals to the didactic and curative powers of acting were pervasive throughout World War II, as military psychiatrists struggled to fuse documentary filmmaking with various forms of therapy. The clinical treatment of war trauma thus provided a major occasion for documentary's ongoing if occasionally controversial embrace of imagination and reconstruction, demonstrating the evidentiary as well as restorative function of acting. Despite its much-discussed centrality to psychiatric treatment, however, film performance represented a point of contention among veterans who struggled to communicate the authenticity of their emotional responses. Appearing in John Huston's Army documentary *Let There Be Light* (1946), which was shot on location at Mason General Hospital in New York, one man begins to cry uncontrollably during an intake interview, prompting a psychiatrist to declare that "a display of emotion is all right" and "sometimes very helpful"—to which the weeping veteran replies, "I'm not doing this deliberately, sir! Please believe me!" In the context of such concerns about credibility, which often doubled as distrust of the documentary legitimacy of certain forms of acting, the art of "playing oneself"—what Joris Ivens (among many others) championed as a vehicle of "authenticity," a tool of social engagement, and an engine of social change—further developed as a key method of rehabilitation and political advocacy.[108]

CHAPTER 5

"Casualties of the Spirit"

Let There Be Light *and Its Contexts*

In the spring of 1945, the War Department announced its intention to oversee the production of a three-part film series that would help veterans secure postwar employment and "make a natural readjustment to civilian life." At the same time, the project—dubbed *The Returning Soldier*—was meant to convince civilians that "returnees will not be a lost [sic] of 'queer cases,' but will be normal Americans who deserve UNDERSTANDING and, in some cases, TACT and TIME."[1] Working closely with the Ad Hoc Committee on Readjustment and Redeployment (part of the Office of the Deputy Chief of Staff for Personnel), the War Department outlined its aims in a memorandum for the Signal Corps, which would be tasked with producing all three films. Emphasizing the War Department's interest in broad spectatorship—in a film series that could educate soldiers as much as civilians, albeit in different ways and to somewhat different ends—the memorandum acknowledges the sheer accessibility and general utility of docudramatic devices, which, in this interpretation, combine fact and fiction in ways meant to guarantee a film's wide exhibition, its appeal to a variety of audience "types." Where a "typical" fiction film, however well-intentioned, might require supplementary pedagogic materials—explanatory pamphlets, perhaps, or contextualizing reviews—in order to promote an understanding of "the facts," *The Returning Soldier* would need to retain the hybridity of many of the military's previous training films, fusing its commitment to veterans with careful attention to the civilian spectators who would soon greet them. Far from ignorant of documentary history and theory, then, the War Department in 1945 seemed to understand the importance of combining various documentary devices (didactic voice-over narration, testimonial interview, staged reenactment, psychodrama) in the representation of war trauma.

"Each part of this film project," the War Department made clear, "is to be a motion picture able to 'stand on its own feet.' In other words, it should be complete within itself and it should not be necessary for an officer to accompany the film when it is shown to the public."[2] Eighteen months later, military police would seize a print of the third and final installment of *The Returning Soldier*, preventing its screening at New York's Museum of Modern Art. The film—John Huston's legendary *Let There Be Light* (1946)—didn't disappear, however. Instead, it immediately entered nontheatrical circulation in a wide range of military and civilian settings, its significance as a document of medical science scarcely in dispute. Standard scholarly accounts of *Let There Be Light* suggest that the film was thoroughly suppressed until 1980, when it was finally granted a commercial public exhibition. Far from hidden, however, the film enjoyed a robust nontheatrical life even as military police stormed MoMA, and its estrangement from commercial cinemas inspired Hollywood to give American spectators a glimpse of its psychiatric subject, translating it into a number of melodramatic, star-centered scenarios.

Let There Be Light records the experiences of several traumatized veterans as they receive a series of psychiatric treatments at Mason General, a military hospital on Long Island, New York. Chief among these treatments is narcosynthesis, described by voice-over narrator Walter Huston as "effective in certain types of acute cases." Involving an intravenous injection of the barbiturate sodium amytal (or any one of a number of other sedatives), narcosynthesis "induces a state similar to hypnosis." As developed by the American psychiatrists Roy Grinker and John Spiegel in Tunisia in the spring of 1943, narcosynthesis was designed to provide a speedy recovery—to enable traumatized soldiers to return to the front as quickly as possible. By relying on sodium amytal and other barbiturates regularly employed as intravenous anesthetics, Grinker and Spiegel ensured that narcosynthesis could be performed by any medical professional; the technique required no familiarity with psychoanalysis.[3] *Let There Be Light* records its use on two occasions, first on a young soldier suffering from "conversion hysteria" (or psychosomatic paralysis), and later on a victim of "battle tension," who stutters uncontrollably. Referring to sodium amytal, Walter Huston's voice-over narration states,

> The use of this drug serves a twofold purpose: like hypnosis, it is a shortcut to the unconscious mind. As the surgeon probes for a bullet, the psychiatrist explores the submerged regions of the mind, attempting to locate and bring to the surface the emotional conflict which is the cause of the patient's distress. The second purpose of this drug is to remove, through suggestion, those symptoms which impede the patient's recovery.

The scenes that feature the use of sodium amytal and the complex process of narcosynthesis are characterized by what Jonathan Kahana has called a "theatrics of psychotherapy." Having "translated into the language of cinema the interrogatory and theatrical techniques of military psychiatry," Huston's film depicts narcosynthesis as "a drug-induced reenactment of the traumatic events" that led to paralysis or stuttering in certain patients at Mason General.[4] Thus even as it lays claim to an observational style, providing the impression of "life caught unawares," *Let There Be Light* showcases the therapeutic potential of reenactment that was so central to military psychiatry as well as to an array of military documentaries in the 1940s.

Let There Be Light was by no means the only such documentary to focus so closely on narcosynthesis as a means of treating war trauma. By 1944, even films produced outside of the armed forces were addressing the procedure, applying the lessons of military psychiatry to various civilian contexts. Produced by the Department of Psychiatry at Bishop Clarkson Memorial Hospital in Omaha, Nebraska, the ten-minute film *Psychoneuroses* (1944) highlights the strategies of Grinker and Spiegel, showing their "civilian uses," particularly in "aid[ing] ventilation of conflict material" and "for relief of anxiety." Arguing that narcosynthesis can reveal "numerous traumatic experiences," the film shows, in observational fashion, the use of sodium pentothal on a series of real patients, from an elderly man who has been displaying "choreic movements" for twenty-four years to an eleven-year-old girl traumatized by her emotionally abusive father. As one title card puts it, narcosynthesis "causes the patient to re-experience emotions originally associated with psychic trauma. The patient synthesizes emotion and memories under light narcosis and develops insight, thus breaking up the neurotic, infantile reactions."

Similar claims are made in several contemporaneous military documentaries. The 1945 Army film *Combat Exhaustion*, a fifty-minute dramatization of "typical psychiatric procedures" that was initially intended for field medics, depicts a military psychiatrist who touts "chemical hypnosis," which, in his words, "produces a state of semi-sleep, or twilight state, in which suggestibility is increased, as it is in true hypnotism." While *Let There Be Light* carefully indicates the partial effectiveness of narcosynthesis—and even its complete ineffectiveness in some cases— through Walter Huston's occasionally equivocating voice-over narration, *Combat Exhaustion* offers the bold claim that the procedure can decisively "cure" psychoneurosis. Both films suggest, however tendentiously, the immediate effectiveness of narcosynthesis; no sooner has a patient received an injection, it seems, than he is able to recover and "work through" the psychic source of his symptoms, shedding those symptoms in a matter of minutes. While Grinker and Spiegel stressed the capacity of narcosynthesis to enable a speedy recovery, they had in mind a few days, not mere minutes.[5] *Let There Be Light* thus appears to take considerable liberties with a procedure that it presents as immediately effective, and it is only through Walter Huston's narration that the film gestures toward what John Hersey, writing in 1945, called "merely a makeshift" procedure, a sort of stopgap:

> As with all tools used in scientific progress, narco-synthesis is used differently by different doctors—naturally with varying results. Consequently, according to their individual experience, various doctors place various degrees of confidence in it, from utmost faith to utter scorn. Narco-synthesis is, in any case, never used alone, but only in conjunction with other techniques of psychotherapy. *It cannot, therefore, be regarded as a cure, but only as a step along the road.*[6]

Despite the seemingly miraculous cures depicted in *Let There Be Light*—each credited to a single session of narcosynthesis—the procedure does not "get at the deeper causes of the illness"; in Hersey's words, it "only hints and points the way for the more time-consuming techniques of psychotherapy."[7] While *Let There Be Light*, like *Combat Exhaustion*, depicts multiple therapeutic strategies (including hypnosis, interviews, Rorschach tests, occupational therapy, and group discussion sessions), it rests on the impression that narcosynthesis can be immediately effective, an impression that both lends the film a strikingly "cinematic" quality and contributes to its strategic valorization of military psychiatry as a near-miraculous profession.

For its part, *Combat Exhaustion*, which reenacts (and thus reproduces) psychiatric instruction, features a scene in which a medical officer reviews "some of the drugs used in narcotherapy and chemical hypnosis." Noting that "the drugs of choice are the barbiturates," he places

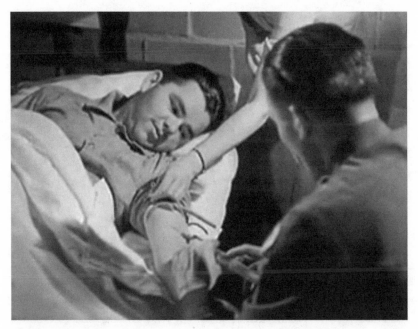

FIGURE 20. A psychiatric patient is given an injection of sodium pentothal in the Army's *Combat Exhaustion* (1945). Courtesy of the U.S. National Library of Medicine.

a heavy emphasis on the effectiveness of sodium amytal ("There's an ample supply of it in your #2 chest," he informs the diegetic and extra-diegetic medical trainees). Complicating the film's condensed dramatization of the value of narcosynthesis, however, he carefully explains that doses of sodium amytal must be "repeated, and the narcosis thus continued as long as necessary": "Patients with fully developed varieties of combat exhaustion will require a *minimum* of twenty-four hours of continuous narcosis; some will require forty-eight to seventy-two hours." The fifty-minute *Combat Exhausion* is at pains to visualize this slow process, however, and it eventually opts for an illustration of "sudden recovery": a patient suffering from back problems of a psychosomatic nature is given an injection of sodium pentothal, after which he is able to recall the source of his trauma—an especially frightening combat experience—and agree, at the prompting of a psychiatrist, that his symptoms have no "organic basis."

If this brief depiction of "successful narcosynthesis" suggests that the procedure can be immediately effective, the dialogue track and voice-over narration provide a contrasting impression. Thus despite the economy of

FIGURE 21. A medical officer interacts with a patient in the Army's *Combat Exhaustion* (1945). Courtesy of the U.S. National Library of Medicine.

its visual storytelling—a trait that it shares with the skillfully edited *Let There Be Light*—*Combat Exhaustion* can hardly be said to offer an unqualified endorsement of narcosynthesis as an agent of rapid psychic recovery. "Sometimes it is necessary to coax the patient to relive the stresses which produced his hysteria, but it is more common for it to happen spontaneously, as it did here," claims the on-camera psychiatrist, pointing to his patient and praising the capacity of sodium pentothal to "restore memory." Emphasizing the traumatic dimensions of this "retrieved" memory, the psychiatrist says, "Now he has it off his chest, and this is the time for suggestive therapy." He proceeds to "feed lines" to the patient: "Your back is straight and strong! Your back is fine and straight!"

While the film risks accentuating its own docudramatic stiltedness at such histrionic moments, it also evokes many of the arguments of Grinker and Spiegel, particularly their claim that, in order for narcosynthesis to work effectively, the administering physician may need to "act out" various scenarios and thereby "trigger" additional responses from the patient. At one point in *Combat Exhaustion*, the psychiatrist pretends to be a commanding officer, ordering his patient to "walk like a soldier!" The ploy works: the young man, still under the influence of sodium pentothal, follows the order, his posture finally restored to "normal." "Treatment is not complete in this case," the psychiatrist then warns, calmly explaining that a "general reconditioning program" will be required to give the patient confidence and to "complete what we started here this morning."

If *Let There Be Light* seems, by contrast, positively Hollywoodian in its polished, economical presentation of purported psychiatric triumphs, the film's partly observational, proto-*vérité* style suggests authenticity of a different sort, one that sets it apart from the rather stagy docudrama of *Combat Exhaustion*. Through its diverse documentary devices, *Let There Be Light* helped both to crystalize and to catalyze representations of combat trauma in the military as well as in Hollywood, serving as a key (if somewhat occluded) mediator between the two institutions.[8] But it was far from the only military-produced documentary of the period to grapple, in observational fashion, with the effects of combat trauma, recording various therapeutic methods and enjoying a broad nontheatrical exhibition. Its institutional and filmic contexts form the subject of this chapter.

THE LEGEND OF *LET THERE BE LIGHT*

Long mythologized as "too strong for the army,"[9] "too much for the Army,"[10] "*too* effective. . .so powerful that the army decided to suppress it,"[11] "too disturbing,"[12] "too unsettling,"[13] and "so shock[ing],"[14] *Let There Be Light* is widely believed to have been "suppressed because it documented . . . psychiatric treatment"—as though no other military documentary had done the same.[15] James Agee established the tenor of accounts to come when, in May 1946, he wrote, "John Huston's *Let There Be Light*, a fine, terrible, valuable non-fiction film about psychoneurotic soldiers, has been forbidden civilian circulation by the War Department."[16] Writing in the early 1950s, Richard Griffith went so far as to claim, with no evidence, that the War Department "never intended a film of this sort to be made anyway, that Huston 'pulled a fast one.'"[17] (Griffith would have done well to consult the widely read publications of William C. Menninger, "undoubtedly the most influential psychiatrist during the war and the immediate postwar era," who monitored the production of Huston's film and heartily approved the finished product.)[18] The legend of *Let There Be Light* thus depends upon ignorance of nontheatrical nonfiction film—and of the military's Psychiatric Film

Program in particular—in order to sustain it. Only Elaine Showalter, in her controversial *Hystories*, manages to suggest (albeit in passing and without explicit reference to nontheatrical distribution) the wide and immediate influence of *Let There Be Light*, writing that the film "helped change public attitudes about the legitimacy of war neurosis and the efficacy of psychiatric treatment."[19]

Even when other military documentaries are cited in scholarly and popular writings (which is rare enough in itself), they are typically linked to *Let There Be Light* as a sort of urtext—the singular source of things to come. Not only did similar works long predate the film, but later documentaries that are said to be indebted to *Let There Be Light*— such as the Army's *Shades of Gray* (1947), long if somewhat incorrectly understood as a remake of Huston's film—are equally indebted to the Navy's *The Inside Story of Seaman Jones* (1944) and the Army's *Psychiatric Procedures in the Combat Area* (1944).[20] In fact, *Shades of Gray* remakes aspects of all three documentaries (along with parts of the Navy's *The N.P. Patient* [1944]), with *Let There Be Light* providing the inspiration for less than 10 percent of the film's total running time.

Retrospectively deemed "too raw and too powerful for its time," Huston's film has long been held captive by a myth that insists on its having "opened a whole Pandora's box of the evils of war"—a box that had to be shut quickly, and left entirely unopened until 1980.[21] In reality, however, this carefully commissioned film received an abundance of praise from the military establishment, which received it as a major contribution to a long line of institutional documentaries whose production had begun several years earlier. When George S. Goldman, the military psychiatrist who had overseen the military's Psychiatric Film Program from the Office of the Surgeon General, was awarded the Army Commendation Ribbon in 1946, the citation referred to *Let There Be Light* as a "remarkably successful psychiatric film"—one of which the Army could be proud.[22] Unaware of this history—or simply unwilling to admit its significance—scholars have painted a quaint portrait of Huston as a heroic genius, cannily capable of circumventing the military's restrictions on representation only to see his film punitively shelved for decades.

Let There Be Light has long been used to prop up a false dichotomy rooted in ignorance of the military's complex coding and classification systems, which situate information on a continuum at the extreme ends of which are such familiar categories as "declassified" and "top secret." In military terms, films can be suppressed—or shared—by degrees. For

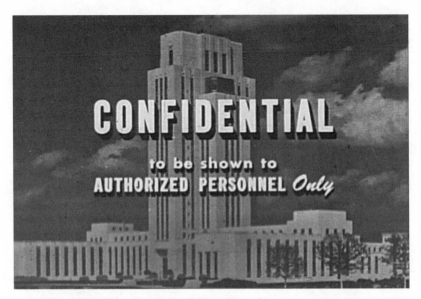

FIGURE 22. The Navy's *The N.P. Patient* (1944) was initially classified as "confidential," which limited its distribution to the service's patients and medical professionals (including social workers). Courtesy of the U.S. National Library of Medicine.

example, to label something "confidential" is to give it a lower classification than "top secret." By this institutional logic, "confidential" information can be leaked to the press or otherwise shared under a public-relations rubric that respects the anonymity of military sources and other participants while ostensibly satisfying a certain, generalized "right to know."[23] This was the institutional context in which *Let There Be Light* circulated as early as the spring of 1946. As a noncommercial product whose exhibition would not require standard forms of publicity, with their commitment to crude forms of identification, Huston's film was relatively free to be distributed nontheatrically, provided some pedagogic or therapeutic justification for its exhibition could be supplied. Accounts of the film's "shocking" effect on spectators appear to be largely apocryphal: *Let There Be Light* echoed such earlier (and equally widely distributed) Army documentaries as *Psychiatric Procedures in the Combat Area* and *Combat Exhaustion*—not to mention a host of films produced by the Navy and imported from the British military—and archival evidence suggests that even civilian audiences, viewing the film in 1946, were well prepared for its depictions of traumatized veterans.[24]

First-person accounts of war trauma, such as the often-wrenching testimonials that punctuate *Let There Be Light*, were hardly new to the American public in 1946. A quarter-century earlier, *The Atlantic Monthly* had published an eleven-page testimonial by an anonymous veteran of World War I, who described his traumatic symptoms (auditory hallucinations, dizziness, insomnia, extreme fatigue), his treatment at Walter Reed Hospital, and his interest in inspiring Americans to better understand—and even directly assist—the "shell-shocked."[25] The article was quickly adopted by medical educators as a supplementary guide to war trauma, much as such professionals would later adopt films like *Psychiatric Procedures in the Combat Area* and *Let There Be Light* for use in classes and symposia. In the spring of 1946, the Veterans Administration (VA) obtained the negative of *Let There Be Light*, from which it would strike hundreds of prints for use in medical facilities and training centers across the country. With professional training "the most pressing medical problem" facing the VA—at least according to the agency's chief of psychiatry—documentary films in general, and *Let There Be Light* in particular, were heartily embraced as teaching tools.[26] Precisely because of its observational character, Huston's film, like the equally observational *Psychiatric Procedures*, proved especially useful: by shooting actual patients rather than actors, Huston provided a proto-*vérité* record of numerous symptoms (including, significantly, those that *Let There Be Light* does not actually identify but that were recognizable to psychiatrists trained to discern the telltale signs of particular "trauma reactions"). When, in March of 1946, the War Department ordered the Signal Corps to ship the negative of *Let There Be Light* to the VA, the agency was just launching an "ambitious four-year training program in clinical psychology," one designed to "train two hundred individuals in twenty-two different universities."[27] The VA was thus able to strike prints of Huston's film for use at these universities, as well as in any number of other facilities where clinicians received training.

The pronounced pedagogic utility of *Let There Be Light* derived from the film's partly observational character, as numerous medical professionals pointed out as early as 1946. In 1953, after the film had been in circulation for seven years, a team of physicians and medical educators highlighted this aspect of *Let There Be Light*, reserving special praise for the filmmakers' refusal to replace actual patients with actors— a decision that would, of course, prove intensely controversial. "A perfect synthesis of visual and verbal elements occurs in John Huston's

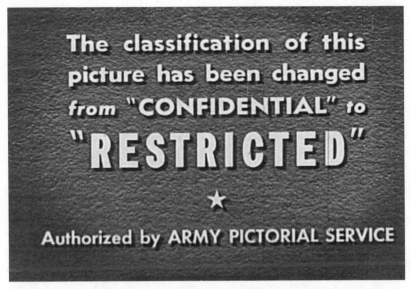

The classification of this picture has been changed from "CONFIDENTIAL" to "RESTRICTED"

★

Authorized by ARMY PICTORIAL SERVICE

FIGURE 23. The classification of Navy's *The N.P. Patient* (1944) was changed from "confidential" to "restricted" in 1945, which meant that it could be distributed to medical groups, journalists, and other "interested parties" outside of the Navy; its "restriction" was merely to noncommercial contexts. Courtesy of the U.S. National Library of Medicine.

Let There Be Light," they wrote. "Here, in unrehearsed interview and treatment episodes, a searching and knowing camera caught a wide range of emotional disturbance and recovery." The writers were hardly naïve, however, and they would go on to acknowledge "the way in which the filmmaking procedure itself affects the actions of the filmed subject, and thereby the authenticity of the phenomena to be recorded." In their estimation, "certain types of mental patients appear indifferent to this procedure," and "those in *Let There Be Light* behave as if they were alone with the psychiatrist." The writers recognized the value of reenactment, highlighting its role in a number of other "psychiatric documentaries." Of course, they maintained, "actual violent or suicidal patients could hardly be used for systematic demonstrations of physical restraint procedures," and the depiction of cases "more severe" than those shown in Huston's film "obviously requires re-enactment."[28] Arguing that the "non-re-enacted" *Let There Be Light* offers "a powerfully motivating experience," the writers concluded that it remained, in 1953, "of sufficient scientific validity to justify its use as an instructional tool for professionally interested groups."[29]

Such groups were hardly confined to medical educators. Indeed, a growing number of audience "types" were engaging with *Let There Be Light* by the early 1950s. As the abovementioned manual pointed out, the film's "authorized" audience included "physicians in general, psychiatrists, residents in psychiatry, medical students and interns, nurses, psychiatric hospital personnel, psychologists and students of clinical psychology, social workers and students in the field, occupational therapists, personnel supervisors, and civic groups."[30] Given the dramatic postwar growth of psychiatry and psychology, it is reasonable to surmise that (at the very least) tens of thousands of Americans watched *Let There Be Light* in the immediate postwar period. That these spectators included members of "civic groups" is telling—a reminder that Huston's film was hardly "kept from the general public" but was, instead, strategically disseminated to many noncommercial formations of this public. "Non-medical or non-scientific groups" had only to request "special permission to use the film"—requests that were often effectively couched in terms of the public "right to know," or that expressed grave concerns about the lasting effects of war trauma. All such public groups were instructed to "address loan requests" to the Surgeon General, "according to location of film user." Any one of the six officer branches of the Army Medical Department—located in New York, Maryland, Georgia, Texas, Illinois, and California—could, and often did, provide the film on a temporary loan basis.[31]

Still other groups were able to purchase their own prints of *Let There Be Light* directly from the VA. These included, perhaps most significantly, the executive branch of the government of Minnesota. Beginning in 1947 (the year he was inaugurated), Governor Luther Youngdahl, hoping to cultivate popular support for a new mental-health program, "toured the state" with *Let There Be Light*, prints of which his administration received from the VA. The film was billed as a "special attraction" at, among other locations, a St. Paul hotel where large crowds of state legislators and their constituents gathered to watch Huston's documentary, the better to understand Youngdahl's plans for improving medical facilities (for which, in the governor's estimation, Mason General provided a model).[32] Youngdahl's public uses of *Let There Be Light*, which exposed the film to thousands of Minnesotans between 1947 and 1951, were hardly unique. In the first few years following the film's completion, the Mental Hygiene Association of Westchester County hosted public screenings of *Let There Be Light*, all of them premised on the notion that it could help audiences understand the importance of seeking psychiatric treatment for their "troubles." Promoting "mental hygiene as a community project," the association adopted several other military documentaries (including *Introduction to Combat Fatigue* and *The Inside Story of Seaman Jones*) as models for how to think and talk about mental illness and psychotherapy.[33]

The comprehensibility of *Let There Be Light* to non-specialist audiences was arguably abetted by a number of Hollywood fiction films that sought to dramatically condense aspects of Huston's subject— particularly the significance of narcosynthesis and its reliance on drugs like sodium pentothal.[34] Numerous films produced between 1938 and 1958 present pentothal as a near-miraculous means of accessing traumatic pasts. These include the RKO musical *Carefree* (Mark Sandrich, 1938), staring Fred Astaire and Ginger Rogers; Curtis Bernhardt's *High Wall* (1947), which focuses, in *noir* fashion, on a traumatized veteran of the Army Air Forces who reluctantly undergoes narcosynthesis; Bernhardt's *Possessed* (1947), which allegorizes combat trauma through its melodramatic emphasis on love as a "battlefield" that sends a woman to a mental hospital; *The Snake Pit* (Anatole Litvak, 1948), which was partly shot on location at the Camarillo State Hospital in California, and which was produced with the cooperation of multiple practicing psychiatrists, eventually receiving endorsements from the Committee of American Psychologists and the California Citizens Committee for Mental Hygiene; *Home of the Brave* (Mark Robson, 1949), based on Arthur Laurents' 1946 play; the low-budget *The Judge* (Elmer Clifton, 1949), from Ida Lupino's Emerald Productions, in which a psychiatrist cheerfully refers to pentothal as "the stuff we started using during the war"; and *Harvey*, which allegorizes the drug as the fantastical "Formula Number 977"—a "special serum" that promises to "shock" the title character "back to reality." Described as "the truth serum" in *Kiss Me Deadly* (Robert Aldrich, 1955) and "that truth stuff" in *Touch of Evil* (Orson Welles, 1958), pentothal is presented as potentially fatal in the reactionary thriller *Big Jim McLain* (Edward Ludwig, 1952), which stars John Wayne as an investigator for the House Un-American Activities Committee, and which depicts the deadly misuse of pentothal—and of the lessons of wartime military psychiatry more generally—by the members of a communist cell in Hawaii. Jacques Tourneur's *Night of the Demon* (1957) similarly warns against narcosynthesis. It features a man who, severely traumatized by his exposure to witchcraft, "has lost all contact with reality" and "fails to respond to any normal stimulation"; in "a state of absolute catatonic immobility," he is given an injection of sodium pentothal, which immediately "awakens" him but proves too effective, triggering a panic attack that leads to suicide. Tourneur's film thus evokes the claims of psychiatrist M. Ralph Kaufman and other prominent detractors, who warned that narcosynthesis could, in some instances, actually create or exacerbate anxiety.[35] In the science fiction films *Them!* (Gordon Douglas, 1954) and *The Angry Red Planet* (Ib Melchior, 1959), however, narcosynthesis is upheld as a miraculous procedure—a means of restoring speech in the former, and humanity's "only hope" in the latter.[36]

That all of these films focus on pentothal at the expense of amytal is telling, recalling some of the representational devices of the Army's *Combat Exhaustion*.[37] Expressing a preference for pentothal over amytal, Army psychiatrist Alfred O. Ludwig offered a vivid description of barbiturate abreaction, whose purpose, he claimed, was to "recall to the patient the original traumatic situation in battle":

> [The patient] was told that he was again on the battlefield, and the statement was reinforced by loud warning, such as 'Look out,' or 'Watch those shells,' or 'Duck,' or by whistling to mimic approaching shells and jarring the cot [on which the patient lay]. Usually the patient responded with a dramatic startle pattern, cowered on the couch, sought cover, and at times jumped to the floor to dig in or take flight. He then relived his battle experiences and talked to the therapist as if he were some officer or comrade who was with him at the time. Such recitals, *highly realistic and dramatic*, were often accompanied by a great outburst of emotion and expressions of resentment, hatred, or previously suppressed fear.[38]

A number of military films, from *Psychiatric Procedures in the Combat Area* to *Let There Be Light*, emphasize this "realistic and dramatic" process, presenting it as analogous to various documentary techniques. *Let There Be Light* goes so far as to confine the "recitals" that Ludwig describes—the dramatic recreations of "battle experiences"—to Walter Huston's voice-over commentary, as when Huston powerfully recreates the sibilant menace of German artillery fire ("*ss-ss-ss-ss-ss*"). No therapist who appears in the film actually engages in the transformative, role-playing recreation of combat; all such men instead preserve the boundaries between past and present, patient and therapist, thus allowing the documentary form itself to express some of the distinction-blurring complexities of treatment—outsourcing them to Walter Huston, as it were.

However widely used—and however widely represented on film—pentothal was not universally praised by military psychiatrists. M. Ralph Kaufman, the psychoanalyst who co-directed the 1945 documentary

Hypnosis: Okinawa, was an increasingly outspoken critic of pentothal and other sedative-hypnotic drugs, which, he believed, actually impeded the recovery of traumatic memory by engendering lethargy and confusion.[39] In charge of psychiatry during the 10th Army's campaign against the Japanese, Kaufman studiously applied the lessons of Roy Grinker and John Spiegel, consistently leaning on sodium pentothal until one patient, awaiting an injection of the drug, began to "open up" on his own, leading Kaufman to renounce narcohypnosis in favor of "natural" hypnosis.[40] It was the latter procedure, which relied solely upon suggestion, that Kaufman and Lindsay Beaton placed at the center of their film *Hypnosis: Okinawa*, which thus served, in a sense, to rebut *Let There Be Light* in advance of the latter film's production, suggesting that barbiturates could, in contrast to their growing reputation as "memory drugs," in fact exacerbate amnesia.[41]

Kaufman and Beaton were hardly alone in questioning the usefulness of barbiturates, and their pronounced hostility to pentothal, which took at least an hour to administer, helps explain the zeal with which so many fiction and nonfiction films propagandized on behalf of the drug during and after the war. As Alison Winter argues, the "filmlike" aspects of memory's sudden activation—the triggering of "flashbacks" through barbiturate abreaction—rendered narcosynthesis especially amenable to cinematic representation.[42] Planned as a documentary on "narcohypnosis," the British film *The Seventh Veil* (Compton Bennett, 1945) ultimately became a fictional thriller that doubled as an advertisement for the procedure. The Oscar-winning screenplay goes so far as to highlight its "curative" potential, as naysayers are forced to "come around." *High Wall*, *Possessed*, and *The Snake Pit* (among many other Hollywood films) similarly contest Kaufman's claims about the iatrogenic effects of sodium pentothal, not only upholding narcosynthesis as an effective engine for the recovery of traumatic memory, but also presenting it as a most humane treatment method. Tendentiously ignoring Kaufman's emphasis on the effectiveness of drug-free hypnosis, these films suggested that to disallow barbiturate abreaction was to open the door to such gruesome, potentially deadly procedures as insulin-coma therapy and electroshock treatment.

With its reliance on (relatively) abundantly available drugs, narcosynthesis was, fundamentally, a response to wartime psychiatric shortages. "Like some other therapeutic achievements," noted William C. Menninger, "its development was related to the fact that there never were nearly enough psychiatrists. . . . Psychotherapy under sedation was a short cut, a time-saving device."[43] A number of documentary films continued to couch it as such well into the 1950s. For instance, *We, the Mentally Ill* . . . (1955)—portions of which were shot, in proto-*vérité* style, at the crowded, understaffed Manhattan State Hospital—records the experiences of a patient named Sally, whose symptoms include a speech disorder. Produced with support from the American Medical Association, which organized screenings of *Let There Be Light* as early as 1946, *We, the Mentally Ill* . . . vividly evokes Huston's film in its depiction of the sheer tongue-loosening utility of narcosynthesis, even as it shows how drugs like pentothal and amytal are gradually being replaced by more "advanced medications" like Promazine and other antipsychotics. The film's claims about the remarkable effectiveness of these drugs is unsurprising, given that it was sponsored by the pharmaceutical company Smith, Kline, & French, but they recall the occasionally hyperbolic faith that some military psychiatrists placed in pentothal and amytal during World War II. Alfred Ludwig, for instance, claimed that pentothal was effective on a whopping 95 percent of the Army patients on which it was used, but others disagreed, with some military psychiatrists pointing out that the recovery of traumatic memory hardly guaranteed relief from "chronic and acute anxiety states resulting from combat."[44]

As Abram Kardiner and Herbert Spiegel noted in 1947, pentothal was far from the "wonder drug" that Hollywood films were portraying: "The drug acts as an anesthetic for the operation. It is not the cure."[45] Spiegel, then an instructor in the School of Military Neuropsychiatry at Mason General, had reason to critique the growing cultural emphasis on narcosynthesis, having witnessed firsthand Huston's disproportionate focus on the procedure during the making of *Let There Be Light*. Never a fan of Huston's film, Spiegel's dissenting opinion regarding its documentary value was reflected in the closing paragraph of the second edition of the book *War Stress and Neurotic Illness*, which he co-authored with Kardiner in 1947: "There is still too little knowledge of psychodynamics and too much reliance upon the barbiturate interview. Claims for the latter in producing effective and permanent cures seem at present indications to have been greatly exaggerated."[46] These words appear, however indirectly, to damn not just Huston's optimistic film but also the institutional routines that it uncritically recorded. For Spiegel, Huston erred not merely in contributing to the myopic valorization of barbiturate abreaction that had begun, in earnest, in the 1930s (as the film *Carefree* so vividly attests), but also in centralizing it at the expense of a range of other procedures more commonly carried out at Mason General, such as the sort of hypnosis in which Spiegel himself specialized, and which he had developed while serving as a battalion surgeon with the First Infantry in North Africa. (Huston's film does include a seven-minute scene in which the Army psychiatrist Benjamin Simon performs hypnosis on an amnesiac survivor of the Battle of Okinawa.) Thanks to Spiegel's efforts, *Shades of Gray*, a brief portion of which is an almost shot-by-shot remake of *Let There Be Light*, offers a somewhat less resounding endorsement of narcosynthesis, as the narrator makes clear that it is "*not* a magic cure-all."

Huston was hardly alone in offering so disproportionate a focus on narcosynthesis. Far from a pioneering work, *Let There Be Light* merely restaged incidents and recapitulated claims familiar from earlier documentary films, including those imported from Britain, which similarly insisted on the dramatic power of barbiturate abreaction. *Neuropsychiatry 1943* (Michael Hankinson, 1943), which, along with the aforementioned *Combat Exhaustion*, had become a staple teaching tool at Mason General by 1944, provided a clear road map for Huston and his associates, including Signal Corps Captain Charles Kaufman.[47] Indeed, each iteration of the script by Huston and Kaufman—including those scribbled in pencil on hotel stationery—reads like a deliberate retread of *Neuropsychiatry 1943*. Take, for instance, the latter film's voice-over narration, which clearly anticipates the audio track that Walter Huston would record on Stage C at the Signal Corps Photographic Center on October 30, 1945: "Narco-analysis is reserved for hysterical patients with acute memory disturbances or conversion symptoms. This man has such a severe hysterical stammer that he's almost mute." "Narco-analysis"—the term coined by British psychiatrist John Stephen Horsley in the mid-1930s and later "Americanized" by Grinker and Spiegel as "narcosynthesis"—effectively "loosens [the patient's] tongue," allowing him to recite the days of the week at the prompting of his doctor, who explains, "You're speaking perfectly well, and that is because you're now properly relaxed."[48] The narrator then cautions that "the removal of the symptom by this means is only a prelude to dealing with the difficulties that caused it. If these difficulties are not resolved, the patient will break down again." In *Let There Be Light*, Walter Huston's reminder that a successful session of narcosynthesis "does not mean that [the patient's] neurosis has been cured," but merely that "the way has been opened for the therapy to follow," clearly echoes this aspect of *Neuropsychiatry 1943*.

Perhaps the most striking resemblance between the two films lies in their depiction of "hysterically paralyzed" men who learn to walk again while under the influence of barbiturates. In *Neuropsychiatry 1943*, a timid young man—described by the narrator as "very dependent on his family," is also described as having been unable to adjust to life in the Army. Eventually, "hysterical symptoms supervened in the form of a weakness and tremor in the left leg." As a result, the patient is barely able to walk, much like Robert Gerardi, the young man who, in Huston's film, suffers from "conversion hysteria." In both films, narcosynthesis leads to unexpectedly fluent strides around the treatment room, as the narrator intervenes to explain that time-consuming psychoanalysis must follow this sudden ambulatory success.[49] In appearing to remake this sequence of *Neuropsychiatry 1943*, *Let There Be Light* also replays a climactic episode of *Combat Exhaustion*, in which narcosynthesis helps a "hysterically paralyzed" veteran "walk like a soldier," as well as several sequences from *Psychiatric Procedures in the Combat Area*, including a long take of an actual patient undergoing narcosynthesis— and, like Gerardi in Huston's film, expressing anxiety at the sight of a hypodermic needle.

Huston's reiteration of these earlier military documentaries was standard practice, but it still rankled some at the Signal Corps—particularly those who had, in 1944, faced hostile members of the House of Representatives Committee on Appropriations, many of whom were committed to "exposing" redundancies in state-sponsored filmmaking. While conservative opponents of the military's documentary enterprise wanted it scrapped altogether, believing that works produced by commercial newsreel companies could suffice as teaching tools, others were simply aware of the many psychiatric methods, traumatic symptoms, and inspirational strategies that were *not* being reflected in film after film about the "miracle" of narcosynthesis.[50] Rather than peddling the conservative preference for, say, the privately financed *The Returning Veteran* (a *March of Time* entry from 1945) over the state-sponsored *Let There Be Light*, these men tried to prevent the latter from being produced at all, hoping to replace it with a project that would cover something other than well-trodden territory.

RESISTING REDUNDANCY

When the War Department summarized its plans for *The Returning Soldier* in the spring of 1945, it made no mention of previous military documentaries on the subject of readjustment. Paying particular attention to "the exaggerated picture that has already been given to the public through the press, magazine and radio stories," the War Department memorandum omitted cinematic precedents altogether—including the military's own.[51] One week earlier, however, a Signal Corps official, aware of the War Department's plans, had prepared a statement on "overlapping projects"—those military documentaries that "already did" what *The Returning Soldier*, in its three parts, was supposed to do. Decrying "the number of directives received from different agencies of the War Department"—the many bureaucratic entanglements that seemed to preclude clear communication—the Signal Corps official, Colonel Emanuel Cohen, endeavored to explain why *The Returning Soldier*, as planned, would be nothing short of redundant. Cohen's complaint would later be echoed by those for whom *Let There Be Light*, far from a path-breaking work of heroic auteurism, was merely the latest in a long line of films about the treatment of traumatized veterans. The War Department was requesting three films—one on "the average returnee," one on "the physically wounded," and one on "the nervously wounded (or psychoneurotic)"—despite the fact that, as Cohen made clear, all three subjects had already been abundantly covered by the Signal Corps alone, a reality that seemed to elude the strategically amnesiac War Department in its zealous planning for *The Returning Soldier*.[52]

As an executive producer of documentaries for the Signal Corps, Cohen understood just how frequently and just how thoroughly (within certain institutional constraints) his own division had tackled the subject of the returning soldier—both the "normal" man and his "nervously wounded" counterpart—in films earmarked for military and, eventually, civilian audiences. In a report to Colonel Edward L. Munson, chief of the Army Pictorial Service, Cohen addressed each of the War Department's specific aims, explaining the costly redundancies that would result from the realization of those aims.[53] The War Department, in the words of Major A.M. Whitlock, wanted the first film in its requested series to "give a clear and honest picture of the average men and women who will be returning from the Army to civilian life"; to "point out emphatically that the large majority will <u>not</u> be abnormal, that they will <u>not</u> be fundamentally changed"; and, perhaps most importantly, to emphasize that "the returnees will be [the] greatest single potential pool of high-grade employees for years to come," and that, even though "a small proportion will be nervously wounded" and "physically maimed," all will have acquired considerable practical skills, making them "the hope of every American community and business of the future."[54] According to Cohen, all of these claims had been covered in a series of educational filmstrips that the Signal Corps had produced in 1944, as well as in the Pathé documentary *Honorable Discharge* (1944), which was produced in collaboration with the War Department and received a commercial public release. Furthermore, no fewer than five films "on the problem of getting jobs" had been made for the Army's Information and Education Division, and the subject of post-service employment was similarly covered in the 1944 Signal Corps documentary *He Has Seen War*, which also, for good measure, addressed the incidence of psychoneurosis among combat veterans, identifying the sight of death as one of its primary sources.[55]

If the Signal Corps filmstrips had received a relatively limited distribution—and were seen to lack the artistry and emotional persuasiveness of moving pictures—a film like *He Has Seen War* was granted a wide circulation so as to encourage military and civilian spectators to dispense with the negative stereotypes associated with "shellshock" and other ailments. Indeed, *He Has Seen War* was frequently distributed "to special groups in order to enlist their interest in the returning soldier," and it became a key part of campaigns to "assuage" and "reassure"—to "counsel" potential employers frightened of possibly "damaged" veterans.[56] The rhetoric surrounding *He Has Seen War* suggests that, in the military's own view, such employers were as much in need of a therapeutic intervention as psychoneurotic soldiers. Documentary film—a category broad enough to encompass artistry and emotionality as well as instruction and attention to "practical matters"—was seen as a key vehicle of such intervention, a way of helping soldiers by "adjusting" those who might squeamishly resist their return to civilian life.[57]

In May 1945, just as the War Department was issuing its instructions for *The Returning Soldier*, *The March of Time* released *The Returning Veteran*, a short film that examines the importance of psychiatry not merely for demobilization but also for the veteran's life thereafter. It begins with a long shot of a train speeding through a wintry landscape, accompanied by dramatic music that further evokes the then-popular suspicion that demobilization may have been occurring, as James T. Sparrow puts it, "at a pace that was only just shy of ruinous."[58] But the rushing train is soon replaced by a shot of two men seated at a conference table, one of them a psychiatrist and the other a journalist. Evoking the Griersonian conception of documentary as a journalistic vehicle through which specialist knowledge may reach a broad public, it is the latter's job to transcribe and disseminate the statements of the former, which include the following: "We psychiatrists have a much tougher time trying to persuade employers to use our patients"—that is, to hire them despite their having undergone psychiatric treatment.

Referring to "a boy I'm working with now," the psychiatrist explains that this "boy" saw combat in the Pacific, experiencing an "acute traumatic shock" that required immediate treatment in the field. As the psychiatrist, who is played by an actor, explains the case in voice-over, the film incorporates both actual combat footage and staged reenactments, shifting from images of the physically wounded (sourced from the archives of *The March of Time*) to those of the emotionally distressed (simulated on the producer's sound stages). *The Returning Veteran* offers a complex recreation of the process by which a particular field psychiatrist, confronted with a combat-traumatized soldier, would attempt to ease the man's symptoms and facilitate his transportation back to the United States and a more adequate psychiatric facility. The film's reenactments show the psychiatrist administering to a helpless young man who stares blankly into the distance, as the doctor's voice-over explains that this treatment "patched him up wonderfully—uh, mentally—but, of course, that was only temporary." Sent back home, the soldier was finally given "the right psychotherapy and recreation," and "the trick was turned." In the next shot, the soldier, now as accustomed to advanced psychotherapeutic treatment as even the most privileged of civilians, is seen reading Hugo Münsterberg's *Psychology and Life*, first published in 1899. "He was in no condition to go back to the Army, but he was perfectly capable of functioning in civilian life as well as many people," claims the psychiatrist, who proceeds to detail the prejudices that the young man continued to face—particularly from potential employers:

> The word got around town that he had been in a mental hospital. Wherever he went looking for work, he was turned down. People got the idea that he was mentally unbalanced. Now, that's wrong! Right now, this boy still comes to visit me in my office, simply because he feels the need of someone with whom he can discuss his emotional upsets—someone who will understand his moods and his fears and make him understand them too. Most civilians have no idea of the effect of the tremendous pressure of modern warfare, and the horrors these boys have experienced.

As the psychiatrist speaks these words, the film incorporates close-ups of the veteran as he sweats profusely, tossing and turning on the analyst's couch. The film then transitions, via a lap dissolve, into the

FIGURE 24. A psychiatric patient reads Hugo Münsterberg's *Psychology and Life* in the *March of Time* short *The Returning Veteran* (1945). Courtesy of the National Archives and Records Administration.

scenes playing out in the young man's mind—scenes that unfold in typical *March of Time* style, as a combination of actual combat footage and reenactments. Guns are fired. Bombs explode. Tanks roll across a desolate landscape, loud and threatening. Men land on the beaches of the Pacific Theater, encountering Japanese corpses stiffly stuck in the sand. Flames are thrown, transforming the landscape into a vision of hell. "The things this boy has gone through will remain in his mind for years to come," claims the psychiatrist in voice-over. "He'll have bad days occasionally—who doesn't?" With this rhetorical question, the psychiatrist emphasizes the essential psychic continuity between soldiers and civilians—something that Emanuel Cohen would stress in his response to the War Department's unintentionally pathologizing approach to the "nervously wounded."

The stakes of such an approach are made clear in *The Returning Veteran*, as the psychiatrist describes the difficulty of convincing employers to accept those ex-servicemen who seem "different":

When I went to see this boy's former employer, I had to use some pretty high-powered salesmanship to get him to agree to take my patient back at all. Finally he gave in and now he admits that this boy is one of the best men he has. And what's more, this boy's success in his job is helping to improve his adjustment. It's remarkable, you know, the powers of adjustment we all have, no matter what's happened to us.

With these words, the film confirms its commitment to presenting the "psychologistic" equivalence between soldiers—even combat-traumatized ones—and civilians, as it inveighs against the unreasonable prejudice of employers, echoing a host of similarly themed military documentaries. "I think I could do machine-shop work all right if they'd just give me a chance," proclaims a character in the Navy's *Combat Fatigue: Assignment Home* (1945), discussing the prejudices that he faces as a former neuropsychiatric patient. "That's where the rub comes in." For its part, the VA documentary *What's My Score?* (1946) follows a group of disabled ex-servicemen as they travel to New York City to demonstrate their skills before six hundred "top men in industry." As the film's voice-over narrator puts it, disabled veterans are "ready for all kinds of jobs"; "all they're asking is a chance to prove it—prove it to you." Despite their verifiable accomplishments, such men continue to be the victims of discrimination—a state of affairs that *What's My Score?* was intended to help transform. Released five years earlier, the thriller *The Face Behind the Mask* (Robert Florey, 1941), which opens with a message about the traumatic experiences of refugees from Hitler's Europe, presciently allegorizes this predicament in its depiction of a Hungarian immigrant—an Army veteran, former factory worker, and self-proclaimed "mechanical genius," played by Peter Lorre—who is cruelly refused employment after his face is badly burned in a hotel fire. (Ironically, Lorre had earlier played a surgeon who "cures mutilated soldiers" in the horror film *Mad Love* [Karl Freund, 1935].) Like *The Face Behind the Mask*, *The Returning Veteran* advocates compassion in the "handling" of those traumatized either visibly or invisibly, pushing for more "humane" hiring practices.

Completely ignoring the widely distributed interventions of *The March of Time*, the War Department—which had, in fact, authorized and assisted the production of *The Returning Veteran*—explained in the spring of 1945 that the third and final film in the Army's *Returning Soldier* series would need to address the precise relationship between combat and psychoneurosis, the better to clarify the condition's anomalous contours while still endeavoring to de-stigmatize it. For the War Department, a "film on the nervously wounded (or psychoneurotic)" veteran would need to point out that only "a small proportion" of soldiers fell into this category. In order to "eliminate the stigma now attached to the psychoneurotic," the film would need to offer "a thorough examination of the condition and what it really is," and to explain that "in many cases the reason that makes a psychoneurotic unsatisfactory for the Army is the very reason for which this same person could be a real success in civilian life." In an attempt to substantiate the latter claim, the War Department cited unnamed veterans—all of them suffering from the effects of combat trauma—who claimed that "those qualities which made them a success as a civilian were the very things that made them carck [sic] up as a soldier."[59] The War Department offered no elaboration, and the ambivalence and ambiguity that characterized this statement on "the success of failure" would scarcely be incorporated into *Let There Be Light*, the final installment in the *Returning Soldier* series and a film that firmly suggests that psychotherapeutic treatment—not some "civilian-like" aversion to combat—could ensure the postwar productivity of the traumatized veteran. In this way, *Let There Be Light* echoes numerous other Army documentaries (particularly *He Has Seen War* and *Welcome Home*) in insisting that military service, however traumatizing, can confer upon a soldier any number of marketable skills, and that psychoanalysis can serve as a bridge between "uniformed service" and "postwar work"—a way of surmounting the traumas experienced in combat.

THE REPRESENTABILITY OF PSYCHONEUROSIS

During the production of what would become *Let There Be Light*, John Huston's celebrity was sufficient to attract the attention of mass-circulation magazines, two of which—*Life* and *Harper's Bazaar*—covered the director's efforts at Mason General. In addition to production stills and film frames, the resulting *Life* piece consisted of a short story by John Hersey—"a typical case history in fiction form," titled "A Short Talk with Erlanger" and based upon the use of narcosynthesis at Mason General and other military hospitals—as well as a sidebar explaining that the Army had, by the date of publication, treated over one million servicemen for neuropsychiatric disorders. "Suffering from what is popularly, but not strictly accurately, called combat fatigue," these servicemen had, the sidebar claims, "provided an enormous amount of laboratory material for advance of the science of psychiatry."[60] Huston's own images, which accompany Hersey's prose, are captioned with information about *Let There Be Light*—especially regarding the film's capacity to "show how Army psychiatrists use narcosynthesis."[61]

It is by now well known that, in justifying its decision to withhold *Let There Be Light* from commercial public exhibition (against the wishes of the ambitious Huston), the War Department cited the right to privacy of the dozens of men who appear as patients in the film. Huston maintained (correctly) that most of these men had signed releases, but he did not mention that they had also done so for *Life* magazine, granting the publication permission to print photographs of them alongside Hersey's text. In published form, "A Short Talk with Erlanger" features a total of eleven supplementary stills, six of which show moments from Huston's film—those in which patients Robert Gerardi and Eric Hofmeister undergo narcosynthesis for the treatment of "hysterical paralysis" and a speech disorder, respectively. In October 1945, both men had cabled the magazine to authorize its use of their images. These cables do not, however, reference *Let There Be Light* (or *The Returning Soldier—Psychoneurotics*, as it was then known). Instead, they refer to "Signal Corps movies," the plural form here indicating a telling reality that has previously gone unmentioned in writing on Huston's film—the inescapable fact that both Gerardi and Hofmeister, far from being suddenly "transformed" into unwitting documentary subjects by Huston alone, were by the fall of 1945 quite accustomed to appearing before Signal Corps cameras.

Serving as one of the nation's major schools of neuropsychiatry during the war, Mason General Hospital had long been an important filmmaking site. It began functioning as a specialist psychiatric center in July 1943, boasting over three thousand beds. Its teaching staff included M. Ralph Kaufman (who supervised the making of the Army documentaries *Hypnosis: Okinawa* and *Ward Care of Psychotic Patients*, and who would later exert his influence upon *Let There Be Light*) and W. H. Dunn. Both Kaufman and Dunn were in the habit of filming treatment sessions (as was done at such other facilities as Fitzsimmons Army Hospital, Don Ce-Sar Place, and St. Elizabeths Hospital), shipping the exposed film to Deluxe Laboratories for processing, and then screening the results (however bland and repetitive) for students—a clear precedent for the Signal Corps' later infiltrations of Mason General (and, for that matter, for the largely medical uses of *Let There Be Light*).[62] When Gerardi and Hofmeister cabled *Life*, they likely understood that the magazine wished to use a variety of images of them—frames, that is, from any number of "Signal Corps movies."

The sheer proliferation of filmmaking activities at Mason General does not, however, resolve a far thornier matter: whether individuals undergoing psychiatric treatment are truly capable of offering fully informed consent. In the history of documentary film, a number of works have raised urgent questions about consent and its relationship to a public "right to know," none of them more controversial than Frederick Wiseman's *Titicut Follies* (1967), made at the Massachusetts Correctional Institution at Bridgewater, a combined prison and mental hospital. Of the sixty-two inmate-patients filmed by Wiseman, only twelve were able to complete consent forms, the admissibility of which was almost immediately called into question. Since "mental incompetence" was the very basis for the men's incarceration, their "consent" was tenuous at best—and, at worst, cruelly oxymoronic, at least as solicited by the ambitious Wiseman.[63] Like *Let There Be Light* before it, Wiseman's film was withheld from commercial exhibition but was widely seen by mental health professionals, thus demonstrating how, in Brian Winston's words, "ethical problems, such as invasion of privacy and the tenuous nature of consent," can be "assuaged by the specialized nature" of a given audience.[64]

Let There Be Light offers a somewhat different case, however, in that the general "mental competence" of its subjects was scarcely in question by the time the film was made. Suffering not from an inability to distinguish reality from fantasy, or "right" from "wrong," the men at Mason General—or, more accurately, those relatively "mild cases" filmed by Huston (in contrast to the hospital's far more severely disturbed, antagonistic, even psychotic candidates for lobotomy, insulin-coma therapy, and electroshock treatment)—were troubled "only" by their traumatic memories and the challenge of coping with them. Perhaps irresolvable, these debates about consent motivated not the "suppression" of *Let There Be Light* but, rather, the film's careful rebranding as a noncommercial document of medical science, one that could widely circulate as such. Denied a commercial public release, *Let There Be Light* was thereafter presented as something other than a commodity, despite the fact that prints of the film were occasionally rented or purchased outright from the Army and the Veterans Administration by various professional groups and state agencies. The film could thus be used to satisfy a public "right to know" only in certain noncommercial, pedagogic, and even political circumstances.

A number of documentary films produced in the wake of *Let There Be Light* tellingly reflect aspects of this contentious history. *Shades of*

Gray, for instance, opens with a resounding endorsement of reenactment as an ethical vehicle of documentary truth. "Although actual patients are not shown," reads a title card, "their expressions, reactions, gestures, and speech have been carefully reproduced." This insistence on the ethical dimensions of reenactment did not originate with *Shades of Gray*, however. It can be found in a number of documentary and realist films produced earlier in the decade. MGM's short documentary *The Woman in the House* (Sammy Lee, 1942), part of John Nesbitt's *Passing Parade* series, is a case in point. The film earnestly attributes the development of psychiatry to the "shock" of World War II, and it proceeds to suggest the war's traumatic impact on soldiers and civilians alike. "For obvious reasons, we cannot give real names and places," announces the narrator, after which the film explicitly presents reenactment as a suitable means of avoiding the unnecessary exposure of the mentally ill, preserving the anonymity of "case histories" through a process of "historical reconstruction."

Later films, many of them patterned on *Let There Be Light* but carefully structured to avoid its controversial character, share this embrace of reenactment as a means of believably communicating psychiatric realities. Huston's sentimental emphasis on baseball as a form of group therapy—and a way of confirming a patient's progress—recurs in *Man to Man* (Irving Jacoby, 1954), a production of the Mental Health Film Board. Shot at the Fairfield State Hospital in Newtown, Connecticut, the film features hospital staff members in the roles of their patients, thus circumventing the question of fully informed consent while insisting on the verisimilar character of these performances, which are based, as a closing text tells us, on staff members' intimate knowledge of their patients' behavior (if not on any obvious acting talent). For its part, the Army's own *Combat Psychiatry: The Battalion Medical Officer* (1954) opens, like the earlier *Shades of Gray*, with a disclaimer intended to assure the film's spectators that it crosses no lines of propriety in examining the eponymous profession. Reflecting the Army's lasting awareness of the controversies surrounding *Let There Be Light*, *Combat Psychiatry* offers a blunt articulation of its own scrupulous avoidance of morally suspect methods: "No actual casualties are seen in this film," reads an opening title card. "Professional actors and Marine Corps personnel portray patients."

By 1944, numerous military psychiatrists believed that "exposing" patients to the scrutiny of cinema spectators represented a necessary evil—the only way to truly advance the psychiatric profession through documentary pedagogy. In June 1945, the Neuropsychiatry Consultants Division, in heartily recommending the production of "carefully developed motion pictures of neuropsychiatric activities," noted, "These would in some instances, of necessity, include 'identifiable' patients."[65] At stake in this commitment to observational realism was the capacity of actual patients to subtly suggest—through vocal inflections as much as through the microphysiognomy of their faces—emotional responses to trauma and psychotherapy that simply could not be captured by actors, however proficient.

Like the observational *Psychiatric Procedures in the Combat Area,* which shows a range of actual psychiatric interviews, *Let There Be Light* emphasizes the value of various "authentic" speech acts, including those performed under sedation. In remaking both films, *Shades of Gray* insists on the capacity of skilled actors to capture all signs of psychoneurosis, opening with a text that reads, in part, "This film is based upon official case histories faithfully re-enacted. Although actual patients are not shown, their expressions, reactions, gestures, and speech have been carefully reproduced." The histrionics that follow suggest otherwise, however, and the film certainly cannot compete with the observational character of parts of *Psychiatric Procedures* and *Let There Be Light.* The latter films appear to reflect Freud's fundamental challenge to Jean-Martin Charcot's biologism (through which the neurologist advanced his ideas about the sources and treatment of "hysteria"), as well as the shift—occasioned by psychoanalysis itself—from visuality (particularly the empiricist insistence that neurosis was inscribed on the surface of the body and eminently detectable in the body's movements) to sound and audition.[66]

Narcosynthesis played a significant role in motivating this shift from the visual to the aural. One military psychiatrist pointed out that, while some sedated patients "will readily get up and act," most "will be too drowsy because of the hypnotic and will continue to lie down, giving *only a verbal* account of their story."[67] What's more, psychiatrists were often forced to keep their hypodermic needles in the veins of their patients in order "to regulate the depth of the narcosis," which invariably restricted the patients' movements, limiting them to *"spoken* confession."[68] What Lisa Cartwright calls "the sensory hierarchy of psychoanalysis" is thus on ample display in films like *Psychiatric Procedures* and *Let There Be Light,* which place a premium on speech acts as diagnostic, historiographic, and therapeutic instruments.[69] In recording the actions of psychiatrists who carefully pose questions to their patients, these films also suggest an investment in the act of listening as a powerful clinical tool. As an Army technical manual put it in 1950, "The skilled interviewer learns early that listening in an interview situation is not the same as in a social situation. In most social situations the manifest content of the conversation is what the listener hears," but in a psychiatric interview "a different kind of listening is required."[70] Evoking the remit of documentary film, with its familiar capacity to reveal the "meaning *behind* the thing and the significance *underlying* the person," the psychiatric interview was designed not merely to elicit information but also to "expose the [traumatized] underside" of a patient's institutional identity.[71] In filming these interviews, documentaries like *Psychiatric Procedures* and *Let There Be Light* revealed a proto-*vérité* flair for uncovering traumatic realities and, in the process, promoting the transference of mindful audition from on-screen psychiatrist to off-screen spectator.

DISCIPLINES OF LISTENING

By 1945, the theme of listening had become central to a number of state-sponsored documentaries concerned with the rehabilitation of traumatized veterans. Produced by the Division of Motion Pictures at the Department of the Interior, the Veterans Administration film *Service to Those Who Served* (1945) emphasizes the importance of "sympathetic listening" to the VA's efforts to meet the needs of troubled ex-servicemen, many of whom repair to any number of local VA offices where they are interviewed by committed case workers. "There must be real humanity in these interviews," explains the voice-over narrator, pointing to the therapeutic potential of "genuine" interactions and providing a blueprint for the dramatization of such "personal exchanges" in Fred Zinnemann's *Teresa* (1951), parts of which are set (and were shot) in an actual VA facility in New York, and Arnold Laven's *The Rack* (1956), set and shot in and around Letterman General Hospital in San Francisco. Describing the hospital's patients—all of them newly liberated from prisoner-of-war camps—a psychiatrist in the latter film reminds their visiting family members, "These men have been through a series of very shocking experiences, and they have left their mark. If they want to unload, let them. But don't ask questions—don't pry. Be patient." Defining wars as "human holocausts," *Service to Those Who Served* anticipates *Teresa*, *The Rack*, and especially *Let There Be Light* in its attention to "problems of readjustment," which require careful and patient listening. (In this respect, the film also echoes *Neuropsychiatry 1943*, whose narrator claims that "every [psychiatric] interview with the patient is organized both to elicit information and to strengthen therapeutic rapport.") Describing attempts to "modernize and speed up services" for ex-combatants, a spokesman for the VA argues that "nothing in the postwar period is more important than that communities provide intelligent counsel and neighborly advice to returning veterans." Some of the professional responsibilities of psychiatrists, psychologists, and social workers thus become the "everyday duties" of all Americans—a process of translation that the film self-consciously seeks to facilitate.

Nontheatrical nonfiction films of the immediate postwar period are steeped in this insistence on the therapeutic and community-building value of listening. These include *Psychotherapeutic Interviewing Techniques* (1949), a series of three feature films produced by the Veterans Administration and distributed by Pennsylvania State University[72]; *Psychotherapeutic Interviewing Series, Part One: Introduction—1950* (1950), an eleven-minute film produced for the VA's Department of Medicine and Surgery by Presentation Division, prints of which were purchasable from United World Films and rentable through the National Medical & Biological Film Library[73]; and the Navy's *Preventative Psychiatry: In or Out* (1961), in which the intake interview "brings into sharp focus preexisting conditions," as the voice-over narrator puts it. Highlighting the importance of recognizing psychiatric disorders "as soon as possible," *Preventative Psychiatry* features actual recruits who "play themselves" in scripted scenes in which they each meet with a psychiatrist, the latter posing such questions as "How come you never finished school?" and "How many times were you in trouble with the police?" The psychiatrist, who also "plays himself," then models "effective listening" for the medical professionals—including psychiatric social workers—for whom the film was initially intended.

What these and other state-sponsored documentaries do not address—what they seem designed to evade and displace—is the harsh reality of thousands of ex-servicemen being denied psychiatric treatment due to the "belatedness" of their traumatic symptoms. A central tenet of trauma theory—namely, the sheer "untimeliness" of trauma, its capacity to produce effects unexpectedly and, in some cases, long after the moment of initial traumatization—was thus unrecognizable to (or rendered bureaucratically inadmissible by) various state facilities. The VA, for instance, required that traumatic symptoms evince a so-called "service connection"—proof (usually in the form of a military-psychiatric paper trail) of the symptoms' rootedness in active military duty.[74] Men whose symptoms did not appear until after discharge, or who failed (or were, owing to severe psychiatric shortages, unable) to obtain any form of medical treatment while in uniform, were thus prohibited from taking advantage of many of the services so proudly depicted in the above-mentioned films. By insisting on the importance of listening, these films tended to suggest a rather conservative, proto-neoliberal investment in its practice not by the state but by individuals willing to shoulder the burden of "hearing and healing," to quote *Psychotherapeutic Interviewing Techniques*. For its part, *Service to Those Who Served* seems both to celebrate and to undercut the VA, identifying its contributions while also seeking to attribute them to "neighborliness" (a "quality of the community" rather than a provision of the state). Still, the shared capacity of these films to reflect the "sensory hierarchy of psychoanalysis"— what had, by 1945, become a clear commitment to speaking and listening over and against an empiricism based strictly on visual scrutiny—is remarkable, and well worth considering in further detail.

In the late 1940s, psychoanalyst Theodor Reik would emphasize this "shift in the ranking of the senses" through his focus on speech and audition as primary therapeutic instruments.[75] Reik's theory of "the third ear" has major implications for the study not simply of *Let There Be Light* but of the on-camera, synch-sound interview more generally, a device that can be traced back to (among other works) Esfir Shub's *Komsomol—Leader of Electrification* (1932), Dziga Vertov's *Three Songs of Lenin* (1934), and Arthur Elton and Edgar Anstey's *Housing Problems* (1935), which all, to varying degrees, feature confessional speech as a means of capturing and even mastering psychological trauma. In Vertov's film, for instance, a shock worker carefully describes a nearly disastrous accident, and if her radiant smile suggests health and happiness, her speech tells a far different story, compelling the viewer to place a premium on the act of listening and to value the voice as a source of documentary truth. During World War II, *I Was There*, a special segment of the biweekly *Army-Navy Screen Magazine*, would similarly deploy the on-camera, synch-sound interview, offering dramatic eyewitness commentaries typically delivered in the flat, affectless voices of nonactors, as in *I Was There: Corregidor* (1943), in which an Army nurse stiffly describes the trauma of a recent aerial attack. For its part, the Army's *All-American* (1943), which is addressed to "the aircraft workers of America," purports to offer this "special audience" something "entirely new": following a nearly two-minute sequence showing

FIGURE 25. In a seven-minute take, a series of on-camera, synch-sound interviews suggest the trauma of a recent bombing raid in the Army's *All-American* (1943). Note the visibility of the boom microphone. Courtesy of the National Archives and Records Administration.

a bombing raid over Germany, the narrator announces, "For the first time, you'll be permitted to sit in on the interrogation of the crew of one of the bombers that made the raid. Their story will be more than the routine details of the action—it'll tell the whole saga of young America meeting the greatest crisis in our history." What follows is a remarkable series of on-camera, synch-sound interviews—a seven-minute take in which fourteen flyers are asked by an officer to describe, in their own words, the experience of the raid, their unrehearsed answers indeed providing "more than the routine details," expressing at times the personal traumas of "total war."

Reik's psychoanalytic notion of "the third ear," a faculty of listening uniquely attuned to what is "whispered between sentences" and "expressed almost noiselessly," resonates with Jonathan Kahana's notion of an "ear of documentary"—a cultural-critical faculty that complicates Bill Nichols's famous definition of a "voice of documentary" by drawing attention to the empathic, diagnostic, and even therapeutic function of a film like *Let There Be Light*.[76] Huston's documentary reflects the growing commitment of the Signal Corps to the on-camera, synch-sound interview as a supplement to other devices—an engine of self-reflection that often complicates the "objective" claims of a voice-over narrator. Consider, for instance, the Army's *The Atom Strikes!* (1945), which features a nearly seven-minute interview with a Jesuit priest who survived the bombing of Hiroshima, and who gives a detailed, at times wrenching account of his experience of the blast, describing some of its physical as well as psychological effects. Contrasting "official figures" with "the knowledge of special groups" (including the group of Jesuits to which he himself belongs), the priest suggests how the documentary interview can create a split or aporia, disrupting the rhetorical thrust of a film committed to limiting the meanings of atomic destruction.

In implicit recognition of this disruptive power, the priest ultimately resorts to reading a prepared statement of support for the use of atomic weapons, claiming that "in total war, as carried on in Japan, there was no difference between civilians and soldiers, and that the bomb itself was an effective force tending to end the bloodshed, warning Japan to surrender and thus to avoid total destruction." Here, the testimonial voice is itself split into two voices, one "personal" and autobiographical and the other institutional or ventriloquial. Starting out as the source of a seemingly extemporized, idiosyncratic narrative of traumatization at the hands of the atomic bomb, the priest becomes, toward the end of his seven minutes of screen time, a mere mouthpiece for the military establishment—unsurprisingly, given that this is an official Army film. Yet *The Atom Strikes!* also suggests the sheer therapeutic power of this institutionally approved performance: the priest's prepared statement, which echoes official governmental claims about the necessity of the bomb and its paradoxically life-saving properties, becomes a doubly therapeutic instrument—a potentially calming, incantatory influence on both the film's subject (here, the priest in his post-traumatic state) and its audience (forced to confront visible evidence of atomic destruction). The seemingly contradictory but perhaps compatible speech acts that make up this section of *The Atom Strikes!* had, by the time of the film's production, long been central to military documentaries. In fact, *Let There Be Light* was far from the first such film to employ the on-camera, synch-sound interview in order to reflect some of the objectives of military psychiatry. Nearly two years before Huston first visited Mason General, the psychiatrists Frederick Hanson, Calvin Drayer, and Stephen Ranson, while stationed in the Mediterranean, made *Psychiatric Procedures in the Combat Area*, a film that features a total of nine "psychiatric interviews," many of them shot using the dynamic two-camera setup for which Huston and cinematographer Stanley Cortez would later receive credit for "pioneering."

Shot under the supervision of seasoned Signal Corps filmmakers, *Psychiatric Procedures* vividly illustrates that, far from the product of an auteur's ingenuity, the striking formal devices of *Let There Be Light* were simply the components of an institutional style that predated the efforts of Huston and Cortez. Encountering cases of combat fatigue in North Africa and Italy, Hanson (the psychiatric consultant for the entire Mediterranean Theater), Drayer, and Ranson were among the military psychiatrists tasked with interviewing these soldiers upon their arrival at various training and rehabilitation centers. The first such interview shown in *Psychiatric Procedures* involves a soldier suffering from what the narrator describes as "a mild anxiety state." "Tell me, soldier, what's your trouble?" asks the on-camera interviewer. The patient proceeds to describe a recent experience of "pretty heavy shelling," and the uncontrollable crying that it produced in him. The psychiatrist prescribes two days of rest, after which the interview is resumed on camera. Other patients are, following their intake interviews, prescribed five days of "reconditioning" activities designed to prepare them for future combat, after which they are returned to psychiatrists for yet more interviews.

Psychiatric Procedures carefully records these encounters between doctors and their patients, often lavishing visual attention on the latter but occasionally including reverse shots of the former. One patient, suffering from "reactive depression," describes the gruesome horrors of war to a psychiatrist whose inscrutable reactions to this confessional speech are briefly shown in close-up. "I just can't stand seeing people killed," the patient says. "I can't stand seeing dead people. It scares me." Like *Let There Be Light*, *Psychiatric Procedures* somberly acknowledges that swiftly "bouncing back" from war trauma is not a possibility, but it goes much further than Huston's film by detailing the relative resistance to treatment of one of its on-camera subjects—the aforementioned "depressed case," whose lifelong anxiety the narrator describes, concluding, "His present condition, together with his past history of neurotic fears, leaves little hope of a rapid recovery." In the film, some patients "regain health" more swiftly, but that does not mean that they may return to combat. This is especially true of "seriously shaken men" who, while responsive to treatment, have simply seen too much fighting. The narrator describes them as "old veterans who have been excellent soldiers but have reached the limit of their endurance." Known colloquially as "old sergeant syndrome," their "chronic anxiety state" precludes a return to the front lines. One man reports that he has seen 320 days of combat, confessing, "I've gone about as far as I can go. . . . I can't stand the shelling any more." Toward the end of his 320 days on the front lines, he discovered, much to his surprise, that a single round of shelling made him cry uncontrollably all through the night. As the narrator puts it, "Even the best man can stand only so much. In the old veteran, anxiety reactions become chronic and fixed."

With these sequences devoted to "old sergeant syndrome," *Psychiatric Procedures* was intended, in part, to endorse the recent recommendations of psychiatrist John Appel, who, having served in an "exhaustion center" near the Cassino and Anzio battlefields, concluded that the average man could sustain no more than 240 days of combat. Eventually, Appel proposed a limited "tour of duty" of 210 days—a proposal that, as Ben Shephard points out, would prove extremely influential in the long run, even if its immediate impact was negligible, thus necessitating the principled and empirically grounded intervention of *Psychiatric Procedures*, which would circulate in the Army for at least the next three decades.[77] Produced without Appel's direct participation, the film was meant to advocate on his behalf, with Hanson, Drayer, and Ranson all heartily concurring with his findings, including as on-camera subjects. (In the film, they are among the psychiatrists seen interviewing patients near the front lines.) *Psychiatric Procedures* thus suggests another, heretofore-unacknowledged purpose for which trauma-themed military documentaries were produced, beyond but not unrelated to the objectives of instruction, normalization, and therapy. That purpose was advocacy on behalf of a particular psychiatric proposal, one that threatened to be lost or discredited amid the turf wars characteristic of the era, and that an individual film could vividly substantiate through proto-*vérité* encounters with "men who have reached their limit." With this film, Hanson, Drayer, and Ranson were plainly taking sides, aligning themselves with Appel and, in the process, conceivably helping to inspire the one-year tour of duty belatedly adopted by the Army during the war in Vietnam (and anticipated by an Army psychiatrist in *The Manchurian Candidate*, recognizing that Frank Sinatra's traumatized protagonist is, at least in part, "suffering a delayed reaction to eighteen months of continuous combat in Korea"). As the narrator of *Psychiatric Procedures* so succinctly puts it, "It must be remembered that good and able soldiers also lose their grip after long and hard combat."

The five-reel *Psychiatric Procedures* is unique in detailing the forms of therapy prescribed at multiple sites "behind the lines." These sites— identified via animated maps and carefully described by the narrator— include the initial clearing station, where the physically wounded are separated from their "neuropsychiatric" counterparts; the T&R (Training and Rehabilitation) Center, where "reconditioning" exercises take place in anticipation of a return to combat; the N.P. (Neuropsychiatric) Clearing Station; the Base Section N.P. Hospital; and the Replacement Center. The farther one travels along this line of stations and centers, the more likely one is to be sent to a mental hospital in the United States. The narrator is quick to point out, however, that, of the men who end up at the Base Section N.P. Hospital, "only a few are sent back to the United States"; most are sent to the Replacement Center for "assignment to jobs in the rear area." The on-camera, synch-sound interviews that punctuate *Psychiatric Procedures* were shot at three sites—the T&R Center, the N.P. Clearing Station, and the Base Section N.P. Hospital. At the N.P. Clearing Station, an interviewee from the first site is shown submitting to another round of questioning, as a new psychiatrist attempts to better understand the sources of the patient's depression and anxiety. This follow-up interview leads to a confession: "My biggest trouble is I can't stand seeing people get killed. Been that way all my life. I can't kill anyone, either. I tried. I couldn't do it. And when they started to get killed around me, and I started seeing people dead, all around, it did something to me—I couldn't stand it." The narrator interrupts to claim that "this soldier has improved considerably since his interview at the T&R Center yesterday," but there is still the matter of his childhood neurosis to discuss. The psychiatrist's probing questions produce a startling confession: the patient begins to self-diagnose as suffering from "an inferiority complex," one that has plagued him all his life. Having calmly described his history of depression and anxiety, the patient is given a better sense of how to proceed with his treatment.

If the patients shown in *Psychiatric Procedures* seem considerably more restrained than those in *Let There Be Light*, it may well be because, as Herbert Spiegel argued, Huston was not on hand to direct them. Spiegel, who worked at Mason General but is not featured in Huston's film (though his hypnosis techniques are), later confessed that, in his opinion, Huston did more than merely "intrude" on treatment sessions, multiple cameras and an experienced cinematographer in tow (part of Huston's twenty-man filmmaking crew, which included six cameramen).[78] He also "slobbered over" the patients, directing them to "act like cry-babies"—an assertion that echoes condemnatory accounts of Method acting, particularly those that centered on Elia Kazan's direction of James Dean in *East of Eden* (1955), and that lends credence to the familiar claim that what is most disturbing about *Let There Be*

Light, at least to some spectators, is Huston's depiction of men who weep.[79] This is not to deny or downplay the many other similarities between Huston's film and the earlier *Psychiatric Procedures.* The latter, which Huston likely saw either at the Signal Corps Photographic Center or at Mason General, insists that a range of traumatic symptoms are "perfectly normal," and it proceeds to linger on cases that "require" narcosynthesis. These the narrator describes as "a few tense, uncertain patients [who] cannot start on their road to recovery because the specific sources of their anxiety have been obscured in the depths of an hysterical amnesia."

One man "recalls readily his anxiety during the first three days of an attack on the Gothic Line, until he was blown out of his foxhole. But he can't tell what happens from that time, until he came to in an aid station." The narrator's confusion of tenses, which produces a disordered syntax ("can't tell what happens . . . until he came"), is less a slip of the tongue than a deliberate reflection of the temporal juxtapositions characteristic of narcosynthesis. Roy Grinker and John Spiegel had famously described the procedure in terms of its "delicate manipulations" of past and present, through which different tenses may "intrude" upon one another, "filling out," however awkwardly, a patient's recollection of the past, producing spontaneous utterances whose grammatical transgressions were the essence of their cathartic power.[80] The narrator of *Psychiatric Procedures* suggests some of the historiographic challenges associated with narcosynthesis when he says, "Dramatic precipitation into the patient's battle experiences results in the reliving of the forgotten scenes, but the therapist often may have to lead the patient back to the subject in order to get a consecutive story." If the patient is eventually "able to tell a connected story," it is only through the sort of "patching up" of narrative holes that takes place after the pentothal has worn off, when temporality is stabilized and tenses settled into coherent agreement.[81] As Grinker and Spiegel put it in their descriptions of this post-pentothal process, "the patient actually synthesizes the emotions and memories connected with his experience, putting together what has lain fragmented between consciousness and unconsciousness into a complete whole, which corresponds in almost every detail with the original experience."[82]

Grinker and Spiegel often stressed the importance of getting patients to "act out the traumatic parts of the battle scene"—an often histrionic process that *Psychiatric Procedures* directly depicts.[83] (The film thus contrasts with, say, *Narcosynthesis,* which promotes a more "soothing" approach involving "reassurance" and "positive suggestion.") Describing the therapeutic power of performance in language that Jacob Moreno and other proponents of psychodrama theater likely appreciated, Grinker and Spiegel sought to establish the centrality of acting to narcosynthesis, thereby dampening the emergent cultural enthusiasm for sodium pentothal as a sort of "miracle drug":

> The patient is told in a matter-of-fact manner that he is on the battlefield, in the front lines. Depending upon the amount of known history, specific details are added corresponding to the actual situation at the time of the trauma. If little or nothing is known of the original situation, a typical scene is depicted. The patient is told that mortar shells are flying about; that one has just landed close by; that enemy planes are overhead, or that tanks are approaching from the flank; and that he must tell what is happening.[84]

If a patient resists, the authors continue, "the stimulation is made more dramatic and realistic," requiring the participation of all members of the "psychiatric team," including nurses and social workers, who must "act out the traumatic parts of the battle scene."[85]

This is precisely what *Psychiatric Procedures* depicts. In a stunning long take that lasts nearly ten minutes, the film shows one man undergoing narcosynthesis, crying hysterically even during the initial injection of sodium pentothal, as he counts slowly and in step with two psychiatrists. After the patient has been "adequately narcotized," one of the psychiatrists begins to perform, shouting, "You're back on the battlefield! Now!" The doctor's elaborate act involves mimicking the sounds of shellfire and shouting, "Look out! Duck!" Having participated in this simulation, shaking and flinching and generally attempting to evade the imagined shells, the patient comes to describe, in anguished terms, his harrowing experiences under actual fire, during which he saw his friends killed and had to cower in holes in order to save his own life.

This psychodramatic approach sometimes backfired, as Grinker and Spiegel discovered after informing a narcotized patient that he was back on the battlefields of Gafsa. "He immediately reacted, screaming, 'Gafsa?' and sat bolt upright in bed, terrified. He had so much terror that he was unable to talk."[86] No extant military documentary shows such clinical failures, but numerous films detail the sort of post-traumatic speech disorder that develops in the Gafsa veteran, and that would play a memorable part in Anthony Mann's drama *Men in War* (1957), in which a character played by Robert Keith is rendered mute by his experiences in Korea. Suggesting military-psychiatric failure of a sort, Otto Preminger's *Whirlpool* (1949) centers on a civilian psychiatrist,

Dr. William Sutton (Richard Conte), who must pick up where the military left off, treating a traumatized veteran who "can't talk." "It's difficult to begin unloading fears and secrets and guilts," Dr. Sutton observes. "Poor fellow. The war was an easier conflict than the one he's in now." Jean Renoir's *The Woman on the Beach* (1947) suggests a similar dilemma in its depiction of a combat-traumatized veteran: asleep in his bed, Lieutenant Scott Burnett (Robert Ryan), now a mounted patrolman in the United States Coast Guard, suffers from combat-themed nightmares. "They're coming back again, every night, and I can't stand it," he confesses. "When they let me out of the hospital, they said, 'Lieutenant, your wounds are all healed. You're sound in body and mind.' But my head isn't! Let's face it—I'm not well!" Exhibiting what Erving Goffman would later call "release anxiety"—the conviction that he is "too 'sick' to reassume the responsibility from which the total institution [in this case, the military hospital] freed him"—Scott implicates the clinical shortcomings of military psychiatrists. Where once he couldn't talk, now he talks too much, hysterically narrating his nightmares for anyone in earshot.[87]

Like *Let There Be Light*, *Psychiatric Procedures* shows patients who suffer from "major hysteria" and cannot talk, or whose speech is marked by stuttering—problems that both films present as characteristic of war trauma.[88] (As Henry James observed in response to World War I, "The war has used up words; they have weakened, they have deteriorated like motorcar tires."[89]) MGM's *Random Harvest* (Mervyn LeRoy, 1942) features a combat-traumatized veteran plagued by a speech disorder—"a result of shock," a psychiatrist calls it. In *Psychiatric Procedures*, one patient fidgets uncontrollably, unable to speak. Describing his dysphonia, the narrator claims that "speech disorders in general are very resistant to therapy." Three pentothal interviews are insufficient to produce speech in the patient (in stark contrast to the single injection that, in *Let There Be Light*, prompts a man to proclaim, "Oh, God, listen, I can talk!"), and he must undergo sessions of "faradic stimuli," in which electrical currents are applied to his larynx, along with "strong suggestion." "Only then," the narrator notes, "did his voice begin to improve significantly, and only then could his basic problem be approached" through psychoanalysis.

This concession to the curative power of an "older method" like faradic therapy sets *Psychiatric Procedures* apart from the far less forthcoming *Let There Be Light*, which sidesteps not only the effectiveness but also the very existence of electroshock treatment (a common procedure at Mason General). As the narrator of *Psychiatric Procedures* puts it, "Electroshock treatments sometimes are necessary to speed recovery." The film stresses that some patients have become psychotic and "pseudo-psychotic," including a man who saw his close friend disemboweled by a shell fragment. Shock therapy, which wasn't authorized by the military until April 1943, here proves particularly useful as a treatment for psychosis.[90] *Psychiatric Procedures* does not acknowledge its controversial character, but simply presents it as an effective "last resort" in "extreme cases."

Describing it as a "mortification of the self by way of the body," Erving Goffman would later situate shock therapy among the "physical indignities" that "may lead many [patients] to feel that they are in an environment that does not guarantee their physical integrity."[91] If wartime and postwar military documentaries only rarely addressed the procedure, it was not because their makers shared Goffman's concerns. Numerous Army psychiatrists made clear the lack of "cinematic appeal" of electroconvulsive treatment, in the aftermath of which "patients groan and moan and sometimes mutter, sometimes scream, for an hour at a time."[92] The British import *Neuropsychiatry 1943*, much of which is difficult to watch, seems to prove this point. Of the multiple treatment methods that the documentary depicts, electroshock therapy is perhaps the most disturbing, particularly as filmed in a direct, observational style that leaves little to the imagination, as a female patient is seen convulsing while three nurses and two psychiatrists grip various parts of her body, preventing her from falling off the bed on which she is being treated. Because of this scene, *Neuropsychiatry 1943* was circulated with a "special note," its use in the American military largely restricted to psychological professionals and their students, including at Mason General and other wartime schools of neuropsychiatry: "Because of the shock therapy scenes, it seems advisable to show this film only to students who have had a previous course in psychology and to adults who have had a preliminary explanation."[93] Acquiring the film in the immediate postwar period, various nontheatrical distributors (including the NYU Film Library) declared that it was "unsuitable for nonscientific audiences"; as a result, they also acquired a twenty-minute abridged version (entitled simply *Neuropsychiatry*), which was "more suitable for the general public," since the scenes of electroshock therapy had been excised.[94]

If *Let There Be Light*, like *Psychiatric Procedures* and *Neuropsychiatry 1943*, suggests a precedent of sorts for *cinéma vérité*, that precedent lies as much in its production methods as in the negative responses that they generated. The *cinéma vérité* style that seemed to dominate American documentary filmmaking in the 1960s was, even at the time, critiqued for what Thomas Waugh has called "its persistent pretense of impartiality," and for the impression that it often created of aggressive documentarists pushing their subjects to the breaking point (emotional breakdown constituting the coin of the *vérité* realm, the crux of its claims to authenticity).[95] For Herbert Spiegel, Huston was guilty of performing what many practitioners of *vérité* would later disavow: the emotional manipulation of documentary subjects, a manipulation rooted as much in the injunction against looking at or otherwise acknowledging the camera as in persistent inducements to emote. Huston, in Spiegel's telling, went too far in actively encouraging his subjects to cry—a claim that seems farfetched strictly on the basis of those scenes in *Let There Be Light* in which patients do produce tears. It is difficult to believe, for instance, that the man of color who cries during his intake interview— the new patient who describes the pain of "nostalgia," of constant longing for the wife who, perhaps alone among the individuals in his life, loves and believes in him, against the implicit backdrop of structural racism and inequality—is doing so strictly at Huston's bidding.

At the same time, however, it would be naïve to suggest that Huston exerted no influence whatsoever over the patients who, in all likelihood, remained well aware of his presence at Mason General. Anticipating a later form of *vérité*, Huston's film foregrounds the recording process in a scene in which the hospital's patients are told that "there is no need to be alarmed at the presence of these cameras, as they are making a photographic record of your progress at this hospital from the date of admission to the date of discharge." Unlike those *vérité* practitioners invested in "systematically snipp[ing] out all looks at the camera in order to preserve the representational illusion"—the façade of non-interventionism—Allan King would later echo *Let There Be Light*, and implicitly defend Huston's methods, in his film *Warrendale* (1967). Shot at an experimental home for emotionally troubled youth, *Warrendale* repeatedly signals the presence of King and his colleagues, though it is a measure of the impact of certain *vérité* myths that David MacDougal, in his 1975 essay "Beyond Observational Cinema," could classify King's film as being "without reference to the presence of the film crew." In fact, references to the crew abound in *Warrendale*—the children who are among its subjects are on a first-name basis with the off-screen King—and one staff member, discussing the shooting process at length, concludes that, since the children are "used to all of the [filmmakers]," who, he says, "work very sensitively with [them]," "it would be more natural" to have the crew film a special and potentially upsetting meeting "than not to have them film it."

Let There Be Light encourages a similar reading of observational filmmaking as an institutionally approved—even institutionally central —practice. Indeed, the sense that Huston and others were "natural" rather than alien elements is further buttressed by archival evidence— particularly the aforementioned telegrams that indicate patients' habituation to the presence of film crews at Mason General. Given his own, longstanding involvement in filmmaking at the hospital, Spiegel's denunciation of Huston—his dismissal of *Let There Be Light*—suggests less a dogmatic aversion to filmic interventionism than the skepticism of an expert toward a documentary that, in Griersonian terms, borrows and adapts professional knowledge for the intended edification of the masses. Spiegel's proprietary expertise—what he obtained through years of research and service, including near the front lines in North Africa—became, in a sense, Huston's sentimental pedagogy, marking *Let There Be Light* as an inevitably inadequate record of what actually transpired at Mason General. According to Spiegel, Huston's greatest sin, apart from (allegedly) instructing his subjects to cry, was in falsely intimating that all of the men depicted in *Let There Be Light* were combat casualties—patients traumatized by their participation in battle— rather than "deficient" soldiers unable to "cope" with racism, classism, time away from home and family, and the general rigors of military service.[96]

According to Spiegel, *Let There Be Light* is additionally problematic for what it does not show—namely, electroconvulsive therapy (ECT), which the doctors at Mason General routinely administered to "severe cases," such as schizophrenics and catatonics.[97] (For its part, the earlier *Combat Exhaustion* had directly depicted the administration of what its voice-over narrator refers to as "electrical shock treatment," which is reserved for "patients who show marked symptoms of reactive depression" and used only in combination with "insulin and narcosis therapy.") Huston's film thus belongs to an American stylistic tradition that, as Krin Gabbard and Glen O. Gabbard argue, entails "a striking overrepresentation of 'the talking cure' and an equally striking underrepresentation of treatments such as electroconvulsive therapy."[98] While *Let There Be Light* does allude, through its emphasis on sodium amytal, to the utility of pharmacotherapy—another option that, Gabbard and

Gabbard suggest, American films often strategically exclude in their sanitizing approach to psychiatric treatment—it nevertheless omits what, in Spiegel's account, constituted the less photogenic procedures at Mason General, shifting tendentiously toward a representational tradition that, in Hollywood as well as in the military, was well established by 1946.

If Huston elided the function of electroconvulsive therapy at Mason General, his evasive approach was entirely in keeping with military policy. ECT was among the procedures that were rarely mentioned in official dispatches to the public, simply because it was deemed too shocking, and thus an unacceptable advertisement for military psychiatry, whatever its clinical effectiveness. Editing an account of the treatment of combat-traumatized pilots for public release, one military psychiatrist ordered that the following sentence be deleted: "Electric shock therapy was used experimentally and successfully in the case of anxiety neuroses with claustrophobic symptoms."[99] *Let There Be Light* is by no means strictly censorious or euphemistic, however, and those aspects of Walter Huston's narration that stress the stubborn intractability of trauma were the result of longstanding efforts among military psychiatrists to promote the honest, "scientific presentation" of psychoneurosis, even—perhaps especially—in films intended for the general public. Responding, in part, to the production of institutional documentaries about war trauma, the Air Forces psychiatrist John M. Murray called for a sober, "ethical" recognition of those patients who "do not recover"—who are unresponsive to "rest treatment" and who prove impervious even to psychotherapy.[100]

Psychiatric Procedures is perhaps closer to what Murray had in mind than the far more optimistic *Let There Be Light*. For Murray, the documentary value of "psycho films" and other dispatches to the public were pronounced if they managed to suggest how men become "worn out with the stresses of combat," but a "note of optimism" such as that so consistently injected in *Let There Be Light* by Walter Huston's narration, as well as by the staging of a triumphant baseball game, may well have been "out of line with a scientific presentation."[101] The public had a "right to know" that not everyone recovered; that some men would, in fact, be unemployable; that others would have to remain hospitalized indefinitely. In a report co-authored by M. Ralph Kaufman, who drew on the experience of making *Hypnosis: Okinawa* on the titular island, Murray later reiterated his instructions to those seeking to "inform the public" about war trauma, writing, "The limitations of treatment under trying conditions must be made clear and limited aims established for such situations."[102]

By the mid-1930s, national film-reform discourses had succeeded in drawing firm distinctions "between what constitutes decency for an audience of the general public and what constitutes decency for a restricted audience."[103] *Let There Be Light*, with the added weight of salient questions concerning the consent of those undergoing psychiatric treatment, was certainly not immune to these debates. But it would be wrong to continue to view the film's segregation from "the general public" as a function of military necessity—a phobic institutional response to the "shame" of emotional distress. More to the point, it would be wrong to view this segregation as entirely effective. Was not a "general public" constituted by Governor Youngdahl's constituents, who repeatedly gathered at his behest to watch Huston's film in a range of nontheatrical settings and as part of the politician's efforts to cultivate popular support for statewide reforms?[104] The shortcomings of film histories that restrict their conception of "the general public" to paying audiences in commercial movie theaters have unduly burdened *Let There Be Light*, which should instead be seen as a kind of limit case for what counts as "general exhibition" in the first place.[105] The complicated career of Huston's film proves that the reach of a work can exceed even the grasp of those commercial circuits from which it has been carefully withheld. Just how "available" was a film that could not be purchased or rented from commercial firms—only "requested" (and, on occasion, acquired at cost) from the Army and the Veterans Administration? Widely available indeed, even if its noncommercial, largely nontheatrical itineraries have tempted film historians to suggest otherwise. *Let There Be Light* thus frustrates the binary opposition between theatrical and nontheatrical maintained by those who insist on a qualitative difference in terms of "impact," often citing box-office revenues and other markers of commercial success. Huston's film was not "hidden"; it just wasn't a commodity in the traditional economic sense.[106]

This is not to deny that the film was, in some significant ways, suppressed, its circulation carefully circumscribed by concerns regarding consent and the right to privacy of its subjects, most of whom were, by 1946, pursuing the sort of postwar productivity that the film was designed, in part, to ensure. But it was precisely by turning the film into a noncommercial product—by rendering it the opposite of a commodity— that the Army managed to guarantee its exposure to something resembling a general public, one limited not by professional categories (of journalism or medicine, for instance) but by the willingness of politicians and their constituents to pursue mental health education. By all accounts,

Youngdahl's "reform rallies" and other public events were exceptionally well-attended, and there is no reason to believe that crowds dispersed as soon as his assistants struck up their 16mm projectors in order to show *Let There Be Light*, or shielded their eyes from the sight of so many traumatized veterans. In fact, such hotels as the Nicollet in Minneapolis and the Lowry in St. Paul could barely contain the thousands of Minnesotans who "thronged" to the widely publicized screenings of Huston's film, which quickly became standing-room-only affairs, forcing spillover crowds to wait for later showings in the hotels' vast banquet halls.[107] As these and other examples attest, nontheatrical distribution is a vitally important part of the story that we need to tell about the military's relationship to cinema. Pretending otherwise—perpetuating myths of squeamishness and scarcity—is unacceptable.

Conclusion

Traumatic Returns

There is a moment in Clint Eastwood's *American Sniper* (2014) in which Bradley Cooper, as historical figure Chris Kyle, interacts with a number of physically wounded Iraq War veterans—many of them played by actual veterans whose combat-altered bodies, displayed for the camera in blunt tableaux of suffering and recovery, externalize the traumas that appear to haunt Cooper's Kyle.[1] The moment, which takes place in a Veterans Affairs recreation center, thus unites two discrepant yet related traumatic registers, bringing together a beefed-up Hollywood star, with his skillful, neo-Method evocation of psychological damage, and a series of "real people" who, in a sense (and regardless of their intentions), "play themselves," allowing their maimed bodies to bear the burden of representing war trauma. Cooper's expert acting, telegraphing Kyle's anguished interiority and thus elevating *American Sniper* above the staid biopic it might otherwise have been, bespeaks traumas too entrenched to be denied, while his nonprofessional costars, comparatively affectless, index traumas of a different order—traumas that may yet share aspects of Kyle's "invisible" symptomatology.[2]

However responsive to the unique realities of the Iraq War, Eastwood's film is steeped in the psychological rhetoric of an earlier conflict, one that occasioned widespread debates about the relationship between organic and psychogenic factors in war trauma, and that seemed to demand that military-sponsored filmmakers "make the invisible visible" even while insisting on the many "mysteries of the mind." Showing the complex imbrication of paradigms of observational realism and dramatic reconstruction, Eastwood cannot help but evoke such earlier films as Fred Zinnemann's *The Men* (1950), in which the young Marlon Brando skillfully simulates war trauma while surrounded by paraplegic nonprofessionals, and William Wyler's *The Best Years of Our Lives* (1946), in which the inner turmoil that Dana Andrews must convey is counterpoised to the eminently visible traumatic condition of double amputee Harold Russell (the subject of the 1945 Army documentary *Diary of a Sergeant*). In *American Sniper*, Cooper must perform war trauma without the aid of a simulated physical injury, while his amateur costars, lacking the actor's virtuosity, are on hand to literalize Kyle's psychic condition, making the character's pain all the more visible through—paradoxically—their own missing limbs.

Eastwood's amalgamating strategy, with its fusion of observation and reconstruction, autobiographical display and actorly transformation, has long served as the crux of efforts to both visualize and "manage" war trauma in documentary and realist films. While the star-driven *American Sniper* would not seem to lay claim to a documentary character, it nevertheless partakes of representational devices that fleetingly lend it a documentary value in excess of its basic biographical and realist intentions. Bradley Cooper may strive to make psychological trauma "real" for the audience, but that audience must be capable of reading the signs of his performance—the subtle behavioral tics that bespeak trauma even (perhaps especially) in Kyle's quieter moments. Cooper's amputee costars demand considerably less cognitive labor, however, their maimed bodies not only obvious guarantors of authenticity—of, specifically, the men's status as actual veterans (and actual amputees)—but also readily readable symbols of the high costs of combat.

That *American Sniper* is very much a vehicle for Bradley Cooper does not diminish its documentary potential, for Cooper is merely modeling, in his own, "able-bodied" way, the traumatic effects so starkly evident in the film's use of actual veterans. It is precisely as a commentary on trauma's diverse character that *American Sniper* may be aligned with earlier efforts to test the boundaries of documentary as a form of instruction, therapy, artistry, and advocacy. For the dialectic of visibility and invisibility with which Eastwood must wrestle, and that appears to have demanded that he supplement Bradley Cooper's star performance with "real people" instantly recognizable not only as such but also, and more specifically, as victims of war trauma, is nothing less than a basic challenge of documentary. How to make the realities of trauma intelligible to spectators? How to blend the "working through" of staging with the stark actuality of "simply being"? Cooper, as Kyle, is one source of historical reconstruction, literally reenacting events narrated in Kyle's autobiography, on which the film is based; the amputees, by contrast, are objects of observation—ambassadors of the "real" that ostensibly serve a legitimating function, drawing Cooper (and the film itself) into their unsimulated orbit.

It is when addressing war trauma that *American Sniper* invites us to engage with it as (if it were) a documentary, recalling an earlier period of filmmaking in which war trauma stood as a dominant challenge not merely to representation itself but also to any number of seemingly axiomatic distinctions between fiction and nonfiction. Indeed, *American Sniper* merely extends into star-driven, twenty-first-century territory the very devices characteristic of efforts to define war trauma during and in the wake of World War II. Eastwood's combination of, in John Corner's terms, the "captured" and the "constructed"—the former a function of employing "real people" and placing them in a setting to which they are presumably accustomed (a VA rec center), the latter a matter of star performance and effects-driven studio filmmaking—has important roots in the 1940s, when the United States military, facing unprecedented levels of psychological distress among enlisted personnel, utilized film in a concerted effort to address the epidemic of war trauma.[3] "Tragic as it was that so many men became psychiatric casualties, there was an intangible benefit in the common knowledge about them," wrote the psychiatrist William C. Menninger in 1948.[4] As conduits of this knowledge—the very tools that worked to make it "common" in Menninger's sense—documentary and realist films were key elements of what the sociologist Philip Rieff called "the triumph of the therapeutic."[5] They helped bridge gaps between professional expertise and everyday concerns, bringing psychiatric insights to schools, churches, factories, civic organizations, and community centers nationwide. Yet their success as instruments of the military-industrial state cannot be explained by presentist methods that insist on the naïveté and sheer camp value of wartime and postwar propaganda films—an approach popularized by *The Atomic Café* (Jayne Loader, Kevin Rafferty, and Pierce Rafferty, 1982) and other compilation films, including the Army's own *The 20th Anniversary of the Army Pictorial Center* (1962), which pokes fun at the titular studio, downplaying its erstwhile importance and offering an abundance of farcical outtakes from the 1940s.

A certain resistance to the totalizing dimensions of the modernist project—an awareness of its limitations and, by extension, those of the documentary tradition itself—is evident in military films about war trauma: psychoneurosis flourishes in the face of modernism's emphasis on rationality, a direct and obstreperous result of the technologized commitment to imposing order on the world, including through "total war"; traumatic symptoms linger, some of them unaccountably and indefinitely; and trauma itself exceeds and defies conventional descriptive and interpretive gestures, placing considerable burdens on documentary as an "instrument of rationality." Thus even as they endeavor to distill, with a familiar pedagogic drive, the essence of particular branches of military psychiatry, documentaries about war trauma are obliged to concede that a complete recovery is not possible for all patients, that trauma is inconsistent and sometimes elusive, and that many of the tools of science, however exalted in certain quarters, remain controversial—subject to revision, oppositional hypotheses, and outright attacks.

Heartily embraced by the likes of Roy Grinker and John Spiegel, narcosynthesis was rejected by others as a "crude mental enema."[6] Likewise, the dramatic reenactments that played so prominent a part in Grinker and Spiegel's clinical practice, and which saw them plausibly assuming the roles of actual and imagined combatants, were dismissed by some as mere "playacting."[7] Even John Huston's *Let There Be Light*, for all its insistence on the miracles of modern medicine, allows for (but does not directly represent) certain exceptions, such as psychiatric methods that are ineffective for some patients; communicated through Walter Huston's voice-over narration, such exceptions signal the impossibility of making sweeping claims about military psychiatry, even in a film that otherwise, in its teleological presentation of the psychiatric treatment of traumatized veterans, evokes a kind of New Deal confidence.[8]

Despite these challenges and inconsistencies, however, documentary and realist films about war trauma tend to maintain a remarkably stable relationship with the military-industrial state, consistently advocating on behalf of the traumatized veteran's reintegration into its therapeutic fold. In the 1960s, however, some nontheatrical films began to draw attention to the military's institutional role in creating and exacerbating trauma. Produced by Studio One Animation for the Minnesota Department of Public Welfare and based, in part, on Erving Goffman's *Asylums*, the animated film *Dehumanization and the Total Institution* (Don Bajus, 1966) links the military to the mental hospital in its capacity to "adversely affect human dignity." "Do we confuse conformity to rules with mental health?" asks the narrator.

By the 1970s, military facilities had been transformed into woefully inadequate sites in American cinema—places where traumatized Vietnam veterans could not possibly achieve recovery. The male protagonist of Hal Ashby's Coming Home (1978) must escape the clutches of the VA in order to find fulfillment—erotic, intellectual, and otherwise—with a civilian woman "on the outside." Both the Marines and the Veterans Administration refused to cooperate with the making of the film, marking a new era in Hollywood's docudramatic depictions of trauma and rehabilitation—a clean break from such state-sponsored works as Zinnemann's The Men, which was shot at a VA hospital in California, and William Wyler's The Best Years of Our Lives, which enjoyed ample support from the armed forces. Partly shot on location at a VA hospital in Cleveland, Ohio, Michael Cimino's The Deer Hunter (1978) depicts VA facilities as overcrowded netherworlds where clumsy nurses spill pills and where "therapy" is limited to excruciatingly boring bingo nights—a far cry from the clinically sophisticated sites portrayed in Service to Those Who Served, Shadow in the Sky (Fred M. Wilcox, 1952), and any number of other films produced in the wake of World War II.

Numerous state-sponsored nontheatrical films of the 1970s attempted to counteract the antiwar climate of the decade, offering a strategic return to earlier discourses of trauma and psychotherapy. The ill-fated film Vietnam! Vietnam! (Sherman Beck, 1971), produced for the United States Information Agency (USIA) and "presented" by John Ford, is a case in point: designed to convince "world opinion" of the political importance and moral necessity of the war in Vietnam, the film would serve simply as a key (if relatively little-seen) example of tone-deaf state propaganda. One hundred sixty-one prints of the film were shipped to the USIA's foreign outposts, the majority of which, besieged by violent antiwar protests, promptly shipped them back, never having screened them.[9] Restricted (until 1990) to media professionals, members of Congress, and other government officials, Vietnam! Vietnam! would seem to represent a unique example in the history of state-sponsored documentary, but the film follows many of the discursive patterns described in this book, particularly in its insistence that the U.S. military is a reliable source of physical and psychological rehabilitation—in this case, for South Vietnamese children as well as for the American soldiers who endeavor to "protect" them. Antiwar protesters, far from the proponents of sustained psychiatric treatment that so many of them actually were, are here depicted as obstacles to soldiers' physical and emotional recovery. One hospitalized serviceman, wheeled out to describe his ordeal for the filmmakers, goes so far as to suggest his ongoing victimization at the hands of "ignorant" activists. The antiwar sentiments of famed pediatrician Benjamin Spock, who speaks of the moral and legal traumas of the war in Vietnam, are set against the more familiar (and purportedly more palatable) sentiments of Secretary of State Dean Rusk, who calls for "more compassion and more sympathy"—not merely for the beleaguered South Vietnamese but also for the American war veterans who, recovering in VA hospitals, testify to their convalescent conditions, telling the camera that physical and psychological traumas are a small price to pay for protecting "freedom," particularly given the state's alleged commitment to rehabilitation.

Conceivably, the disastrous global reception of *Vietnam! Vietnam!* helped throw into stark relief the strategic presentation of psychotherapy in earlier films that sought to normalize war trauma and the permanence of America's large-scale military force—and that, unlike *Vietnam! Vietnam!*, had been widely circulated, including to secondary schools. Directed by Sherman Beck, who had served in the Signal Corps during World War II, *Vietnam! Vietnam!* follows the longstanding military formula of depicting the horrors of war and their careful "containment" by the armed forces. Rooted in the public relations value of the "strategy of truth" as much as in a certain conception of documentary as a reliable vehicle of traumatic realities, this formula would seem to have been undermined by the poorly received *Vietnam! Vietnam!* and other films of its state-sponsored ilk. But recent developments prove its staying power, demonstrating that it is anything but archaic. When, for instance, U.S. military personnel develop audiovisual narratives—including television soap operas—for the entertainment, edification, and emotional rehabilitation of Iraqi audiences, they are operating very much in the therapeutic vein of their 1940s predecessors, counting on the restorative effects of media screened nontheatrically and according to precise psychiatric and psychological prescriptions.[10] Likewise, today's "Hire a Hero" job fairs, which tout employers' commitment to veterans (including "wounded warriors"), rest upon the discursive work performed by films that, circulated nontheatrically for decades, credibly insisted on the sanity and employability of battle-scarred ex-servicemen.[11]

It may seem as if the steady privatization of care—coupled with the kind of sentiment encapsulated in Ronald Reagan's famous remark that "government is the problem, not the solution"—has diminished the demand for anything like the state-sponsored production that this book recounts.[12] "The nine most terrifying words in the English language are 'I'm from the government and I'm here to help,'" Reagan declared in 1986, echoing the arguments of so many post-Vietnam films that, like *The Deer Hunter*, thematize a masculinist and white-supremacist sense of "personal responsibility" in the wake of massive state failures.[13] Amidst this triumph of neoliberalism, however, the military has only broadened its influence over popular understandings of trauma and psychotherapy, enforcing a docudramatic return to the VA hospital as a praiseworthy site of recovery in such films as *American Sniper* and *When the Game Stands Tall* (Thomas Carter, 2014), which show the state successfully rehabilitating Iraq War veterans.[14]

An increasingly conspicuous feature of Army posts and other military installations, "simulation centers" look a lot like the psychodrama theaters of yesteryear, and provide military personnel—including combat-traumatized soldiers—with opportunities to "work through" various emotional obstacles via virtual reality. New technologies have hardly replaced flesh-and-blood psychiatrists and other psychological experts, however. Instead, these technologies merely supplement—and are in fact structured by—the work of such experts, who often share spaces of simulation previously reserved for face-to-face encounters recorded by film cameras. The style of psychodrama theater pioneered by psychiatrists and social workers at such places as St. Elizabeths Hospital (where Gene Kelly impersonated a traumatized patient in preparation for the film *Combat Fatigue: Irritability*) and Fitzsimons Army Hospital (where Lewis Barbato oversaw the filming of "drama therapy") thus survives to this day, albeit in technologically altered form, with digital networked technologies replacing celluloid film. Despite the growing therapeutic reliance on computer graphics and web-enabled activities, the most conspicuous change is, perhaps, merely terminological, as Grinker and Spiegel had predicted. Terms like "drama therapy" and "psychodrama theater" are, of course, no longer in vogue, having been supplanted by (among others) "simulation therapy," "immersion therapy," and "exposure therapy," just as "PTSD" has reliably replaced "combat fatigue."

The basic premise of psychodrama theater—that "role play" can effect therapeutic change precisely by recreating traumatic combat conditions—remains central to the military's treatment of PTSD (or, more accurately, to the procedures carried out under its auspices, including by private contractors). So, too, have Griersonian ideals of documentation and public education, which informed the filming of psychiatric patients during and in the wake of World War II, carried over into the use of analog and digital video to record encounters between therapists and those suffering from PTSD—or between the latter and their own traumatic memories. Harun Farocki's dual-channel video installation *Serious Games III: Immersion* (2009) documents a workshop demonstration of a new virtual reality "psychotechnology" for the treatment of combat-related PTSD. Part of a four-part series of video installations that reflects Farocki's interest in the seemingly fading distinctions between reality and its simulation, particularly within military contexts, *Immersion* shows how the University of Southern California's Institute of Creative Technologies (ICT), which is sponsored by the Department of Defense and functions in collaboration with the U.S. Army Research Laboratory, has used VR technology in the treatment of PTSD.

Like the other works in Farocki's series, *Immersion* suggests the extent to which the military's contemporary training and therapeutic exercises are reliant upon—even isomorphic with—commercial video games, much as earlier iterations of these exercises seemed indistinguishable (to some observers, at least) from Hollywood fiction films. With funding from the U.S. Office of Naval Research, Albert "Skip" Rizzo, a psychologist at ICT and one of the subjects of *Immersion*, co-developed a "psychotechnology" called "Virtual Iraq" that repurposed computer graphics previously seen in commercial video games like 2004's *Full Spectrum Warrior* and its sequel. Developed for the Navy with the requirement that they be made immediately available for commercial use via the Xbox platform, these graphics were thus "repatriated" to the military in the form of Virtual Iraq, which, as Pasi Väliaho puts it, "produces individually tailored scenarios that re-create the settings where the patients' traumatic events originally occurred." Rather than traveling back to the specific geographical sites of his traumatization (San Pietro, Munich, Berlin, Fallujah), the combat soldier is now required merely to experience a "virtual return" via new technologies that digitally simulate desert scenes and Humvees. "The therapeutic assumption," writes Väliaho, "is that reliving traumatic experiences in the virtual world will help patients significantly reduce if not banish the flashbacks, hallucinations, and dreams of the experiences that torment them and that give rise to fears, anxieties, and stress in their present-day lives."[15] VR goggles thus function for Farocki's Iraq War veterans the way that injections of sodium amytal did for the subjects of Huston's *Let There Be Light*— as, that is, vehicles of traumatic return.

Immersion documents a workshop demonstration of Virtual Iraq for U.S. Army psychologists at Madigan Army Medical Center in January 2009, and it vividly evokes, however unintentionally, the dramaturgical experiments carried out over six decades earlier in Margaret Hagan's psychodrama theater at St. Elizabeths Hospital, as well as in Barbato's Fitzsimons facilities, and its many similarities to military documentaries of the 1940s verge on the uncanny. A traumatized veteran, trying virtual reality exposure therapy (VRET) for the first time, anxiously asks if it has "ever made anyone worse," thus echoing one of the patients in the Army's *Psychiatric Procedures in the Combat Area*, who worries about the possibly iatrogenic effects of narcosynthesis. Throughout *Immersion*, Farocki suggests "the unparalleled visual economy that has emerged in the biopolitical taking charge of the psyches of soldiers," as Väliaho puts it. But this "taking charge" is firmly rooted in capitalist gain—a reality that is beyond the scope, and perhaps irrelevant to the purpose, of Farocki's installation. As Tim Lenoir points out, the Department of Defense "has been the major source of long-term funding for 3-D graphics and work on VR," making it difficult if not impossible to avoid recognizing how the military-industrial complex has reliably extended to encompass the work of video game companies.[16]

Fittingly, perhaps, these companies have increasingly been charged with the responsibility of recreating actual battle conditions, including for the purposes of therapeutic reenactment. In 1991, the Institute for Defense Analyses sought to recreate the Battle of 73 Easting (a tank battle in the Gulf War) "based on in-depth debriefings of 150 survivors." The purpose of this computer-generated recreation—documentary reenactment by new technological means—was "to get timeline-based experiences of how individuals felt, thought, and reacted to the dynamic unfolding of the events—their *fears and emotions* as well as actions—and to render the events as a fully three-dimensional simulated reality that any future cadet could enter and relive."[17] In lieu of transporting traumatized veterans back to "the ruins of recent battlefields" in Italy and North Africa, as in *San Pietro* and *Psychiatric Procedures in the Combat Area*, the military could now rely on VR to furnish such a therapeutic return.

If Virtual Iraq represents the latest outsourcing of psychotherapy for the combat-traumatized, it still rests on precedents set by the military during and in the immediate aftermath of World War II. Today, key players in the privatized military industry, such as Strategic Communication Laboratories (which specializes in psychological warfare) and other sources of "psychological operations," are explicitly built upon the earlier work of psychiatrists and other psychological experts.[18] Created in 2007, the United States Africa Command—or AFRICOM—has regularly pursued various mental-health initiatives throughout the continent, often explicitly invoking the therapeutic strategies pioneered by military-sponsored psychological professionals in the 1940s.[19] The history of the RAND Corporation offers numerous examples of the influence of Menninger, Barbato, Grinker, Spiegel, and other psychiatrists who served in the military during World War II. RAND military historian Bernard Brodie, the man credited with the concept of nuclear deterrence, was an outspoken proponent of psychoanalysis, which quickly became "almost de rigueur" at the think tank—a means of "grappling with the aftermath of World War II and the anxieties of the new Cold War."[20] The continued utility of psychoanalysis is evident in the military's responses to the latest methods and means of waging war. Often denounced as an amoral extension of video game culture, distance killing—particularly the use of unmanned combat aerial vehicles—has hardly reduced the incidence of psychological trauma among military personnel. A 2011 report commissioned by the Air Force found high rates of "clinical distress" among drone pilots—a reality subsequently dramatized in such films as *Good Kill* (Andrew Niccol, 2014), *Eye in the Sky* (Gavin Hood, 2015), and *Drone* (Jason Bourque, 2017).[21]

The subject of this book—the treatment of war trauma and psychotherapy in documentary and realist films—could be viewed as a key if understudied component of the postwar "liberal consensus," in that the films in question helped transform the traumatized into a political collective with strong moral and economic claims on the national body. "American liberalism has had many 'protean' forms," writes Jefferson Cowie, "but the version generated by the trauma of the Depression and World War II proved extraordinary because it was not about morality or individual rights or regulation alone, but about *collective economic rights*."[22] Indeed, if there is a common claim in the films examined in this book, it concerns precisely these economic rights and the sheer obscenity of withholding them from anyone touched by war trauma.

It is the durability of these films—enabled by the resilience and reproductive potential of particular nontheatrical distribution networks—that has lent war trauma a lasting urgency even in the face of political attacks on state psychiatric facilities. In 1979, the psychologist John Wilson began organizing therapeutic film screenings at various Veterans Association outreach centers—a project that received a considerable shot in the arm when, in the following year, President Carter signed the Mental Health Systems Act, with its careful attention to community mental health centers.[23] Reagan's subsequent disregard for the act—and his general antipathy to psychiatry as he endeavored to dramatically slash funding for the nearly one hundred veteran centers established during Carter's presidency—could not, of course, prevent the screening of therapeutic films in other settings, from church basements to private homes.[24] The survival of these state-sponsored films *despite* the actions of the state is thus a testament to the enduring, idiosyncratic power of nontheatrical film.

Notes

INTRODUCTION

1. Howard P. Rome, "Therapeutic Films and Group Psychotherapy," in *Group Psychotherapy: A Symposium* (Beacon, NY: Beacon House, 1945), 247–252 [248].

2. Ibid.

3. Ibid.

4. Quoted in Jack C. Ellis, *John Grierson: Life, Contributions, Influence* (Carbondale and Edwardsville: Southern Illinois University Press, 2000), 59.

5. *Movie Lot to Beach Head: The Motion Picture Goes to War and Prepares for the Future by the Editors of Look* (Garden City, NY: Doubleday, Doran, 1945), 268.

6. Unsigned letter, April 29, 1945, Box 12, Folder 14, John M. Murray Papers, Sigmund Freud Collection, Manuscript Division, Library of Congress, Washington, DC (hereafter John M. Murray Papers).

7. "Permanent U.S. Visual Office," *Business Screen*, vol. 6, no. 4 (April 5, 1945), 42.

8. André Bazin, *What Is Cinema? Volume 1*, edited and translated by Hugh Gray (Berkeley: University of California Press, 1967).

9. MGM's *Rage in Heaven* (W.S. Van Dyke II, 1941) features a psychiatrist (Oscar Homolka's Dr. Rameau) at a "private clinic for the insane," who takes an explicitly postempirical approach to trauma: "Evidence, evidence—I spit on evidence!" he cries, dismissing "circumstantial rubbish" as "too convenient, too perfect." Earlier, he carefully (and somewhat contradictorily) explains how "surfaces deceive," pointing to the case of an outwardly "perfect" yet severely disturbed patient: "To you as a layman, he will appear to be a normal, charming, highly intelligent young man. But if you'll watch him closely, you'll notice a certain curious lack of emotion—a certain tonelessness in his speech. To the expert,

these indications confirm that he is suffering from what we call paranoia—[he is] a nervous case."

10. In *Silent Spring*, Rachel Carson would note that strontium 90, "released into the air through nuclear explosions, comes to earth in rain or drifts down as fallout, lodges in soil, enters into the grass or corn or wheat grown there, and, in time, takes up its abode in the bones of a human being, there to remain until his death." Rachel Carson, *Silent Spring* (New York: Mariner Books, 2002 [1962]), 6. Consider, as well, the "shadows of death" described in Sekigawa Hideo's 1953 docudrama *Hiroshima*.

11. David Culbert, "'Why We Fight': Social Engineering for a Democratic Society at War," in *Film & Radio Propaganda in World War II*, ed. K.R.M. Short (Knoxville: University of Tennessee Press, 1983), 173–191 [175].

12. For more on Marshall's report, see Nathan G. Hale, Jr., *The Rise and Crisis of Psychoanalysis in the United States: Freud and the Americans, 1917–1985* (New York: Oxford University Press, 1995), 201.

13. While accepted as a legitimate condition treatable through psychotherapy, war trauma is also played for laughs in *The Big Hangover* (Norman Krasna, 1950): a veteran (played by Van Johnson) has developed a pronounced fear of alcohol—a product of his having been trapped for fourteen hours in a basement in France, in which, during an air raid, several barrels of brandy broke open, flooding the space and nearly drowning him. Embarrassed, the veteran at first refers cryptically to "something that happened to [him] during the war," but he later elaborates, describing his sudden fear of booze: "The Army psychoanalyst thought it was funny . . . Turned out I had recall—you know, fellas who were in explosions get frightened when a match is struck. Well, with me, it's just being susceptible to liquor. Even the smell gets me dizzy, brings it back to my nervous system, or something." He notes that his strange condition has been "written up in a medical journal—two and a half columns and my picture: 'The Biggest Hangover in the History of Medical Science.'" It takes an aspiring psychoanalyst (played by Elizabeth Taylor) to diagnose his "true" condition, which, it turns out, has little to do with brandy per se: "You've been through a war," she explains, "and your best friend died in your arms."

14. "I suppose horses have as much of a right to go crazy as men have," observes an officer of a "shell-shocked" animal in Sam Fuller's *The Big Red One* (1980).

15. In John Ford's Navy documentary *The Battle of Midway* (1942), even the atoll's birds "seem nervous," according to one of the film's narrators.

16. By 1947, a small-town character in *The Long Night* (1947), Anatole Litvak's remake of Marcel Carné's *Le jour se lève* (1939), can casually (if uncharitably) observe, "Yeah, a lot of vets go crazy, you know." Other townspeople are considerably more sensitive, however—including a little girl who calmly, empathically asks the traumatized protagonist, "What happened to you, Joe?" Her earnest effort to understand the plight of the war veteran is shared by the film itself, with its emphatic endorsement of the scores of citizens who fill the town square in support of the suffering Joe. "All these people—they want to know what it's all about," says Joe in voice-over, attesting to the epistemological drive that turns war trauma into a community problem with solutions to be

arrived at collectively. "Please do something for Joe," the little girl begs the chief of police, later learning that no one man, however influential, can "cure" psychoneurosis—that collective action (here couched as "community support") is required. "They know all about you," Joe's girlfriend tells him, giving voice to the film's insistence that war trauma can be understood by one and all. "What happened to you over there in the war that you came back so different?" asks a sympathetic bartender of an alcoholic former journalist in Columbia's *The Guilt of Janet Ames* (Henry Levin, 1947). By contrast, *Kiss the Blood Off My Hands* (Norman Foster, 1948) suggests the destructive impact of civilian ignorance (presented as isomorphic with a patent lack of empathy): "What's the matter with you?" asks an exasperated Joan Fontaine of severely traumatized war veteran Burt Lancaster. "Why can't you be like everybody else?"

17. Roy R. Grinker and John P. Spiegel, *Men Under Stress* (Philadelphia: Blakiston, 1945), 55. "You'll have to get used to that," one character says of his "war jitters" in Monogram's *Below the Deadline* (William Beaudine, 1946). "I haven't sat still in years—in the army they call me Jumpy Joe."

18. Catherine Lutz, *Homefront: A Military City and the American Twentieth Century* (Boston: Beacon Press, 2001), 46.

19. Columbia's *The Guilt of Janet Ames* (Henry Levin, 1947) dramatizes this creative principle, as a "pack of lies" becomes therapeutically sufficient, "curing" the title character's "hysterical paralysis."

20. Rome, "Therapeutic Films and Group Psychotherapy," 486.

CHATPER 1

1. John Milne Murray, "Accomplishments of Psychiatry in the Army Air Forces," March 1947, 598, Box 12, Folder 4, John M. Murray Papers.

2. Ellen Herman, *The Romance of American Psychology: Political Culture in the Age of Experts* (Berkeley: University of California Press, 1995), 86.

3. The report went on to explain that "the reasons for this lie partly in the fact that medical science has not yet discovered ways and means of curing these patients as rapidly as other forms of medical ills, and partly because the resources devoted to such conditions are far short of those devoted to medical and surgical conditions." Daniel Blain, "Priorities in Psychiatric Treatment of Veterans," 1–22 [2], in Box 17, Folder 7, John M. Murray Papers.

4. Rebecca Jo Plant, "Preventing the Inevitable: John Appel and the Problem of Psychiatric Casualties in the US Army During World War II," in *Science and Emotions After 1945: A Transatlantic Perspective*, ed. Frank Biess and Daniel M. Gross (Chicago: University of Chicago Press, 2014), 209–238 [210].

5. Blain, "Priorities in Psychiatric Treatment of Veterans," 1.

6. Ibid. See also *Review of the Month*, the VA's "monthly progress report"—particularly the July 31, 1946 issue, in Box 17, Folder 6, John M. Murray Papers; and John M. Murray, "The Syndrome of Operational Fatigue in Flyers" (ca. 1942), in Box 18, Folder 5, John M. Murray Papers.

7. See, for instance, Richard Dyer MacCann, *The People's Films: A Political History of U.S. Government Motion Pictures* (New York: Hastings House, 1973), 119.

8. Michael Renov, *The Subject of Documentary* (Minneapolis: University of Minnesota Press, 2004), xix–xx.

9. Renov, *The Subject of Documentary*, xviii.

10. Jonathan Michel Metzl, *Prozac on the Couch: Prescribing Gender in the Era of Wonder Drugs* (Durham, NC: Duke University Press, 2003), 201n2. "Madness," says Peter Lorre's character in Fox's *Crack-Up* (Malcolm St. Clair, 1936), "is a very common malady." Consider, as well, the opening lines of Columbia's *Blind Alley* (Charles Vidor, 1939), which are uttered by a professor of "experimental psychology," Dr. Shelby (played by Ralph Bellamy), who is also a practicing psychiatrist ("cur[ing] sick minds by psychoanalysis"): "So, you see, most people don't know how abnormal they are. Most people don't know they're abnormal. . . . The difference between the normal mind and the abnormal is so slight—the thread supporting them so delicate—it would take an extremely acute perception to distinguish between the two." "Furthermore," he continues, "abnormality is more or less relative to the person, time, and place." Later, Dr. Shelby says to the escaped killer holding him hostage, "You'd go far in the Army"—a line that is omitted from the otherwise remarkably faithful 1949 remake, *The Dark Past* (directed by Rudolph Maté), along with Dr. Shelby's glib "I cure screwballs."

11. Quoted in Martin Halliwell, *Therapeutic Revolutions: Medicine, Psychiatry, and American Culture, 1945–1970* (New Brunswick, NJ: Rutgers University Press, 2013), 24.

12. William C. Menninger, *Psychiatry in a Troubled World: Yesterday's War and Today's Challenge* (New York: Macmillan, 1948), 9.

13. Ibid., 19.

14. Ibid., xiii.

15. Quoted in Eli Ginzberg, John L. Herma, and Sol W. Ginsburg, *Psychiatry and Military Manpower Policy: A Reappraisal of the Experience in World War II* (New York: King's Crown Press, 1953), 35.

16. John Milne Murray, "Accomplishments of Psychiatry in the Army Air Forces," March 1947, 598, Box 12, Folder 4, John M. Murray Papers.

17. Metzl, *Prozac on the Couch*, 201n2.

18. John G. Watkins, *Hypnotherapy of War Neuroses: A Clinical Psychologist's Casebook* (New York: Ronald Press, 1949).

19. Ibid., 94, 97.

20. Funded by a teachers' union, Sekigawa Hideo's *Hiroshima* (1953) features, "as themselves," various survivors of the atomic bomb, their keloid scars exposed to the camera—presented as eminently visible analogs of psychic distress. (Released the previous year, Kaneto Shindo's *Children of Hiroshima*—shot on location in the titular city—also features actual, heavily scarred survivors.)

21. Jonathan Kahana, *Intelligence Work: The Politics of American Documentary* (New York: Columbia University Press, 2008), 9.

22. Ibid., 46. William Stott defines social documentary in terms of "the primacy of feeling": "the whole idea of documentary . . . makes it possible to see, know, and feel the details of life, to feel oneself part of some other's experience" (8). Stott's claim that social documentary "educates one's feelings"—that it "shows man at grips with conditions neither permanent nor necessary" (20) and

"deals with facts that are alterable" (26)—resonates with the fundamental frameworks within which military films about trauma and psychotherapy were understood and disseminated during and after World War II. William Stott, *Documentary Expression and Thirties America* (New York: Oxford University Press, 1973). The impermanence of certain traumatic conditions was a point that numerous military psychiatrists stressed—along with the unknowability of trauma's true incidence in the American population at large—in their interactions with filmmakers. "The number of veterans having neurological and psychiatric conditions is not definite and cannot be definite," wrote VA psychiatrist Daniel Blain in 1947. Blain, "Priorities in Psychiatric Treatment of Veterans," 1.

23. Alice Lovejoy, *Army Film and the Avant Garde: Cinema and Experiment in the Czechoslovak Military* (Bloomington: Indiana University Press, 2015), 16.

24. Thomas Waugh, *The Conscience of Cinema: The Works of Joris Ivens 1926–1989* (Amsterdam: Amsterdam University Press, 2016), 306, 308, 323–333.

25. Kahana, *Intelligence Work*, 46.

26. John Stuart, Jr., "The Memphis Belle," *Motion Picture Herald*, vol. 154, no. 13 (March 25, 1944): 75.

27. See, for instance, "Norway Replies," *Motion Picture Herald*, vol. 154, no. 10 (March 4, 1944): 94.

28. Some prints use the shortened title *The Inside Story*; emphasis added.

29. Howard P. Rome, "Audio-Visual Aids in Psychiatry," *Business Screen*, no. 5 (1945), 68, 104.

30. For a brief account of the film's reception in secondary schools, see Harold Wright Bernard, *Toward Better Personal Adjustment* (New York: McGraw-Hill, 1951), 417. The industrial metaphors on which *Seaman Jones* relies were rooted in earlier discursive efforts. Exploring the application "to the American Army [of] the logics of biomechanical efficiency initially developed for the factory floor," Florian Hoof suggests how, beginning in the 1910s, military films epitomized "the exchange of ideas between the military and the industrial sector," functioning as "building block[s] for the evolving military-industrial complex." Florian Hoof, "Between the Front Lines: Military Training Films, Machine Guns, and the Great War," in *Cinema's Military Industrial Complex*, ed. Haidee Wasson and Lee Grieveson (Berkeley: University of California Press, 2018), 177–191 [177–178]. See also Noah Tsika, "From Wartime Instruction to Superpower Cinema: Maintaining the Military-Industrial Documentary," in *Cinema's Military Industrial Complex*, 192–209.

31. Quoted in Leonard Mosley, *Zanuck: The Rise and Fall of Hollywood's Last Tycoon* (Boston: Little, Brown, 1984), 210–211.

32. See also Zoë Druick and Jonathan Kahana, "New Deal Documentary and the North Atlantic Welfare State," in *The Documentary Film Book*, ed. Brian Winston (London: Palgrave, 2015), 153–158.

33. See Mickey Rooney's remarkable portrait of a traumatized Korean War veteran in *The Strip* (László Kardos, 1951). "It was in Korea," explains Rooney's character. "I was in some . . . hospitals. Finally ended up in a VA in Kansas."

34. Gloria Waldron, *The Information Film: A Report of the Public Library Inquiry* (New York: Columbia University Press, 1949), 12.

35. Charles F. Hoban, Jr., *Movies That Teach* (New York: Dryden, 1946), 68, 67, italics in original.

36. Peter Maslowski, *Armed with Cameras: The American Military Photographers of World War II* (New York: Free Press, 1993), 89–90.

37. Curtis Mitchell to Colonel Barrett, "Report From the Aleutians," August 11, 1943; Emanuel Cohen to Mr. Ray Little, Eastman Kodak Company, August 23, 1943, Box 3, *It's Your War Too* folder, Record Group 111 (hereafter RG 111), National Archives and Records Administration (hereafter NARA).

38. Brian McAllister Linn, *Elvis's Army: Cold War GIs and the Atomic Battlefield* (Cambridge, MA: Harvard University Press, 2016), 256–257.

39. John M. Murray to Dr. Lawrence Kolb, January 12, 1948, in Box 12, Folder 4, John M. Murray Papers. For more on Becker's "Mr. Everyman," see Kahana, *Intelligence Work*, 64–66. In the early 1970s, William Stott offered an influential conception of documentary as the genre of and for the "common man," writing, "Documentary is a radically democratic genre. It dignifies the usual and levels the extraordinary. Most often its subject is the common man." Stott identifies Edward R. Murrow's radio broadcasts during the Battle of Britain as emblematic of this tendency—especially given Murrow's repeated question "How does Commonman feel?" Stott, *Documentary Expression and Thirties America*, 49–50.

40. See also Columbia's *Bad for Each Other* (Irving Rapper, 1953), in which a former Army doctor (a veteran of the Korean War, played by Charlton Heston) complains of having to treat "spoiled" civilians. "In the Army, I'm a doctor, treating real patients"—as opposed to the wealthy, "neurotic" society women of Pittsburgh, who develop what he dismissively terms "imaginary illnesses."

41. "Lady in the Dark," *Motion Picture Herald*, vol. 154, no. 7 (February 12, 1944): 67; William R. Weaver, "Studios Turn to Psychiatry as New Picture Theme," *Motion Picture Herald*, vol. 155, no. 10 (June 3, 1944): 28; David Bordwell, *Reinventing Hollywood: How 1940s Filmmakers Changed Movie Storytelling* (Chicago: University of Chicago Press, 2017), 314.

42. J. L. Moreno, *Psychodrama: First Volume* (New York: Beacon House, 1959 [1946]), 392.

43. For more on the cultivation of television's therapeutic dimensions, see Joy V. Fuqua, *Prescription TV: Therapeutic Discourse in the Hospital and at Home* (Durham, NC: Duke University Press, 2012).

44. For a summary of these ads, see "Television a Reality, NBC Ads Insist," *Motion Picture Herald*, vol. 155, no. 6 (May 6, 1944): 23.

45. See, for instance, Winfield W. Riefler, "Our Economic Contribution to Victory," *Foreign Affairs*, vol. 26, no. 1 (October 1947): 9–103.

46. Herbert I. Schiller, *Mass Communications and American Empire* (New York: Augustus M. Kelley, 1969), 93.

47. Anna McCarthy, *The Citizen Machine: Governing by Television in 1950s America* (New York: New Press, 2010).

48. Herbert I. Schiller and Joseph D. Phillips, "Introduction: The Military-Industrial Establishment: Complex or System?" in *Super-State: Readings in the*

Military-Industrial Complex (Urbana: University of Illinois Press, 1970), 1–28 [27, 1, 26]."

49. "Exploiting the New Films," *Motion Picture Herald*, vol. 155, no. 6 (May 6, 1944): 60.

50. Manny Farber, "The Lady and the Belle," in *Farber on Film: The Complete Writings of Manny Farber*, ed. Robert Polito (New York: Library of America, 2009), 155–157.

51. Douglas Cunningham, "Imaging/Imagining Air Force Identity: 'Hap' Arnold, Warner Bros., and the Formation of the USAAF First Motion Picture Unit," *The Moving Image*, vol. 5, no. 1 (Spring 2005): 95–124.

52. Ibid., 99–100.

53. Aeron Davis, *Promotional Cultures: The Rise and Spread of Advertising, Public Relations, Marketing and Branding* (Malden, MA: Polity Press, 2013).

54. George Creel, *How We Advertised America: The First Telling of the Amazing Story of the Committee on Public Information that Carried the Gospel of Americanism to Every Corner of the Globe* (New York: Harper & Brothers, 1920), 155. Tanner Mirrlees has commented on the military's marketing efforts, writing, "From the First World War throughout the wars of the twentieth century and to this day, PR strategies initially designed to support capitalism's sales effort have converged with and become indistinguishable from large-scale national security state campaigns aimed at selling America and war policy to the world." Tanner Mirrlees, *Hearts and Mines: The US Empire's Culture Industry* (Vancouver: UCB Press, 2016), 68.

55. Tsika, "From Wartime Instruction to Superpower Cinema."

56. Woodruff S. Post, memorandum, Project 11,929, October 1, 1946, RG 111, Box 10, *Employing Disabled Veterans in Industry* folder, NARA.

57. Floyde E. Brooker to Signal Corps Photographic Center, June 13, 1946, RG 111, Box 10, *Employing Disabled Veterans in Industry* folder, NARA.

58. Colonel E.M. DeYoung, "Memorandum for Director, Information & Education Division, War Department," March 28, 1946, in ibid.

59. Florian Hoof notes that, by the end of World War I, the "growing importance of film for the military not only led to new film units inside the military organization but also presented promising business opportunities for external consultants and film professionals." Hoof, "Between the Front Lines," 182. Making military documentaries represents a "cushy job" for Melvyn Douglas's character in *My Own True Love* (Compton Bennett, 1949), in explicit contrast to the traumatizing combat experiences of his pilot son, who returns from the war both physically and mentally "damaged."

60. Kahana, *Intelligence Work*, 8.

61. George's 1948 U.S. Army film *Toward Independence* would win the Academy Award for Best Documentary (Short Subject). For more on Grierson's transnational influence, see Christie Milliken, "Continence of the Continent: The Ideology of Disease and Hygiene in World War II Training Films," in *Cultural Studies: Medicine and Media*, ed. Lester D. Friedman (Durham, NC: Duke University Press, 2004), 280–298 [288]. Milliken misleadingly claims that the U.S. Army Signal Corps would produce "more than two hundred" films; in fact, the subdivision would produce well over two thousand.

62. John Trumpbour, *Selling Hollywood to the World: U.S. And European Struggles for Mastery of the Global Film Industry* (Cambridge: Cambridge University Press, 2002), 125.

63. Kahana, *Intelligence Work*, 12.

64. Hoban, Jr., *Movies That Teach*, 153.

65. While the term "military-industrial complex" is closely associated with Dwight D. Eisenhower, who memorably employed it in his last speech as president in January 1961, Eisenhower did not coin the term, and its appearance in these pages is hardly anachronistic: as James Ledbetter has revealed, the term has a rich history that long predates Eisenhower's speech, and its explanatory utility intensified in response to World War II (thanks, in part, to the work of economist Winfield W. Riefler in 1947). James Ledbetter, *Unwarranted Influence: Dwight D. Eisenhower and the Military-Industrial Complex* (New Haven, CT: Yale University Press, 2011).

66. Hoban, Jr., *Movies That Teach*, 36.

67. Michael Chanan, *The Politics of Documentary* (London: BFI, 2008), 7.

68. Tsika, "From Wartime Instruction to Superpower Cinema."

69. Waldron, *The Information Film*, 116.

70. In 1949, an estimated five thousand screenings sponsored by the National Conference were held in Hartford, Connecticut alone. Waldron, *The Information Film*, 121.

71. See, for instance, Lillian Wachtel, "We Use Films in Our Program," *Film News*, vol. 8, no. 4–5 (September/October, 1947): 24; and Lillian Wachtel, "We Use Films In Our Program: League of Women Voters of the U.S.A.," *Film News*, vol. 8, no. 5–6 (November/December, 1947): 18.

72. Ibid., 120–123, 126.

73. Memorandum to the chancellor and council of New York University, from the board of the Educational Film Institute and New York University Film Library, June 8, 1945, Box 39, Folder 9, Administrative Papers of Chancellor Harry Woodburn Chase, 1933–1951, Record Group 3.0.5, Series II: Administrative Correspondence, New York University Archives (hereafter Harry W. Chase Papers).

74. Robert Gessner, "In the Post-War World Educational Films Will Illuminate the Classroom," Box 39, Folder 9, Harry W. Chase Papers.

75. June Bingham, *The Inside Story: Psychiatry and Everyday Life* (New York: Vintage Books, 1953). At least one earlier film shares this approach to "matters of the mind." In Columbia's *Blind Alley* (Charles Vidor, 1939), Ralph Bellamy, with pencil and paper, sketches the conscious and unconscious minds— as well as "the censor band" separating the two—for the severely traumatized, diversely symptomatic escaped killer who is holding him hostage. The figure Bellamy draws "could be anybody—let's say it's *you*."

76. Damion Searls, *The Inkblots: Hermann Rorschach, His Iconic Test, and the Power of Seeing* (New York: Crown, 2017), 201.

77. Ellen Dwyer, "Psychiatry and Race during World War II," *Journal of the History of Medicine and Allied Scientists*, vol. 61, no. 2 (April 2006): 117–143 [119].

78. Quoted in Allan Bérubé, *Coming Out Under Fire: The History of Gay Men and Women in World War II* (New York: Plume, 1990), 11.

79. "Governor Urges Speed in Mental Hospital Aid," *Minnesota Welfare*, vol. 4, no. 8 (February, 1949): 3.

80. Thomas Doherty, *Projections of War: Hollywood, American Culture, and World War II*, rev. ed. (New York: Columbia University Press, 1999 [1993]), 201; Mark Harris, *Five Came Back: A Story of Hollywood and the Second World War* (New York: Penguin, 2014), 413. Tanner Mirrlees goes so far as to allege that *all* of Huston's Army documentaries "were not released to the public, on the grounds that they would demoralize America and harm future recruitment efforts." Mirrlees, *Hearts and Mines*, 169.

81. Internal memorandum, May 21, 1946 (handwritten addendum dated May 22, 1946), Box 11, *Let There Be Light* folder, RG 111, NARA.

82. See Nancy Katz and Robert Katz, "Documentary in Transition, Part 1: The United States." *Hollywood Quarterly*, vol. 3, no. 4 (1948): 426–435.

83. The Netflix miniseries *Five Came Back* (2016) and the Mark Harris book on which it is based are obvious examples of this tendency. "Anti-Retro: Michel Foucault in Interview with Pascal Bonitzer and Serge Toubiana," trans. Annwyl Williams, in *Cahiers du Cinéma, Volume Four*, ed. David Wilson (New York: Routledge, 2000), 159–171 [161].

84. Haidee Wasson, "Protocols of Portability," *Film History*, vol. 25, no. 1–2 (2013): 236–247 [240]. See also Haidee Wasson, "Experimental Viewing Protocols: Film Projection and the American Military," in *Cinema's Military Industrial Complex*, 25–43.

85. "Anti-Retro," 161–162.

86. Michael Rogin, "'Make My Day!': Spectacle as Amnesia in Imperial Politics." *Representations*, no. 29 (Winter, 1990): 99–123 [114].

87. Untitled document, ca. 1946, 14, Box 6, Folder 4, John M. Murray Papers. See also the case history of a severely traumatized veteran of the Siege of Bastogne, who, under the influence of sodium pentothal, said to a psychiatrist, "Fucking Army. Teach you in the damn book how to fight—why you fight. It's a damn lie. You just go up to the front with a gun. You don't know where your objective is or where you are at—nobody does. Think more of a jeep than they do a battalion of men. Fucking me up." "Pentothal Interview," May 23, 1945, Box 17, Folder 1, John M. Murray Papers. Confusion regarding "why we fight" is common in transcriptions of such "pentothal interviews." Diagnosed with severe anxiety and a "schizoid personality," one man screamed, "What the hell are we fighting for? Shit, shit on a stick!" "Case History: Majcher, Leonard," 1, Box 17, Folder 1, John M. Murray Papers.

88. Paul Virilio, *War and Cinema: The Logistics of Perception*, trans. Patrick Camiller (London: Verso, 1989), 13.

89. Ibid., 34.

90. Lovejoy, *Army Film and the Avant Garde*, 7.

91. Haidee Wasson and Charles R. Acland, "Introduction: Utility and Cinema," in *Useful Cinema*, ed. Charles R. Acland and Haidee Wasson (Durham: Duke University Press, 2011), 1–14.

92. David Serlin, "Introduction: Toward a Visual Culture of Public Health," in *Imagining Illness: Public Health and Visual Culture*, ed. David Serlin (Minneapolis: University of Minnesota Press, 2010), xi–xxxvii [xxiii].

93. Walter Benjamin, "Theses on the Philosophy of History," in *Illuminations*, trans. Harry Zohn, ed. Hannah Arendt (New York: Schocken Books, 1968), 253–264 [255].

94. In Barbara Berch, "Gold in Them Chills," *Collier's*, January 29, 1944, 66.

95. Penny Coleman, *Flashback: Posttraumatic Stress Disorder, Suicide, and the Lessons of War* (Boston: Beacon Press, 2006), 50–51.

96. Plant, "Preventing the Inevitable," 210.

97. William C. Menninger, "The Military Psychiatrist," *Bulletin of the Menninger Clinic* 7 (July 4, 1943): 129–136 [129].

98. Rosa Brooks, *How Everything Became War and the Military Became Everything: Tales from the Pentagon* (New York: Simon & Schuster, 2016), 189.

99. Herman, *The Romance of American Psychology*, 242–243.

100. Eva S. Moskowitz, *In Therapy We Trust: America's Obsession with Self-Fulfillment* (Baltimore, MD: Johns Hopkins University Press, 2001).

101. Herman, *The Romance of American Psychology*, 67.

102. Searls, *The Inkblots*, 198–199.

103. Eric Jaffe, *A Curious Madness: An American Combat Psychiatrist, a Japanese War Crimes Suspect, and an Unsolved Mystery from World War II* (New York: Scribner, 2014), 148.

104. Charles Wolfe, "Mapping *Why We Fight*: Frank Capra and the US Army Orientation Film in World War II," in *American Film History: Selected Readings, Origins to 1960*, ed. Cynthia Lucia, Roy Grundmann, and Art Simon (West Sussex: Wiley Blackwell, 2016), 326–340 [328].

105. Plant, "Preventing the Inevitable," 214. *The Long Night* (1947), Anatole Litvak's remake of Marcel Carné's *Le jour se lève* (1939), presents war trauma as "absolutely normal"—the psychological flipside of physical wounds (like the blindness that results from one character's combat injuries). The first film that Litvak made after his wartime contributions to the Army Signal Corps, *The Long Night* deviates from its predecessor in ways that emphasize American faith in psychotherapy—in, specifically, the availability and effectiveness of psychiatric treatment for "nervously wounded" veterans. Instead of committing suicide, like Jean Gabin's character in Carné's original film, Henry Fonda's protagonist is coaxed out of hiding by the promise of community support and psychotherapy, and *The Long Night* ends with war trauma accepted and small-town values restored.

106. John W. Appel, "Prevention of Loss of Manpower from Psychiatric Disorders: A Report of the Surgeon General," Special Technical Bulletin no. 3, December 1, 1944, file 147, box 1310, RG 112, NARA, 1.

107. In RKO's *Crack-Up* (Irving Reis, 1946), a veteran played by Pat O'Brien says that he has "seen a lot of good guys crack up in this war. Cool, composed cookies one day, and the next, snapped like a tight violin string. It's the one fear everybody had—they kept thinking, 'It might happen to me.'" As a doctor later puts it, "Even the finest minds have their saturation point."

108. Herman, *The Romance of American Psychology*, 244.

109. Ibid., 87.

110. Ibid., 90.

111. Neuropsychiatry Consultants Division memorandum, quoted in William C. Menninger, "Public Relations," in *Neuropsychiatry in World War II: Vol. I—Zone of Interior*, ed. R. S. Anderson, A. J. Glass, and R. J. Bernucci (Washington, DC: U.S. Government Printing Office, 1966), 129–151 [147].

112. "Forgotten?" *Film News*, vol. 8, no. 5–6 (November/December 1947): 31.

113. Herman, *The Romance of American Psychology*, 83.

114. Judith Butler writes of official efforts to render "insensate certain losses whose open mourning might challenge the rationale of war itself." Military-sponsored films about trauma and recovery are thus among the "cultural modes of regulating affective and ethical dispositions" regarding war and its waging. Judith Butler, *Frames of War: When Is Life Grievable?* (London: Verso, 2016), xvi, 1.

115. Fredric Jameson, *The Political Unconscious: Narrative as a Socially Symbolic Act* (Ithaca: Cornell University Press, 1981), 10.

116. Ibid., 10–11. Butler has similarly considered "how war waging acts upon the senses so that war is thought to be an inevitability, something good, or even a source of moral satisfaction." Butler notes that "the frame is always throwing something away, always keeping something out, always de-realizing and de-legitimating alternative versions of reality, discarded negatives of the official version. . . . Even as the frames are actively engaged in redoubling the destruction of war, they are only polishing the surface of a melancholia whose rage must be contained, and often cannot." Butler, *Frames of War*, ix, xiii.

117. Schiller and Phillips, "Introduction," 6–7.

118. Mimi White, *Tele-Advising: Therapeutic Discourse in American Television* (Chapel Hill: University of North Carolina Press, 1992), 22–24.

119. In Michel Foucault, *Power/Knowledge: Selected Interviews and Other Writings, 1972–1977*, ed. Colin Gordon (New York: Random House, 1980), 61. Butler calls for efforts "to distinguish between instrumental forms of reasoning and normative justifications." Butler, *Frames of War*, xv.

120. Menninger, "Public Relations," 136.

121. Ibid., 142.

122. J. R. Rees, *The Shaping of Psychiatry by War* (New York: W. W. Norton, 1945).

123. Norman C. Meier, *Military Psychology* (New York: Harper & Brothers, 1943), 279.

124. Eleanor Roosevelt, "My Day, October 6, 1942," *Eleanor Roosevelt Papers Digital Edition* (2008), accessed 5/20/2017, https://www2.gwu.edu/~erpapers/myday/displaydoc.cfm?_y=1942&_f=mdo56309.

125. Alison Winter, "Film and the Construction of Memory in Psychoanalysis, 1940–1960." *Science in Context*, vol. 19, no. 1 (2006): 111–136 [115].

126. For more on *Combat Exhaustion*, see Kaia Scott, "Managing the Trauma of Labor: Military Psychiatric Cinema in World War II," in *Cinema's Military Industrial Complex*, 116–136. See also Winter, "Film and the Construction of Memory in Psychoanalysis."

127. E. Fuller Torrey, *American Psychosis: How the Federal Government Destroyed the Mental Illness Treatment System* (New York: Oxford University Press, 2014), 26–29.

128. William C. Menninger, "Education and Training," in *Neuropsychiatry in World War II: Vol. I*, 53–66 [66].

129. Menninger, "Public Relations," 139.

130. Ibid., 140.

131. Ibid., 143.

132. Menninger, "Education and Training," 66.

133. Winter, "Film and the Construction of Memory in Psychoanalysis," 118; Robert J. Carpenter and S. Bayne-Jones, quoted in Menninger, "Public Relations," 148.

134. Carpenter and Bayne-Jones, quoted in Menninger, "Public Relations," 148.

135. Carl R. Rogers and John L. Wallen, *Counseling with Returned Servicemen* (New York: McGraw-Hill, 1946), 19. See also Carl R. Rogers, *Counseling and Psychotherapy: Newer Concepts in Practice* (Boston: Houghton Mifflin, 1942).

136. This approach is parodied in Columbia's *The Wife Takes a Flyer* (Richard Wallace, 1942), in which a buffoonish German officer believes that any affliction—including "a nervous breakdown"—can be overcome through "willpower."

137. Subtitled *A Psychoanalytic Film*, Pabst's *Secrets of a Soul* was made under the supervision of "technical consultants" Drs. Karl Abraham and Hanns Sachs, and it opens with a series of title cards that tout its documentary value: "The events in this film are taken from life," reads one. "They do not deviate in any important factual way from the actual medical case history."

138. Agnieszka Piotrowska, *Psychoanalysis and Ethics in Documentary Film* (London: Routledge, 2014), 7.

139. *Movie Lot to Beach Head*, 109.

140. Ibid., 45.

141. Ibid., 52, 105.

142. Lt. Comdr. Philip Solomon, "Military Aspects of Mental Disease," *Marine Corps Gazette*, December 1945, 45–50.

143. Samuel Fuller, with Christa Lang Fuller and Jerome Henry Rudes, *A Third Face: My Tale of Writing, Fighting, and Filmmaking* (New York: Alfred A. Knopf, 2002), 114.

144. Daniel Lang, "Fallout," *New Yorker*, July 16, 1955, 31–41.

145. See also MGM's *The Beginning or the End* (Norman Taurog, 1947), a docudramatic recounting of the Manhattan Project, in which footage of the test at Los Alamos is screened for pilots in the Marianas, who respond with considerable shock.

146. Winter, "Film and the Construction of Memory in Psychoanalysis," 124.

147. Brian Winston, "Introduction," *The Documentary Film Book*, 25. My exploration of these dialectics of visibility and invisibility is indebted to Kirsten Ostherr, *Cinematic Prophylaxis: Globalization and Contagion in the Discourse*

of World Health (Durham, NC: Duke University Press, 2005). "I carry the war with me," says the traumatized protagonist of *Confidential Agent* (Herman Shumlin, 1945). "Perhaps I ought to wear a bell, like the old lepers."

148. Roy R. Grinker and John P. Spiegel, *Men Under Stress* (Philadelphia: Blakiston, 1945), 371.

149. This is Cathy Caruth's translation of Jacques Derrida, "Prière d'insérer," *Mal d'Archive*, in Caruth, *Literature in the Ashes of History* (Baltimore, MD: Johns Hopkins University Press, 2013), 77.

150. Jacques Derrida, *Archive Fever: A Freudian Impression*, trans. Eric Prenowitz (Chicago: University of Chicago Press, 1996), 30.

151. Rebecca Jo Plant, "William Menninger and American Psychoanalysis, 1946–48." *History of Psychiatry*, vol. 16, no. 2 (2005): 181–202 [182].

152. Solomon, "Military Aspects of Mental Disease," 48.

153. Marlisa Santos, *The Dark Mirror: Psychiatry and Film Noir* (New York: Lexington Books, 2010), 37.

154. Orville Goldner, "Films in the Armed Services," in *Film and Education*, 386.

155. McCarthy, *The Citizen Machine*, 5.

156. Quoted in ibid., 7.

157. Wasson and Acland, "Introduction," 4.

158. I hope, therefore, to complicate the notion that "industrial, sponsored, or educational films are better explained in terms of use and functionality, rather than meaning or style." Patrick Vonderau, "Introduction: On Advertising's Relation to Moving Pictures," in *Films that Sell: Moving Pictures and Advertising*, ed. Bo Florin, Nico de Klerk, and Patrick Vonderau (London: Palgrave, 2016), 1–18 [4].

159. Dominic LaCapra, *History in Transit: Experience, Identity, Critical Theory* (Ithaca: Cornell University Press, 2004), 133. As one character puts it in the B movie *Crime Doctor* (Michael Gordon, 1943), "Psychiatry and politics don't mix very well."

CHAPTER 2

1. Menninger, "Education and Training," 65–66.

2. John Milne Murray, "Accomplishments of Psychiatry in the Army Air Forces," March 1947, 598, Box 12, Folder 4, John M. Murray Papers.

3. Donald W. Hastings, memorandum to General Grant, January 29, 1945, 6, Box 12, Folder 5, John M. Murray Papers.

4. Nichtenhauser, Coleman, and Ruhe, *Films in Psychiatry, Psychology, and Mental Health*, 151.

5. Ibid., 152.

6. See Documents M-367–M-369, *Film and Propaganda in America: A Documentary History, Volume 5* [microfiche supplement].

7. James J. Gibson, ed., *Motion Picture Testing and Research: Report No. 7* (Santa Ana: Army Air Forces Aviation Psychology Program Research Reports, 1947), 267.

8. Jones, "*Neuro Psychiatry 1943*," 300.

9. Charles Tepperman, *Amateur Cinema: The Rise of North American Moviemaking, 1923–1960* (Berkeley: University of California Press, 2014), 12.

10. After serving in North Africa and Italy, the patient began complaining of severe depression, irritability, intolerance of others, loss of interest in everything, anorexia, suicidal ideas, and a loss of about 40 pounds. "Case Report," 1–11 [4], Box 17, Folder 1, John M. Murray Papers.

11. Hale, *The Rise and Crisis of Psychoanalysis in the United States*, 15.

12. Fuqua, *Prescription TV*, 29.

13. Haidee Wasson, *Museum Movies: The Museum of Modern Art and the Birth of Art Cinema* (Berkeley: University of California Press, 2005), 50.

14. Jennifer Horne, "'Neutrality-Humanity': The Humanitarian Mission and the Films of the American Red Cross," in *Beyond the Screen: Institutions, Networks, and Publics of Early Cinema*, ed. Charlie Keil, Rob King, and Paul S. Moore (New Barnet, UK: John Libbey, 2012): 11–18 [13–14].

15. *The Sportsman*, November 1928, 71.

16. "Films for Sale," *Movie Makers*, vol. 3, no. 7 (July 1928): 482.

17. Quoted in Haidee Wasson, "The Reel of the Month Club: 16mm Projectors, Home Theaters and Film Libraries in the 1920s." In *Going to the Movies: Hollywood and the Social Experience of Cinema*, ed. Richard Maltby, Melvyn Stokes, and Robert C. Allen (Exeter: University of Exeter Press, 2007), 217–234 [225].

18. Ibid., 226.

19. H. Bruce Franklin, *War Stars: The Superweapon and the American Imagination* (Amherst: University of Massachusetts Press, 2008), 94.

20. A. B. Feuer, *The U.S. Navy in World War I: Combat at Sea and in the Air* (Westport, CT: Praeger, 1999).

21. Edgar Jones, "War Neuroses and Arthur Hurst: A Pioneering Medical Film about the Treatment of Psychiatric Battle Casualties," *Journal of the History of Medicine and Allied Sciences*, vol. 67, no. 3 (July 2012): 345–373.

22. For more on the CPI's production, distribution, and attempted social management of film material, see Lee Grieveson, "War, Media, and the Security of State and Capital," in *Cinema's Military Industrial Complex*, 261–280. As Michael Kazin points out, the CPI "was nearly as active abroad as at home—with bureaus all over the globe, producing documents in nearly every major language and several minor ones too," thus laying some of the practical and discursive groundwork for later efforts to circulate military-sponsored films to global audiences. Michael Kazin, *War Against War: The American Fight for Peace, 1914–1918* (New York: Simon & Schuster, 2017), 339n5.

23. "Recruiting by Moving Pictures," *Literary Digest*, vol. 46 (June 28, 1913): 1424–1425 [1425].

24. Quoted in ibid., 1425.

25. The Assistant Secretary of War to the National Board of Censorship, June 5, 1915. In *Film and Propaganda in America: Volume I—World War I*, 38–42 [39].

26. Ibid., 76.

27. Ibid., 85.

28. Ibid., 86. The CPI made its own feature films, as well—part of an aggressive multimedia effort to normalize and celebrate American involvement in the Great War. Kazin, *War Against War*, 188–189.

29. Some of those involved with the CPI would later change their tune, publicly acknowledging the importance of recognizing and treating war trauma. Honored by the American Psychological Association in 1949, Edward Bernays, who had served in the CPI, spoke of the need to "regiment the public mind every bit as much as an army regiments the bodies of its soldiers." Quoted in Noam Chomsky, *Profit Over People: Neoliberalism and Global Order* (New York: Seven Stories, 1999), 53. For more on the CPI's efforts to promote certain styles of self-governance, see Sue Collins, "Star Testimonies: World War and the Cultural Politics of Authority," in *Cinema's Military Industrial Complex*, 281–304.

30. "National Issue when Pennsylvania Calls 3 Films Unpatriotic," *Motion Picture News*, May 5, 1917. In *Film and Propaganda in America*, 217.

31. Ibid., 218.

32. Its plot set in motion by two men who served as military psychiatrists during World War II, Sam Fuller's much later *Shock Corridor* (1963) would refine this reliance on the traumatic flashback, using actuality footage to suggest the painful memories of a deeply disturbed Korean War veteran, the footage's color cinematography powerfully punctuating the stark black-and-white proceedings of the film's present tense. See also Burt Lancaster's panic attack in a zoo in *Kiss the Blood Off My Hands* (Norman Foster, 1948): the zoo's commotion proves too much for him, as do the stark reminders of his two years in a prisoner-of-war camp (he identifies with the caged animals desperate to escape). For more on *In Paris, A.W.O.L.*, see Winter, "Film and the Construction of Memory in Psychoanalysis," 129.

33. John Whiteclay Chambers II, "The Peace, Isolationist, and Anti-Interventionist Movements and Interwar Hollywood," in *Why We Fought: America's Wars in Film and History*, ed. Peter C. Rollins and John E. O'Connor (Lexington: University Press of Kentucky, 2008), 196–225 [201–202]. For more on *Lives Wasted* and *Dealers in Death*, see Tepperman, *Amateur Cinema*.

34. As the protagonist of *Crime Doctor* (Michael Gordon, 1943) puts it, "Anything might help—perhaps even reenactment." Paramount's *The Accused* (William Dieterle, 1949) similarly depicts the transformative powers of reenactment, as its traumatized protagonist—a psychology professor who killed a student in self-defense—re-creates the killing by bludgeoning a dummy, in the process "going too far" (i.e., beyond the merely functional experiment designed by a group of investigators). "Reliving" a past experience, she both exposes her traumatic condition and incriminates herself.

35. Raoul Walsh's *The Roaring Twenties* (1939) examines the plight of unemployed, agitated veterans who, back from the battlefields of Europe, are forced to turn to criminal activities. One veteran explains, "We can't sit still. We've seen too much action, too much blood. They think after that we can just sit around and twiddle our thumbs. Well, they're crazy—we can't!"

36. Alice Lovejoy's work on the Czechoslovak military is exemplary in this respect, demonstrating the need for nuance in addressing any national context and its militarized relationship to cinema. Lovejoy, *Army Film and the Avant Garde*.

37. Ibid., 7, 6; Richard Maxwell and Toby Miller, "Film and Globalization," in *Communications Media, Globalization and Empire*, ed. Oliver Boyd-Barrett (Eastleigh, UK: John Libbey, 2006), 33–52. "That the military became an

ever-expansionist apparatus is," writes Florian Hoof, "also a result of its ability to provide business opportunities for third parties and thus to also economically expand and integrate with civilian economies." Hoof, "Between the Front Lines," 179. See also Patrick Vonderau, who writes of the diversity of sponsored films as being "best represented as a spectrum, rather than a binary division between institutional/non-institutional or theatrical/non-theatrical." Vonderau, "Introduction," 7.

38. Writers' War Board Monthly Report, no. 27, July 1, 1945, RG 111, Box 10, *Concentration Camp Atrocities* folder, NARA.

39. For an extended discussion of the Navy's oversight of *The Blue Dahlia*, see James Naremore, *More Than Night: Film Noir in Its Contexts* (Berkeley: University of California Press, 2008).

40. David Bordwell, *The Rhapsodes: How 1940s Critics Changed American Film Culture* (Chicago: University of Chicago Press, 2016), 30.

41. Dan Streible, Martina Roepke, and Anke Mebold, "Introduction: Non-theatrical Film," *Film History*, vol. 19 (2007): 339–343 [342].

42. Gerald N. Grob, *From Asylum to Community: Mental Health Policy in Modern America* (Princeton, NJ: Princeton University Press, 1991).

43. "Army Seeks Increased Output Thru Use of Incentive Films," *Billboard*, June 24, 1944, 50.

44. Dana Polan, *Scenes of Instruction: The Beginnings of the U.S. Study of Film* (Berkeley: University of California Press, 2007), 234. For more on Morkovin's wartime experiments in "diagnostic and therapeutic cinema," see Boris Vladimir Morkovin, *Life-Situation Speech-Reading Through the Cooperation of Senses: Audio-Visual-Kinesthetic-Rhythmic Approach ("AVK" Method)* (Los Angeles: University of Southern California Press, 1948).

45. Morkovin, *Life-Situation Speech-Reading Through the Cooperation of Senses*.

46. Robert Gessner to Chancellor Chase, December 3, 1943, Box 39, Folder 9, Harry W. Chase Papers.

47. NYU School of Military Neuropsychiatry notes (April 17, 1944 to July 8, 1944), Box 12, Folder 18, John M. Murray Papers.

48. *Educational Screen*, vol. 15, no. 1 (January 1936): 57.

49. Charles R. Acland, "Classrooms, Clubs, and Community Circuits: Cultural Authority and the Film Council Movement, 1946–1957," in *Inventing Film Studies*, ed. Lee Grieveson and Haidee Wasson (Durham, NC: Duke University Press, 2008), 149–181 [155–156].

50. Thomas Cripps, *Making Movies Black: The Hollywood Message Movie from World War II to the Civil Rights Era* (Oxford: Oxford University Press, 1993), 158.

51. Herbert B. Dorau, "Memorandum to the Chancellor and the University Council," August 2, 1944, Box 39, Folder 9, Harry W. Chase Papers, 1.

52. David Culbert, "Introduction," *Film and Propaganda in America: A Documentary History, Volume 2: World War II, Part 1* (Westport, CT: Greenwood Press, 1990), xv–xvi.

53. Menninger, "Public Relations," 140.

54. Richard Koszarski, "Subway Commandos: Hollywood Filmmakers at the Signal Corps Photographic Center." *Film History*, vol. 14 (2002): 296–315.

55. Anthony Slide, *Before Video: A History of the Non-Theatrical Film* (New York: Greenwood Press, 1992), 48, 94.

56. Ibid., 101.

57. Maslowski, *Armed with Cameras*, 282.

58. *Psychiatric Quarterly*, vol. 20, no. 1 (January 1946): 205.

59. Orville Goldner, "Films in the Armed Services," in *Film and Education*, 398.

60. Ibid., 399.

61. Albert Wertheim, *Staging the War: American Drama and World War II* (Bloomington: Indiana University Press, 2004), 198–200.

62. Ibid.

63. *Business Screen*, no. 5 (1945), 99.

64. Document M-216, *Film and Propaganda in America: A Documentary History, Vol. 5* [microfiche supplement].

65. John Dollard, *Fear in Battle* (New Haven, CT: Institute of Human Relations, Yale University, 1943), 19.

66. "Army & Navy: Who's Afraid?" *Time*, November 22, 1943, 69.

67. *Military Psychiatric Social Work*, Department of the Army Technical Manual TM 8-241, March 1950 (Washington, DC: United States Government Printing Office, 1950), 2.

68. Orville Goldner, "The Story of Navy Training Films," *Business Screen*, no. 5 (1945), 33.

69. David Culbert, "Introduction," *Film and Propaganda in America: A Documentary History, Volume 3—World War II, Part 2* (Westport, CT: Greenwood Press, 1990), xx.

70. Ibid., xix.

71. Menninger, *Psychiatry in a Troubled World*, 538.

72. Halliwell, *Therapeutic Revolutions*, 4.

73. Paul Rotha, *Documentary Film* (Boston: American Photographic Publishing Co., 1936 [1935]), 131, emphasis in the original.

74. *War Department Field Manual FM 21-7, January 1946: List of War Department Films, Film Strips, and Recognition Film Slides* (Washington, DC: United States Government Printing Office, 1946), 1.

75. Waugh, *The Conscience of Cinema*, 291, 306–308, 323–331.

76. Raymond Evans, Chief of the Division of Motion Pictures, U.S. Department of Agriculture, quoted in Slide, *Before Video*, 48.

77. John Grierson, "First Principles of Documentary," in *The Documentary Film Reader: History, Theory, Criticism*, ed. Jonathan Kahana (Oxford: Oxford University Press, 2016), 217–225 [217–218].

78. Richard Griffith, "The Use of Films by the U.S. Armed Services," Appendix I in Paul Rotha, *Documentary Film* (London: Faber and Faber, 1952), 344–358 [349].

79. Ibid., 358.

80. Ibid.

81. Charles Musser, "Carl Marzani and Union Films: Making Left-Wing Documentaries during the Cold War, 1946–53," *Moving Image*, vol. 9, no. 1 (Spring 2009): 104–160 [119].

82. Cathy Caruth, *Trauma: Explorations in Memory* (Baltimore, MD: Johns Hopkins University Press, 1995), 8–9.

83. Abram Kardiner, *The Traumatic Neuroses of War* (Menasha, WI: George Banta, 1941), 82.

84. Janet Walker, *Trauma Cinema: Documenting Incest and the Holocaust* (Berkeley: University of California Press, 2005).

85. See Document 25, *Film and Propaganda in America: A Documentary History, Volume 3: World War II, Part 2*.

86. Quoted in William Guynn, *A Cinema of Nonfiction* (Cranbury, NJ: Associated University Presses, 1990), 23.

87. Maslowski, *Armed with Cameras*, 78–94.

88. See the NYU Film Library catalogues in Box 39, Folder 9, Harry W. Chase Papers.

89. Originally titled *Neuropsychiatry 1943*, the film was retitled by the Army, which added an "updated psychiatric crawl" to the head of distribution prints (to which the NYU Film Library then added its own logo). "*Psychiatry in Action*," June 1944, Box 39, Folder 9, Harry W. Chase Papers.

90. Maslowski, *Armed with Cameras*, 82.

91. Brian Winston, "Introduction: The Documentary Film," in *The Documentary Film Book*, 1–29 [8].

92. Ibid., 8.

93. Brian Winston, "Life as Narrativized," in *The Documentary Film Book*, 89–97 [95].

94. In Guynn, *A Cinema of Nonfiction*, 19.

95. Nichtenhauser, Coleman, and Ruhe, *Films in Psychiatry, Psychology, and Mental Health*, 49–50.

96. Quoted in Justin Horton, "Mental Landscapes: Bazin, Deleuze, and Neorealism (Then and Now)," *Cinema Journal*, vol. 52, no. 2 (Winter 2013): 23–45 [27].

97. "You must make them understand you were suffering from battle fatigue," says one character to another in the World War II combat film *Never So Few* (John Sturges, 1959). "You must make them realize this."

98. Robert Stam, *Reflexivity in Film and Literature: From Don Quixote to Jean-Luc Godard* (New York: Columbia University Press, 1992), 14.

99. Zadie Smith, "A Note by Zadie Smith," in *The 40s: The Story of a Decade*, ed. Henry Finder with Giles Harvey (New York: Random House, 2014), 585–589 [587]. The words "trauma" and "traumatic" can be heard in any number of Hollywood films of the early 1940s. For instance, a doctor confidently diagnoses a patient with "traumatic shock" in RKO's *The Falcon's Brother* (Stanley Logan, 1942).

100. Paul Lerner and Mark S. Micale, "Trauma, Psychiatry, and History: A Conceptual and Historiographical Introduction," in *Traumatic Pasts: History, Psychiatry, and Trauma in the Modern Age, 1870–1930*, ed. Paul Lerner and Mark S. Micale (Cambridge: Cambridge University Press, 2001), 1–27 [9].

101. Office of the Surgeon General report on war trauma, November 25, 1942, Box 12, Folder 12, John M. Murray Papers, 16–17.

102. Abram Kardiner and Herbert X. Spiegel, *War Stress and Neurotic Illness* (New York: Paul B. Hoeber, 1947), 2.

103. Ibid., 6.

104. Menninger, *Psychiatry in a Troubled World*, 256.

105. Louis L. Tureen and Martin Stein, "The Base Section Psychiatric Hospital," *Bulletin of the U.S. Army Medical Department*, vol. 9 (November 1949): 105–136 [106].

106. Menninger, *Psychiatry in a Troubled World*, 259.

107. Ibid., 261, 259.

108. Ibid., 262, 263.

109. Roger Luckhurst, *The Trauma Question* (New York: Routledge, 2008), 49 – 50. Malarial fever was frequently identified as an exacerbating factor in the "psychoneurotic anxiety states" of servicemen. See, for instance, "Case History: Koslowsky, Alfred," Box 17, Folder 1, John M. Murray Papers.

110. Menninger, *Psychiatry in a Troubled World*, 141.

111. The term "mentally ill" is also central to Joseph Losey's *M* (1951).

112. Kardiner and Spiegel, *War Stress and Neurotic Illness*, 44.

113. Ibid., 80.

114. Naoko Wake, "The Military, Psychiatry, and 'Unfit' Soldiers, 1939–1942." *Journal of the History of Medicine and Allied Sciences*, vol. 62, no. 4 (October, 2007): 461–494 [480]. "I am aware that I have some latent homosexual impulses," confessed a first lieutenant under psychiatric observation in the Army Air Forces. "I need a man to inspire me. I move for love of him . . . I am terrified by the Army machine." Greenson, June 8, 1945 and June 1, 1945, Box 17, Folder 1, John M. Murray Papers.

115. John W. Appel, "Prevention of Loss of Manpower from Psychiatric Disorders: A Report of the Surgeon General," Special Technical Bulletin no. 3, December 1, 1944, file 147, Box 1310, RG 112, NARA. "Though the exclusions would lead to untold injustices and horrors in later years," writes Randy Shilts, "they were initially written as an enlightened and even compassionate treatment of homosexuality." Randy Shilts, *Conduct Unbecoming: Gays & Lesbians in the U.S. Military* (New York: St. Martin's, 1993), 17.

116. Wake, "The Military, Psychiatry, and 'Unfit' Soldiers, 1939–1942."

117. In Janet Walker, "Rights and Return: Perils and Fantasies of Situated Testimony after Katrina," in *Documentary Testimonies: Global Archives of Suffering*, ed. Bhaskar Sarkar and Janet Walker (London: Routledge, 2010), 83–114 [94].

118. Quoted in Ginzberg, Herma, and Ginsburg, *Psychiatry and Military Manpower Policy*, 35.

119. Yvonne Tasker, *Soldiers' Stories: Military Women in Cinema and Television Since World War II* (Durham, NC: Duke University Press, 2011). "The army that prided itself on giving credit where credit was due created and maintained the delusion that military women served only in safe areas, were excluded from service in combat zones, and did not share the dangers of war on or near the front lines," argue Evelyn M. Monahan and Rosemary Neidel-Greenlee.

"Few Americans of the day realized that military women had lost their lives in combat situations and had won military decorations, including the Purple Heart, the Bronze Star, the Silver Star, and the Distinguished Service Medal" (108). They continue, "WACs would experience artillery attacks, bombing raids, strafing, and V-1 and V-2 rocket attacks while serving in a combat zone in a theater of war. Army nurses would be survivors of hospital ships sunk by the German Luftwaffe, six army nurses would be killed by enemy fire in 1944 in Italy, and six by a Japanese suicide plane that aimed for and hit their hospital ship, which was treating wounded soldiers in the Southwest Pacific Theater of War. Army flight nurses would be killed while caring for wounded and ill soldiers, sailors, and marines on medical evacuation flights" (119). Evelyn M. Monahan and Rosemary Neidel-Greenlee, *A Few Good Women: America's Military Women from World War I to the Wars in Iraq and Afghanistan* (New York: Alfred A. Knopf, 2010).

120. For a later example of this approach, see Columbia's *Escape in the Fog* (Budd Boetticher, 1945), in which Nina Foch plays a combat-traumatized nurse suffering from "night terrors."

121. Similarly, in *The Secret Heart* (Robert Z. Leonard, 1946), it is civilian women—June Allyson and Claudette Colbert—who require the attentions of Lionel Barrymore's psychiatrist, and not the newly returned Navy veteran to whom the two women are related. And yet the film also acknowledges the considerable psychic costs of combat. As Colbert's character says of war veterans, "All those boys have been through a lot. They don't talk about it, but it's there inside."

122. Herman, *The Romance of American Psychology*, 89.

123. Bérubé, *Coming Out Under Fire*, 28–33.

124. Therese Benedek, *Insight and Personality Adjustment: A Study of the Psychological Effects of War* (New York: Roland Press Company, 1946), 67–68.

125. Benedek, *Insight and Personality Adjustment*, 274, 277, 280.

126. The Mental Hygiene Unit, Army Air Base, Drew Field, Florida, "A Manual of Organization and Procedure for a Mental Hygiene Unit," January 1944, Box 12, Folder 17, John M. Murray Papers, 61.

127. Menninger, *Psychiatry in a Troubled World*, 115.

128. Ginzberg, Herma, and Ginsburg, *Psychiatry and Military Manpower Policy*, 32.

129. Dwyer, "Psychiatry and Race during World War II," 125.

130. Herman, *The Romance of American Psychology*, 73–74. "Just before and during the Second World War, many of my friends fled into the service, all to be changed there, and rarely for the better, many to be ruined, and many to die," wrote James Baldwin in 1962. "I am far from convinced that being released from the African witch doctor was worthwhile if I am now—in order to support the moral contradictions and the spiritual aridity of my life—expected to become dependent on the American psychiatrist." James Baldwin, "Letter from a Region in My Mind," in *The Sixties: The Story of a Decade*, ed. Henry Finder (New York: Random House, 2016), 22–32 [24, 28].

131. Sanford Gifford, "From the Second World War to Vietnam: Historical, Clinical, and Personal Reflections on Post-Traumatic Stress Disorder," *Ameri-*

can Imago, vol. 72, no. 1 (Spring 2015): 1–26 [7]. For an example of how the military's complex public relations apparatus sought to convince Americans of the curative effects of service even for black men, see *This Is the Army* (Michael Curtiz, 1943), in which Sergeant Joe Louis, playing himself, says, "I quit worrying the day I got into uniform. All I know is I'm in Uncle Sam's Army, and we on God's side."

132. Anatole Litvak's *The Long Night* (1947) ends with its combat-traumatized protagonist, Joe (played by Henry Fonda), turning to his black friend, Freddie (Robert A. Davis), and saying, "I think we'll make it, Freddie—just about make it." (Earlier, Joe pointedly declares, "Everybody ought to be free and equal.")

133. Dementia praecox literally means "premature dementia"; today, it's known as schizophrenia.

134. Fantel, *Psychodrama in an Evacuation Hospital*, 22–23.

135. For more on the origins of this pathologizing approach, see Shilts, *Conduct Unbecoming*, 15.

136. Wendell Willkie, "The Case for the Minorities," *Saturday Evening Post*, June 27, 1942, 14.

137. Toni Morrison, *Home* (New York: Alfred A. Knopf, 2012), 19.

138. Nichtenhauser, Coleman, and Ruhe, *Films in Psychiatry, Psychology, and Mental Health*, 154.

139. Hans Pols, "War Neurosis, Adjustment Problems in Veterans, and an Ill Nation: The Disciplinary Project of American Psychiatry During and After World War II." *Osiris*, vol. 22, no. 1 (2007): 72–92 [73].

140. Kardiner and Spiegel, *War Stress and Neurotic Illness*, 51.

141. Brian Winston, "The Tradition of the Victim in Griersonian Documentary," in *The Documentary Film Reader*, 763–775 [768].

142. Bhaskar Sarkar and Janet Walker, "Introduction: Moving Testimonies," in *Documentary Testimonies*, 1–34 [4].

CHAPTER 3

1. Tracey Loughran, "Shell Shock, Trauma, and the First World War: The Making of a Diagnosis and Its Histories," *Journal of the History of Medicine and Allied Sciences*, vol. 67, no. 1 (2010): 94–119 [108].

2. George B. Wellbaum to Major Warren Wade, September 14, 1945, Box 11, *Let There Be Light* folder, NARA.

3. Ibid.

4. David S. Ruhe, "Buy Them and Edit Them," *Journal of Medical Education* 27 (July 1952): 282. For its part, the military-approved MGM docudrama *The Beginning or the End* (Norman Taurog, 1947) depicts the centrality of "top corporations" to the Manhattan Project ("the biggest job ever undertaken by men"). At one point, a series of corporations are introduced as citizens in their own right; they include Union Carbide, the Kellex Corporation, General Electric, DuPont, and Chrysler. See also General Electric's short film *Turbosupercharger: Master of the Skies*, which GE made for the Army Air Forces in 1943.

5. Schiller, *Mass Communications and American Empire*, 31.

6. Quoted in Anton Kaes, *Shell Shock Cinema: Weimar Culture and the Wounds of War* (Princeton, NJ: Princeton University Press, 2009), 34.

7. Set in the future, RKO's *The Master Race* (Herbert J. Biberman, 1944) features a U.S. Army major who, overseeing the rebuilding of a bombed-out Belgian town, looks forward to a lifetime of military occupation and exploration: "All I used to think of was getting home and forgetting the whole thing. But not now. I've got a life ambition now." Made under the watchful eye of technical adviser Lt. Col. Gerard N. Byrne of the U.S. Army, the film speaks self-consciously to the "humanitarian" ambitions of the American military-industrial state.

8. Tracy C. Davis, *Stages of Emergency: Cold War Nuclear Civil Defense* (Durham, NC: Duke University Press, 2007), 106.

9. In Sidney Lens, *Permanent War: The Militarization of America* (New York: Schocken Books, 1987), 4.

10. For more on "the mass moving-image culture of the bomb" (213), see Susan Courtney, "Framing the Bomb in the West: The View from Lookout Mountain," in *Cinema's Military Industrial Complex*, 210–226.

11. Dana Polan, *Power and Paranoia: History, Narrative, and the American Cinema, 1940–1950* (New York: Columbia University Press, 1986), 18.

12. Ibid., 17.

13. For a compelling account of the US military's distribution of nonfiction films in South Korea during the occupation period (1945–1948), see Sueyoung Park-Primiano, "Occupation, Diplomacy, and the Moving Image: The US Army as Cultural Interlocutor in Korea, 1945–1948," in *Cinema's Military Industrial Complex*, 227–240.

14. Based in Oakland, California, the organization American Relief in Korea (ARK) produced a two-minute film entitled *After Autumn . . .* (1952), in which Douglas Fairbanks, Jr. exhorts the viewer to help "the people of Korea—the 10 million displaced men, women, and children who have been driven from their homes by war. Whether it's life or death for them depends on *us.*"

15. "Life is cheap," complained a severely traumatized veteran of the Battle of Bastogne while under the influence of sodium pentothal. "They think more of a jeep than of a battalion of men." "Progress Notes," January 21, 1944, Box 17, Folder 1, John M. Murray Papers.

16. A. M. Whitlock to Ralph Nelson, "Film Project No. 12903, 'The Returning Soldier,'" May 7, 1945, Box 11, *Let There Be Light* folder, NARA.

17. *Business Screen*, no. 1 (1944), 14.

18. *Business Screen*, no. 5 (1945), 83.

19. Harry M. Hague, *Use of Training Films in Department and Specialty Stores* (Boston: Division of Research, Graduate School of Business Administration, Harvard University, 1948), v.

20. John Milne Murray, memorandum, May 8, 1944, 6, Box 12, Folder 8, John M. Murray Papers.

21. Ibid.

22. Ibid.

23. Maurice N. Walsh to John M. Murray, February 12, 1949, Box 12, Folder 11, John M. Murray Papers.

24. Columbia's *The Dark Past* (Rudolph Maté, 1949), which insists that psychological problems can have physical effects (including "hysterical paralysis"), features a psychiatrist (played by Lee J. Cobb) who adopts these very metaphors, referring to troubled young men as broken tools: "A little understanding and guidance, [and] maybe we can salvage some of this waste."

25. Alison Winter, "Film and the Construction of Memory in Psychoanalysis, 1940–1960." *Science in Context*, vol. 19, no. 1 (2006): 111–136 [115–116]. "Surely," writes Judith Butler, "common sense tells us that persons wage war, not the instruments they employ. But what happens if the instruments acquire their own agency, such that persons become extensions of those instruments?" Butler, *Frames of War*, x.

26. J.A. Ulio, War Department memorandum no. W600-22-43, March 5, 1943, Box 12, Folder 14, John M. Murray Papers.

27. In Halliwell, *Therapeutic Revolutions*, 28.

28. Willard Waller, *The Veteran Comes Back* (New York: Dryden, 1944), 231, 302.

29. Irvin L. Child and Marjorie van de Water, eds., *Psychology for the Returning Serviceman* (New York: Penguin, 1945); Charles G. Bolté, *The New Veteran* (New York: Reynal & Hitchcock, 1945).

30. Charles G. Bolté, "The New Veteran," *Life*, December 10, 1945, 66.

31. Kardiner and Spiegel, *War Stress and Neurotic Illness*, 405.

32. "War's good for business," says James Dean's character in *East of Eden* (Elia Kazan, 1955).

33. E.E. Southard, "The Movement for a Mental Hygiene of Industry," *Mental Hygiene* 4 (January 1920): 43–64 [45].

34. Ibid., 47–48.

35. Ibid., 61.

36. The big-budget biopic *Wilson* (Henry King, 1944), one of many Hollywood films to allegorize World War II through a depiction of World War I, has the eponymous president stiffly denying that business interests are at play in the state's prosecution of war, telling a group of soldiers, "I know there are some people who say that this is just another war to protect the great fortunes, or for some other economic reason, but don't believe them!"

37. Mary C. Jarrett, "Shell-Shock Analogues: Neuroses in Civil Life Having a Sudden or Critical Origin." *Medicine and Surgery*, vol. 2, no. 2 (March 1918): 266–280 [266]; Thomas W. Salmon, "Some New Problems for Psychiatric Research in Delinquency," *Mental Hygiene*, vol. 4 (1920): 29–42 [31, 35].

38. Arthur Edwin Krows, "Motion Pictures—Not For Theaters," *Educational Screen*, vol. 18, no. 3 (March 1939): 85–88 [88].

39. Larry Wayne Ward, *The Motion Picture Goes to War* (Ann Arbor, MI: UMI Research Press, 1985), 35, 39, 42.

40. Pare Lorentz, *Lorentz on Film: Movies, 1927 to 1941* (New York: Hopkinson and Blake, 1975), 82–83.

41. Torrey, *American Psychosis*, 23.

42. M. Guy Thompson, *The Truth About Freud's Technique: The Encounter with the Real* (New York: NYU Press, 1994), 195.

43. Andrew J. Bacevich, "Introduction," in *The Long War: A New History of U.S. National Security Policy Since World War II*, ed. Andrew J. Bacevich (New York: Columbia University Press, 2007), vii–xiv [xi].

44. Quoted by his widow, Frances H. Flaherty, in Patricia Aufderheide, *Documentary Film: A Very Short Introduction* (Oxford: Oxford University Press, 2007), 29.

45. Untitled document, 14, Box 6, Folder 4, John M. Murray Papers.

46. *U.S. Government Films for Public Educational Use—1960* (Washington, DC: U.S. Government Printing Office, 1961), 175.

47. *United States Navy Film Catalog* (Arlington County, VA: United States Bureau of Naval Weapons, May 1, 1966), 304. The canny transformation of the film from a "patient's version" into a "working man's version" vividly illustrates Patrick Vonderau's insistence that we view sponsored films as ever-changing objects, "rather than finite artifacts—subject to constant re-versioning and reinterpretation, as they continue to circulate in society." Vonderau, "Introduction," 4.

48. Howard A. Rusk, M.D., and Eugene J. Taylor, "A Directory of Agencies and Organizations Concerned with Rehabilitation and Services to the Handicapped" (New York: New York Times, 1947), 108.

49. Grieveson and Wasson, "The Academy and Motion Pictures," xxi.

50. Eric Hoyt, *Hollywood Vault: Film Libraries Before Home Video* (Berkeley: University of California Press, 2014), 10.

51. *U.S. Government Films for Public Educational Use*, 175.

52. Advertisement in *Business Screen*, no. 5 (1945), 1.

53. Advertisement in *Business Screen*, vol. 6, no. 4 (April 5, 1945), 33.

54. The film *Lonelyhearts* (Vincent J. Donehue, 1958) features a character whose "husband is a cripple. He was hurt in the war, he told me, but after we'd been married three years he said that was a lie, that he fell working in the shipyards. I said I didn't mind, because, in a way, that *was* being in the war. Making planes and ships—it's helping to win the war."

55. Solomon, "Military Aspects of Mental Disease," 48.

56. Quoted in Ginzberg, Herma, and Ginsburg, *Psychiatry and Military Manpower Policy*, 44.

57. In Clayton R. Koppes and Gregory D. Black, *Hollywood Goes to War: How Politics, Profits, and Propaganda Shaped World War II Movies* (New York: Free Press, 1987), 142.

58. Sidney Lens, *The Military-Industrial Complex* (Philadelphia: Pilgrim Press, 1970), 110.

59. "The UAW-CIO Pioneers Use of Films Among Labor Unions," *Business Screen*, vol. 6, no. 4 (April 5, 1945), 46.

60. Untitled memorandum, John M. Murray Papers, Box 12, Folder 14.

61. Alfred O. Ludwig, "Psychiatry at the Army Level," *Bulletin of the U.S. Army Medical Department*, vol. 9 (November 1949), 74–104 [99].

62. Meier, *Military Psychology*, 279.

63. The Warner Bros. drama *Wings for the Eagle* (Lloyd Bacon, 1942) exemplifies this approach in its depiction of "the battle of production." As one character—a Lockheed executive—says to a group of "war workers," "you are the soldiers in that fight, without uniforms, but just as essential to victory as the

men who fight in the planes you build." The film is set at a Lockheed factory in Burbank, and it includes ample documentary footage of war production. Dedicated "to our airplane factory workers," it explicitly presents defense work as potentially traumatic. As a foreman puts it, speaking of a "discharged" worker, "the going around here got too tough for him, and he couldn't take it."

64. This is true even of contemporary films. "There is no cure for trauma," says a VA therapist in Jason Hall's *Thank You for Your Service* (2017). Identifying the goal of symptom management, she recommends that a traumatized veteran "work with tanks," and she proceeds to tell him about a job opening at a heavy ordinance range.

65. "This too is a battlefield," reads a factory sign in Akira Kurosawa's 1944 film *The Most Beautiful*, which was shot on location in an actual optics plant, and which suggests the global currency of this equation, at least for the war's principal belligerents. "Production lines are battle lines!" reads a poster in RKO's *The Falcon in Danger* (William Clemens, 1943), which features a remarkable "lying" flashback motivated by the tall tales of its villain, an industrialist whose war plant conceals some illicit activities.

66. Thomas Arthur Ryan *Work and Effort: The Psychology of Production* (New York: Ronald Press, 1947).

67. "He may be shell-shocked, but he's not helpless," says one character of another in the postwar comedy *Come September* (Robert Mulligan, 1961).

68. Waller, *The Veteran Comes Back*, 169.

69. For more on this growing commitment, and on the role of films as "bearers of the message of liberal capitalism" (315) in liberated Europe in particular, see Alice Lovejoy, "'A Treacherous Tightrope': The Office of War Information, Psychological Warfare, and Film Distribution in Liberated Europe," in *Cinema's Military Industrial Complex*, 305–320.

70. Lens, *The Military-Industrial Complex*, 16.

71. James Agee, *Agee on Film* (Boston: Beacon Press, 1958), 236.

72. Parker Tyler, *Magic and Myth of the Movies* (New York: Simon and Schuster, 1970 [1947]), 170.

73. Herman, *Romance*, 83. Kaia Scott rightly emphasizes the lasting utility of film amid these efforts, citing the medium's capacity to bridge gaps between military and civilian practice: "As the large cohort of newly trained psychiatrists began to look to civilian society and postwar rehabilitation when their jobs in military service began to end, some of them continued to see film as a ready tool for breaking new professional ground." Scott, "Managing the Trauma of Labor," 129.

74. Such efforts are applied to a different national context in the Stanley Kramer production *The Juggler* (Edward Dmytryk, 1953), in which a physician, heartily recommending psychiatry, argues that "healthy minds" are necessary for the strength of the newly established State of Israel; the film ends with the desperate plea of its traumatized protagonist—a belated confession that doubles as a declaration of psychiatry's therapeutic promise: "I'm sick. I need help."

75. "We're pawns, that's all—pawns in the interests of imperialism!" proclaims one soldier in MGM's *Yellow Jack* (George B. Seitz, 1938) as he languishes in Cuba in the immediate aftermath of the Spanish-American War.

76. Catherine Lutz, "Epistemology of the Bunker: The Brainwashed and Other New Subjects of Permanent War." In *Inventing the Psychological: Toward a Cultural History of Emotional Life in America*, ed. Joel Pfister and Nancy Schnog (New Haven, CT: Yale University Press, 1997), 245–270 [245].

77. Melvin Sabshin, "Twenty-Five Years after *Men under Stress*," in *Modern Psychiatry and Clinical Research: Essays in Honor of Roy R. Grinker, Sr.*, ed. Daniel Offer and Daniel X. Freedman (New York: Basic Books, 1972), 94–101 [98].

78. "Wars, conflict—it's all business," says Charlie Chaplin's title character in *Monsieur Verdoux* (1947), the filmmaker's sly critique of the military-industrial complex. Sekigawa Hideo's *Hiroshima* (1953), a docudramatic recreation of the bombing and its aftermath, depicts the emotional impact of Chaplin's film on a young man named Endo. Evacuated to the mountains before the attack on Hiroshima, which kills his parents and brother, Endo later joins a group of juvenile delinquents before being placed in an asylum. Upon his release, Endo goes to work in a factory located near a cinema that is showing *Monsieur Verdoux*. Chaplin's film, with its antiwar message, inspires Endo to quit after the factory begins manufacturing shells and other "weapons of war."

79. Menninger, "Emotional Reactions Created by the War," in *A Psychiatrist for a Troubled World*, 475–494 [478–479]; Menninger, "The Role of Psychiatry in the World Today," *American Journal of Psychiatry* 104 (September 1947): 155–163 [156].

80. Herman, *Romance*, 77.

81. William D. Hartung, *Prophets of War: Lockheed Martin and the Making of the Military-Industrial Complex* (New York: Nation Books, 2011), 223.

82. Torrey, *American Psychosis*, 75.

83. Harry P. Warner, "Clearances on 'Let There Be Light,'" March 11, 1946, *Let There Be Light* folder, NARA.

84. Lutz, "Epistemology of the Bunker," 253.

85. Arthur Edwin Krows, "Motion Pictures—Not For Theaters," *Educational Screen*, vol. 18, no. 4 (April 1939): 121–124 [123].

86. Herman, *Romance*, 84.

87. Torrey, *American Psychosis*, 25.

88. Quoted in Ralph E. Lapp, "The Military-Industrial Complex: 1969," in *The Military-Industrial Complex and United States Foreign Policy*, ed. Omer L. Carey (Pullman: Washington State University Press, 1969), 42–54 [42].

89. Herman, *Romance*, 245.

90. Samuel P. Huntington, *The Soldier and the State: The Theory and Politics of Civil-Military Relations* (Cambridge, MA: Harvard University Press, 1957), 364.

91. Lutz, "Epistemology of the Bunker," 247.

92. Lens, *Permanent War*, 16.

93. Lutz, "Epistemology of the Bunker," 253.

94. Lens, *Permanent War*, 14.

95. Ibid., 13.

96. Samuel P. Huntington, "The Defense Establishment: Vested Interests and the Public Interest," in *The Military-Industrial Complex and United States Foreign Policy*, 1–14 [4].

97. *Broadcasting*, vol. 52 (1957): 89.

98. Ledbetter, *Unwarranted Influence*, 80.

99. Joel Pfister, "On Conceptualizing the Cultural History of Emotional and Psychological Life in America," in *Inventing the Psychological: Toward a Cultural History of Emotional Life in America*, ed. Joel Pfister and Nancy Schnog (New Haven, CT: Yale University Press, 1997), 17–62 [36].

100. Benedek, *Insight and Personality Adjustment*, 77.

101. Ledbetter, *Unwarranted Influence*, 113.

102. "Allies Release War Films to Spur Production, Fight 'War Is Over' Sentiment," *The Billboard* (September 9, 1944): 45.

103. Walter J. Klein, *The Sponsored Film* (New York: Hastings House, 1976), 123.

104. Ibid.

105. Edward L. Munson, "Request for Motion Picture, 'Combat Team,'" Box 10, *Combat Team* folder, NARA.

106. C. C. Keller to War Activities Committee, October 18, 1943, RG 111, Box 3, *It's Your War, Too* folder, NARA.

107. *United Nations Bulletin* (vol. 6, United Nations Department of Public Information, 1950), 406.

108. Herbert E. Rubin and Elias Katz, "Auroratone Films for the Treatment of Psychotic Depressions in an Army General Hospital," *Journal of Clinical Psychology*, vol. 2, no. 4 (1946): 333–340 [333].

109. *Motion Picture*, vol. 67, no. 5 (June 1944): 45. For more on the use of moving images in military hospitals, see Andrea Kelley, "Mobilizing the Moving Image: Movie Machines at US Military Bases and Veterans' Hospitals during World War II," in *Cinema's Military Industrial Complex*, 44–60.

110. "Process Wins Some Success," *Billboard*, June 23, 1945, 65.

111. "Musicolor: New Coin Machine?," *Billboard*, December 29, 1945, 78.

112. Helen Westhoff, "Auroratone: Painting With Music," *Best: The Popular Digest*, vol. 4 (1946): 35.

113. *Rosicrucian Magazine*, vol. 39, no. 12 (December 1947): 540, 541.

114. Elias Katz, "A Brief Survey of the Use of Motion Pictures for the Treatment of Neuropsychiatric Patients." *Psychiatric Quarterly*, vol. 20 Supplement 1 (January 1946): 204–216 [207]. Not to be outdone in its pursuit of "corporate social responsibility," DuPont began producing Auroratone-style films in 1950, including the twenty-five-minute *The Case for Color*, which claims to reveal and reproduce "the psychological effects" of various colors. The film transforms Stokes' nonprofit therapeutic experiments (which, as technologically mediated expressions, were already tacit advertisements for color-processing facilities) into an advertisement for DuPont's "color conditioning" painting plan, which purported to identify the "right" colors for schools, factories, hospitals, and homes. DuPont distributed *The Case for Color* on a "free-loan" basis—including to schools and hospitals. *Film World and A-V World News Magazine*, vol. 6 (1950): 421.

115. MGM's *Random Harvest* (Mervyn LeRoy, 1942) opens with a depiction of the earlier expansion of such facilities to cover the treatment of combat-traumatized veterans, as the voice-over narrator calls attention to an English

asylum that is "grimly proud of its new military wing, which barely suffices . . .
to house the shattered minds of the war that was to end war."

116. Rubin and Katz, "Auroratone," 340.

117. See F. Dean McClusky, "Motion Pictures: Characteristics and Use of
Educational Films," in *The Audio-Visual Reader*, ed. James S. Kinder and
F. Dean McClusky (Dubuque, IA: WM. C. Brown, 1954), 103–117 [111].

118. Katz, "A Brief Survey," 215.

119. Wasson and Acland, "Introduction," 6.

120. Katz, "A Brief Survey," 215.

121. "Yule Seal Sales Net $28,000 First Week," *The Leader—Freeport,
N. Y.*, Thursday, December 2, 1948, 7.

122. Herbert B. Dorau, "Memorandum to the Chancellor and the University
Council," August 2, 1944, 1, Box 39, Folder 9, Harry W. Chase Papers.

123. Hoban, Jr., *Movies That Teach*, 86, italics in original.

124. Wolfe, "Mapping *Why We Fight*," 338.

125. Lens, *The Military-Industrial Complex*, 35.

126. See, for instance, Frederick Wiseman with Alan Westin, "'You Start Off
with a Bromide': Conversation with Film Maker Frederick Wiseman," in *The
Documentary Film Reader*, 556–564 [558].

127. Lens, *The Military-Industrial Complex*, 36.

128. Coronet Films, quoted in Lawrence H. Suid, "Introduction," in *Film
and Propaganda in America*, vol. 4: *1945 and After*, xv–xxii [xviii], italics in
original.

129. Quoted in ibid., xviii.

130. Nichtenhauser, Coleman, and Ruhe, *Films in Psychiatry*, 155.

131. F. Dean McClusky, "Principals of Utilizing Audio-Visual Materials in
the Curriculum," in *The Audio-Visual Reader*, 38–41 [40].

132. The United States National Commission for UNESCO, "UNESCO and
You: A Six-Point Program" (Washington, DC, September 1947), 24–25. In Box
12, Folder 1, John M. Murray Papers.

133. Joseph Nye, Jr., *Soft Power: The Means to Success in World Politics*
(New York: Public Affairs, 2009).

134. McClusky, "Principals," 40. See also Wm. W. Wattenberg, "Films Aid
Program of Mental Hygiene," *Library Journal*, vol. 74, no. 12 (June 15, 1949):
924–925, 978.

135. Nichtenhauser, Coleman, and Ruhe, *Films in Psychiatry*, 153.

136. Dubbed AboutFace, the series can be viewed on the VA's dedicated You-
Tube channel: https://www.youtube.com/playlist?list=PLC87C65F04DE484C0.

CHAPTER 4

1. Untitled document, 15, Box 6, Folder 4, John M. Murray Papers. See also
Samuel Stouffer, et al., *The American Soldier: Combat and its Aftermath* (Princeton, NJ: Princeton University Press, 1946), 34.

2. Ibid. Evoking this history, RKO's postwar comedy *Magic Town* (William
A. Wellman, 1947) conveys the difficulty not merely of "accurately" playing
oneself but also of "effectively" communicating particular lessons to one's

audiences. The film focuses on an American small town proudly described as "a sturdy challenge to the evils of the modern era"—a fount of good mental hygiene. "The U.S. in capsule," the town is said to "reflect the nation's thinking," representing "the perfect barometer of public opinion." The apocryphal National Newsreel Company is soon dispatched to the town in order to film its residents, who, asked to "play themselves," are nevertheless given extensive direction: "OK, now," a man says from behind the camera. "You're the typical American—act like it!"

3. Joris Ivens, "Collaboration in Documentary," *Films* 1, no. 2 (1940): 30–42.

4. Ernest Fantel, *Psychodrama in an Evacuation Hospital* (New York: Beacon House, 1946), 3.

5. Ibid.

6. Grinker and Spiegel, *War Neuroses in North Africa*, 161.

7. The psychiatrist Charles Burns used the phrase "crude mental enema." See Ben Shephard, *A War of Nerves: Soldiers and Psychiatrists in the Twentieth Century* (Cambridge, MA: Harvard University Press, 2001), 210.

8. See Grinker and Spiegel's widely read *War Neuroses in North Africa*.

9. Moreno, *Psychodrama and Therapeutic Motion Pictures*, 7.

10. Ibid., 19–20.

11. National Committee for Mental Hygiene, *Annual Report, 1941* (New York: National Committee for Mental Hygiene).

12. Shonni Enelow, *Method Acting and Its Discontents: On American Psycho-Drama* (Evanston, IL: Northwestern University Press, 2015).

13. Lewis Barbato, "Drama Therapy," in *Group Psychotherapy: A Symposium* (Beacon, NY: Beacon House, 1945), 396–398.

14. Erik Barnouw, *Documentary: A History of the Non-Fiction Film* (Oxford: Oxford University Press, [1974] 1993), 121.

15. Quoted in Paula Rabinowitz, *They Must Be Represented: The Politics of Documentary* (New York: Verso, 1994), 92.

16. MacCann, *The People's Films*, 166.

17. Nichtenhauser, Coleman, and Ruhe, *Films in Psychiatry, Psychology, and Mental Health*, 28.

18. Rome, "Audio-Visual Aids in Psychiatry," 104.

19. Ibid.

20. Kaja Silverman, *Male Subjectivity at the Margins* (New York: Routledge, 1992), 57.

21. Z.M. Lebensohn, "Psychoses in Naval Officers: A Plea for Psychiatric Selection." *American Journal of Psychiatry* 101 (January 1945): 511–516.

22. *Bulletin of the U.S. Army Medical Department*, no. 84–89 (Washington, DC: U.S. Government Printing Office, 1945), 44.

23. The influence of *The N.P. Patient* and other widely distributed, trauma-themed military documentaries can be seen in the fiction film *The Caretakers* (Hall Bartlett, 1963), in which Robert Stack's psychiatrist explains to Polly Bergen's patient, "You've been under tremendous emotional pressures and something gave way. Like the way a lung might collapse—or a heart—during periods of great stress."

24. *U.S. Government Films for Public Educational Use—1960*, 225.

25. Ibid.

26. See Adolf Nichtenhauser, *Films in Psychiatry, Psychology & Mental Health* (Health Education Council, 1953), 50.

27. Rome, "Audio-Visual Aids in Psychiatry," 68, 104.

28. Ibid., 396, 398.

29. Vanessa Agnew, "Introduction: What Is Reenactment?," *Criticism*, vol. 46, no. 3 (Summer 2004): 327–339 [330]; Jane Marie Todd, *Autobiographics in Freud and Derrida* (London: Garland Publishing, 1990).

30. See Jean Rouch, *Ciné-Ethnography*, ed. and trans. Steven Feld (Minneapolis and London: University of Minnesota Press, 2003), 153–154.

31. Employing reenactment in order to "work through" the traumas of world war, and dispatching soldiers to "play themselves" as a crucial component of this process, films about the recovery of hospitalized combat veterans powerfully presage such classic works of documentary reenactment as George Stoney's *Palmour Street: A Study of Family Life* (1949) and *All My Babies: A Midwife's Own Story* (1953), both made for the Georgia State Department of Health. But they were also, in their own time, part of an expansive tapestry of global cinematic production that extended to postwar Poland, as evidenced by Wanda Jakubowska's remarkable *The Last Stage* (1948). Filmed on location at Auschwitz-Birkenau, *The Last Stage* represented the efforts of Jakubowska, a former inmate of the camp, to collaborate with fellow survivors in the potentially therapeutic reconstruction of their horrific experiences. See Aaron Kerner, *Film and the Holocaust: New Perspectives on Dramas, Documentaries, and Experimental Films* (New York: Bloomsbury Academic, 2011).

32. Rome, "Therapeutic Films and Group Psychotherapy," 253.

33. Ibid., 253.

34. For more on Rome's beliefs about the potentially "triggering" effects of film spectatorship, see Scott, "Managing the Trauma of Labor," 127.

35. Katz, "A Brief Survey of the Use of Motion Pictures for the Treatment of Neuropsychiatric Patients," 215.

36. Ibid., 210.

37. John Milne Murray, "Accomplishments of Psychiatry in the Army Air Forces," March 1947, 597, Box 12, Folder 4, John M. Murray Papers; Menninger, *Psychiatry in a Troubled World*, 301n16.

38. Grinker and Spiegel, *Men Under Stress*, 191.

39. In this respect, the film vividly recalls a remarkable sequence in Alfred Hitchcock's *Sabotage* (1936), in which Sylvia Sidney's protagonist, distraught over the death of her brother, repairs to a screening of the Disney short *Who Killed Cock Robin?* (David Hand, 1935), which, rather than offering a welcome distraction, ultimately "triggers" her trauma, its animated images of murder suddenly assuming powerfully realistic dimensions.

40. Instructively—and in a strikingly similar fashion—newsreel footage of a series of missile launches precipitates the breakdown of Polly Bergen's character in *The Caretakers*. (Purchasing a ticket to *West Side Story*, and hoping for a reprieve from her anxieties, she instead finds herself forced to confront loud, frightening images of Cold War preparedness, and these drive her out of her

seat—and "out of her mind.") And in Paramount's *The Accused* (William Diet-erle, 1949), a billboard advertising the (apocryphal) film *Murder* is sufficient to exacerbate the post-traumatic condition of the film's protagonist, a psychology professor (played by Loretta Young) who has just killed a sexual assaulter in self-defense.

41. Morrison, *Home*, 78.

42. *Bulletin of the U.S. Army Medical Department*, vol. 9 (Washington, DC: U.S. Government Printing Office, 1949), 15.

43. Moreno, *Psychodrama*, 392.

44. Benjamin, "Theses on the Philosophy of History."

45. The influence of this approach can be seen in any number of later films that combine traumatic reality and its careful, psychoanalytically inflected sim-ulation. In Joseph Losey's *King & Country* (1964), for instance, gruesome pho-tos from the Imperial War Museum punctuate the narrative proceedings, vividly illustrating the causes of the post-traumatic condition from which the protago-nist (a soldier played by Tom Courtenay) suffers. Stuart Cooper's *Overlord* (1975) takes this device a step further, blending footage culled from the Imperial War Museum's audiovisual archives with staged reenactments suggesting the horrors of the eponymous operation.

46. Moreno, *Psychodrama and Therapeutic Motion Pictures*, 18.

47. Ibid.

48. Justin Horton, "Mental Landscapes: Bazin, Deleuze, and Neorealism (Then and Now)," *Cinema Journal*, vol. 52, no. 2 (Winter 2013): 23–45 [27].

49. Ibid., 24.

50. In ibid., 44.

51. Quoted in Shephard, *A War of Nerves*, 245.

52. See Rabinowitz, *They Must Be Represented*, 5.

53. See the film *The N.P. Patient*.

54. Quoted in Shephard, *A War of Nerves*, 244.

55. "Movies Speed Rehabilitation," *Popular Photography*, vol. 18, no. 2 (February 1946): 73.

56. Ibid.

57. Ibid.

58. Alvin Yudkoff, *Gene Kelly: A Life of Dance and Dreams* (New York: Back Stage Books, 1999), 152.

59. "Movies Speed Rehabilitation," 73.

60. David Oshinsky, *Bellevue: Three Centuries of Medicine and Mayhem at America's Most Storied Hospital* (New York: Doubleday, 2016), 2. Universal's *The Sleeping City* (George Sherman, 1950) was also shot on location at Bellevue.

61. "Movies Speed Rehabilitation," 73.

62. Ibid.

63. Ibid.

64. Ibid.

65. In *Pilot #5*, Kelly has a supporting role as an Italian-American "hothead"—a lieutenant who frequently lashes out at others, and whose brother (a member of the resistance to Mussolini) commits suicide after escaping a prison camp, prompting Kelly's character to break down. He is hardly alone in

his neuroses, however. Diagnosed with "neurasthenia" in 1940, Franchot Tone discovers that his application for the Air Corps lists him as suffering from "shock." Kelly's role in *Combat Fatigue: Irritability* suggests the prototype for Dane Clark's performance as a compulsively violent ex-Navy man in *Deep Valley* (Jean Negulesco, 1947). While manning PT boats during the war, Clark's character struck a petty officer, broke the man's jaw, and was court-martialed for it. Aspects of Kelly's characterization carried over into the actor's own postwar roles, as well. "Did anything happen to you overseas?" his character's wife asks in *Living in a Big Way* (Gregory La Cava, 1947), in which Kelly plays an ex-Army lieutenant who commits himself to the plight of homeless veterans.

66. William C. Menninger, "Emotional Reactions Created by the War," in *A Psychiatrist for a Troubled World: Selected Papers of William C. Menninger, M.D.*, ed. Bernard H. Hall (New York: Viking, 1967), 475–494 [489].

67. Ibid.

68. Ibid.

69. Ibid., 490. In her account of postwar social science and its impact on American television, Anna McCarthy writes of such men as Stanley Milgram and Allen Funt, who "shared a sense of theatricality, simulation, and dissimulation as necessary tools for understanding the complex dimensions of human behavior in modern society" (33); their pronounced appreciation for "play" was, McCarthy argues, part of a "cold war elite understanding of the uses of visual culture" (27). Anna McCarthy, "'Stanley Milgram, Allen Funt, and Me': Postwar Social Science and the 'First Wave' of Reality TV," in *Reality TV: Remaking Television Culture* (revised edition), ed. Susan Murray and Laurie Ouellette (New York: New York University Press, 2008), 23–43.

70. "Movies Speed Rehabilitation," 73.

71. Ibid.

72. The Mental Hygiene Unit, Army Air Base, Drew Field, Florida, "A Manual of Organization and Procedure for a Mental Hygiene Unit," January 1944, 21–22, Box 12, Folder 17, John M. Murray Papers.

73. Ibid.

74. Ibid.

75. Ibid.

76. Ibid.

77. In taking the nonextant as seriously as its surviving counterparts, I follow Allyson Nadia Field's methodological lead in looking "beyond decayed and combusted nitrate stock as victims of time and neglect," and "arguing that we have as much to discover and learn from absences as we do from surviving artifacts." Allyson Nadia Field, *Uplift Cinema: The Emergence of African American Film and the Possibility of Black Modernity* (Durham and London: Duke University Press, 2016), 2.

78. "A Manual of Organization and Procedure for a Mental Hygiene Unit," 21–22.

79. Grinker and Spiegel, *Men Under Stress*, 191, 383; John Milne Murray, memorandum, May 8, 1944, 1–6, Box 12, Folder 8, John M. Murray Papers.

80. Sample "postcard," A.A.F. Convalescent Hospital, Don Ce-Sar Place, St. Petersburg, Florida, n.d., Box 12, Folder 18, John M. Murray Papers.

81. J. E. Maynard, memorandum, A.A.F. Convalescent Hospital, Don Ce-Sar Place, St. Petersburg, Florida, October 4, 1944, 1–2, Box 12, Folder 18, John M. Murray Papers.

82. Ibid.

83. John Milne Murray, "Accomplishments of Psychiatry in the Army Air Forces," March 1947, 597, Box 12, Folder 4, John M. Murray Papers.

84. Glass, "Combat Psychiatry."

85. *Military Psychiatric Social Work*, Department of the Army Technical Manual TM 8-241, March 1950 (Washington, DC: United States Government Printing Office, 1950), 36.

86. Katz, "A Brief Survey of the Use of Motion Pictures for the Treatment of Neuropsychiatric Patients," 207.

87. Glass, "Combat Psychiatry."

88. John Milne Murray, memorandum, May 8, 1944, 5, Box 12, Folder 8, John M. Murray Papers.

89. Ibid.

90. Ibid.

91. Ibid.

92. Ibid.

93. Glass, "Combat Psychiatry."

94. Freud, *Beyond the Pleasure Principle*.

95. Kardiner and Spiegel, *War Stress and Neurotic Illness*, 112. "I'm sorry, kid—I didn't mean to bring it back to you," says one character to the traumatized protagonist of *The Fallen Sparrow* (Richard Wallace, 1943), after innocently asking him to "relive" the precise process of his traumatization.

96. Winfred Overholser and James M. Enneis, *Twenty Years of Psychodrama at St. Elizabeths Hospital* (New York: Beacon House, 1959), 284.

97. Margaret Hagan, "Psychodrama as a Medium for Mental Hygiene Education," *Diseases of the Nervous System* 19 (1949): 74–80 [78].

98. "Report of the Subcommittee on Treatment of the Consultants in Neuropsychiatry to the Surgeon General," n.d. (ca. 1947), 2, Box 12, Folder 11, John M. Murray Papers.

99. Ibid.

100. Ibid.

101. John M. Murray, M. Ralph Kaufman, and Alfred Ludwig, "Report on Committee on Treatment of the Consultants to the Surgeon General, U.S. Army," February 23, 1947, 1, Box 12, Folder 11, John M. Murray Papers.

102. Hagan, "Psychodrama as a Medium for Mental Hygiene Education," 78.

103. Rotha, *Documentary Film*, 138.

104. Hagan, "Psychodrama as a Medium for Mental Hygiene Education," 78.

105. *Annual Report of the Board of Health, Territory of Hawaii, for the Fiscal Year 1946*, 29.

106. Anna McCarthy, "Screen Culture and Group Discussion in Postwar Race Relations," in *Learning with the Lights Off*, 397–423 [399].

107. For more on amphetamine, its connection to Smith, Kline, & French, and its wartime military uses, see Nicolas Rasmussen, "Medical Science and the

Military: The Allies' Use of Amphetamine during World War II," *Journal of Interdisciplinary History*, vol. 42, no. 2 (Autumn 2011): 205–233.

108. Ivens, "Collaboration in Documentary."

CHAPTER 5

1. Memorandum for Chief, Army Pictorial Service, May 7, 1945, Box 11, *Let There Be Light* folder, NARA.

2. Ibid.

3. Alison Winter, *Memory: Fragments of a Modern History*, 63.

4. Jonathan Kahana, "Speech Images:*Standard Operating Procedure* and the Staging of Interrogation," *Jump Cut* 52 (2010).

5. Winter, *Memory*, 59.

6. John Hersey, "A Short Talk with Erlanger: The Army Is Using a Dramatic Treatment Called Narco-Synthesis to Help Psychiatric Casualties," *Life*, vol. 19, no. 18 (October 29, 1945): 122, emphasis added.

7. Ibid., 122.

8. I would therefore complicate Kaia Scott's claim that the film "is revealed not as the *beginning* of a communications strategy, but as the *culmination* of a well-developed communications apparatus," since *Let There Be Light*—far from marking the apogee or end point of a certain style of military-psychiatric cinema—immediately inspired a number of filmmaking, film distribution, and film reception strategies, both in and beyond the armed forces. Scott, "Managing the Trauma of Labor," 117.

9. Saverio Giovacchini, *Hollywood Modernism: Film and Politics in the Age of the New Deal* (Philadelphia: Temple University Press, 2001), 149.

10. James Combs and Sara T. Combs, *Film Propaganda and American Politics: An Analysis and Filmography* (New York: Routledge, 1994), 79.

11. Winter, *Memory*, 66, emphasis in original.

12. Andrew R. Heinze, *Jews and the American Soul: Human Nature in the Twentieth Century* (Princeton, NJ: Princeton University Press, 2004), 203.

13. Lawrence Grobel, *The Hustons: The Life and Times of a Hollywood Dynasty* (New York: Skyhorse, 2014 [1989]), 273.

14. Peter C. Rollins, "World War II: Documentaries," in *The Columbia Companion to American History on Film: How the Movies Have Portrayed the American Past*, ed. Peter C. Rollins (New York: Columbia University Press, 2003), 116–124 [121].

15. Robert Niemi, *History in the Media: Film and Television* (Santa Barbara, CA: ABC-CLIO, 2006), 123.

16. Agee, *Agee on Film*, 200.

17. Griffith, "The Use of Films by the U.S. Armed Services," 356.

18. Grob, *From Asylum to Community*, 20, 308n24.

19. Elaine Showalter, *Hystories: Hysterical Epidemics and Modern Media* (New York: Columbia University Press, 1997), 75.

20. Other precedents arguably include the script that Huston co-wrote for the medical biopic *Dr. Ehrlich's Magic Bullet* (William Dieterle, 1940), which insists on the existence of "diseases of the soul" and even has the title character

denouncing racism ("What has race to do with science?"). There are obvious stylistic affinities between *Let There Be Light* and this earlier film, with its preponderance of wipes and crawls, and a climactic sequence in which a patient's sight is "miraculously" restored.

21. Greg Garrett, quoted in Rollins, "World War II," 121; Grobel, *The Hustons*, 273.

Even Kaia Scott insists that, upon its completion, Huston's project "ceased to fit within the evolving paradigm of psychotherapy that best served the military's postwar interests." Scott, "Managing the Trauma of Labor," 130.

22. Quoted in *Bulletin of the Association for Psychoanalytic Medicine*, vol. 43 (Spring 2009): 50.

23. Lutz, "Epistemology," 252.

24. See the many documents contained in Box 11, *Let There Be Light* folder, NARA.

25. Anonymous, "Shell-Shocked—and After," *Atlantic Monthly* (December 1921): 738–749.

26. Dr. Daniel Blain, quoted in Herman, *The Romance of American Psychology*, 243.

27. Ibid., 243.

28. Nichtenhauser, Coleman, and Ruhe, *Films in Psychiatry, Psychology, and Mental Health*, 28.

29. Ibid., 155.

30. Ibid.

31. Ibid., 151.

32. "Large crowds . . . thronged the hotel" for back-to-back screenings of *Let There Be Light* on Mental Health Day, according to *Minnesota Welfare*, a monthly publication of the State of Minnesota Division of Social Welfare of the Department of Social Security. This "special attraction" was purchased from the VA as a series of prints, and its public screenings were sponsored by the Interclub Council and the Ramsey County Citizens Committee on Mental Health. Like Governor Youngdahl, both groups maintained that Huston's film, "which depicts treatment given soldiers suffering from battle fatigue," could "inspire" Minnesotans to immediately pursue statewide mental-hospital reform and general mental-health education. "Governor Urges Speed in Mental Hospital Aid," 3.

33. *Mental Hygiene* 31, no. 3 (July 1947): 513.

34. Re-creating the Battle of San Pietro, Michael Curtiz's 1951 film *Force of Arms* (also known as *A Girl for Joe*) incorporates clips from Huston's 1945 documentary *San Pietro* (some of the very same clips included in *The Story of G.I. Joe* [William A. Wellman, 1945], and here identified, in the closing credits, merely as "actual combat film" from the Department of Defense and the Army). But *Force of Arms* also insistently links *San Pietro* to *Let There Be Light*, as when a character notes that one soldier has "got the jitters," and William Holden's protagonist is forced to confront his own psychosomatic symptoms, complaining of "things knocking around in my head."

35. Shephard, *A War of Nerves*, 210.

36. In addition, MGM's *Dark Delusion* (Willis Goldbeck, 1947) features a young doctor (played by James Craig) who administers sodium pentothal

(which he calls "a truth bringer-outer") to a "neurotic heiress" (played by Lucille Bremer). The latter, who believes herself to have caused her parents' divorce, is suffering from a guilt complex compounded by a head injury, and it is up to her doctor to carefully explain, in vernacular terms, that "there's a thing called narcosynthesis, a technique which might help me talk with all levels of your mind, even the deep subconscious. . . . I don't know what has made you ill, but perhaps you do, without realizing it." As in *Let There Be Light*, narcosynthesis here proves immediately effective, as the sedated patient begins to reveal her darkest secrets.

37. Amytal hardly went unrepresented, however. It is, in fact, at the center of MGM's *Remember?* (Norman Z. McLeod, 1939), in which a team of scientists strive to develop what they call "the opposite of Amytal"—not something to help remember but something to help forget. The film features much talk of the therapeutic power of forgetting, as scientists finally seize upon "the biggest discovery in modern medicine"—what they christen "Mamozine": "It makes the patient forget he's been sick"; "It just makes him forget everything—forget pain, forget the shock of an accident, forget the accident itself." As one man puts it, "Why, every psychiatrist in the world has been looking for something like this!" In the later *Crack-Up* (Irving Reis, 1946), a doctor played by Ray Collins says, "Odd, isn't it, that truth should be a byproduct of war. Because only in the recent war did we perfect a direct method of communication with a man's true self. It's called narcosynthesis. . . . It's placed honesty on a scientific basis. Just one small injection of [sodium amytal], and the brain is illuminated with accuracy. It's relieved the necessity of weighing answers. All inhibitors go, and the subconscious mind takes over."

38. Ludwig, "Psychiatry at the Army Level," 96, emphasis mine.

39. "Treatment is likely to unhinge [the] mind altogether!" warns one character in the British film *The Seventh Veil* (Compton Bennett, 1945), in reference to "narcohypnosis," while *Harvey* (Henry Koster, 1950) features a cabbie who inveighs against "truth serum," which, he claims, makes people "crabby."

40. Hale, *The Rise and Crisis of Psychoanalysis in the United States*, 196.

41. Of course, in fiction films of the period, "natural" hypnosis is often dangerous. The Sherlock Holmes film *The Woman in Green* (Roy William Neill, 1945), for instance, depicts the criminal co-optation of what one character calls "the therapeutic value of hypnotism." In a variation on *The Cabinet of Dr. Caligari* (Robert Wiene, 1920), the film's criminals use modern hypnotic techniques in order to induce various men to commit murder. Instructively, they prey upon a traumatized Army veteran—a sniper who has been given a medical discharge—forcing him through hypnosis to attempt to assassinate Holmes.

42. Winter, *Memory*, 64–65.

43. Menninger, *Psychiatry in a Troubled World*, 309.

44. Louis L. Tureen and Martin Stein, "The Base Section Psychiatric Hospital," in *Combat Psychiatry: Experiences in the North African and Mediterranean Theaters of Operation, American Ground Forces, World War II*, compiled and ed. Frederick R. Hanson, *Bulletin of the U.S. Army Medical Department*, vol. 9, Supplemental Number (November 1949), 122.

45. Kardiner and Spiegel, *War Stress and Neurotic Illness*, 5.

46. Ibid., 413.

47. Jones, "*Neuro Psychiatry 1943*," 321.

48. J. S. Horsley, "Narco-analysis," *Journal of Mental Science* 82 (1936): 416–422.

49. The postwar comedy *Bedtime Story* (Ralph Levy, 1964) parodies this approach in its depiction of a con artist who simulates "hysterical paralysis" resulting from "a traumatic experience."

50. In April 1944, Congressman John Taber of New York asked what the military documentary could do that the commercial newsreel could not. In response to Taber's demand for a definition of documentary that would adequately describe its superiority to the newsreel, Thurman L. Barnard, Assistant Executive Director of the OWI's Overseas Branch, proclaimed that documentary in general was "absolutely authentic," and that the military documentary in particular represented "a complete document on a phase of the American war effort, especially produced and recorded on film." *National War Agencies Appropriation Bill for 1945, Volume 20, Parts 2 and 3: Hearings Before the Subcommittee of the Committee on Appropriations, House of Representatives, Seventy-Eighth Congress, Second Session on the National War Agencies Appropriation Bill for 1945* (Washington, DC: United States Government Printing Office, 1944), 165.

51. Memorandum for Chief, Army Pictorial Service, May 7, 1945, Box 11, *Let There Be Light* folder, NARA.

52. Emanuel Cohen to Edward L. Munson, "Pictures Re: Returning Soldiers," April 30, 1945, Box 11, *Welcome Home* folder, NARA.

53. Ibid.

54. Memorandum for Chief, Army Pictorial Service, May 7, 1945, Box 11, *Let There Be Light* folder, NARA.

55. Emanuel Cohen to Edward L. Munson, "Pictures Re: Returning Soldiers," April 30, 1945, Box 11, *Welcome Home* folder, NARA.

56. Ibid. As William Powell's jobless World War I veteran puts it in *The Hoodlum Saint* (Norman Taurog, 1946), "Employers in this town are seldom in—must be the uniform!"

57. Ibid.

58. James T. Sparrow, *Warfare State: World War II Americans and the Age of Big Government* (New York: Oxford University Press, 2011), 242.

59. Memorandum for Chief, Army Pictorial Service, May 7, 1945, Box 11, *Let There Be Light* folder, NARA.

60. Hersey, "A Short Talk with Erlanger," 122.

61. Ibid.

62. Kaufman's efforts at Mason General mirrored those that had generated *Hypnosis: Okinawa*, which Kaufman and others filmed in a standard field hospital that had been converted into an exhaustion center and special neuropsychiatric hospital. Menninger, *Psychiatry in a Troubled World*, 308.

63. Winston, *Lies, Damn Lies, and Documentaries*, 85.

64. Ibid., 161.

65. Quoted in Menninger, "Public Relations," 147.

66. Cartwright, *Screening the Body*, 50.

67. Fantel, *Psychodrama in an Evacuation Hospital*, 6, emphasis added. Columbia's *The Guilt of Janet Ames* (Henry Levin, 1947) features a paean to (relatively) drug-free forms of hypnosis, which generate what one character calls "vivid word-pictures." In an indication of the era's emphasis on the sheer translatability of military psychiatry, the film features a sort of vernacular or "wild cat" psychoanalysis, practiced by a man (played by Melvyn Douglas) who has no medical training, and who merely relies upon what he calls "the Peter Ibbetson technique," which emphasizes the power of imagination above all else. ("Without imagination, there's no reality," sings Betsy Blair in the film's first dream sequence.) Though she is, at one point, given a gram and a half of a sedative, the title character (played by Rosalind Russell) enters a hypnotic state without the aid of sodium pentothal or sodium amytal. Suffering from "a type of hysteria paralysis," she regains her ability to walk after "imaginatively" describing her past traumas, and she demonstrates her "healthy" gait by walking back and forth in a hospital room (much like Robert Gerardi in *Let There Be Light*).

68. Ibid., emphasis added.

69. Cartwright, *Screening the Body*, 50.

70. *Military Psychiatric Social Work*, Department of the Army Technical Manual TM 8-241, March 1950 (Washington, DC: United States Government Printing Office, 1950), 28.

71. Rotha, *Documentary Film*, 131, emphasis in original.

72. *Mental Health Motion Pictures*, 65.

73. *Canadian Medical Association Journal*, vol. 80, no. 9 (May 1, 1959): 772.

74. Bureaucratically speaking, little has changed for those seeking psychiatric treatment at the VA—a state of affairs that some films manage to convincingly capture. In Jason Hall's 2017 drama *Thank You For Your Service*, the VA denies medical benefits to a severely traumatized veteran—who escaped a burning Humvee in Iraq—because he "didn't report an injury at the time of the incident." The VA proceeds to gather eyewitness testimony from "those who were there," and who might be able to "prove" that the man was, in fact, traumatized in combat.

75. Cartwright, *Screening the Body*, 50.

76. Theodor Reik, *Listening with the Third Ear: The Inner Experience of a Psychoanalyst* (New York: Farrar, Straus and Giroux, 1948), 61; Jonathan Kahana and Noah Tsika, "*Let There Be Light* and the Military Talking Picture," in *Remaking Reality: U.S. Documentary Culture after 1945*, ed. Sara Blair, Joseph B. Entin, and Franny Nudelman (Chapel Hill: University of North Carolina Press, 2018), 14–34. This notion of a "documentary ear" originates with Jonathan, and I am deeply indebted to his insights.

77. Shephard, *A War of Nerves*, 245.

78. Untitled document, August 9, 1945, Box 11, *Let There Be Light* folder, NARA.

79. Quoted in Shephard, *A War of Nerves*, 277.

80. Grinker and Spiegel, *War Neuroses in North Africa*, 289; *Men Under Stress*, 261–262.

81. Ibid., 87.

82. Ibid., 157–158.
83. Ibid., 161.
84. Ibid., 160–161.
85. Ibid., 161.
86. Ibid., 210.
87. Erving Goffman, *Asylums: Essays on the Social Situation of Mental Patients and Other Inmates* (New York: Anchor Books, 1961), 73.
88. The fiction film *Deep Valley* (Jean Negulesco, 1947) depicts a civilian's speech impediment (stuttering) in explicit relation to war trauma. "It's all my fault you can't talk!" screams a man—a traumatized veteran of the First World War—to his daughter, Libby (played by Ida Lupino), who once saw him strike her mother. (For her part, Libby's mother also believes that it was the traumatic sight of spousal abuse that engendered Libby's speech disorder.) But a World War II veteran, familiar with military psychiatry, informs the father that Libby's stuttering is "curable." Libby, for her part, identifies with *another* World War II veteran, a deeply disturbed escaped convict played by Dane Clark. "I had a feeling that I *was* him," she says at one point, as she acknowledges that he is—as he himself puts it—"all messed up" ("I don't know what goes on in my own head!"). But his love for her ultimately cures her speech impediment—a sentimental plot development that recalls *The Enchanted Cottage* (John Cromwell, 1945), with its emphasis on a psychological recovery that occurs in the complete absence of professional psychotherapy, and as a result strictly of "love."
89. In Kaes, *Shell Shock Cinema*, 25.
90. Menninger, *Psychiatry in a Troubled World*, 294.
91. Goffman, *Asylums*, 21–22.
92. Tureen and Stein, "The Base Section Psychiatric Hospital," 114.
93. *Mental Health Motion Pictures: A Selective Guide, 1960* (Washington, DC: United States Government Printing Office, 1960), 65.
94. *Canadian Medical Association Journal*, vol. 80, no. 9 (May 1, 1959), 772.
95. Thomas Waugh, "Beyond *Vérité*: Emile de Antonio," in *The Right to Play Oneself: Looking Back on Documentary Film* (Minneapolis: University of Minnesota Press, 2011), 93–154 [96].
96. Shephard, *A War of Nerves*, 278.
97. Ibid.
98. Krin Gabbard and Glen O. Gabbard, *Psychiatry and the Cinema* (Chicago: University of Chicago Press, 1989), 36.
99. John M. Murray, memorandum for Colonel Walter S. Jensen, "Critique of Paper Entitled 'Integration in Neuropsychiatry as a Treatment Unit in Air Force Station Hospitals,'" n.d. (ca. 1944), Box 12, Folder 9, John M. Murray Papers.
100. Ibid.
101. John M. Murray, memorandum for Colonel Walter S. Jensen, "Articles for Publication," n.d. (ca. 1944), Box 12, Folder 9, John M. Murray Papers.
102. M. Ralph Kaufman Murray and Alfred Ludwig, "Report on Committee on Treatment of the Consultants to the Surgeon General, U.S. Army," February 23, 1947, 3, Box 12, Folder 11, John M. Murray Papers.
103. Ostherr, *Cinematic Prophylaxis*, 44.

104. In 1947, the 54th annual Minnesota Welfare Conference, held at the Nicollet Hotel in Minneapolis, boasted 1,400 attendees, a significant number of which would have seen *Let There Be Light* as part of a special Veterans Administration session on the "mental care" of ex-servicemen. Two years later, an estimated 2,600 Minnesotans attended back-to-back screenings of *Let There Be Light* on Mental Health Day in St. Paul. "1,400 Attend Welfare Conference," *Minnesota Welfare*, vol. II, no. 10 (June 1947): 5; "Governor Urges Speed in Mental Hospital Aid," 3.

105. As Brian Larkin has argued, "the relation between cinema and the commodity form should be seen as contingent rather than necessary." Brian Larkin, *Signal and Noise: Media, Infrastructure, and Urban Culture in Nigeria* (Durham, NC: Duke University Press, 2008), 121.

106. Active from 1941 until 1946, the U.S. Office of Education's Division of Visual Aids for War Training often required that "therapeutic films" be screened only "where no charge is made." Floyde E. Brooker to Signal Corps Photographic Center, 13 June 1946, RG 111, Box 10, Folder "Employing Disabled Veterans in Industry," NARA.

107. "Governor Urges Speed in Mental Hospital Aid," 3.

CONCLUSION

1. The amputees include Jacob Schick, an Iraq War veteran whose encounter with a triple-stacked anti-tank mine cost him his left hand, left arm, and right leg. Like other members of the cast, Schick suffers from post-traumatic stress disorder (PTSD). The grandson of a World War II veteran, Schick is heavily involved in efforts to raise awareness about war trauma and suicide prevention, as is his costar Bryan Anderson, an Iraq War veteran who lost both of his legs as well as his left arm in a roadside bomb explosion.

2. Anatole Litvak's *The Long Night* (1947) prefigures this doubling of physical and psychological trauma in its depiction of a pair of World War II veterans—Frank Dunlap (Elisha Cook, Jr.), who was blinded in battle, and Joe Adams (Henry Fonda), who, having survived both the Battle of Anzio and the Invasion of Normandy, suffers from a "hidden" condition strongly evocative of combat fatigue.

3. John Corner, *The Art of Record: A Critical Introduction to Documentary* (Manchester: Manchester University Press, 1996).

4. Menninger, *Psychiatry in a Troubled World*, 362.

5. Philip Rieff, *The Triumph of the Therapeutic: Uses of Faith After Freud* (Harmondsworth, UK: Penguin, 1966).

6. The psychiatrist Charles Burns used the phrase "crude mental enema." See Shephard, *A War of Nerves*, 210.

7. Menninger addresses such criticisms in *A Psychiatrist for a Troubled World*, 490.

8. As Ben Shephard writes, "*Let There Be Light* conjures up today a lost world of New Deal idealism, confidence and hope. There is a moving sense of common enterprise, an assumption that the gifted, the intelligent and the strong are helping their fellow men in a spirit of purpose and authority." Shephard, *A War of Nerves*, 277.

9. Fred Kaplan, "*Vietnam! Vietnam!,*" *Cineaste*, vol. 7, no. 3 (1976): 20–23.

10. Brooks, *How Everything Became War and the Military Became Everything*, 13–14.

11. Ibid., 15.

12. In Alex Abella, *Soldiers of Reason: The RAND Corporation and the Rise of the American Empire* (New York: Harcourt, 2008), 57. Lee Grieveson contends that the "unrelenting expansion of the market system has mostly left behind the kinds of didactic media" characteristic of early efforts to normalize liberal capitalist "democracy": "For media is now more fully, militantly, liberal, and these values are carried through a relentlessly banal media culture suffused by individualist and consumerist logics that are incapable of picturing the kinds of collective actions necessary to realize humane transformation." Lee Grieveson, *Cinema and the Wealth of Nations: Media, Capital, and the Liberal World System* (Berkeley: University of California Press, 2018), 333.

13. In Jefferson Cowie, *The Great Exception: The New Deal & the Limits of American Politics* (Princeton, NJ: Princeton University Press, 2016).

14. An exception is Jason Hall's somber *Thank You for Your Service* (2017), parts of which were shot at an actual Department of Veterans Affairs center, with actual veterans assembled to "play themselves" (mostly as extras). In Hall's film, the VA is overcrowded, understaffed, and generally stymied by a constipated bureaucracy. A severely traumatized applicant for psychiatric care is told that he needs to produce a VA card. One staff member complains that the facility is "backed up," and that each veteran will have to wait six to nine months to see a therapist. "This shit could give me PTSD," the protagonist says of the VA's obvious shortcomings. An officer runs into him shortly thereafter, and berates him for seeking professional help; psychological distress, he says, is "bad for morale—bad for Big Army." As this book has suggested, it has been anything *but* bad for "Big Army." In *Thank You For Your Service*, however, the VA is so crowded, so inefficient, that the best option is a private facility—The Pathways Home, located in California and run by a veteran who established it in the immediate aftermath of the Vietnam War.

15. Pasi Väliaho, *Biopolitical Screens: Image, Power, and the Neoliberal Brain* (Cambridge, MA: MIT Press, 2014), 62.

16. Tim Lenoir, "All But War Is Simulation: The Military-Entertainment Complex," *Configurations*, vol. 8, no. 3 (Fall 2000): 289–335 [314].

17. Ibid., 329–300, emphasis added.

18. P. W. Singer, *Corporate Warriors: The Rise of the Privatized Military Industry* (Ithaca, NY: Cornell University Press, 2003), 14, 62, 99.

19. Brooks, *How Everything Became War and the Military Became Everything*, 83–84.

20. Abella, *Soldiers of Reason*, 90.

21. Rachel Martin, "Report: High Levels of 'Burnout' in U.S. Drone Pilots," NPR, December 18, 2011, http://www.npr.org/2011/12/19/143926857/report-high-levels-of-burnout-in-u-s-drone-pilots.

22. Cowie, *The Great Exception*, 9.

23. Luckhurst, *The Trauma Question*, 60.

24. Ibid., 59.

Select Bibliography

ARCHIVES AND COLLECTIONS

The British Film Institute National Archive, London, UK.
Colonial Film: Moving Images of the British Empire: http://www.colonialfilm
   .org.uk/.
Imperial War Museum Film and Video Archive, London, UK.
The Library of Congress, Washington, DC, US.
Margaret Herrick Library, Academy of Motion Picture Arts and Sciences, Los
   Angeles, CA, US.
Media History Digital Library: http://mediahistoryproject.org/.
Motion Picture Films and Sound and Video Recordings, National Archives at
   College Park, MD, US.
Motion Picture Producers and Distributors of America, Inc., 1922–1939, Digi-
   tal Archive, Flinders University, Australia, https://mppda.flinders.edu.au/.
Moving Image Research Center, Motion Picture, Broadcasting and Recorded
   Sound, Library of Congress, Washington, DC, US.
The National Archives, College Park, MD, US.
The National Archives, Washington, DC, US.
The National Library of Medicine, Bethesda, MD, US.
New York Public Library for the Performing Arts, Dorothy and Lewis B. Cull-
   man Center, New York, US.
Prelinger Archives, https://archive.org/details/prelinger/.
The Schomburg Center for Research in Black Culture, New York, US.
The Steven A. Schwarzman Building of the New York Public Library, New
   York, US.

PUBLISHED WORKS

Abella, Alex. *Soldiers of Reason: The RAND Corporation and the Rise of the American Empire* (New York: Harcourt, 2008).

Acland, Charles R. "Classrooms, Clubs, and Community Circuits: Cultural Authority and the Film Council Movement, 1946–1957," in *Inventing Film Studies*, edited by Lee Grieveson and Haidee Wasson (Durham, NC: Duke University Press, 2008), 149–181.

Agnew, Vanessa. "Introduction: What Is Reenactment?," *Criticism*, vol. 46, no. 3 (Summer 2004): 327–339.

Alexander, William. *Film on the Left: American Documentary Film from 1931 to 1942* (Princeton, NJ: Princeton University Press, 1981).

Arthur, Paul. "Jargons of Authenticity (Three American Moments)," in *Theorizing Documentary*, edited by Michael Renov (New York: Routledge, 1993), 108–134.

Bacevich, Andrew J. "Introduction," in *The Long War: A New History of U.S. National Security Policy Since World War II*, edited by Andrew J. Bacevich (New York: Columbia University Press, 2007), vii–xiv.

Bacevich, Andrew J. *Washington Rules: America's Path to Permanent War* (New York: Metropolitan Books, 2010).

Ball, Karyn. "Introduction: Traumatizing Psychoanalysis," in *Traumatizing Theory: The Cultural Politics of Affect In and Beyond Psychoanalysis*, edited by Karyn Ball (New York: Other Press, 2007), xvii–li.

Barbato, Lewis. "Drama Therapy," in *Group Psychotherapy: A Symposium* (Beacon, NY: Beacon House, 1945), 396–398.

Barber, James Alden, Jr. "The Military-Industrial Complex," in *The Military and American Society: Essays and Readings*, edited by Stephen E. Ambrose and James A. Barber, Jr. (New York: Free Press, 1972), 43–60.

Barnouw, Erik. *Documentary: A History of the Non-Fiction Film* (Oxford: Oxford University Press, [1974] 1993).

Barsam, Richard M. *Non-Fiction Film: A Critical History, Revised and Expanded* (Bloomington and Indianapolis: Indiana University Press, 1992 [1973]).

Becker, Carl. "Everyman His Own Historian," *American Historical Review* 37, no. 2 (January 1932): 221–236.

Benedek, Therese. *Insight and Personality Adjustment: A Study of the Psychological Effects of War* (New York: The Roland Press Company, 1946).

Benjamin, Walter. "Theses on the Philosophy of History," in *Illuminations*, translated by Harry Zohn, edited by Hannah Arendt (New York: Schocken Books, 1968), 253–264.

Benson, Thomas W. and Carolyn Anderson. "The Ultimate Technology: Frederick Wiseman's *Missile*," in *Communication & the Culture of Technology*, edited by Martin J. Medhurst, Alberto Gonzalez, and Tarla Rai Peterson (Pullman: Washington State University Press, 1990), 257–283.

Bernard, Harold Wright. *Toward Better Personal Adjustment* (New York: McGraw-Hill, 1951).

Bérubé, Allan. *Coming Out Under Fire: The History of Gay Men and Women in World War II* (New York: Plume, 1990).

Bingham, June. *The Inside Story: Psychiatry and Everyday Life* (New York: Vintage Books, 1953).

Bolté, Charles G. *The New Veteran* (New York: Reynal & Hitchcock, 1945).

Bordwell, David. *Reinventing Hollywood: How 1940s Filmmakers Changed Movie Storytelling* (Chicago: University of Chicago Press, 2017).

Bordwell, David. *The Rhapsodes: How 1940s Critics Changed American Film Culture* (Chicago: University of Chicago Press, 2016).

Brandell, Jerrold R., ed. *Celluloid Couches, Cinematic Clients: Psychoanalysis and Psychotherapy in the Movies* (Albany: State University of New York Press, 2004).

Brooks, Rosa. *How Everything Became War and the Military Became Everything: Tales from the Pentagon* (New York: Simon & Schuster, 2016).

Butler, Judith. *Frames of War: When Is Life Grievable?* (London: Verso, 2016).

Campbell, Russell. *Cinema Strikes Back: Radical Filmmaking in the United States, 1930–1942* (Ann Arbor: UMI Research Press, 1982).

Caruth, Cathy *Literature in the Ashes of History* (Baltimore, MD: Johns Hopkins University Press, 2013).

Caruth, Cathy. *Trauma: Explorations in Memory* (Baltimore, MD: Johns Hopkins University Press, 1995).

Chambers II, John Whiteclay. "The Peace, Isolationist, and Anti-Interventionist Movements and Interwar Hollywood," in *Why We Fought: America's Wars in Film and History*, edited by Peter C. Rollins and John E. O'Connor (Lexington: University Press of Kentucky, 2008), 196–225.

Chanan, John. *The Politics of Documentary* (London: BFI, 2008).

Child, Irvin L. and Marjorie van de Water, eds., *Psychology for the Returning Serviceman* (New York: Penguin, 1945).

Chomsky, Noam. *Profit Over People: Neoliberalism and Global Order* (New York: Seven Stories Press, 1999).

Coleman, Penny. *Flashback: Posttraumatic Stress Disorder, Suicide, and the Lessons of War* (Boston: Beacon Press, 2006).

Collingwood, R. G. *The Idea of History* (Oxford: Oxford University Press, 1946).

Combs, James and Sara T. Combs. *Film Propaganda and American Politics: An Analysis and Filmography* (New York: Routledge, 1994).

Corner, John. *The Art of Record: A Critical Introduction to Documentary* (Manchester: Manchester University Press, 1996).

Courtney, Susan. "Framing the Bomb in the West: The View from Lookout Mountain," in *Cinema's Military Industrial Complex*, edited by Haidee Wasson and Lee Grieveson (Berkeley: University of California Press, 2018), 210–226.

Cowie, Elizabeth. *Recording Reality, Desiring the Real* (Minneapolis: University of Minnesota Press, 2011).

Cowie, Jefferson. *The Great Exception: The New Deal & the Limits of American Politics* (Princeton, NJ: Princeton University Press, 2016).

Creel, George. *How We Advertised America: The First Telling of the Amazing Story of the Committee on Public Information that Carried the Gospel of Americanism to Every Corner of the Globe* (New York: Harper & Brothers, 1920).

Cripps, Thomas. *Making Movies Black: The Hollywood Message Movie from World War II to the Civil Rights Era* (Oxford: Oxford University Press, 1993).

Culbert, David. "'Why We Fight': Social Engineering for a Democratic Society at War," in *Film & Radio Propaganda in World War II*, edited by K. R. M. Short (Knoxville: University of Tennessee Press, 1983), 173–191.

Cunningham, Douglas. "Imaging/Imagining Air Force Identity: 'Hap' Arnold, Warner Bros., and the Formation of the USAAF First Motion Picture Unit," *The Moving Image*, vol. 5, no. 1 (Spring 2005): 95–124.

Davis, Aeron. *Promotional Cultures: The Rise and Spread of Advertising, Public Relations, Marketing and Branding* (Malden, MA: Polity Press, 2013).

Davis, Tracy C. *Stages of Emergency: Cold War Nuclear Civil Defense* (Durham, NC: Duke University Press, 2007).

Derrida, Jacques. *Archive Fever: A Freudian Impression*, translated by Eric Prenowitz (Chicago: University of Chicago Press, 1996).

Doherty, Thomas. *Projections of War: Hollywood, American Culture, and World War II*, rev. ed. (New York: Columbia University Press, 1999 [1993]).

Dollard, John. *Fear in Battle* (New Haven, CT: Institute of Human Relations, Yale University, 1943).

Druick, Zoë and Jonathan Kahana, "New Deal Documentary and the North Atlantic Welfare State," in *The Documentary Film Book*, edited by Brian Winston (London: BFI, 2015), 153–158.

Dwyer, Ellen. "Psychiatry and Race during World War II," *Journal of the History of Medicine and Allied Scientists*, vol. 61, no. 2 (April 2006): 117–143.

Ellis, Jack C. *John Grierson: Life, Contributions, Influence* (Carbondale and Edwardsville: Southern Illinois University Press, 2000).

Enelow, Shonni. *Method Acting and Its Discontents: On American Psycho-Drama* (Evanston, IL: Northwestern University Press, 2015).

Fantel, Ernest. *Psychodrama in an Evacuation Hospital* (New York: Beacon House, 1946).

Farber, Manny. "The Lady and the Belle," in *Farber on Film: The Complete Writings of Manny Farber*, edited by Robert Polito (New York: Library of America, 2009), 155–157.

Field, Allyson Nadia. *Uplift Cinema: The Emergence of African American Film and the Possibility of Black Modernity* (Durham, NC: Duke University Press, 2016).

Florin, Bo, Nico de Klerk, and Patrick Vonderau (eds.). *Films that Sell: Moving Pictures and Advertising* (London: Palgrave, 2016).

Franklin, H. Bruce. *War Stars: The Superweapon and the American Imagination* (Amherst: University of Massachusetts Press, 2008).

Fuqua, Joy V. *Prescription TV: Therapeutic Discourse in the Hospital and at Home* (Durham, NC: Duke University Press, 2012).

Gaines, Jane M. "Political Mimesis," in *Collecting Visible Evidence*, ed. Jane M. Gaines and Michael Renov (Minneapolis: University of Minnesota Press, 1999), 84–102.

Gaines, Jane M. "The Real Returns," in *Collecting Visible Evidence*, ed. Jane M. Gaines and Michael Renov (Minneapolis: University of Minnesota Press, 1999), 1–18.

Gibson, James J. (ed.). *Motion Picture Testing and Research: Report No. 7* (Santa Ana: Army Air Forces Aviation Psychology Program Research Reports, 1947).

Ginzberg, Eli, John L. Herma, and Sol W. Ginsburg. *Psychiatry and Military Manpower Policy: A Reappraisal of the Experience in World War II* (New York: King's Crown Press, 1953).

Giovacchini, Saverio. *Hollywood Modernism: Film and Politics in the Age of the New Deal* (Philadelphia: Temple University Press, 2001).

Goffman, Erving. *Asylums: Essays on the Social Situation of Mental Patients and Other Inmates* (New York: Anchor Books, 1961).

Gordon, Marsha. *Film is Like a Battleground: Sam Fuller's War Movies* (New York: Oxford University Press, 2017).

Grierson, John. "First Principles of Documentary," in *The Documentary Film Reader: History, Theory, Criticism*, edited by Jonathan Kahana (Oxford: Oxford University Press, 2016), 217–225.

Grieveson, Lee. *Cinema and the Wealth of Nations: Media, Capital, and the Liberal World System* (Berkeley: University of California Press, 2018).

Grieveson, Lee. "War, Media, and the Security of State and Capital," in *Cinema's Military Industrial Complex*, edited by Haidee Wasson and Lee Grieveson (Berkeley: University of California Press, 2018), 261–280.

Grieveson, Lee and Haidee Wasson, eds. *Cinema's Military-Industrial Complex* (Berkeley: University of California Press, 2018).

Griffith, Richard. "The Use of Films by the U.S. Armed Services," Appendix I in Paul Rotha, *Documentary Film* (London: Faber and Faber, 1952), 344–358.

Grinker, Roy R. and John P. Spiegel. *Men Under Stress* (Philadelphia: Blakiston, 1945).

Grob, Gerald N. *From Asylum to Community: Mental Health Policy in Modern America* (Princeton, NJ: Princeton University Press, 1991).

Guynn, William. *A Cinema of Nonfiction* (Cranbury, NJ: Associated University Presses, 1990).

Hagan, Margaret. "Psychodrama as a Medium for Mental Hygiene Education," *Diseases of the Nervous System* 19 (1949): 74-80.

Hague, Harry M. *Use of Training Films in Department and Specialty Stores* (Boston: Division of Research, Graduate School of Business Administration, Harvard University, 1948).

Hale, Jr., Nathan G. *The Rise and Crisis of Psychoanalysis in the United States: Freud and the Americans, 1917–1985* (New York: Oxford University Press, 1995).

Halliwell, Martin. *Therapeutic Revolutions: Medicine, Psychiatry, and American Culture, 1945–1970* (New Brunswick, NJ: Rutgers University Press, 2013).

Harris, Mark. *Five Came Back: A Story of Hollywood and the Second World War* (New York: Penguin, 2014).

Hediger, Vinzenz and Patrick Vonderau (eds.). *Films that Work: Industrial Film and the Productivity of Media* (Amsterdam: Amsterdam University Press, 2009).

Heinze, Andrew R. *Jews and the American Soul: Human Nature in the Twentieth Century* (Princeton, NJ: Princeton University Press, 2004).

Herman, Ellen. *The Romance of American Psychology: Political Culture in the Age of Experts* (Berkeley: University of California Press, 1995).

Hersey, John. "A Short Talk with Erlanger: The Army Is Using a Dramatic Treatment Called Narco-Synthesis to Help Psychiatric Casualties," *Life*, vol. 19, no. 18 (October 29, 1945).

Hill, Annette. "Ambiguous Audiences," in *The Documentary Film Book*, edited by Brian Winston (London: BFI, 2015), 83–88.

Hoban, Jr., Charles F. *Movies That Teach* (New York: Dryden Press, 1946).

Hoof, Florian. "Between the Front Lines: Military Training Films, Machine Guns, and the Great War," in *Cinema's Military Industrial Complex*, edited by Haidee Wasson and Lee Grieveson (Berkeley: University of California Press, 2018), 177–191.

Horne, Jennifer. "'Neutrality-Humanity': The Humanitarian Mission and the Films of the American Red Cross," in *Beyond the Screen: Institutions, Networks, and Publics of Early Cinema*, edited by Charlie Keil, Rob King, and Paul S. Moore (New Barnet, Herts, UK: John Libbey, 2012), 11–18.

Horsley, J. S. "Narco-analysis," *Journal of Mental Science* 82 (1936), 416–422.

Horton, Justin. "Mental Landscapes: Bazin, Deleuze, and Neorealism (Then and Now)," *Cinema Journal* 52:2 (Winter 2013): 23–45.

Hoyt, Eric. *Hollywood Vault: Film Libraries Before Home Video* (Berkeley: University of California Press, 2014).

Huntington, Samuel P. *The Soldier and the State: The Theory and Politics of Civil-Military Relations* (Cambridge, MA: Harvard University Press, 1957).

Ivens, Joris. "Collaboration in Documentary," *Films* 1, no. 2 (1940): 30–42.

Jaffe, Eric. *A Curious Madness: An American Combat Psychiatrist, a Japanese War Crimes Suspect, and an Unsolved Mystery from World War II* (New York: Scribner, 2014).

Jameson, Fredric. *The Political Unconscious: Narrative as a Socially Symbolic Act* (Ithaca, NY: Cornell University Press, 1981).

Jarrett, Mary C. "Shell-Shock Analogues: Neuroses in Civil Life Having a Sudden or Critical Origin." *Medicine and Surgery*, vol. 2, no. 2 (March 1918): 266–280.

Jones, Edgar. "War Neuroses and Arthur Hurst: A Pioneering Medical Film about the Treatment of Psychiatric Battle Casualties," *Journal of the History of Medicine and Allied Sciences*, vol. 67, no. 3 (July 2012): 345–373.

Kaes, Anton. *Shell Shock Cinema: Weimar Culture and the Wounds of War* (Princeon, NJ: Princeton University Press, 2009).

Kahana, Jonathan. *Intelligence Work: The Politics of American Documentary* (New York: Columbia University Press, 2008).

Kahana, Jonathan. "Introduction: What Now?: Presenting Reenactment," *Framework*, vol. 50, no. 1 & 2 (Spring & Fall 2009): 46–60.

Kahana, Jonathan. "Speech Images:*Standard Operating Procedure* and the Staging of Interrogation," *Jump Cut* 52 (2010).

Kahana, Jonathan and Noah Tsika. "*Let There Be Light and the Military Talking Picture*," in *Remaking Reality: U.S. Documentary Culture after 1945*, edited by Sara Blair, Joseph B. Entin, and Franny Nudelman (Chapel Hill: University of North Carolina Press, 2018), 14–34.

Kaplan, Fred. "*Vietnam! Vietnam!*," *Cineaste*, vol. 7, no. 3 (1976): 20–23.

Kardiner, Abram. *The Traumatic Neuroses of War* (Menasha, WI: George Banta, 1941).

Kardiner, Abram and Herbert X. Spiegel, *War Stress and Neurotic Illness* (New York: Paul B. Hoeber, 1947).

Katz, Elias. "A Brief Survey of the Use of Motion Pictures for the Treatment of Neuropsychiatric Patients." *Psychiatric Quarterly*, vol. 20, Supplement 1 (January 1946): 204–216.

Katz, Nancy and Robert Katz, "Documentary in Transition, Part 1: The United States." *Hollywood Quarterly*, vol. 3, no. 4 (1948): 426–435.

Kazin, Michael. *War Against War: The American Fight for Peace, 1914–1918* (New York: Simon & Schuster, 2017).

Kerner, Aaron. *Film and the Holocaust: New Perspectives on Dramas, Documentaries, and Experimental Films* (New York: Bloomsbury Academic, 2011).

Klein, Walter J. *The Sponsored Film* (New York: Hastings House, 1976).

Koppes, Clayton R. and Gregory D. Black. *Hollywood Goes to War: How Politics, Profits, and Propaganda Shaped World War II Movies* (New York: Free Press, 1987).

Koszarski, Richard. "Subway Commandos: Hollywood Filmmakers at the Signal Corps Photographic Center." *Film History*, vol. 14 (2002): 296–315.

Krows, Arthur Edwin. "Motion Pictures—Not For Theaters," *Educational Screen*, vol. 18, no. 3 (March 1939): 85–88.

LaCapra, Dominic. *History in Transit: Experience, Identity, Critical Theory* (Ithaca, NY: Cornell University Press, 2004).

Lapp, Ralph E. "The Military-Industrial Complex: 1969," in *The Military-Industrial Complex and United States Foreign Policy*, edited by Omer L. Carey (Pullman: Washington State University Press, 1969), 42–54.

Lebensohn, Z. M. "Psychoses in Naval Officers: A Plea for Psychiatric Selection." *American Journal of Psychiatry* 101 (January 1945): 511–516.

Ledbetter, James. *Unwarranted Influence: Dwight D. Eisenhower and the Military-Industrial Complex* (New Haven, CT: Yale University Press, 2011).

Lenoir, Tim. "All but War Is Simulation: The Military-Entertainment Complex," *Configurations*, vol. 8, no. 3 (Fall 2000): 289–335.

Lens, Sidney. *The Military-Industrial Complex* (Philadelphia: Pilgrim Press, 1970).

Lens, Sidney. *Permanent War: The Militarization of America* (New York: Schocken Books, 1987).

Lerner, Paul and Mark S. Micale. "Trauma, Psychiatry, and History: A Conceptual and Historiographical Introduction," in *Traumatic Pasts: History, Psychiatry, and Trauma in the Modern Age, 1870–1930*, edited by Paul Lerner and Mark S. Micale (Cambridge: Cambridge University Press, 2001), 1–27.

Leys, Ruth. *Trauma: A Genealogy* (Chicago: University of Chicago Press, 2000).

Linn, Brian McAllister. *Elvis's Army: Cold War GIs and the Atomic Battlefield* (Cambridge, MA: Harvard University Press, 2016).

274 | Select Bibliography

Lorentz, Pare. *Lorentz on Film: Movies, 1927 to 1941* (New York: Hopkinson and Blake, 1975).

Loughran, Tracey. "Shell Shock, Trauma, and the First World War: The Making of a Diagnosis and Its Histories," *Journal of the History of Medicine and Allied Sciences*, vol. 67, no. 1 (2010): 94–119.

Lovejoy, Alice. *Army Film and the Avant Garde: Cinema and Experiment in the Czechoslovak Military* (Bloomington and Indiana: Indiana University Press, 2015).

Lovejoy, Alice. "'A Treacherous Tightrope': The Office of War Information, Psychological Warfare, and Film Distribution in Liberated Europe," in *Cinema's Military Industrial Complex*, edited by Haidee Wasson and Lee Grieveson (Berkeley: University of California Press, 2018), 305–320.

Luckhurst, Roger. *The Trauma Question* (New York: Routledge, 2008).

Ludwig, Alfred O. "Psychiatry at the Army Level," *Bulletin of the U.S. Army Medical Department*, vol. 9 (November 1949): 74–104.

Lutz, Catherine. "Epistemology of the Bunker: The Brainwashed and Other New Subjects of Permanent War." In *Inventing the Psychological: Toward a Cultural History of Emotional Life in America*, edited by Joel Pfister and Nancy Schnog (New Haven, CT: Yale University Press, 1997), 245–270.

Lutz, Catherine. *Homefront: A Military City and the American Twentieth Century* (Boston: Beacon Press, 2001).

MacCann, Richard Dyer. *The People's Films: A Political History of U.S. Government Motion Pictures* (New York: Hastings House, 1973).

Maslowski, Peter. *Armed with Cameras: The American Military Photographers of World War II* (New York: Free Press, 1993).

Maxwell, Richard and Toby Miller, "Film and Globalization," in *Communications Media, Globalization and Empire*, edited by Oliver Boyd-Barrett (Eastleigh, UK: John Libbey, 2006).

McCarthy, Anna. *The Citizen Machine: Governing by Television in 1950s America* (New York: New Press, 2010).

McCarthy, Anna. "Screen Culture and Group Discussion in Postwar Race Relations," in *Learning with the Lights Off: Educational Film in the United States* (Oxford and New York: Oxford University Press, 2012), 397–423.

McCarthy, Anna. "'Stanley Milgram, Allen Funt, and Me': Postwar Social Science and the 'First Wave' of Reality TV," in *Reality TV: Remaking Television Culture* (revised edition), edited by Susan Murray and Laurie Ouellette (New York: New York University Press, 2008), 23–43.

McClusky, F. Dean. "Motion Pictures: Characteristics and Use of Educational Films," in *The Audio-Visual Reader*, edited by James S. Kinder and F. Dean McClusky (Dubuque, IA: WM. C. Brown, 1954), 103–117.

Meier, Norman C. *Military Psychology* (New York: Harper & Brothers, 1943).

Menninger, William C. *Psychiatry in a Troubled World: Yesterday's War and Today's Challenge* (New York: Macmillan, 1948).

Menninger, William C. "Education and Training," in *Neuropsychiatry in World War II: Vol. I*, 53–66.

Menninger, William C. "Emotional Reactions Created by the War," in *A Psychiatrist for a Troubled World: Selected Papers of William C. Menninger, M.D.*, edited by Bernard H. Hall (New York: Viking, 1967), 475–494.

Menninger, William C. "The Military Psychiatrist," *Bulletin of the Menninger Clinic* 7 (July 4, 1943), 129–136.

Menninger, William C. "Public Relations," in *Neuropsychiatry in World War II: Vol. I—Zone of Interior*, edited by R. S. Anderson, A. J. Glass, and R. J. Bernucci (Washington, DC: U.S. Government Printing Office, 1966), 129–151.

Menninger, William C. "The Role of Psychiatry in the World Today," *American Journal of Psychiatry* 104 (September 1947): 155–163.

Metzl, Jonathan Michel. *Prozac on the Couch: Prescribing Gender in the Era of Wonder Drugs* (Durham, NC: Duke University Press, 2003).

Milliken, Christie. "Continence of the Continent: The Ideology of Disease and Hygiene in World War II Training Films," in *Cultural Studies: Medicine and Media*, edited by Lester D. Friedman (Durham, NC: Duke University Press, 2004), 280–298.

Minh-ha, Trinh T. "The Totalizing Quest of Meaning," in *Theorizing Documentary*, edited by Michael Renov (New York: Routledge, 1993), 90–107.

Mirrlees, Tanner. *Hearts and Mines: The US Empire's Culture Industry* (Vancouver: UCB Press, 2016).

Monahan, Evelyn M. and Rosemary Neidel-Greenlee, *A Few Good Women: America's Military Women from World War I to the Wars in Iraq and Afghanistan* (New York: Alfred A. Knopf, 2010).

Moran, James M. "A Bone of Contention: Documenting the Prehistoric Subject," in *Collecting Visible Evidence*, ed. Jane M. Gaines and Michael Renov (Minneapolis: University of Minnesota Press, 1999), 255–273.

Moreno, J. L. *Psychodrama: First Volume* (New York: Beacon House, 1959 [1946]).

Morgan III, C. A. "From *Let There Be Light* to *Shades of Grey*: The Construction of Authoritative Knowledge About Combat Fatigue (1945–48)," in *Signs of Life: Medicine & Cinema*, edited by Graeme Harper and Andrew Moor (London and New York: Wallflower Press, 2005), 132–152.

Morrison, Toni. *Home* (New York: Alfred A. Knopf, 2012).

Moskowitz, Eva S. *In Therapy We Trust: America's Obsession with Self-Fulfillment* (Baltimore, MD: Johns Hopkins University Press, 2001).

Movie Lot to Beach Head: The Motion Picture Goes to War and Prepares for the Future by the Editors of Look (Garden City, NY: Doubleday, Doran, 1945).

Mowitt, John. "Trauma Envy," in *Traumatizing Theory: The Cultural Politics of Affect In and Beyond Psychoanalysis*, edited by Karyn Ball (New York: Other Press, 2007), 349–376.

Musser, Charles. "Carl Marzani and Union Films: Making Left-Wing Documentaries during the Cold War, 1946–53," *The Moving Image*, vol. 9, no. 1 (Spring 2009): 104–160.

Naremore, James. *More Than Night: Film Noir in Its Contexts* (Berkeley: University of California Press, 2008).

Nichtenhauser, Adolf. *Films in Psychiatry, Psychology & Mental Health* (Health Education Council, 1953).

Nichols, Bill. "'Getting to Know You': Knowledge, Power, and the Body," in *Theorizing Documentary*, edited by Michael Renov (New York: Routledge, 1993), 174–192.

North, Edmund. "The Secondary or Psychological Phase of Training Films," *Journal of the Society for Motion Picture Engineers* vol. 42, no 2. (February 1944): 117–122.

Nye, Jr., Joseph. *Soft Power: The Means to Success in World Politics* (New York: Public Affairs, 2009).

Orgeron, Devin, Marsha Orgeron, and Dan Streible. "Introduction," in *Learning with the Lights Off: Educational Film in the United States* (Oxford: Oxford University Press, 2012), 3–14.

Oshinsky, David. *Bellevue: Three Centuries of Medicine and Mayhem at America's Most Storied Hospital* (New York: Doubleday, 2016).

Ostherr, Kirsten. *Cinematic Prophylaxis: Globalization and Contagion in the Discourse of World Health* (Durham, NC: Duke University Press, 2005).

Overholser, Winfred and James M. Enneis. *Twenty Years of Psychodrama at St. Elizabeths Hospital* (New York: Beacon House, 1959).

Park-Primiano, Sueyoung. "Occupation, Diplomacy, and the Moving Image: The US Army as Cultural Interlocutor in Korea, 1945–1948," in *Cinema's Military Industrial Complex*, edited by Haidee Wasson and Lee Grieveson (Berkeley: University of California Press, 2018), 227–240.

Pfister, Joel. "On Conceptualizing the Cultural History of Emotional and Psychological Life in America," in *Inventing the Psychological: Toward a Cultural History of Emotional Life in America*, edited by Joel Pfister and Nancy Schnog (New Haven, CT: Yale University Press, 1997), 17–62.

Piotrowska, Agnieszka. *Psychoanalysis and Ethics in Documentary Film* (London: Routledge, 2014).

Plant, Rebecca Jo. "Preventing the Inevitable: John Appel and the Problem of Psychiatric Casualties in the US Army During World War II," in *Science and Emotions After 1945: A Transatlantic Perspective*, edited by Frank Biess and Daniel M. Gross (Chicago: University of Chicago Press, 2014), 209–238.

Plant, Rebecca Jo. "William Menninger and American Psychoanalysis, 1946–48." *History of Psychiatry*, 16.2 (2005): 181–202.

Polan, Dana. *Power and Paranoia: History, Narrative, and the American Cinema, 1940–1950* (New York: Columbia University Press, 1986).

Polan, Dana. *Scenes of Instruction: The Beginnings of the U.S. Study of Film* (Berkeley: University of California Press, 2007).

Pols, Hans. "War Neurosis, Adjustment Problems in Veterans, and an Ill Nation: The Disciplinary Project of American Psychiatry During and After World War II." *Osiris*, vol. 22, no. 1 (2007), 72–92.

Prelinger, Rick. *The Field Guide to Sponsored Film* (San Francisco: National Film Preservation Foundation, 2006).

Rabinowitz, Paula. *They Must Be Represented: The Politics of Documentary* (New York: Verso, 1994).

Rasmussen, Nicolas. "Medical Science and the Military: The Allies' Use of Amphetamine during World War II," *Journal of Interdisciplinary History*, vol. 42, no. 2 (Autumn 2011): 205–233.

Rees, J. R. *The Shaping of Psychiatry by War* (New York: W. W. Norton, 1945).

Reik, Theodor. *Listening with the Third Ear: The Inner Experience of a Psychoanalyst* (New York: Farrar, Straus and Giroux, 1948).

Renov, Michael. "Domestic Ethnography and the Construction of the 'Other' Self," in *Collecting Visible Evidence*, ed. Jane M. Gaines and Michael Renov (Minneapolis: University of Minnesota Press, 1999), 140–155.

Renov, Michael. "Introduction: The Truth About Non-Fiction," in *Theorizing Documentary*, edited by Michael Renov (New York: Routledge, 1993), 1–11.

Renov, Michael. *The Subject of Documentary* (Minneapolis: University of Minnesota Press, 2004).

Renov, Michael. "Toward a Poetics of Documentary," in *Theorizing Documentary*, edited by Michael Renov (New York: Routledge, 1993), 12–36.

Rieff, Philip. *The Triumph of the Therapeutic: Uses of Faith After Freud* (Harmondsworth, UK: Penguin, 1966).

Rogers, Carl R. and John L. Wallen. *Counseling with Returned Servicemen* (New York: McGraw-Hill, 1946).

Rogers, Carl R. *Counseling and Psychotherapy: Newer Concepts in Practice* (Boston: Houghton Mifflin Company, 1942).

Rogin, Michael. "'Make My Day!': Spectacle as Amnesia in Imperial Politics." *Representations*, No. 29 (Winter 1990): 99–123.

Rollins, Peter C. "World War II: Documentaries," in *The Columbia Companion to American History on Film: How the Movies Have Portrayed the American Past*, edited by Peter C. Rollins (New York: Columbia University Press, 2003), 116–124.

Rome, Howard P. "Therapeutic Films and Group Psychotherapy," in *Group Psychotherapy: A Symposium* (Beacon, NY: Beacon House, 1945).

Rotha, Paul. *Documentary Film* (Boston: American Photographic Publishing, 1936 [1935]).

Rouch, Jean. *Ciné-Ethnography*, edited and translated by Steven Feld (Minneapolis : University of Minnesota Press, 2003).

Rubin, Herbert E. and Elias Katz, "Auroratone Films for the Treatment of Psychotic Depressions in an Army General Hospital," *Journal of Clinical Psychology*, vol. 2, no. 4, (1946): 333–340.

Ruhe, David S. "Buy Them and Edit Them," *Journal of Medical Education* 27 (July 1952).

Ryan, Thomas Arthur. *Work and Effort: The Psychology of Production* (New York: Ronald Press, 1947).

Sabshin, Melvin. "Twenty-five Years after *Men under Stress*," in *Modern Psychiatry and Clinical Research: Essays in Honor of Roy R. Grinker, Sr.*, edited by Daniel Offer and Daniel X. Freedman (New York: Basic Books, 1972), 94–101.

Santos, Marlisa. *The Dark Mirror: Psychiatry and Film Noir* (New York: Lexington Books, 2010).

Sarkar, Bhaskar and Janet Walker. "Introduction: Moving Testimonies," in *Documentary Testimonies: Global Archives of Suffering*, edited by Bhaskar Sarkar and Janet Walker (London: Routledge, 2010), 1–34.

Schiller, Herbert I. *Mass Communications and American Empire* (New York: Augustus M. Kelley, 1969).

Schiller, Herbert I. and Joseph D. Phillips, "Introduction: The Military-Industrial Establishment: Complex or System?" in *Super-State: Readings in the Military-Industrial Complex* (Urbana: University of Illinois Press, 1970), 1–28.

Scott, James. *Seeing Like a State: How Certain Schemes to Improve the Human Condition Have Failed* (New Haven, CT: Yale University Press, 1998).

Scott, Kaia. "Managing the Trauma of Labor: Military Psychiatric Cinema in World War II," in *Cinema's Military Industrial Complex*, edited by Haidee Wasson and Lee Grieveson (Berkeley: University of California Press, 2018), 116–136.

Searls, Damion. *The Inkblots: Hermann Rorschach, His Iconic Test, and the Power of Seeing* (New York: Crown, 2017).

Serlin, David. "Introduction: Toward a Visual Culture of Public Health," in *Imagining Illness: Public Health and Visual Culture*, edited by David Serlin (Minneapolis: University of Minnesota Press, 2010), xi–xxxvii.

Shephard, Ben. *A War of Nerves: Soldiers and Psychiatrists in the Twentieth Century* (Cambridge, MA: Harvard University Press, 2001).

Shilts, Randy. *Conduct Unbecoming: Gays & Lesbians in the U.S. Military* (New York: St. Martin's Press, 1993).

Showalter, Elaine. *Hystories: Hysterical Epidemics and Modern Media* (New York: Columbia University Press, 1997).

Silverman, Kaja. *Male Subjectivity at the Margins* (New York: Routledge, 1992).

Slide, Anthony. *Before Video: A History of the Non-Theatrical Film* (New York: Greenwood Press, 1992).

Smith, Ken. *Mental Hygiene: Classroom Films, 1945–1970* (New York: Blast Books, 1999).

Singer, P. W. *Corporate Warriors: The Rise of the Privatized Military Industry* (Ithaca, NY: Cornell University Press, 2003).

Southard, E. E. "The Movement for a Mental Hygiene of Industry," *Mental Hygiene* 4 (January 1920): 43–64.

Sparrow, James T. *Warfare State: World War II Americans and the Age of Big Government* (New York: Oxford University Press, 2011).

Stam, Robert. *Reflexivity in Film and Literature: From Don Quixote to Jean-Luc Godard* (New York: Columbia University Press, 1992).

Stott, William. *Documentary Expression and Thirties America* (New York: Oxford University Press, 1973).

Stouffer, Samuel et al., *The American Soldier: Combat and its Aftermath* (Princeton, NJ: Princeton University Press, 1946).

Streible, Dan, Martina Roepke, and Anke Mebold, "Introduction: Nontheatrical Film," *Film History*, vol. 19 (2007): 339–343.

Tasker, Yvonne. *Soldiers' Stories: Military Women in Cinema and Television Since World War II* (Durham, NC: Duke University Press, 2011).

Tepperman, Charles. *Amateur Cinema: The Rise of North American Moviemaking, 1923–1960* (Berkeley: University of California Press, 2014).

Thompson, M. Guy. *The Truth About Freud's Technique: The Encounter With the Real* (New York: NYU Press, 1994).

Todd, Jane Marie. *Autobiographics in Freud and Derrida* (London: Garland Publishing, 1990).

Torrey, E. Fuller. *American Psychosis: How the Federal Government Destroyed the Mental Illness Treatment System* (New York: Oxford University Press, 2014).

Trumpbour, John. *Selling Hollywood to the World: U.S. And European Struggles for Mastery of the Global Film Industry* (Cambridge: Cambridge University Press, 2002).

Tsika, Noah. "From Wartime Instruction to Superpower Cinema: Maintaining the Military-Industrial Documentary," in *Cinema's Military Industrial Complex*, edited by Haidee Wasson and Lee Grieveson (Berkeley: University of California Press, 2018), 192–209.

Tureen, Louis L., and Martin Stein. "The Base Section Psychiatric Hospital," *Bulletin of the U.S. Army Medical Department*, vol. 9 (November 1949): 105–136.

Tyler, Parker. *Magic and Myth of the Movies* (New York: Simon and Schuster, 1970 [1947]).

Väliaho, Pasi. *Biopolitical Screens: Image, Power, and the Neoliberal Brain* (Cambridge, MA: MIT Press, 2014).

Virilio, Paul. *War and Cinema: The Logistics of Perception*, translated by Patrick Camiller (London: Verso, 1989).

Vonderau, Patrick. "Introduction: On Advertising's Relation to Moving Pictures," in *Films that Sell: Moving Pictures and Advertising*, edited by Bo Florin, Nico de Klerk, and Patrick Vonderau (London: Palgrave, 2016), 1–18.

Wake, Naoko. "The Military, Psychiatry, and 'Unfit' Soldiers, 1939–1942." *Journal of the History of Medicine and Allied Sciences*, vol. 62, no. 4 (October 2007): 461–494.

Waldron, Gloria. *The Information Film: A Report of the Public Library Inquiry* (New York: Columbia University Press, 1949).

Walker, Janet. "Rights and Return: Perils and Fantasies of Situated Testimony after Katrina," in *Documentary Testimonies: Global Archives of Suffering*, edited by Bhaskar Sarkar and Janet Walker (London: Routledge, 2010), 83–114.

Walker, Janet. *Trauma Cinema: Documenting Incest and the Holocaust* (Berkeley: University of California Press, 2005).

Waller, Willard. *The Veteran Comes Back* (New York: Dryden Press, 1944).

Ward, Larry Wayne. *The Motion Picture Goes to War* (Ann Arbor, MI: UMI Research Press, 1985).

Wasson, Haidee. "Experimental Viewing Protocols: Film Projection and the American Military," in *Cinema's Military Industrial Complex*, edited by Haidee Wasson and Lee Grieveson (Berkeley: University of California Press, 2018), 25–43.

Wasson, Haidee. *Museum Movies: The Museum of Modern Art and the Birth of Art Cinema* (Berkeley: University of California Press, 2005).

Wasson, Haidee. "Protocols of Portability," *Film History*, vol. 25, no. 1–2 (2013): 236–247.

Wasson, Haidee. "The Reel of the Month Club: 16mm Projectors, Home Theaters and Film Libraries in the 1920s." In *Going to the Movies: Hollywood and the Social Experience of Cinema*, edited by Richard Maltby, Melvyn Stokes, and Robert C. Allen (Exeter: University of Exeter Press, 2007), 217–234 [225].

Wasson, Haidee and Charles R. Acland. "Introduction: Utility and Cinema," in *Useful Cinema*, edited by Charles R. Acland and Haidee Wasson (Durham: Duke University Press, 2011).

Wasson, Haidee and Lee Grieveson (eds.). *Cinema's Military Industrial Complex* (Berkeley: University of California Press, 2018).

Watkins, John G. *Hypnotherapy of War Neuroses: A Clinical Psychologist's Casebook* (New York: Ronald Press, 1949).

Waugh, Thomas. "Beyond *Vérité*: Emile de Antonio," in *The Right to Play Oneself: Looking Back on Documentary Film* (Minneapolis: University of Minnesota Press, 2011), 93–154.

Waugh, Thomas. *The Conscience of Cinema: The Works of Joris Ivens 1926-1989* (Amsterdam: Amsterdam University Press, 2016).

Wertheim, Albert. *Staging the War: American Drama and World War II* (Bloomington: Indiana University Press, 2004).

White, Mimi. *Tele-Advising: Therapeutic Discourse in American Television* (Chapel Hill: University of North Carolina Press, 1992).

Winter, Alison. "Film and the Construction of Memory in Psychoanalysis, 1940–1960." *Science in Context*, vol. 19, no. 1 (2006): 111–136.

Winston, Brian. *Claiming the Real II: Documentary: Grierson and Beyond* (London: BFI, 2008).

Winson, Brian. "The Documentary Film as Scientific Inscription," in *Theorizing Documentary*, edited by Michael Renov (New York: Routledge, 1993), 37–57.

Winston, Brian. "Introduction: The Documentary Film," in *The Documentary Film Book*, edited by Brian Winston (London: BFI, 2015), 1–29.

Winston, Brian. "Life as Narrativised," in *The Documentary Film Book*, edited by Brian Winston (London: BFI, 2015), 89–97.

Wolfe, Charles. "Mapping *Why We Fight*: Frank Capra and the US Army Orientation Film in World War II," in *American Film History: Selected Readings, Origins to 1960*, edited by Cynthia Lucia, Roy Grundmann, and Art Simon (West Sussex, UK: Wiley Blackwell, 2016), 326–340.

Zimmermann, Patricia R. *States of Emergency: Documentaries, Wars, Democracies* (Minneapolis: University of Minnesota Press, 2000).

Index

Parsons, Ernest, 39
Pathé, 188
Patterson, Robert, 58
Patton, George S., 5
Peace Films Caravan, 55
Peace Films Foundation, 54–55
Pete Kelly's Blues (1955), 104
pharmaceutical companies, 34, 161, 166–7, 184
Phil Silvers Show, The (1955–1959), 78
Phillips, Joseph, 37
Photographic Science Laboratory (US Navy), 62
Pilot #5 (1943), 150, 255n65
Plant, Rebecca Jo, 9, 35, 44
Plow That Broke the Plains, The (1936), 19
Polan, Dana, 59, 85
Possessed (1947), 181, 183
post-traumatic stress disorder (PTSD), 8, 47, 125, 220, 221 264n, 265n14
Presentation Division, 198
Preston, Robert, 84–85
Preventative Psychiatry: In or Out (1961), 78, 198
Private Buckaroo (1942), 95
Private Snafu series (1942–1945), 154
Private Worlds (1935), 26–27
Production Code, 150
Promazine, 165–7, 184
Psychiatric Film Program, Office of the Surgeon General, 39, 176
Psychiatric Procedures in the Combat Area (1944), 45, 59, 100–102, 105, 110, 176–8, 182, 186, 196, 201, 222
Psychiatry in Action (1943), 69–70
psychodrama, 7, 13, 78, 126–68, 170, 206–7, 220–2, 262n67
Psychological Test Film Unit (Army Air Forces), 49, 144–5
Psychologists' Peace Manifesto (1945), 107
Psychoneuroses (1944), 171
Psychotherapeutic Interviewing Series, Part One: Introduction—1950 (1950), 198
Psychotherapeutic Interviewing Techniques (1949), 198–9
psychotropic drugs, 165–7
Pyle, Ernie, 139

Rack, The (1956), 109, 110, 156, 197–8
Radio Corporation of America (RCA), 21–22
Rage in Heaven (1941), 225n9
Rand, Ayn, 75
RAND Corporation, 115–223

Random Harvest (1942), 207, 251n115
Ranson, Stephen, 201–3
Ray-Bell Films, 88
Raytheon, 105
Reagan, Ronald, 137, 219–20, 224
Recognition of the Japanese Zero Fighter (1943), 96, 137
Red Cross Motion Picture Bureau (1916–1922), 51
Redlich, Fritz, 29–30
reenactment, as documentary method, 2–3, 12, 14, 19, 43, 84, 90, 179, 189–90, 195; as therapy, 55, 127–68, 170–1, 217, 222, 239n34, 254n31, 255n45
Rees, J. R., 39
Reik, Theodor, 199–200
"release anxiety," 207
Remember? (1939), 260n37
Renov, Michael, 10–11
Report from the Aleutians (1943), 20, 119
Rescue Dawn (2006), 156–7
Returning Veteran, The (1945), 186, 188–92
Return to Guam (1944), 120
Rieff, Philip, 216
River, The (1937), 19
Rizzo, Albert "Skip," 221
Roaring Twenties, The (1939), 239n35
Robbins, Lewis L., 152–3
Rogers, Carl, 41
Rogers, Ginger, 21, 181
Rogin, Michael, 33
Role of the Combat Cameraman, The (1952), 58–59
Rome, Howard P., 7, 121, 131, 140, 148
Roosevelt, Eleanor, 39
Rose, Nikolas, 46
Rotha, Paul, 14, 65, 66, 67, 160
Rubin, Herbert E., 121
Ruhe, David S., 83
Rusk, Dean, 219
Russell, Harold, 73, 215
Ryan, Thomas Arthur, 102

Sabotage (1936), 254n39
Salmon, Thomas, 93
Salter, Andrew, 108
Salute to the Navy! (1941), 86–87
San Pietro (1945), 20, 69, 222, 259n34
Santos, Marlisa, 45
Sarkar, Bhaskar, 81
Schiller, Herbert, 22, 37, 83
School of Military Neuropsychiatry (Army), 9, 59, 184